Springer Series in Game Theory

The Springer Series in Game Theory is devoted to new developments in game theory and its applications. Since von Neumann and Morgenstern's work, game theory has been established in economics as a powerful tool to study issues of competition and strategic interaction. In addition, game theoretic approaches have been increasingly embraced to study a wide variety of phenomena in other subject areas, including political science, philosophy, computer science, behavioral studies, psychology and life science. The series welcomes game-theoretic contributions from these different subject areas and ensures interdisciplinary expertise through its board of advisory editors. High-profile books such as advanced textbooks and focused research monographs, as well as edited volumes if presented in a coherent and well-balanced way, will be considered for publication. The series is the Official Book Series of the Game Theory Society.

Pierre Dehez

Game Theory for the Social Sciences

Conflict, Bargaining, Cooperation and Power

Springer

Pierre Dehez
Center for Operations Research
and Econometrics (CORE), LIDAM
UCLouvain
Louvain-la-Neuve, Belgium

ISSN 1868-517X ISSN 1868-5188 (electronic)
Springer Series in Game Theory
ISBN 978-3-031-58240-0 ISBN 978-3-031-58241-7 (eBook)
https://doi.org/10.1007/978-3-031-58241-7

This Springer imprint is published by the registered company Springer Nature Switzerland AG
The registered company address is: Gewerbestrasse 11, 6330 Cham, Switzerland

Game theory is a bag of analytical tools designed to help us understand the phenomena that we observe when decision makers interact. The basic assumptions that underlie the theory are that decision makers pursue well-defined exogenous objectives (they are rational) and consider their knowledge or expectations of other decision makers' behavior (they reason strategically).

Martin Osborne and Ariel Rubinstein, A course in game theory, The MIT Press, 1994.

Courtesy David Ross

This book is dedicated to Jacques Drèze (1929–2022), founder of the Center for Operations Research and Econometrics (CORE).

Jacques was an outstanding scholar who has inspired so many of us.

Praise for *Game Theory for the Social Sciences*

"The aim of game theory is to propose solutions to decision problems that involve several individuals with possibly conflicting interests. According to a conventional view, non-cooperative games model in detail the strategic interaction of individuals, while cooperative games describe axiomatically suitable properties of collective decisions. Pierre Dehez reconciles the two points of view by offering a consistent kit of classic game theoretic tools, from equilibrium concepts to bargaining solutions and power indices, all illustrated with insightful examples and applications."

—Françoise Forges, *Professor of Economics, Université Paris Dauphine-PSL*

"In the economy and more generally in our society, the behavior of the system as a whole is the result of direct interaction between individuals who, unlike the actors in the usual framework think about the people with whom they interact. This changes the perspective through which we analyze social science and economics in particular. Game theory allows us to understand this interaction which can be cooperative or non-cooperative and where the term strategic behavior is appropriate. This book is written clearly and pedagogically without resorting to difficult mathematics. It provides many different and interesting examples from problems of fair sharing, bargaining to voting systems and many others. It is a perfect introduction to this subject too often quoted but too often misunderstood."

—Alan Kirman, *Directeur d'études, Ecole des Hautes Etudes en Sciences Sociales, Paris Emeritus Professor, Aix-Marseille University*

Acknowledgments

Preliminary versions of this text have been used by the author over the past 25 years as a support for undergraduate courses in game theory. I am grateful to the students of economic, social and political sciences at the University of Louvain. They helped me, often unknowingly, to build a text that I eventually decided to publish, first in French (Economica, 2017) and later in Italian (Giappichelli, 2021). I am also grateful to my former student and friend Pier Mario Pacini, professor at the University of Pisa, who translated the French version into Italian. In doing so, he helped me improve and expand the initial text, now available in English.

I owe a considerable intellectual debt to many persons with whom I have had the chance to exchange over the years, in particular at the *Center for Operations Research and Econometrics* (CORE) of the University of Louvain, at the *Institute of Theoretical Economics* of the University of Bonn and at the *European University Institute* in Florence. In direct connection with this work, my thoughts are going to my late friend Jean Blondel, well-known political scientist, whom I met in Florence. It is to him that I owe my interest in the use of game theory in political science.

My thanks also go to Carlos Alos-Ferrer, Martin Dufwenberg and Françoise Forges whose comments and suggestions have allowed me to improve my text, and to Johannes Glaeser who kindly guided me through the submission process.

Last but certainly not least, I would like to express my gratitude to Chantal Capouillez and Caroline Colvin for their continuous support.

Contents

1 Introduction

Conflict, bargaining, cooperation and power are words covering issues that are at the heart of the social sciences. Because it studies situations where actors are in direct interaction, game theory offers a consistent framework to analyze these issues: what the actors achieve depends not only on their own course of action, but also on that of others. It is precisely this link between individual behavior and collective consequences that is at the heart of the theory of games. One talks of players, beliefs, strategies and payoffs. Players have preferences, not on their own strategies but on the consequences that result from their combination with the strategies of the other players. It would be more appropriate to talk of a *theory of interactive decision*[1]. We will see that the prime goal of game theory is not so much to offer winning solutions. Its main aim is to offer methods to analyze particular situations, to organize and understand observations. "*...it is crucial that the social scientist recognize that game theory is not descriptive, but rather (conditionally) normative. It states neither how people do behave nor how they should behave in an absolute sense, but how they should behave if they wish to achieve certain ends. It prescribes for given assumptions courses of action for the attainment of outcomes having certain formal "optimum" properties. These properties may or may not be deemed pertinent in any given real-world conflict of interest. If they are, the theory prescribes the choices which must be made to get an optimum*" (Luce & Raiffa, 1957, p. 63).

Game situations are typically of a conflictual nature, although not necessarily antagonistic. In a non-cooperative situation, cooperation between players is not

[1] The title *game theory* has its origin in the mathematical analysis of parlor games started in the 1920s.

P. Dehez, *Game Theory for the Social Sciences*, Springer Series in Game Theory,
https://doi.org/10.1007/978-3-031-58241-7_1

ruled out, on the contrary. Parlor games are particular examples of strict antagonistic situations. They belong to the class of zero-sum games. By contrast, society instead, in its economic, social and political dimensions, often leads to situations where conflict and convergence of interest coexist. The determination of wages between firms and trade unions, the settlement of regional conflicts, the arms race, the choice of monetary policies by central banks, the choice of product quality and prices by firms, auctions and governmental coalition formation, are just a few examples among many others.

There are a number of precursors. Two names come in the forefront, Augustin Cournot and Francis Ysidro Edgeworth. Cournot's book *Recherches sur les principes mathématiques de la théorie des richesses* published in 1838 is often cited as the origin of game theory. His analysis of firms in a competitive context within a market has indeed anticipated the general concept of non-cooperative equilibrium introduced more than a century later by John Nash.[2] Edgeworth's book *Mathematical Psychics. An Essay on the Application of Mathematics to the Moral Sciences* published in 1881 contains an analysis of stable transactions within an exchange economy, anticipating the concept of core introduced by Gillies and Shapley in the early 1950s. The mathematical theory of games was formally started with the work of Zermelo (1912) and Borel (1921) on parlor games, followed by the paper of John von Neumann on zero-sum games and the famous *minimax theorem* dated 1928.[3] The foundational impetus was given by the publication in 1944 of the book of John von Neumann and Oskar Morgenstern "*Theory of games and economic behavior*". It was rapidly followed by the fundamental contributions of Nash and Shapley in the early 1950s. Many papers and books then followed, among which that Duncan Luce and Howard Raiffa *Games and decisions* published in (1957). It remains a source of inspiration today.

Game theory, a domain initially reserved to mathematicians, has gradually opened up to the social sciences: economics first, followed by political science, sociology and law. Presently, there remain few domains of economic theory where game theory does not play a central role. New concepts and results have appeared throughout the years, sometimes together with deep mathematical arguments and intense debates. The paper of Robert Aumann, published in 1985 offers a remarkable epistemological analysis of the theory of games together with a critical analysis of its main concepts.[4] He writes, "*My main thesis is that a solution concept should be judged more by what it does than by what it is; more by its success in establishing relationships and providing insights into the workings of the social processes to which it is applied than by considerations of* a priori *plausibility based on its definition alone*".

[2] Beyond game theory, Cournot is considered as the precursor of the mathematical economics.

[3] See Fréchet (1953) for more details on Borel's contribution.

[4] Aumann uses the term *comprehension* to which he attaches three dimensions: (i) relation between structures, (ii) unification of theories and (iii) simplicity as opposed to complexity. It is a highly recommended reading (after having digested the present book…).

More recently, the experimental approach has offered a source of observations from which the limits of concepts and hypotheses could be evaluated, opening new avenues of research. In particular, the assumption of rationality has been re-evaluated within an interdisciplinary research framework combining psychology and economics, leading to a new discipline, neuroeconomics.[5]

In the 1960s, game theory was intensively used to study the arms control and disarmament question.[6] In the 1990s, game theorists have contributed to the development of auction systems, in particular for the allocation of the frequency spectrum for various usages (radio, television, mobile telephony, internet, ...), in the US, Europe and Australia. These contributions and others have been recognized, in particular by the award of the Nobel Prize in economics game theorists, starting with John Nash[7] (University of Princeton), Reinhard Selten (University of Bonn) and John Harsanyi (University of California, Berkeley) who were honored in 1994 *for their pioneering analysis of equilibria in the theory of non-cooperative games.*[8] Eleven years later, Robert Aumann (University of Jerusalem) and Thomas Schelling (University of Maryland) were rewarded *for having enhanced our understanding of conflict and* cooperation *through game theory analysis*. In 2007, Leonid Hurwicz (University of Minnesota), Eric Maskin (Institute for Advanced Study, Princeton) and Roger Myerson (University of Chicago) were rewarded *for having laid the foundations of mechanism design theory*. In 2012, Lloyd Shapley (University of California, Los Angeles) and Alvin Roth (University of Stanford) were rewarded *for the theory of stable allocations and the practice of market design*, linked to the famous "marriage market", a problem of matching solved by David Gale and Lloyd Shapley (1962). The importance of Lloyd Shapley's contributions to the theory of games, in particular to the theory of cooperative games, had been highlighted by Robert Aumann in his Nobel lecture, speaking of him as the greatest game theorist of all time! The latest prize was awarded in 2020 to Paul Milgrom and Robert Wilson (both at Stanford University) *for improvements to* auction *theory and inventions of new* auction *formats*.

I cannot resist the urge to reproduce an extract from Oskar Morgenstern's preface to the book by Davis (1970). "*Game theory is a new discipline that has aroused much interest because of its novel mathematical properties and its many applications to social, economic, and political problems. [This] is due to the fact that the mathematical structure of the theory differs profoundly from previous attempts to provide mathematical foundations of social phenomena. These earlier efforts were oriented on the physical sciences and inspired by the tremendous success these have had over the centuries. Yet social phenomena are different: people are acting sometimes*

---

[5] See for instance Fehr and Glimcher (2014), Reuter and Montag (2016), Battigalli and Dufwenberg (2022), Camerer (2003) and the beautiful book by Winter (2014) on the rationality of emotions.

[6] In particular by Robert Aumann and Michael Maschler, authors of several reports for the *US Arms Control and Disarmament Agency*.

[7] See the book of Nasar (1998) and the 2001 movie *A beautiful* mind that retraces John Nash's life.

[8] See the web page www.nobelprize.org/prizes/lists/all-prizes-in-economic-sciences.

against each other, sometimes cooperatively with each other; they have different degrees of information *about each other and their aspirations lead them to conflict or* cooperation. *Inanimate nature shows none of these traits. In studying the social world, we are in need of rigorous concepts. We must give precision to such terms as* utility, information, *optimal behavior, strategy, payoff, equilibrium, bargaining, and many more. Without such precise concepts, we could never hope to lift the discussion from a purely verbal state and we would forever be restricted to a very limited understanding if, indeed, we could achieve it at all*".

This is the vision of one of the two "creators" of game theory. While not being recent, it highlights the concern, dear to John von Neumann, to offer a formalization specific to the social sciences. The allusion to physical sciences refers mainly to the *theory of general equilibrium*, initiated by Walras in his book *Eléments d'économie politique pure ou théorie de la richesse sociale* (1874), and later formalized by Kenneth Arrow and Gérard Debreu (1954). There is, however, a paradox: this theory was limited to perfect competition where the *direct* interaction between economic agents, in particular firms, is completely ignored. It is therefore at odds with the work of Joan Robinson (1933) and Edward Chamberlin (1933) who advocated considering the imperfections of competition, and with the very spirit of game theory.[9]

The book is organized as follows. Non-cooperative games are the object of Chap. 2. Its first section is devoted to individual decision-making, allowing for uncertainty, while its second section introduces 2-player non-cooperative games through a few emblematic examples. The next sections formalize the non-cooperative concepts within two representations, the extensive form where players move sequentially and the strategic form where each player, when making a strategic choice, ignores the decision made by the other player. The search for a compromise solution to 2-player non-cooperative games is the object of Chap. 3. It is a first step towards cooperation. Cooperation is the object of Chap. 4 which analyzes the distribution of the fruits of cooperation among any number of players, under the assumptions that utility is transferable and agreements are enforceable. It contains applications to various problems, from the calculation of landing fees and patent royalties to the allocation of liability for damages resulting from joint actions. Finally, Chap. 5 is devoted to the analysis of voting rules within committees and the resulting division of power, with applications to various bodies like the UN Security Council and the EU Council of Ministers.

The book introduces many concepts but four of them stand out as major concepts, namely the Nash equilibrium, the Nash bargaining solution, the core and the Shapley value. This book differs from many others in that it devotes an important part to cooperative game theory. The last two chapters may be read independently from the first two, although the reader is invited to read at least Sect. 2.2 that introduces non-cooperative games through simple examples.

[9] See Myerson (1999) for a study of the concept of Nash equilibrium in a historical perspective.

Game theory is mathematical in its formulation and some of its developments are based on advanced mathematical tools. Unlike advanced game theory books, I do not expect the reader to master them. The level remains elementary and the necessary reminders can be found in the Mathematical appendix. Propositions are stated but proofs are given only for some of them, in particular when the arguments used are interesting and useful. Some sections are marked with a *. They can be bypassed without harming the understanding of what follows.

Game theory: the pioneers

Robert Aumann (1930)
David Gale (1921–2008)
John Harsanyi (1920–2000)
Harold Kuhn (1925–2014)
Duncan Luce (1925–2012)
Michael Maschler (1927–2008)
Oskar Morgenstern (1903–1977)
John Nash (1928–2015)
Guillermo Owen (1938)
Bezalel Peleg (1936–2019)
Howard Raiffa (1924–2016)
Reinhard Selten (1930–2016)
Thomas Schelling (1921–2016)
David Schmeidler (1939–2022)
Martin Shubik (1926–2018)
Lloyd Shapley (1923–2016)
John von Neumann (1903–1957)

To these great names, we should add Augustin Cournot (1801–1877) and Francis Ysidro Edgeworth (1845–1926), the first for having anticipated the non-cooperative concept of Nash equilibrium and the second for having anticipated the cooperative concept of core.

All have to their credit fundamental contributions in game theory but two names stand out, namely John Nash and Loyd Shapley. They are the heroes of this book.

References

Arrow, K. J., & Debreu, G. (1954). Existence of an equilibrium for a competitive economy. *Econometrica, 26*, 265–290.

Battigalli, P., & Dufwenberg, M. (2022). Belief-dependent motivations and psychological game theory. *Journal of Economic Literature, 60*, 833–882.

Borel, E. (1921). La théorie du jeu et les équations intégrales à noyau symmetric. *Comptes rendus de l'Académie des sciences, 173*, 1304–1308. English translation by L. J. Savage (1953) in *Econometrica, 21*, 97–100.

Camerer, C. F. (2003). *Behavioral game theory: Experiments in strategic interaction.* Princeton University Press.

Chamberlin, E. (1933). *The theory of monopolistic competition.* Harvard University Press.

Cournot, A. (1838). *Recherches sur les principes mathématiques de la théorie des richesses*, Hachette. English translation by N. T. Bacon (1927). *Researches into the mathematical principles of the theory of wealth.* MacMillan.

Davis, M. (1970). *Game theory: A nontechnical introduction* (2nd edn.). Basic Books.

Edgeworth, F. Y. (1881). *Mathematical psychics: An essay on the application of mathematics to the moral sciences.* Kegan and co.

Fehr, E., & Glimcher, P. W. (eds.) (2014). *Neuroeconomics: Decision making and the brain.* Academic Press.

Fréchet, M. (1953). Emile Borel, initiator of the theory of psychological games and its application. *Econometrica, 21*, 95–124.

Gale, D. & L. Shapley. (1962) College admissions and the stability of marriage. *The American Mathematical Monthly, 69*, 9–15.

Luce, D., & Raiffa, H. (1957). *Games and decisions.* Wiley.

Myerson, R. B. (1999). Nash equilibrium and the history of economic theory. *Journal of Economic Literature, 37*, 1067–1082.

Nasar, S. (1998). *A beautiful mind.* Simon & Schuster.

Nash, J. F. (1950). Equilibrium points in N-person games. *Proceedings of the National Academy of Sciences of USA, 36*, 48–49.

Reuter, M., Montag, Ch. (eds.) (2016). *Neuroeconomics.* Springer.

Robinson, J. (1933). *The economics of imperfect competition.* Macmillan.

Shapley, L. S. (1951). Notes on the n-person game II: The value of an n-person game, *Research Memoreandum* 670, The Rand Corporation, Santa Monica.

von Neumann, J. (1928). Zur Theorie der Gesellschaftspiel. *Mathematische Annalen, 100*, 295–320. English translation in A. W. Tucker & R. D. Luce (eds.). (1959). Contributions to the Theory of games IV. *Annals of mathematical studies* (pp. 13–42). Princeton University Press.

von Neumann, J., & Morgenstern, O. (1944). *Theory of games and economic behavior.* Princeton University Press (latest edition dated 1953).

Walras, L. (1874). *Eléments d'économie politique pure ou théorie de la richesse sociale.* Guillaumin.

Winter, E. (2014). *Feeling smart. Why our emotions are more rational than we think.* Public Affairs.

Zermelo, E. (1912). *Über eine Anwendung der Mengenlehre auf die Theorie des Schaftspiels.* In E. W. Hobson & A. E. H. Love (eds.) *Proceeding of the fifth international congress of mathematicians* (pp. 501–504). Cambridge University Press.

2 Strategy and Conflict

The present chapter is devoted to non-cooperative games, games in which players are not bound by prior agreements. If prior agreements are possible, they are included in the strategies available to the players. We will see that this non-cooperative framework does not exclude cooperation between players: outside the case of zero-sum games, games often include a mix of conflict and convergence of interest. This is precisely what makes their studies interesting.

We will ourselves to 2-player games. This is actually not a real limitation as far as these games contain most of the ingredients necessary to analyze the conceptual difficulties of non-cooperative games. We will also limit ourselves to games with complete information: each player is assumed to know all the data of the game including the preferences of his opponent. This assumption certainly limits the scope of the analysis, but the study of incomplete information is conceptually difficult and would go beyond the scope of an introductory book.

Individual decision-making is the object of the first section. We define the notion of preference ordering and its utility representation to formalize the problem of choice, with a particular attention to choice under uncertainty. This first section is followed by an informal introduction to non-cooperative games through simple examples. The subsequent sections formalize the previous analysis around the central concept of Nash equilibrium.

P. Dehez, *Game Theory for the Social Sciences*, Springer Series in Game Theory,
https://doi.org/10.1007/978-3-031-58241-7_2

2.1 Preferences, Utility, Choices and Uncertainty

Preferences
Choices
Utility
Lotteries
Saint Petersburg paradox
Expected utility
Cardinal representation
Risk aversion.

We consider a decision-maker facing a set A of alternatives. These alternatives are not necessarily monetary amounts. They could be commodity baskets or candidates to an election, sequences of alternatives over a given time interval or lotteries. The set A may include a finite or infinite number of alternatives, possibly a continuum like for instance a price interval.

Preferences
Our decision-maker has preferences on the set A of alternatives in the form of a binary relation. We adopt the following notations:

$a \succ b$ alternative a is preferred to the alternative b,
$a \sim b$ there is indifference between the alternatives a and b.

We shall use the weak preference relation as a primitive concept:

$a \succsim b$ either alternative a is preferred to alternative b, or there is indifference.
Preference and indifference are then derived from the weak preference relation[1]:

$$a \succ b \quad \Leftrightarrow \quad a \succsim b \text{ and } b \succsim a,$$
$$a \sim b \quad \Leftrightarrow \quad a \succsim b \text{ and } b \succsim a.$$

The weak preference relation $\succsim$ is assumed to satisfy the following assumptions:

Reflexivity: for all alternatives $a \in A$, $a \succsim a$.
Transitivity: if $a, b, c \in A$ are such that $a \succsim b$ and $b \succsim c$, then $a \succsim c$.
Completeness: for all pairs $(a, b) \in A \times A$, either $a \succsim b$ or $b \succsim a$.

These three assumptions characterize a preorder. Reflexivity goes by itself but has to be stated. Transitivity is an assumption of *rationality* that requires preferences to be consistent.[2] Observations indicate that transitivity is often violated when individuals are confronted to sequences of choices. However, when an error is reported, they easily recognize it and try to correct it. Completeness is far stronger a requirement: facing any two alternatives, a decision-maker is assumed to be able to tell which

[1] The equivalence symbol $\Leftrightarrow$ reads *if and only if*.
[2] A reflexive and transitive binary relation is a *preordering*. The relation $\geq$ defined on the real numbers is an *ordering* because it also satisfies the property of symmetry: $x \geq y$ and $y \geq x$ imply $x = y$.

one he prefers or else he is indifferent between them, whatever is the complexity of these alternatives. Let's be careful not to confuse "indifference" and "incapacity to choose": if you are indifferent between two alternatives, then you must accept that the choice be made by someone else or by a random drawing.

Choices

Formally, a *choice structure* is defined by a pair $(A, \succsim)$ formed by a set A of alternatives on which a preference relation $\succsim$ is defined. All the alternatives are not necessarily feasible. It depends upon the context. A *context* is a subset of feasible alternatives. The budgetary constraint faced by a consumer is a typical example. He has a given budget for the acquisition of various commodities, each with a known price. The subset commodity baskets whose value does not exceed his budget then defines the context within which the consumer has to decide.

Given a context $B \subset A$, we associate the *choice set* $C(B)$ that collects the best alternatives among the feasible ones:

$$a^* \in C(B) \text{ if and only if } a^* \succsim a \text{ for all } a \in B.$$

Equivalently, $C(B)$ is the set of alternatives that are not preferred by *any* other feasible alternative:

$$a \succ a^* \text{ implies } a \notin B.$$

Notice that $C(B)$ is a *set*: nothing excludes the case where several alternatives do satisfy the optimality criterion for some B, *in which case there is a need for a selection mechanism.* This is, however, unimportant because the decision-maker is *indifferent* between them. In the case where $C(B)$ is a singleton for all $B \subset A$, it is a function, called *choice function.* If instead $C(B)$ contains several alternatives for some B, $C(B)$ is a *multi-valued function* (or point-to-set mapping), called *choice correspondence*.

Utility

Independently of the degree of complexity of the alternatives, it would be convenient to translate the comparison of alternatives into a comparison of numbers. We say that a preference relation $\succsim$ is represented by a function u if it is possible to associate to each alternative $a \in A$ a real number $u(a)$ such that:

$$a \succsim b \Leftrightarrow u(a) \geq u(b).$$

This defines a real-valued function u: $A \rightarrow \mathbb{R}$ called *utility function.* It automatically verifies the following two equivalent statements:

$$a \succ b \Leftrightarrow u(a) > u(b),$$
$$a \sim b \Leftrightarrow u(a) = u(b).$$

Let's be careful. The sentence "*the* utility *of a is greater than the* utility *of b*" may induce a wrong understanding of the notion of utility. As such, a utility function does not carry additional information on preferences. Actually, there is not a unique representation of a given preference relation: if a function u represents the preference relation $\succsim$ then the function $v = T(u)$ obtained through an *increasing* transformation T of u represents the same relation.[3] $v(a) = T(u(a))$, Indeed, we have the following equivalences:

$$a \succsim b \;\Leftrightarrow\; u(a) \geq u(b) \;\Leftrightarrow\; v(a) \geq v(b).$$

This is a purely *ordinal* representation of preferences: comparing utility differences has no meaning, only the *sign* of utility *differences* matters.

If the set of alternatives is finite, it is easy to associate a utility function to any complete preorder. Consider for example a set of four alternatives $A = \{a, b, c, d\}$ and the preferences $a \succ b \sim c \succ d$. We can then arbitrarily choose numbers to represent these preferences, while respecting the preferences, for instance, $u(a) = 9$, $u(b) = u(c) = 0$, $u(d) = -3$. Any other numbers would do the job if the highest number is allocated to a, the lowest to d and a common number to b and c, located between $u(a)$ and $u(d)$. In general, one proceeds in three stages: first group the alternatives between which the decision-maker is indifferent into *equivalence classes*, then place the equivalence classes in order of decreasing preference, and finally allocate an arbitrary real number to each equivalence class following the ordering of preference. This procedure extends to the infinite countable case without additional assumptions.

If the set of alternatives is a continuum, a preference preorder is not necessarily representable by a utility function. A *continuity* assumption is needed to guarantee the existence of a utility function. It requires that $\{x \in A | x \succsim y\}$ and $\{x \in A | y \succsim x\}$ be *closed* sets for all $y \in A$.[4] Continuity is a sufficient condition that ensures that the resulting utility function is continuous.[5] This is a result due to Debreu (1954).

Proposition 2.1 *Any complete and continuous preorder can be represented by a continuous utility function.*

The *lexicographic* preorder (actually an ordering) defined on $\mathbb{R}^n_+$ is an example of a preference relation that is not continuous and cannot be represented by a utility function. Alternatives are of the form $(x_1, x_2, ..., x_n)$ and preferences are defined according to a given ordering of priority. Assuming that we follow the natural order where the first element has the highest priority, $x \succ y$ if

$$x_1 > y_1 \text{ or } [x_1 = y_1 \text{ and } x_2 > y_2] \text{ or } [x_1 = y_1, x_2 = y_2 \text{ and } x_3 > y_3] \text{ or} \ldots x_n > y_n$$

[3] A transformation T is *increasing* if $x > y$ implies $T(x) > T(y)$. For instance, $T(x) = x^3$ is an increasing transformation while $T(x) = x^2$ is not.

[4] A set is closed if it contains its boundary.

[5] In consumer theory, preferences are defined over baskets of commodities and indifference curves are equivalence classes.

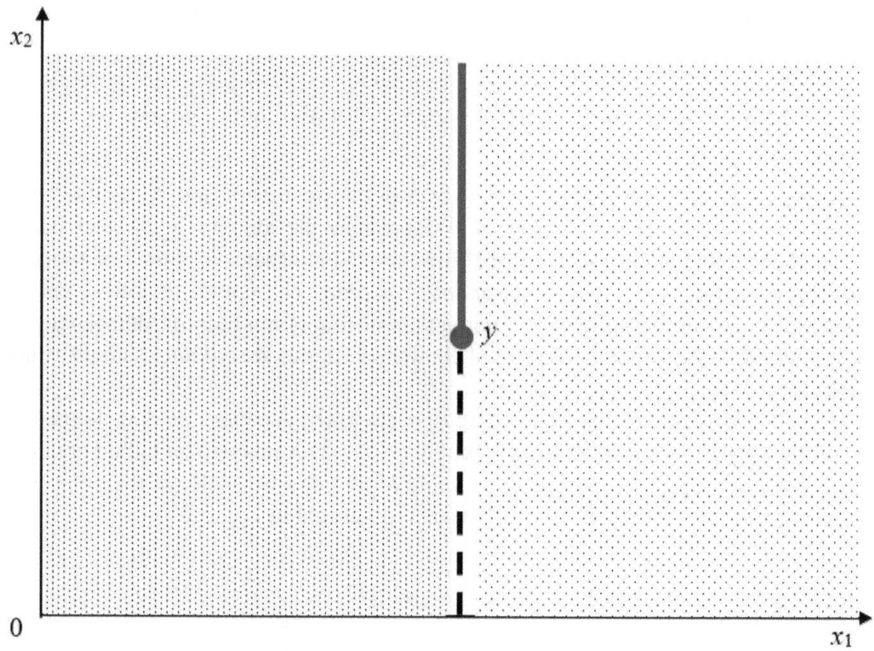

Fig. 2.1 Lexicographic preferences

We observe that indifference occurs *if and only if* $x = y$. Equivalence classes are singletons: $x \sim y$ if and only if $x = y$. As illustrated in Fig. 2.1, for any given $y \in \mathbb{R}_+$, the sets $\{x \in \mathbb{R}_+ | x \succsim y\}$ and $\{x \in \mathbb{R}_+ | y \succsim x\}$ are *not* closed sets. The boundary of the first one includes only the thick portion of the vertical line. The boundary of the second one includes only the dashed portion of the vertical line.

Consider a choice structure $(A, \succsim)$ where the preference relation $\succsim$ can be represented by a utility function u. It can then be replaced by the pair (A, u) and the problem of choice associated with a given context $B \subset A$ is equivalent to the *maximization* of the function u on the set B:

$$a^* \in C(B, u) \quad \Leftrightarrow \quad u(a^*) \geq u(a) \;\; \text{for all } a \in B.$$

The solutions of the maximization of a function coincide with the solutions of the maximization of any increasing transformation of that function. As a consequence, utility maximization is an expression behind which there is nothing more than a reference to the underlying preference relation. The utility function is just a convenient "accessory" introduced to rephrase the problem of choice.

Lotteries

Consider a set $A = \{a_1, a_2, \ldots, a_j, \ldots, a_n\}$ of n alternatives on which is defined as a probability distribution $p = \{p_1, p_2, \ldots, p_i, \ldots, p_n\}$ where p_i denotes the probability that the alternative a_i realizes. We denote by Δ_n the set of all probability distributions on the set A:

$$\Delta_n = \{p = (p_1, p_2, \ldots, p_n)|0 \leq p_i \leq 1 \text{ for all } i \text{ and } \sum_{i=1}^{n} p_i = 1\}.$$

Any probability distribution on the set A defines a *lottery* and Δ_n is the set of lotteries on this set. It has dimension n–1 because the identity $\sum p_i = 1$ has to be satisfied. If the alternatives are real numbers (for instance amounts of money), a lottery is a *discrete real-valued random variable*. The notion of lottery can be extended to an infinite number of alternatives or to a continuum of alternatives. In the latter case, if the alternatives are real numbers, lotteries are *continuous* real-valued random variable.

Consider for instance the case where $A = \{0, 100\}$. A lottery on A is defined by the probability $p_1 = p$ of obtaining 0, with $0 \leq p \leq 1$. A positive gain then obtained with probability $p_2 = 1 - p$. This is a *simple lottery* and we shall use the notation $L = (p \mid 0, 100)$. The lottery $L = (p \mid 0, 100)$ is illustrated in Fig. 2.2.

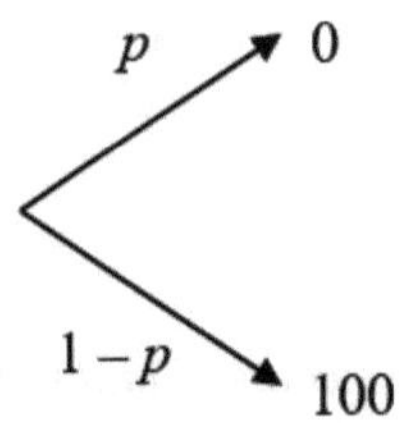

Fig. 2.2 Simple lottery

Lotteries with more than two components can be represented as a combination of simple lotteries. This is illustrated in Fig. 2.3 for the case of a lottery defined on the set $A = \{a, b, c\}$ where $p_3 = 1 - p_1 - p_2$. The initial lottery is equivalent to the following compound lottery:

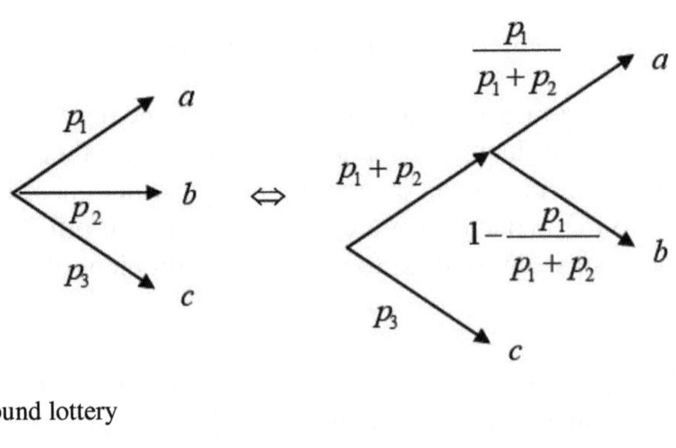

Fig. 2.3 Compound lottery

$$L = \left(p_1 + p_2 \middle| L\left(\frac{p_1}{p_1 + p_2} \mid a, b \right), c \right).$$

In order to compare lotteries involving real numbers, like for instance amounts of money, the first measure that comes to our minds is the *mathematical expectation*, commonly called the *mean*. It is given by the sum of the results weighted by their probabilities:

$$E = \sum_{j=1}^{n} p_j \, x_j$$

The mathematical expectation of the lottery $L = (1/2 \mid 0, 100)$ is equal to 50. From that point of view, it is equivalent to the lottery $L = (3/4 \mid 0, 200)$ but inferior to the lottery $L = (2/3 \mid 0, 200)$.

The following story is often cited as a case where the mathematical expectation is not appropriate as a criterion for comparing lotteries.

Saint Petersburg paradox

The idea of using the mathematical expectation as a criterion of choice dates back to the seventeenth century with a contribution of the famous Dutch scientist Huygens (1657), the first one devoted to the mathematical aspects of games of chance. He published it after having read the exchanges between Blaise Pascal and Pierre de Fermat about a problem posed by the Chevalier de Méré.

Bernoulli (1738), a Swiss mathematician who held a chair at the Saint Petersburg Academic of Science, published a paper where he proposed a solution to a problem invented by his older brother Nicolas[6]: a coin is flipped successively until it produces a tail and the participant then wins an amount equal to 2^n monetary unit where n is the number of times the coin was flipped. This defines a random variable with a countable set of possible values, $\{2, 4, 8, \ldots, 2^n, \ldots\}$, with probabilities $(1/2, 1/4, 1/8, \ldots, 1/2^n, \ldots)$. Indeed, by independence, the probability that flipping the coin n times is needed is given by $(1/2)^n = 1/2^n$. As a consequence, the mathematical expectation of this lottery is infinite:

$$E = \sum_{j=1}^{\infty} \frac{1}{2^j} \, 2^j = 1 + 1 + 1 + \ldots = \infty.$$

[6] Nicolas Bernoulli is the father of the probability distribution that bears his name.

Based on the mathematical expectation, a player would then be willing to pay large amounts of money to have the privilege to participate in this lottery. This is obviously absurd: how much would you be willing to pay?

Daniel Bernoulli's idea was to distinguish the physical value of money from its moral value. The increase in the value (the utility) that we associate with an increase in wealth is smaller the greater is our initial wealth. This is the principle of *decreasing marginal utility*, a well-known principle in economics. More precisely, he assumes that the increase in utility resulting from an increase in wealth is inversely *proportional* to the initial wealth: $\Delta u = \Delta x / x$ or, in terms of infinitesimal variations,

$$\frac{du}{dx} = \frac{1}{x}.$$

It amounts to say that the utility of wealth is equal to its natural *logarithm*. The criterion is not the mathematical expectation of gain but the mathematical expectation of the logarithm of the gain. Applied to the head or tail lottery, it turns out to be finite and reasonable[7]:

$$E = \sum_{j=1}^{\infty} \frac{1}{2^j} (\log\ 2^j) \ = (\log\ 2) \sum_{j=1}^{\infty} \frac{1}{2^j} j \ \simeq 1.39.$$

In this way, Daniel Bernoulli has pre-empted the concept of expected utility formalized later in von Neumann and Morgenstern (1944), as we shall see in the next subsection.

This example is, of course, extreme because it involves a random variable that has *no mean*. For the unconvinced reader, here is another simple example. Consider the lotteries $L = (1/2 \mid 0, 200)$ and $L = (99/100 \mid 0, 10{,}000)$. They both have the same mean, namely 100. They are, however, definitely not equivalent. If, like most of us, you prefer the first lottery that looks less risky, you prove yourself to be *risk-averse*. If instead you prefer the second one, you prove to be *risk-lover*. It is the case of those who play lotto but we are then in a different context where rationality gives way to dreams and emotions.

Expected utility

We have seen that lotteries do not necessarily involve monetary amounts. Moreover, the components of lotteries can be themselves lotteries. Therefore, if preferences are defined over lotteries, we may extend the concepts of choice and utility to lotteries. The following question then comes to mind: is it possible to characterize the preferences over lotteries knowing the preferences on their components? This question is the object of the famous *expected utility theorem* due to von Neumann and Morgenstern (1944).[8]

---

[7] We have used the identity $\log 2^k = k \log 2$ where $\log 2 = 0.693$ and the infinite series converges (quickly) to 2.

[8] A simple proof is given by Varian (1992) under the assumption that there exists a best and a worst lottery.

Proposition 2.2 *Among the utility functions that represent the preferences of a decision-maker over lotteries, there exist utility functions u such that the utility associated with a lottery equals the expected utility of its components:*

$$u(p|a, b) = p\,u(a) + (1 - p)\,u(b) \text{ for all lotteries } (p|a, b). \tag{2.1}$$

This is known as the *Expected Utility Hypothesis.* It implies that a lottery $(p \mid a, b)$ is preferred to a lottery $(q \mid c, d)$ *if and only if* the expected utility of the first is greater than the expected utility of the second:

$$p\,u(a) + (1 - p)\,u(b) > q\,u(c) + (1 - q)\,u(d).$$

Beyond the continuity assumption that ensures the existence of a utility function representing preference preorders, only one additional assumption is needed for this proposition to be true:

If the lotteries L' and L'' are such that $L' \succsim L''$ then $(p|L', L) \succsim (p|L'', L)$ for all probability p, $0 < p \leq 1$, whatever is the "parasitic" lottery L.

This is an *independence condition*: the presence of the lottery L should not affect the preferences over the lotteries L' and L''. Concerning the continuity assumption, it can be reformulated as follows: given any three alternatives a, b and c such that $a \succsim b \succsim c$, there exists a probability p such that $b \sim (p|a, c)$.

When alternatives are expressed in monetary units, the utility function is naturally an increasing function: a greater amount is associated with a greater utility. If the utility function is *linear*, (2.1) involves the mathematical expectation. Indeed, if $u(x) = \alpha + \beta x$ where $\beta > 0$, we have:

$$u(p \mid a, b) = p\,u(a) + (1 - p)\,u(b) = \alpha + \beta(p\,a + (1 - p)\,b).$$

Because $\beta > 0$, the inequality $p\,u(a) + (1 - p)\,u(b) > q\,u(c) + (1 - q)\,u(d)$ can be reduced to the inequality $p\,a + (1 - p)\,b > q\,c + (1 - q)\,d$. This corresponds to the preferences of a *risk-neutral* decision-maker for whom only the mathematical expectation matters in the evaluation of a lottery.

In general, under the assumptions that underlie Proposition 2.2, the comparison of any two random variables (discrete or continuous) reduces to the comparison of their expected utilities:

$$X \succsim Y \quad \Leftrightarrow \quad E[u(X)] \geq E[u(Y)].$$

Since von Neumann and Morgenstern have introduced the Expected Utility Hypothesis, several paradoxes were discovered and alternative approaches were proposed.[9] The Expected Utility Hypothesis remains, however, the simplest and largely used criterion in the analysis of decision-making under uncertainty, in particular in game theory.

[9] The best-known paradox is due to Allais (1953).

Cardinal representation

We have seen that under a continuity assumption, preferences can be represented by an ordinal utility function. Under an additional assumption of independence, we have seen that there exists a subset of utility functions that are compatible with the Expected Utility Hypothesis (2.1). Expected utility is then a possible representation of preferences. This representation has the property that any linear and increasing transformation of the utility function defines a new utility function that satisfies the Expected Utility Hypothesis.[10]

Proposition 2.3 *If a utility function u satisfies the Expected Utility Hypothesis (2.1), then the utility function $v = \alpha + \beta\, u$ where α is an arbitrary real and β is a positive real, also satisfies the Expected* Utility *Hypothesis.*

Proof By linearity of the mathematical expectation, we have $E[v(X)] = \alpha + \beta\, E[u(X)]$ for any random variable X. Now, consider two random variables X and Y such that $X \succsim Y$. The coefficient β being positive, we have the following equivalence:

$$E[u(X)] \geq E[u(Y)] \Leftrightarrow E[v(X)] \geq E[v(Y)]. \blacklozenge$$

Hence, the utility functions representing preferences over lotteries that are compatible with the Expected Utility Hypothesis (2.1) are defined up to a linear and increasing transformation. They form a subset of the set of utility functions that represent these preferences, called *cardinal* representations. As a consequence, we can arbitrarily fix the origin $u(0)$ and the units in which utility is measured. There is indeed no loss of generality in using a utility function v satisfying $v(0) = 0$ by applying the transformation $v(x) = \lambda(u(x) - u(0))$ for some $\lambda > 0$.

With a cardinal representation of preferences, comparing *utility differences* makes sense: if a is preferred to b and c is preferred to d, it is possible to say that a is preferred to b *more intensely* than c is preferred to d:

$$u(a) - u(b) > u(c) - u(d).$$

Indeed, because β is positive, such an assertion remains valid if it is expressed in terms of a transformed utility $v = \alpha + \beta u$:

$$v(a) - v(b) = \beta\, (u(a) - u(b)) > \beta\, (u(c) - u(d)) = v(c) - v(d).$$

Risk aversion

A decision-maker who systematically prefers to receive *with certainty* the mathematical expectation of a lottery, rather than trying his luck by participating in this lottery, is *risk-averse*. If the utility function u represents his preferences, it means that $u(E(X)) > E(u(X))$ for all random variable X, i.e., the utility of the expectation is greater than the expectation of the utility.

[10] *Affine transformation* is the correct mathematical term.

This definition is independent of the utility function chosen. It is therefore a characteristic of the preferences, independently of a particular utility representation. Applying the definition of risk aversion to the simple lottery $(p \mid a, b)$, we have:

$$u(pa + (1-p)b) > pu(a) + (1-p)u(b) \quad \text{for all lotteries } (p \mid a, b),\ 0 < p < 1. \tag{2.2}$$

It shows that risk aversion is equivalent to the *concavity* of the function u. In Fig. 2.4, the cord that joins the points $(a, u(a))$ and $(b, u(b))$ is located *under* the graph of the function u. This is what characterizes a concave function. The probability p determines the position of the expectation $pa + (1-p)b$ between the points a and b. We then apply *Thales' theorem* to determine the position of the expectation $pu(a) + (1-p)u(b)$ between the points $u(a)$ and $u(b)$: ratios are preserved and (2.2) is verified.

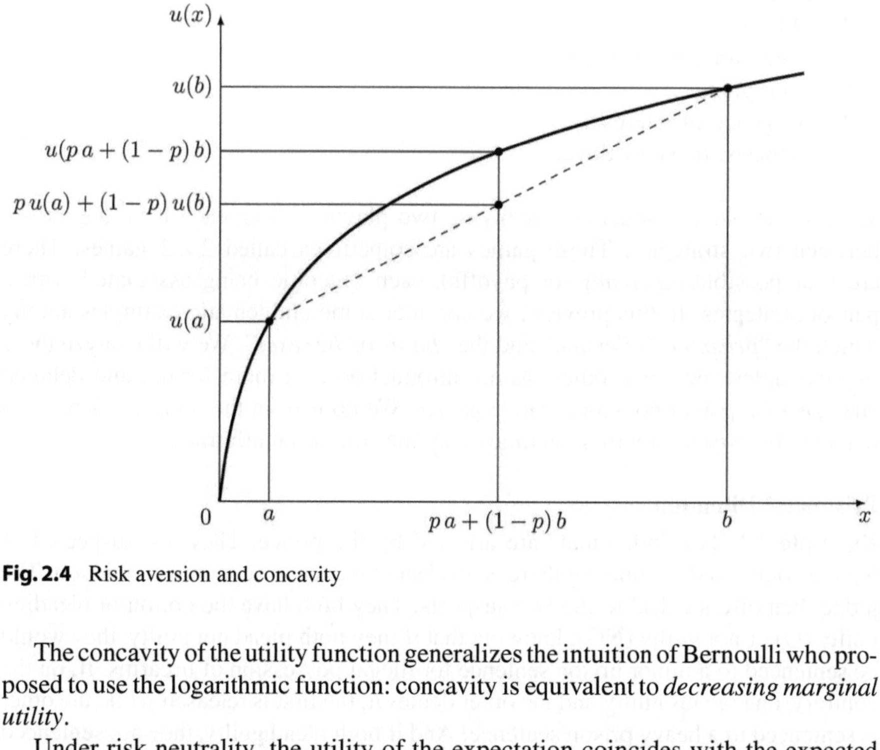

Fig. 2.4 Risk aversion and concavity

The concavity of the utility function generalizes the intuition of Bernoulli who proposed to use the logarithmic function: concavity is equivalent to *decreasing marginal utility*.

Under risk neutrality, the utility of the expectation coincides with the expected utility, for all random variables. The utility functions that represent risk-neutral preferences are then linear. We may simply set $u(x) = x$ and lotteries are then compared only in terms of their mathematical expectations.

Risk aversion is the assumption that is commonly retained. Risk aversion is often assumed to be decreasing, which intuitively means that the utility function is less and less concave. It is sometimes assumed that beyond a certain level of wealth, risk-loving may appear. It means that the utility function is first concave and eventually convex.

2.2 Non-cooperative Games: A Preview

Prisoners' dilemma
Battle of the sexes
Representation of 2-player games
Best reply and dominant strategy
Emergence of cooperation
Prudence: maximin strategy
Equilibrium
The need for coordination
Chicken game
Convergence of interests
A synthesis: hawk or dove.

We consider simple situations involving two players whom each have the choice between two strategies. These games are sometimes called 2×2 games. There are four possible *outcomes* (or payoffs), each outcome being associated with a pair of strategies. In this preview, we consider some emblematic examples among which the "*prisoners' dilemma*" and the "*battle of the sexes*". We will analyze these two examples and some others as an introduction to a more formal and detailed analysis of 2-player non-cooperative games. We do it from the point of view of an outside observer who will sometimes play the role of an arbitrator.

Prisoners' Dilemma

Example 2.1 Two individuals are arrested by the police. They are suspected of having committed a crime but there is no clear evidence to support a conviction. The judge then offers a deal to the two suspects. They both have the option of pleading guilty (G) or not guilty (NG), knowing that if they both plead not guilty, they would be sentenced to a minor prison sentence for illegal possession of firearms. If, on the contrary, one pleads guilty and the other denies it, the first is released while the other is sentenced to a heavy prison sentence! And if both plead guilty, they are sentenced to an intermediate prison term. We then have the following associations where the numbers refer to years of prison:

$$\begin{aligned}(G, G) &\rightarrow (5, 5)\\(NG, G) &\rightarrow (10,\ 0)\\(G, NG) &\rightarrow (0,\ 10)\\(NG, NG) &\rightarrow (1,\ 1)\end{aligned}$$

The preferences of the suspects are easy to imagine. The preferences of the first are given by:

$$(G, NG) \succ (NG, NG) \succ (G, G) \succ (NG, G),$$

and the preferences of the second are given by:

$$(NG, G) \succ (NG, NG) \succ (G, G) \succ (G, NG).$$

Once informed of the deal, they have the possibility to talk to each other before being isolated in their cell to think about their answers. Declaring themselves non-guilty is definitely the best solution from a collective point of view, and this is most probably the conclusion that they may have reached when talking to each other. Do they actually have an interest to commit? No, as we shall see. They will quickly realize that their own interest is to plead guilty and, as a result, they will find themselves behind bars for 5 years! In the choice of the jail terms, what counts is the relative number of years. The sequence 1, 5, 10, 20 would produce the same result as the sequence 0, 1, 5, 10.

Not considering possible prior agreements is what characterizes non-cooperative games.

Battle of the Sexes

Example 2.2 Couples often face a problem of choice between various activities, for instance, where to go for holidays. Consider a couple and two possible destinations, seaside (S) or mountain (M). There are four possible results: they may go together to the seaside or to the mountain, or else they may decide to go separate. The difficulty comes up when they have opposite preferences: he prefers the seaside while she prefers mountain hiking.[11] Of course, they also prefer to be together. And if they end up separate, they prefer to be in their favorite place. Hence, the man's preferences are given by:

$$(S, S) \succ (M, M) \succ (S, M) \succ (M, S),$$

while the woman's preferences are given by:

$$(M, M) \succ (S, S) \succ (S, M) \succ (M, S).$$

[11] The original story has a sexist connotation: the choice is between a football match and a concert, and the man prefers the football ...

We only know the ranking of the four possible results: we have no information on the intensity of preferences. Like in the prisoners' dilemma, the information we have is purely *ordinal.*

If the choices were made sequentially, the outcome is immediate: the one who chooses first proposes to go to his or her preferred place, and the other then follows. The question is then to know who will have the privilege to choose first. If instead, choices are made without knowing the choice made by the other and without any coordination, there is a problem.

We know that the alternative (M, S) is excluded because they both agree that it is the worse situation. We also know that if each stands firm on his or her preferred destination, they will end up separately, the penultimate alternative for both. Clearly, each one has an interest to give up, but who?

This is a *coordination problem.* If the game is repeated through time, a natural solution would be to alternate. If not, the protagonists could decide to flip a coin. This is a fair solution because everyone has *ex-ante* the same probability to end up in his preferred environment and they are sure to be together. This way of solving the problem is equivalent to a sequential choice where the one who chooses first is decided by flipping a coin.

Representation of 2-player games

Players are identified by a *number* (1 or 2), and strategies are identified by a *letter.* Each player has preferences over the outcomes associated with the possible *pairs* of strategies. At this stage, we limit ourselves to two strategies, implying a total of four outcomes, and we assume that no player is indifferent between different outcomes. Being in an ordinal framework, the simplest utility representation of preferences consists in assigning the numbers 1, 2, 3 and 4 to the four outcomes. We could have taken the sequence $(-1, 0, 3, 9)$ to represent the same preferences, in lieu and place of the sequence $(1, 2, 3, 4)$. This information can be summarized in a table whose rows and columns correspond to strategies. By convention, player 1 controls the rows and player 2 controls the columns. Each cell contains two numbers and the first one concerns player 1. The matrix corresponding to the prisoners' dilemma is given in Table 2.1.

Table 2.1 Prisoners' dilemma

	G	*NG*
G	2, 2	4, 1
NG	1, 4	3, 3

If player 1 plays *G* and player 2 plays *NG*, the outcome is (4, 1): the best for player 1 and the worst for player 2. While if they both play *NG*, they both end up in the second-best situation. Similarly, the matrix corresponding to the battle of the sexes is given in Table 2.2.

Table 2.2 Battle of the sexes

	S	*M*
S	4, 3	2, 2
M	1, 1	3, 4

One important point: each player is perfectly informed of the preferences of the other: they are aware of the information summarized in the matrix. In other words, we are in a situation of *complete information*.

Best reply and dominant strategy

In analyzing a game, each player should first identify the strategies that would be best against the strategies of his opponent. These are the best replies. They are conditional. For instance, considering player 1's best replies, *G* is his best reply to *NG* in the prisoners' dilemma, and *M* is her best reply to *M* in the battle of the sexes. But players may also put themselves in the other player's shoes and evaluate his best replies. This is an analysis that each player performs inwardly. There is no sequentiality. Players will finally have to decide on a strategy without knowing the choice of his opponent. It is *as if the players were playing simultaneously.*

One particularity of the prisoners' dilemma is that pleading guilty (*G*) is for both players the best reply to both strategies of the other. Players know that and they know that their opponent knows it. In such a situation, it is easy to guess the outcome: the two players will plead guilty. But this is suboptimal: the pair of strategies (*NG*, *NG*) is indeed preferred by both of them! This justifies the term *dilemma*: pursuing individual interests may not contribute to collective interests. Even if the suspects had agreed to plead non-guilty, none of them has actually an interest to respect his commitment.

The strategy "plead guilty" is the best reply to the strategy "plead guilty", and it is also the best reply to the strategy "plead non-guilty". It is therefore the best strategy because each player would lose by pleading non-guilty, independently of what the other does: "plead guilty" is *the dominant strategy*. In general, if a player has a dominant strategy, it is necessarily *unique* because it is *strictly better* than all other strategies. His opponent is able to guess it and he will then apply his best reply.

The British game show *Golden Balls* where two players have to *Split* or *Steal* a large amount of money is similar to the prisoners' dilemma. It is summarized in Table 2.3 where the numbers are percentages of the sum at stake. If both players choose Steal, they end up with nothing while if the both decide to Split, the sum of money is equally divided. So, it is not exactly a prisoners' dilemma: the best reply to Steal is not clearly established. In the actual play of the game, the tendency is definitely towards an equal division, but not always. Each player tries to convince his opponent that he will play Split but, it happens that one of the players eventually decides to deviate and play in Steal.

Table 2.3 Golden balls

	Split	Steal
Split	50, 50	0, 100
Steal	100, 0	0, 0

In what follows, the best replies will be indicated by *underlining* the corresponding payoff, as illustrated in Tables 2.4 and 2.5 for the prisoners' dilemma and the battle of the sexes. Unlike the prisoners' dilemma, there is no dominant strategy in the battle of the sexes. The best reply is indeed to reproduce the other's strategy.

Table 2.4 Best replies in the prisoners' dilemma

	G	*NG*
G	$\underline{2}, \underline{2}$	$\underline{4}, 1$
NG	$1, \underline{4}$	3, 3

Table 2.5 Best replies in the battle of the sexes

	S	*M*
S	$\underline{4}, \underline{3}$	2, 2
M	1, 1	$\underline{3}, \underline{4}$

Emergence of cooperation

Many real-world situations are in accordance with the parable of the prisoners' dilemma where "pleading non-guilty" is equated with "cooperating" while "pleading guilty" is equated with "defection". If the game is played only once, rational players will implement their dominant strategy, namely defection. If instead the game is repeated through time, the picture changes considerably. Indeed, a repeated game is not the simple juxtaposition of instantaneous games: players have to think about the consequences of their decisions and plan ahead. A player's strategy in a repeated game must specify what the player will do at *each* period, conditionally to *all* possible strategies of his opponent. Hence, a strategy may be quite complex.

If the prisoners' dilemma is repeated a *finite and known* number of times, rationality still imposes to the players to defect at each period. Indeed, no player has an interest to cooperate in the last period and, therefore, no player has an interest to cooperate in the penultimate period. Reasoning retroactively in this way brings us to the conclusion that no player has an interest to cooperate from the beginning.

It goes differently if the game is repeated over an infinite horizon, with possibly a small but positive probability that the game ends at each period. The experimental work conducted by Axelrod (1984) shows that in such a framework cooperation may emerge through two simple strategies, *grim trigger* and *tit-for-tat*. In both cases, players cooperate in the first period. The grim trigger strategy consists for a player to keep cooperating at each subsequent period as long as his opponent cooperates and, in case he defects, to punish him by defecting for ever. The tit-for-tat strategy consists for a player to simply reproduce the last choice of his opponent. Clearly, if both players adopt the same strategy, either grim trigger or tit-for-tat, cooperation will be observed at all periods. Notice that tit-for-tat seems less harsh because it allows for a return to cooperation after some periods of defection, but if *both* players adopt the tit-for-tat strategy, cooperation disappears forever as well once a defection occurs. Axelrod has organized tournaments by inviting game theoreticians to submit strategies. It turned out that the grim-trigger strategy submitted by Rapoport won against all the other strategies.

Prudence: maximin strategy

In a conflicting situation, assuming that no player has a dominant strategy, a player may decide to behave prudently by adopting a strategy that ensures a *minimum* utility whatever his opponent does. The idea is the following. The player first associates with each of his strategies the result that has the lowest utility (the worst-case scenario) and then chooses the strategy that ensures him the largest of these utility levels. This is the *maximin* strategy to which is associated a utility level called *security level*. By adopting this strategy, the player is indeed certain not to end up with a utility below that level. Notice that a dominant strategy is necessarily prudent. It is the case of pleading guilty in the prisoners' dilemma. In the battle of the sexes, the maximin strategy consists for each player to choose his preferred destination. As a result, if both adopt this strategy, they will end up in their preferred destination but separated. So, adopting a maximin strategy may not be a good idea.

Equilibrium

In the battle of the sexes, no particular strategy choice emerges. However, we observe that the strategy profiles (S, S) and (M, M) are *stable* in the sense that no one could gain by deviating *unilaterally*. Indeed, conditional to the choice of the first player to go to the seaside, the best reply of the second player is to go along, and vice versa. Similarly, conditional to the choice of the second player to go to the mountain, the best reply of the first player is to go along, and vice versa. Hence, we have $S \rightarrow S$ and $M \rightarrow M$ as can be seen from Table 2.5.

A pair of strategies where each is a best reply to the other, defines an *equilibrium* strategy profile. If, for whatever reason, the players adopt strategies that form an equilibrium profile, none of them has an incentive to deviate *alone*. This is the idea introduced by Augustin Cournot (1838) to solve his duopoly problem. It was later established as a general concept applied to non-cooperative games by John Nash. This is the reason why economists often use the term "*Cournot–Nash equilibrium*".

In the battle of the sexes, having identified the two equilibria (S, S) and (M, M) does not really help. We only know that being in one or the other situation, no one has an incentive to deviate. And nothing allows an outside observer to privilege one of them, at least without additional information. Remember that we are in an *ordinal* framework. Notice that the profile formed by maximin strategies is not an equilibrium. We will see that it is often so, except when the interests of the two players are systematically opposed. It is the case of zero-sum-games where what one gains is what the other loses.

In the prisoners' dilemma, the strategy profile (G, G) is the unique equilibrium. In terms of best replies, $G \to G$ and $NG \to G$ as can be seen in Table 2.4. Unicity is a consequence of the fact that G is the dominant strategy for both players. In general, if a dominant strategy exists, it is unique and necessarily part of any equilibrium. Therefore, if both players have a dominant strategy, together they define the unique equilibrium.

Example 2.3 The arms race between United States and Soviet Union in the years 1950–1970 offers an illustration of the prisoners' dilemma by assimilating cooperation to disarmament and defection to armament, and assuming that both share the following preferences:

$$\text{military superiority} \succ \text{mutual disarmament} \succ \text{arms race} \succ \text{military inferiority.}$$

In the case where the game is repeated, we have seen that an equilibrium where cooperation occurs obtains if both players adopt the grim trigger strategy. This is equally true if both players adopt the tit-for-tat strategy. Mutual disarmament is eventually what has been observed, after many years of confrontation followed by arduous negotiations.

The need for coordination

Faced with a problem like the battle of the sexes, it appears that coordination between players' actions is desirable. The battle of the sexes being a game that is likely to be repeated, it would be natural to alternate the destinations, the sea side one year and the mountain the year after. This is fair as soon as we do not leave the ordinal framework by introducing intensities of preference. What happens if he suffers from altitude sickness?...

Alternating is a *convention*. In the absence of repetition, an alternative convention could be to rely on chance by flipping a coin. This is the concept of *correlated strategy*. More generally, a correlated strategy is a random mechanism that "suggests" strategies to players. A correlated strategy is in equilibrium if no player has an incentive to deviate from the suggestion he receives. It differs from the notion of *mixed* strategy or *randomized* strategies where each player relies *individually* on a random mechanism: a mixed strategy attaches probabilities to pure strategies. In the battle of the sexes, if each player flips a coin to choose a destination, they end up with their least preferred outcomes with a probability equal to 1/4.

Introducing probabilities on strategies induces an enlargement of the set of strategies. Pure strategies are indeed particular mixed strategies obtained by placing a probability equal to 1 on a pure strategy. Furthermore, mixed strategies induce particular correlated strategies. In terms of *ex-ante* attainable outcomes, *expressed in expected* utilities, we have the following sequence of inclusions: {pure strategies} $\subset$ {mixed strategies} $\subset$ {correlated strategies}.

What can be obtained by playing pure strategies can be obtained by playing mixed strategies, and what can be obtained by playing mixed strategies can be obtained through correlated strategies.

It is important to realize that, in such a probabilistic context, players are facing lotteries and therefore, outcomes are specified in expected utility terms. As a consequence, we move from an ordinal to a cardinal framework in which comparing utility differences has a meaning and the choice of the utility levels associated with pure strategies can no more be arbitrary.

If players decide to cooperate, relying on correlated strategies could be an option to coordinate their actions for a better outcome. Correlation of strategies is indeed a step towards cooperation. It will be the object of Chap. 3 dedicated to bargaining.

Chicken Game

Example 2.4 Imagine two car drivers heading towards each other at high speed on a narrow road. They have two options, either continue or swerve out of the way. In this stupid game, there can be only one winner, the one who continues while the other swerves. The latter is then the "chicken". If they both swerve, there is no winner. And if none swerves, they collide. Let C and S denote the two strategies, "continue" or "swerve". We assume that the preferences of the car drivers are given by:

$$(C, S) \succ (S, S) \succ (S, C) \succ (C, C) \text{ for driver 1,}$$
$$(S, C) \succ (S, S) \succ (C, S) \succ (C, C) \text{ for driver 2.}$$

They agree to consider the frontal crash as the worse outcome. Failing to win, they both place in second position the outcome where they both throw down the gauntlet. The game is summarized in Table 2.6. The situation is similar to the battle of the sexes: there are two equilibria, (C, S) and (S, C), and the coordination problem is fundamentally the same.

Table 2.6 Chicken game

	C	S
C	1, 1	$\underline{4}, \underline{2}$
S	$\underline{2}, \underline{4}$	3, 3

The underlying stories are, of course, quite different! In the Chicken Game, a collision is likely to end up with the death of both participants. The recommendation of an outside observer is self-evident: players should both give up. This is equivalent to convince the players not to play this game. Giving up is also what prudence suggests. However, if one player is sure that his opponent will give up, he has an interest in pursuing. In the battle of the sexes, players should build up a reputation of inflexibility. In the Chicken Game, players should build up a reputation of a hothead.

Given the story, remaining in an ordinal framework may not be appropriate. It would be more realistic to associate a collision with a level of utility in line with the consequences, for instance −1000. However, from an ordinal point of view, the two representations are equivalent, although the recommendation to give up addressed to the players appears to be more justified. The ordinal representation has its limits, even outside a probabilistic reasoning.

Example 2.5 The famous Cuban missiles' crisis of October 1962 can be seen as an illustration of the Chicken Game. The world came close to a nuclear war between the Soviet Union (SU) and the United States (US). The principal actors were Nikita Khrushchev and John Kennedy. The latter has indeed revealed that, at that moment, he had estimated the probability of a conflict to be between 1/3 and 1/2! Mid-October, the CIA discovered that soviets were installing missile ramps on Cuban soil.[12] After analyzing the situation and considered various actions, Kennedy eventually decided to establish a naval blockade of the island of Cuba, without excluding an invasion. Khrushchev then decided to withdraw the missiles on the condition that the US removes their missiles from Turkey (a demand officially denied) and to the engagement not to invade Cuba. It is finally the compromise solution that has prevailed, to the great relief of the world. Only 13 days passed between the discovery of the missiles and the decision to withdraw them.

There are different ways to analyze the problem in strategic terms. Brams (1975) has been the first to study this cold war episode as a *Chicken game* in which "continue" corresponds to "destroy" or "maintain", and "swerve" corresponds to "blockade" or "withdraw". Soviet motivations remain, however, unknown to date.[13] Taylor and Pacelli (2008) have proposed an alternative representation based on Soviet's fear of invasion. We then get two different points of view summarized in Tables 2.7 and 2.8. We observe that the compromise solution corresponds to maximin strategies.

Table 2.7 Cuban missiles: the US point of view

	Maintain missile	Withdraw missiles
Destroy ramps	1, 1	4, 2
Blockade	2, 4	3, 3

Table 2.8 Cuban missiles: the SU point of view

	Maintain missile	Withdraw missiles
Invasion	1, 1	4, 2
No invasion	2, 4	3, 3

[12] One has to keep in mind that Cuba is only 500 miles away from Florida!

[13] See also Brams (1985a, b, 2003) who analyzes a sequential scenario.

Convergence of interests

The situations that we have analyzed so far were all including a mix of possibilities of conflict and opportunities for cooperation. Table 2.9 describes a game where there are two equilibria where, unlike the battle of the sexes or the chicken game, one equilibrium dominates the other *in the sense of Pareto*.

Table 2.9 Game with two comparable equilibria

	A	*B*
A	4, 4	1, 3
B	3, 1	2, 2

The outcome associated with the pair of strategies (*A*, *A*) is indeed preferred by both players to the outcome associated with the pair of strategies (*B*, *B*). There is *unanimity*. This had already been observed in the prisoners' dilemma with, however, an important difference: in the prisoners' dilemma, the equilibrium is unique and includes dominant strategies. In the above example instead, no coordination seems possible without a communication between the players and they could find themselves stuck in the second-best situation.

In the game described in Table 2.9, the strategy pair (*A*, *A*) is a *focal point*, to use the terminology introduced by Schelling (1960). The idea of the focal point is simple and feeds on the following parable. Two persons get lost in a city and seek to find each other. Will they succeed in guessing where the other will go? This, of course, depends on what each person knows about the other. To be a focal point, it must be unique and require a minimum of logical reasoning, similar to the one that underlies the concept of best reply. The *Chicken Game* and its application to the Cuban missiles' crisis offers another example of focal point. In these examples, players are facing a decision under uncertainty. We will come back to this question when discussing risk-dominance.

This game also covers the case of two firms whose activities are complementary. They contemplate the possibility of entering a new market. They both prefer entering together in order to benefit fully of their complementarities. Failing to enter together, a firm prefers to enter alone, what the other considers as the worse outcome.

Example 2.6 The stag hunt parable that appears in the second part of the *Discours sur l'origine et les fondements des inégalités*, Jean-Jacques Rousseau offers an illustration of this game.

> This is how men could insensibly acquire some crude idea of mutual commitments and of the advantage of fulfilling them, but only as much as the prèsent and sensible interest required; for foresight was nothing for them, and far from dealing with a distant future, they did not even think of the next day. Was it a question of capturing a stag, everyone felt well that he had to keep his post faithfully; but if a hare would pass within the reach of one of them, there is no doubt that he would pursued him without scruples, and that having reached his prey he did not care very much to make his companions miss theirs.

The hunters have the possibility of capturing the stag if they coordinate themselves but they also have the possibility to capture a hare in which case they lose the stag. Table 2.10 illustrates this situation where *A* corresponds to ignoring the hare and *B* corresponds to capturing it.

Table 2.10 Stag hunt game

	A	*B*
A	$\underline{4}, \underline{4}$	$\underline{3}, 1$
B	$1, \underline{3}$	$2, 2$

The interests of both players are clearly convergent: cooperation is the most plausible outcome because *A* is a dominant strategy for both players. As a consequence, the pair of strategies (*A*, *A*) defines the unique equilibrium. Unlike the prisoners' dilemma, the implementation of these individually rational strategies leads to a solution that is collectively rational.

A synthesis: hawk or dove

The preceding examples can be placed within a single framework. Imagine two nations that covet a territory. They have two options: *Hawk* or *Dove.* If they both behave as doves, they share the territory peacefully. If only one behaves as a hawk, the other gives up. And if they both behave as hawks, a war follows, with all its disastrous consequences for the people concerned.

It remains to specify the preferences, remaining in a symmetric context. We may assume that both nations prefer to take over the territory or to sign a peace treaty than go to war or to give up. In terms of the preferences of the first nation, we then have:

$$(H, D) \succ_1 (H, H), \ (D, D) \succ_1 (H, H), \ (H, D) \succ_1 (D, H), \ (D, D) \succ_1 (D, H).$$

This leaves room for four symmetric configurations. Consider first the most frequent but unfortunate case where taking over the territory is placed on top. Depending on where nations place war, we then have two possibilities:

$$(H, D) \succ_1 (D, D) \succ_1 (D, H) \succ_1 (H, H),$$

or

$$(H, D) \succ_1 (D, D) \succ_1 (H, H) \succ_1 (D, H)$$

Player 2's ranking follows by symmetry. If war is placed last, we obtain a Chicken Game with two equilibria as illustrated in Table 2.11.

Table 2.11 Hawk or dove: war placed last

	Hawk	Dove
Hawk	1, 1	4, 2
Dove	2, 4	3, 3

If instead going to war is preferred to give up, we obtain a prisoners' dilemma as illustrated in Table 2.12. There is a unique equilibrium and it involves dominant strategies.

Table 2.12 Hawk or dove: war preferred to give up

	Hawk	Dove
Hawk	2, 2	4, 1
Dove	1, 4	3, 3

Now, let's be optimistic and consider the virtuous case where peace and coexistence are placed on top. We then have two possibilities:

$$(D, D) \succ_1 (H, D) \succ_1 (D, H) \succ_1 (H, H)$$
$$\text{or } (D, D) \succ_1 (H, D) \succ_1 (H, H) \succ_1 (D, H).$$

There is a convergence of interests in both cases, as illustrated in Tables 2.13 and 2.14.

Table 2.13 Hawk or dove: peace and coexistence on top, war last

	Hawk	Dove
Hawk	1, 1	3, 2
Dove	2, 3	4, 4

Table 2.14 Hawk or dove: peace and coexistence on top followed by war

	Hawk	Dove
Hawk	2, 2	3, 1
Dove	1, 3	4, 4

In the case where the two nations place war in the last position, there is a unique equilibrium and it involves dominant strategies: peace will prevail. The second case corresponds to the stag hunt Game. There are two equilibria and it may be that, for historical reasons, the two nations find themselves stuck in the least favorable equilibrium, namely war. This is all too often the case in regional conflicts, where the energy and perseverance of the international community are needed to bring the belligerents to the point of peace.

Finally, consider an asymmetric situation where only one nation places war in the last position, as illustrated in Table 2.15.

Table 2.15 Hawk or dove: an asymmetric situation

	Hawk	Dove
Hawk	2, 1	4, 2
Dove	1, 4	3, 3

Hawk is then the dominant strategy for the nation that prefers going to war than to giving up, and there is a unique equilibrium where the other nation gives up. This confirms the value of posing as a falcon.

So far, we have considered games with at least one equilibrium. Actually, there is no guarantee that a game possesses an equilibrium. Table 2.16 describes a situation where there is no equilibrium:

Table 2.16 Hawk or dove: no equilibrium case

	A	*B*
A	4, 1	1, 4
B	3, 3	2, 2

We will later see that all games have an equilibrium once we allow for mixed strategies, in which case we leave the ordinal framework adopted so far.

Vilfredo Pareto is a philosopher, economist, sociologist, political scientist and engineer of the end of the nineteenth century, who succeeded Léon Walras at the Chair of political economy of the University of Lausanne. He is the author of the *Cours d'économie politique* published in 1896. His name is associated with the comparison of states of society.

A state of society specifies the situation of each of its members, measured by his or her level of well-being. A state a dominates *in the sense of Pareto* a state b if each member is in a better or equivalent situation in the first state, and at least one is in a better situation. This definition does not allow for a comparison of *all* states. It only allows a partial ranking.

To formalise this definition, consider a society composed of a set $N = \{1,\ldots,n\}$ of individuals and a set of states $X = \{a, b, c, \ldots\}$ on which they all have preferences. Then, a state a dominates a state b *if and only if* they all prefer a to b or are indifferent, and at least one prefers a to b:

$$a \succsim_i b \text{ for } \textit{all } i \in N \text{ and } a \succ_i b \text{ for } \textit{at least one } i \in N$$

or, alternatively,

$$u_i(a) \geq u_i(b) \text{ for } \textit{all } i \in N \text{ and } u_i(a) > u_i(b) \text{ for } \textit{at least one } i \in N$$

2.3 The Extensive Form

Game trees
Strategies in game trees
Common knowledge, complete information and perfect information
Backward induction.

We continue, limiting ourselves to 2-player games and assuming *complete information:* players know all the details of the game they play, including the preferences of their opponent. The games analyzed in the Preview were *one-shot* games. Here instead, we start with games that are being played *sequentially*. These are *dynamic games* or *games in extensive form* that include a detailed description of the game progress. The games that we analyzed in the Preview are *games in strategic form (or normal form)* which specify the strategies of the players and their preferences over the possible outcomes. We will see that a game in strategic form can be associated with a game in extensive form. However, the strategic form is a reduced form: the information on the sequentiality is indeed lost in the reduction process.

Game trees

The extensive form of a game is a complete description of the game that includes its sequential structure. Each step is attached to the name of one of the players. It specifies the *actions* available to that player and the information he has accumulated at that step. A tree made of *nodes* and *branches* (oriented) is used to graphically represent the sequential structure. There is one *initial node* and several *terminal nodes*. Branches do not overlap and there is no loop. Each non-terminal node belongs to one of the players and the branches that emanate from that node correspond to the actions (moves) available to that player. Outcomes (payoffs) are associated with terminal nodes. We will see later how to incorporate the information that each player has at each node and how it evolves as the game progresses.

Example 2.7 Simple Game Tree. Figure 2.5 illustrates a simple game in extensive form. Player 1 may intervene twice, depending on his action at the initial node and

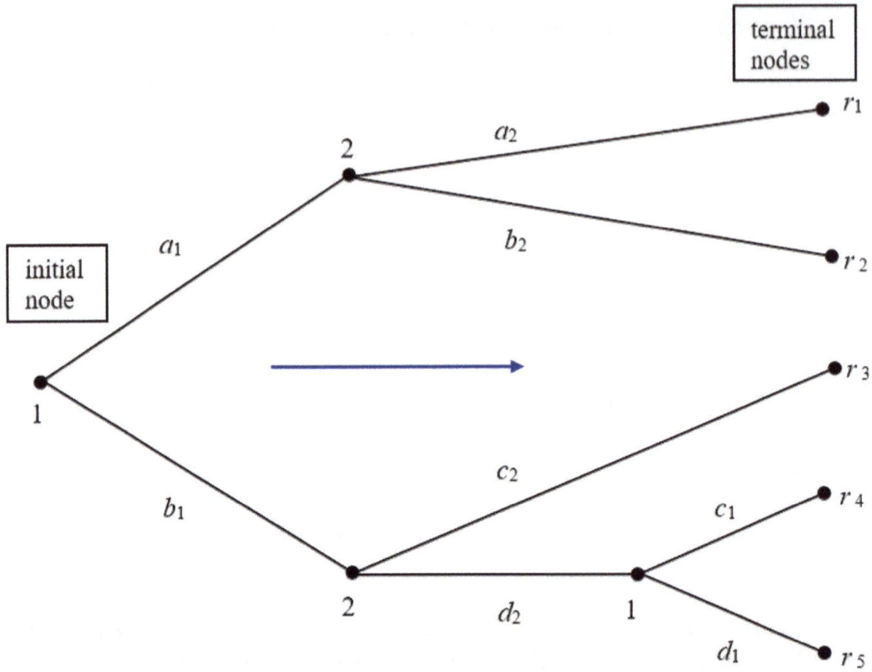

Fig. 2.5 A simple game tree

on subsequent actions of his opponent. At each non-terminal node, players have the choice between two actions. The game ends with five possible outcomes.

Player i has preferences $\succsim_i$ defined on the outcomes of the game. We do not rule out the case where a player is indifferent between several outcomes. The preferences of player i are represented by a utility function u_i and $u_i(r)$ is *the* utility or *payoff* associated with the outcome r.[14]

Referring to the game in Fig. 2.5, assume that players rank the five outcomes as follows:

$$r_4 \succ_1 r_1 \succ_1 r_2 \sim_1 r_3 \sim_1 r_5 \text{ for player 1,}$$
$$r_5 \succ_2 r_3 \succ_2 r_1 \succ_2 r_4 \succ_2 r_2 \text{ for player 2.}$$

Possible payoffs are given in Fig. 2.6:

$$u_1(r_1) = 3, \quad u_1(r_2) = u_1(r_3) = 0, \quad u_1(r_4) = 5, \quad u_1(r_5) = 0,$$
$$u_2(r_1) = 3, \quad u_2(r_2) = 0, \quad u_2(r_3) = 4, \quad u_2(r_4) = 2, \quad u_2(r_5) = 5.$$

[14] Payoffs may be expressed in monetary terms and a negative payoff indicates a loss.

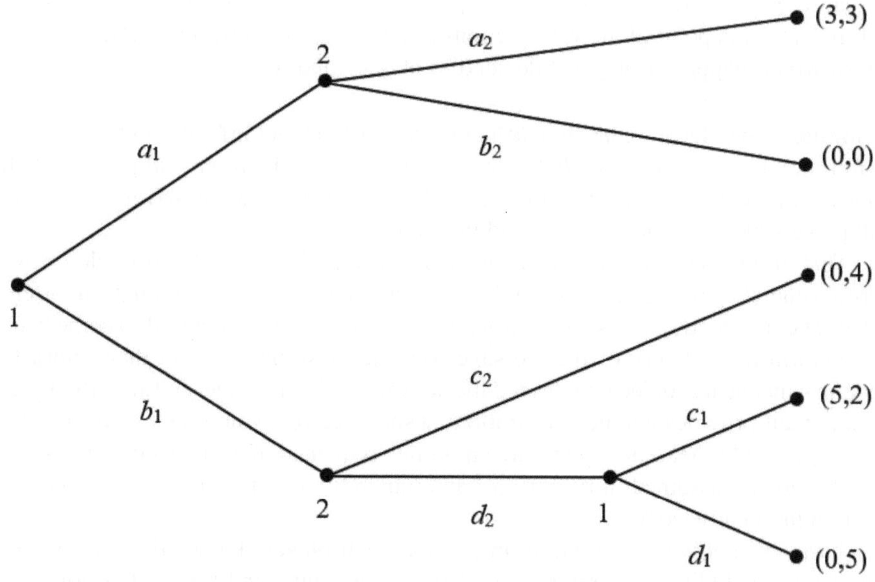

Fig. 2.6 Game tree: specifying the payoffs

Players maximize their utility. This only means that players try to achieve the largest payoff. The difficulty lies in the fact that players can only control their own actions. Their final payoff depends on the actions of the other player.

Strategies in game trees
In sequential games, a strategy for a player must specify a list of actions, an action *at each and every non-terminal node that concerns that player*. As a consequence, it is possible to associate with each pair of strategies with a *unique* path joining the initial node to a terminal node. Put differently, an outcome can be associated with each pair of strategies, like in a game in strategic form.

Example 2.7 (continued) In the game illustrated in Fig. 2.5 and 2.6, each player has four strategies:

$$S_1 = \{a_1c_1,\ a_1d_1,\ b_1c_1,\ b_1d_1\} \text{ for player 1,}$$
$$S_2 = \{a_2c_2,\ a_2d_2,\ b_2c_2,\ b_2d_2\} \text{ for player 2.}$$

For instance, the outcome $r_1 = (3, 3)$ is associated with the pair $(a_1c_1,\ a_2c_2)$.

It is important to understand why a strategy of a player requires the specification of an action at *each* node that belongs to that player, even if some of the actions may actually not be activated. For instance, in the pair of strategies (a_1c_1, a_2c_2), the actions c_1 and c_2 are not activated. This information is, however, essential because we then know what would happen if player 1 decided to play b_1 instead of a_1. From his point of view, the actions c_1 and c_2 are *threats*. Similarly, we know what would happen if player 2 decided to play d_2 and not c_2.

Common knowledge, complete information and perfect information
Information is *common knowledge* among players if it is known by all players, if all players know that all players know it, if all players know that all players know that all players know it, and so forth... ad infinitum.

This infinite sequence of statements is needed as shown by the example of two army generals positioned in two different places and willing to coordinate an offensive. The first sends a messenger through enemy lines. He is supposed to come back to confirm the delivery of the message. But the messenger should then return to confirm that he has indeed confirmed the delivery of the message, and so forth. Electronic mail provides another illustration: absolute certainty about the delivery of a message would theoretically require an infinite sequence of acknowledgements.

Players are assumed to be *rational* and rationality of each player is assumed to be common knowledge.

There is *complete information* in a game if all players know all the details of the game, including the preferences of the participants, and that fact is common knowledge.

We distinguish complete information from perfect information. There is *perfect information* in a game if, at each step of the game, players know the past actions of their opponents as well as their own past actions.

In the present book, we will limit ourselves to complete information games and analyze situations of imperfect information where, at some step, a player ignores the choice made by the player preceding him. We will, however, assume *perfect recall*: all along a game, players are assumed to have a perfect memory of their past actions.

The concept of *information set* is used to represent imperfect information. An information set groups several nodes of a given player that cannot be distinguished on the basis of the information available. As a consequence, *identical actions* must be associated with each of these nodes and information is perfect if all information sets are singletons.

Example 2.8 Game Tree with Imperfect Information. Figure 2.7 covers a modification of Example 2.7, assuming that player 2, when asked to play, ignores the choice made by player 1.

Backward induction
If information is perfect (and complete), backward induction is a simple method to "solve" a game in extensive form. It consists in starting from the terminal nodes and to ride up to the initial node, assuming that, at each step, the player concerned chooses the best action *and* this is common knowledge.

Example 2.7 (continued) Fig. 2.8 illustrates the reasoning behind backward reduction for the game illustrated by Fig. 2.6:

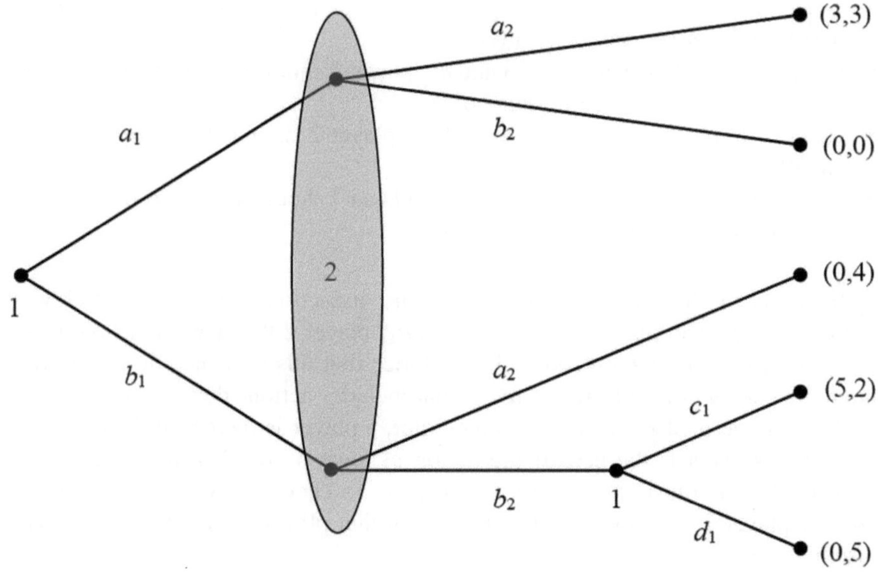

Fig. 2.7 A game tree with imperfect information

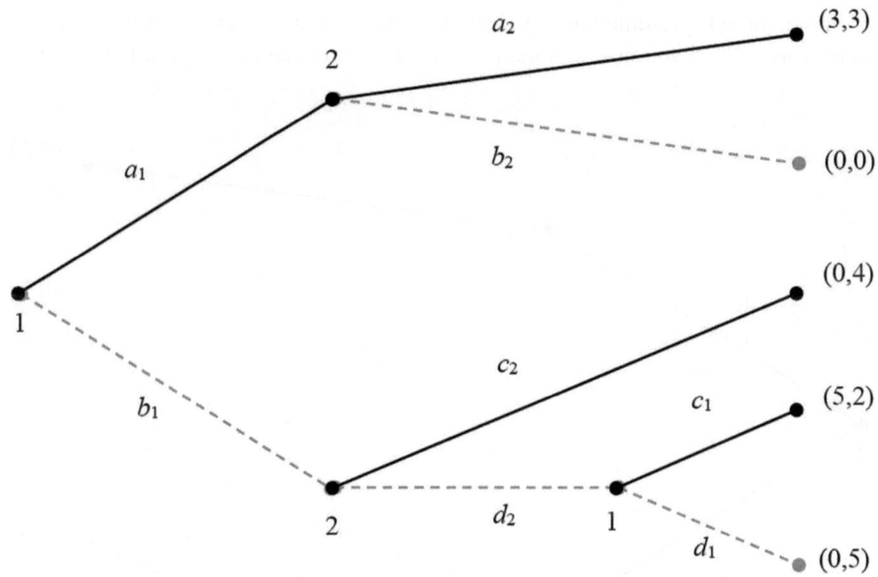

Fig. 2.8 Backward induction under perfect information

- faced with the choice between c_1 and d_1, player 1 should choose c_1 to which a payoff of 5 is associated, instead of 0,
- faced with the choice between c_2 and d_2, player 2 should *then* choose c_2 to which a payoff of 4 is associated, instead of 2,
- faced with the choice between a_2 and b_2, player 2 should choose a_2 to which a payoff of 3 is associated, instead of 0,
- faced with the choice between a_1 and b_1, player 1 should *then* choose a_1 to which a payoff of 3 is associated, instead of 0.

In terms of the game progress, backward induction produces the following sequence of choice: player 1 choose action a_1, player 2 then choose action a_2 and the game ends with the outcome (3, 3). Notice that this sequence of actions rests upon the pair of strategies (a_1c_1, a_2c_2) that includes actions that are *not* activated.

This simple method fails if, at some point, a player is *indifferent* between several actions. This is the case if the action c_2 gave player 2 a utility equal to 2 instead of 4, as illustrated in Fig. 2.9. Having to choose between the actions a_1 and b_1, player 1 is unable to guess the action that player 2 will choose following his choice of b_1.

It is therefore not always possible to identify a *unique* path joining the initial node to a terminal node. It remains, however, possible to identify actions at some nodes that a rational player will never choose.

In the game represented at Fig. 2.9, the actions c_2 and d_2 are equally optimal. If there were a third action available, producing a lower payoff, it would be rejected.

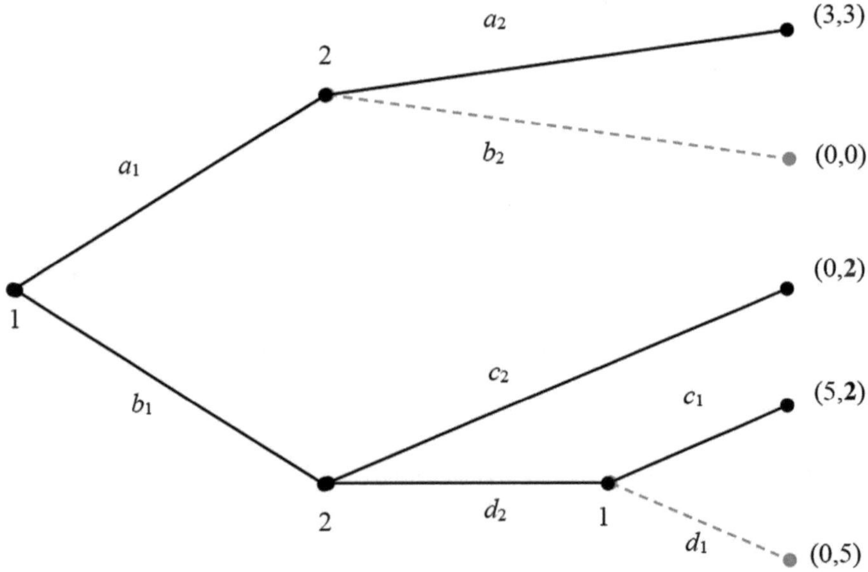

Fig. 2.9 Incomplete backward induction under perfect information

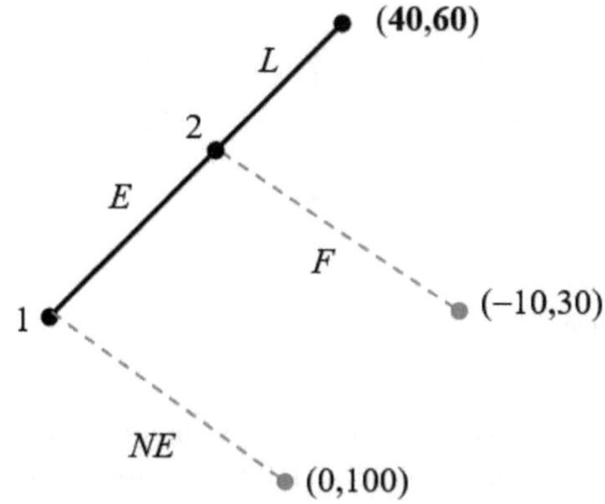

Fig. 2.10 Location of a sales outlet

We will come back later to this question of optimal choices with the notion of *subgame perfection.*

Example 2.9 Location of a Sales Outlet. A petroleum company contemplates the possibility to install a gas station near another gas station owned by a competing company. If the entry (E) occurs, the incumbent company has two options: fight back (F) by running an aggressive price policy, costly for both companies, or laissez-faire (L) and share the market. If instead, the installation does not take place (NE), nothing changes.

The simple game tree in Fig. 2.10 illustrates the situation where payoffs are indicative:

- 100 is the profit obtained by the incumbent when there is a single gas station,
- if the entry takes place and the incumbent defends himself, the latter loses a good part of his profits, while the entrant makes a loss,
- if they share the market, the profit is divided, with possibly an advantage to the incumbent.

What matters in the specification of the payoffs is the way each company orders the outcomes.

There is no surprise when using backward induction: the incumbent has no interest in fighting back and this is anticipated by the entrant who then decides to install the new gas station and share the market with the incumbent.

Example 2.10 Centipede (Rosenthal, 1981). Players act successively, one after the other. There are six rounds and, at each round, the player concerned has the possibility to pass the hand (C) or to stop the game (S). The payoffs are given in Fig. 2.11.

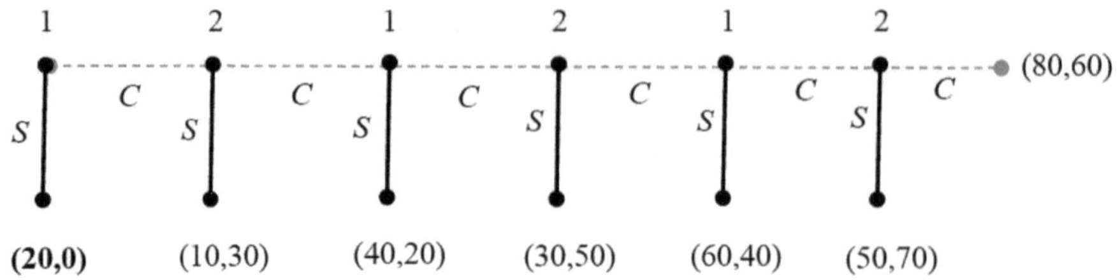

Fig. 2.11 Centipede game

Clearly, players have a *common interest* in pursuing the game until the end, with (80, 60) as an outcome. However, a rational analysis retains only one pair of strategies, namely (*SSS*, *SSS*). As a result, the game ends immediately, with a poor outcome compared to (80, 60). It is indeed what backward induction reveals. The optimal choice of player 2 at the last step would be to stop. He gets 70 instead of 60. Player 1 would then anticipate that choice and decide to stop the game. He gets 60 instead of 50. This is anticipated by player 2. And so on until the first step where player 1 decides to stop, getting 20 instead of 10.

Backward induction generally fails when information is imperfect.

Example 2.8 (continued) In the game illustrated by Fig. 2.7, player 2 ignores the choice made by player 1 at the outset of the game but he can still anticipate that player 1 would opt for c_1 if he had to play a second time.

In this particular example, it turns out that a_2 is optimal because the resulting payoffs are greater in both cases, given the choice of c_1 by player 1. Player 1 can figure it out and play a_1, leading to the final outcome (3, 3).

Figure 2.12 is a modified version where 4 is replaced by 1. Backward induction then fails to produce a solution in this game.

Chance can be introduced in a game by inserting a fictitious player, called "Chance", whose choices are defined by a probability distribution over a set of branches.

For example, at the outset of a game, the choice of the player who will start could be determined by flipping a coin. It gives rise to a tree in two parts, each one having a probability 1/2, as illustrated in Fig. 2.13 representing a game based on the battle of the sexes. We may then apply backward induction to both games. The player who is invited to play first will naturally choose his preferred destination. Ex-ante, in expected utility terms, each player's payoff is equal to 3/2. We will see later that the same result can be obtained through the use of correlated strategies.

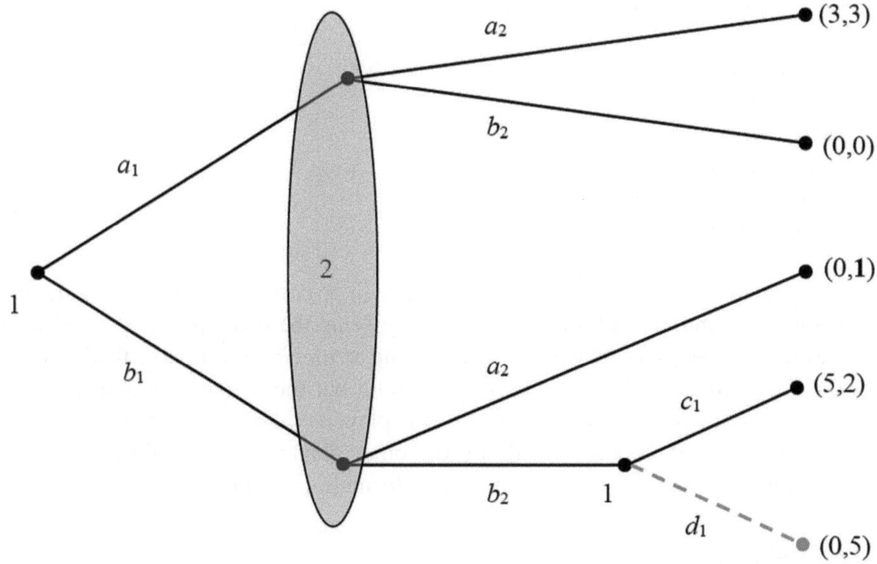

Fig. 2.12 Backward induction with imperfect information

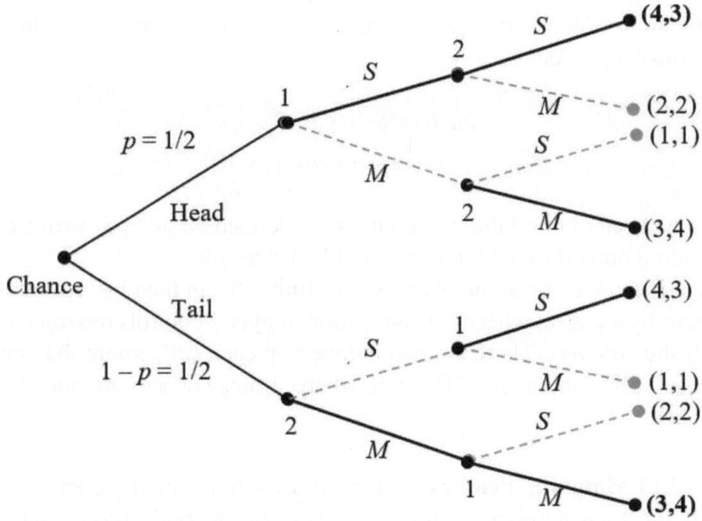

Fig. 2.13 Chance as a fictitious player

2.4 The Strategic Form

The strategic form
Zero-sum games
Mixed strategies
Behavioral strategies *
Correlated strategies
Prudent strategies.

Any game in extensive form can be written in a compact form by listing the strategies available to each player and by specifying the outcomes associated with the resulting strategy combinations. This is the *strategic form* (also called *normal form*). As a reduced form, it is easier to handle but the dynamic structure of the game is lost. In a game in strategic form, players make their strategy choices without knowing the choices made by the other players. It is *as if* players were acting simultaneously. As a consequence, information is *imperfect.*

The strategic form
A 2-player game in strategic form is defined by four elements (S_1, S_2, u_1, u_2) where the sets S_1 and S_2 specify the strategies available to each player and the utility functions u_1 and u_2 represent their preferences on the set of outcomes resulting from the combination of their strategic choices. Utility functions are real-valued defined on the Cartesian product $S_1 \times S_2$:

$$u_i : S_1 \times S_2 \to \mathbb{R}$$
$$(s_1, s_2) \to u_i(s_1, s_2).$$

One must keep in mind that preferences are defined *on pairs of strategies* via the corresponding outcomes, and *not* on individual strategies.

A game is *finite* if the strategy spaces are finite. It can then be represented, as in the Preview, by a matrix where, by convention, player 1 controls the *rows* and player 2 controls the *columns*. There are two numbers in each cell, where the first number refers to the utility of player 1. The case where strategy spaces are not finite will be analyzed later.

Example 2.11 Matching Pennies. Players must simultaneously display one or two fingers. If the total number of fingers is even, the second player pays 1 unit of money to the first. If instead the number of fingers is odd, the transfer goes in the opposite direction. Hence, this is a *zero-sum game*. Penalty kicks in football is similar, assuming that the choices of the goalkeeper and of the kicker are between right (R) or left (L), these directions referring to the goalkeeper. The extensive form of the game is illustrated at Fig. 2.14 where player 1 is the goal keeper. The associated strategic form is given in Table 2.17. These are two perfectly equivalent representations.

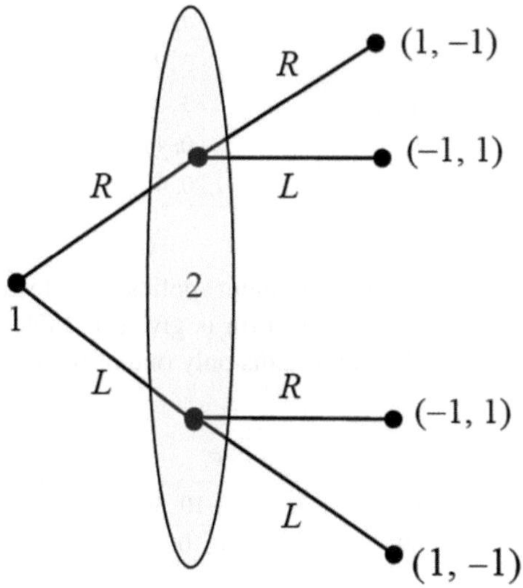

Fig. 2.14 Matching pennies: extensive form

Table 2.17 Matching pennies: strategic form

	R	L
R	$\underline{1}, -1$	$-1, \underline{1}$
L	$-1, \underline{1}$	$\underline{1}, -1$

Example 2.7 (continued) The strategic form associated to the games in extensive form represented by Fig. 2.6 is given in Table 2.18.

Table 2.18 Strategic form associated with the game tree with perfect information

	a_2c_2	a_2d_2	b_2c_2	b_2d_2
a_1c_1	$\underline{3}, \underline{3}$	$3, \underline{3}$	$\underline{0}, 0$	$0, 0$
a_1d_1	$\underline{3}, \underline{3}$	$3, \underline{3}$	$\underline{0}, 0$	$0, 0$
b_1c_1	$0, \underline{4}$	$\underline{5}, 2$	$\underline{0}, \underline{4}$	$\underline{5}, 2$
b_1d_1	$0, 4$	$0, \underline{5}$	$\underline{0}, 4$	$0, \underline{5}$

Following what we did in the Preview, best replies are underlined.

Example 2.8 (continued) Fig. 2.7 is a game tree with imperfect information. The associated strategic form is given in Table 2.19.

There are three equilibria in the first version and two in the second. We will see later how to exclude some equilibria based on rational behavior. For instance, using backward induction in the perfect information case allows retaining only one equilibrium, namely (a_1c_1, a_2c_2).

Table 2.19 Strategic form associated to the game tree with imperfect information

	a_2	b_2
a_1c_1	$\underline{3}, \underline{3}$	0, 0
a_1d_1	$\underline{3}, \underline{3}$	0, 0
b_1c_1	$0, \underline{4}$	$\underline{5}, 2$
b_1d_1	0, 4	$0, \underline{5}$

Example 2.9 (continued) The same argument applies to the location of a sales outlet, described in Fig. 2.10, whose strategic form is given in Table 2.20. There are two equilibria while backward induction retains only one of them.

Table 2.20 Location of an outlet: strategic form

	F	L
E	$-10, 30$	$\underline{40}, \underline{60}$
NE	$\underline{0}, \underline{100}$	$0, \underline{100}$

Games may involve infinite strategy spaces, countable or continuous. Here are examples where the strategy spaces are subsets of the real line.

Example 2.12 Sealed-bid Auctions. An object is offered for sale and there are two potential buyers. Each buyer attributes a value to the object, v_1 for the first and v_2 for the second. These values are reservation prices: no buyer will be willing to pay more than the value he attributes to the object, because he would otherwise make a loss. Bids are placed in sealed envelopes. If a buyer wins and pays a lower price, he makes a *gain* that is equal to the difference. The strategy spaces are therefore given by $S_1 = [0, v_1]$ and $S_2 = [0, v_2]$.

Utility functions depend on the way the auction is conducted. In the *first price bid auction*, the winner just pays what he has bidden. When $p_1 = p_2$, we assume that the buyers share the object if divisible. If not, the object is allocated following the flip of a coin, in which case utilities are expressed in expected terms. The utility functions are then given by:

$$u_1(p_1, p_2) = \begin{cases} v_1 - p_1 & \text{if } p_1 > p_2, \\ 0 & \text{if } p_1 < p_2, \\ (v_1 - p_1)/2 & \text{if } p_1 = p_2. \end{cases}$$

and

$$u_2(p_1, p_2) = \begin{cases} v_2 - p_2 & \text{if } p_2 > p_1, \\ 0 & \text{if } p_2 < p_1, \\ (v_2 - p_2)/2 & \text{if } p_2 = p_1. \end{cases}$$

In the *second price bid auction*, the winner pays the price bidden by the other player.[15] The utility functions are then given by:

$$u_1(p_1, p_2) = \begin{cases} v_1 - p_2 & \text{if } p_1 > p_2, \\ 0 & \text{if } p_1 < p_2, \\ (v_1 - p_1)/2 & \text{if } p_1 = p_2. \end{cases}$$

and

$$u_2(p_1, p_2) = \begin{cases} v_2 - p_1 & \text{if } p_2 > p_1, \\ 0 & \text{if } p_2 < p_1, \\ (v_2 - p_2)/2 & \text{if } p_2 = p_1. \end{cases}$$

Vickrey (1961) has shown that, in such auctions, buyers have an interest in quoting a price equal to their valuation of the object. In doing so, they may gain and never lose. This corresponds to the notion of *weakly* dominant strategies that will be formally defined later.

The finite version obtains when offers must be a multiple of some given number, say 10. If the players' values are $v_1 = 32$ and $v_2 = 52$ we obtain the following matrices for the two types of auctions. Table 2.21 applies in the first price bid auction while Table 2.22 applies to the second price bid auction.

Table 2.21 First price bid auction

	10	20	30	40	50
10	11, 21	0, 32	0, 22	0, 12	0, 2
20	12, 0	6, 16	0, 22	0, 12	0, 2
30	2, 0	2, 0	1, 11	0, 12	0, 2

Table 2.22 Second price bid auction

	10	20	30	40	50
10	11, 21	0, 42	0, 42	0, 42	0, 42
20	22, 0	6, 16	0, 32	0, 32	0, 32
30	22, 0	12, 0	1, 11	0, 22	0, 22

Example 2.13 Price Competition (Bertrand duopoly) In a critique of Augustin Cournot analysis of a duopoly, the mathematician Bertrand (1883) analyzed a situation where two firms produce the same commodity at an identical and constant

[15] Second price auctions are well-known in the philatelic world since 1893. It is also used on eBay.

unit cost $c \geq 0$, without any fixed cost. They face a large number of potential buyers and the demand side is described by a demand function $q = D(p)$ that expresses the quantity demanded as a function of the price. To avoid losses, no firm will set a price below the unit cost c. Each firm is assumed to be able to serve the whole market at a price equal to c. Buyers are perfectly informed about the prices set by each firm and they know that the commodities produced by the two firms are perfect substitutes. As a consequence, the firm that announces a price lower than its competitor captures the whole market. In case where they announce the same price, we assume that demand divides itself equally between the two firms. The strategy spaces are identical. They are given by: $S_1 = S_2 = \{p \in \mathbb{R} | p \geq c\}$. The difference between the price and the unit cost defines the *unit margin* and the profit of a firm is taken as a measure of utility. They are respectively given by:

$$u_1(p_1, p_2) = \begin{cases} (p_1 - c)D(p_1) & \text{if } p_1 < p_2, \\ 0 & \text{if } p_1 > p_2, \\ (p_1 - c)D(p_1)/2 & \text{if } p_1 = p_2. \end{cases}$$

and

$$u_2(p_1, p_2) = \begin{cases} (p_2 - c)D(p_2) & \text{if } p_2 < p_1, \\ 0 & \text{if } p_2 > p_1, \\ (p_2 - c)D(p_2)/2 & \text{if } p_2 = p_1. \end{cases}$$

We will see that in such a situation, the firms enter in a price war that eventually ends up when they both quote the lowest possible price: $p_1 = p_2 = c$: the margin is zero. The two firms make no profit or losses. As we shall see, it is the *unique* equilibrium of this game.

In reality, prices cannot be any real number. Consider instead the case where the unit cost c and prices are natural numbers. If we limit prices to take the values c, $c + 1$ and $c + 2$, the resulting game is given in Table 2.23.

Table 2.23 Bertrand duopoly

	c	$c + 1$	$c + 2$
c	0, 0	0, 0	0, 0
$c + 1$	0, 0	$D(c + 1)/2, D(c + 1)/2$	$D(c + 1), 0$
$c + 2$	0, 0	$0, D(c + 1)$	$D(c + 2), D(c + 2)$

We will see later that in this situation there are two equilibria and this remains true if higher prices are considered.

Two games in strategic form are *strategically equivalent* if they involve the same players with identical strategy spaces and if their payoffs are *increasing transformations* of each other. Formally, the games (S_1, S_2, u_1, u_2) and (S_1, S_2, v_1, v_2) are strategically equivalent if there exists increasing functions T_1 and T_2 such that:

$$v_1(s_1, s_2) = T_1(u_1(s_1, s_2)) \text{ for all } (s_1, s_2) \in S_1 \times S_2,$$
$$v_2(s_1, s_2) = T_2(u_2(s_1, s_2)) \text{ for all } (s_1, s_2) \in S_1 \times S_2.$$

Example 2.1 (continued) Table 2.24 is another representation of the prisoners' dilemma that is equivalent to its original representation given by Table 2.1.

Table 2.24 Modified prisoners' dilemma

	a_2	b_2
a_1	1, 1	−1, $\underline{2}$
b_1	$\underline{2}$, −1	$\underline{0}$, $\underline{0}$

Strategic equivalence applies when considering pure strategies and is consistent with the ordinal framework in which utility levels are defined. It is no longer valid once we leave the ordinal framework. This is the case when considering mixed or correlated strategies. In a cardinal framework, two games are strategically equivalent if they involve the same players with identical strategy spaces and if their payoffs are *linear and increasing* transformations of each other. Formally, the games (S_1, S_2, u_1, u_2) and (S_1, S_2, v_1, v_2) are strategically equivalent *in a cardinal utility framework* if there exists α_i and $\beta_i > 0$ $(i = 1, 2)$ such that

$$v_1(s_1, s_2) = \alpha_1 + \beta_1\, u_1(s_1, s_2) \text{ for all } (s_1, s_2) \in S_1 \times S_2,$$
$$v_2(s_1, s_2) = \alpha_2 + \beta_2\, u_2(s_1, s_2) \text{ for all } (s_1, s_2) \in S_1 \times S_2.$$

Zero-sum games

A 2-player games in which the preferences of the players are systematically opposed is a *strictly competitive game*. Formally, a game in strategic form (S_1, S_2, u_1, u_2) is strictly competitive if

$$u_1(s_1, s_2) \geq u_1(t_1, t_2) \;\Leftrightarrow\; u_2(s_1, s_2) \leq u_2(t_1, t_2).$$

Consequently, we may choose the utility function $u_2 = -u_1$ to represent the preferences of player 2. Hence, we have the following identity:

$$u_1(s_1, s_2) + u_2(s_1, s_2) = u_1(s_1, s_2) - u_1(s_1, s_2) = 0 \text{ for all } (s_1, s_2) \in S_1 \times S_2$$

It justifies the name *zero-sum game*. These duels cover very particular situations and have interesting properties that are not verified in general.

Example 2.11 (continued) Matching pennies is an example of a zero-sum game. Parlor games like chess are other examples of zero-sum games.

In order to define a zero-sum game, it is sufficient to know the preference of one of the players, say player 1. A zero-sum game is therefore defined by the strategy spaces of the two players, S_1 and S_2, and a single utility function u defined on $S_1 \times S_2$, knowing that the preferences of the players are represented by the utility functions $u_1 = u$ and $u_2 = -u$: for a given pair of strategies (a_1, a_2), $u(a_1, a_2)$

is the gain of player 1 and the loss of player 2. Thus, player 1 tries to maximize u, while player 2 tries to minimize it. Indeed, maximizing an arbitrary function f is *equivalent* to minimizing the function $-f$.

Clearly, nonzero-sum games cover more interesting situations where conflict and convergence of interest can coexist. However, conflict does not rhyme with zero sum. In the preface of the second edition (1980) of his book *Strategy of Conflict*, Thomas Schelling explains how John Strachey, a former UK defense minister, had been influenced by reading his book. "*Until he read this book, he had simply not comprehended that an inherently non-zero-sum conflict could exist. He had known that conflict could coexist with common interest but had thought, or taken for granted, that they were essentially separable, not aspects of an integral structure*". Surprising for "*a scholar concerned with monopoly capitalism and class struggle, nuclear strategy and alliance politics, working late in his career on arms control and peacemaking*".

Mixed strategies

It may be profitable for a player to fool his opponent by playing randomly, more precisely, by assigning probabilities to his strategies. Doing so enlarges the set of strategies available to the player. This is the concept of *mixed strategy*. The outcomes are then lotteries that are compared ex-ante in terms of expected utility.

Formally, if a player has two strategies, a and b, he may decide to play a with probability p_1 $(0 \le p_1 \le 1)$ and b with probability $p_2 = 1 - p_1$. We then move from a finite strategy space to a continuum:

$$S = \{a, b\} \quad \rightarrow \quad \Delta = \{(p_1, p_2) | 0 \le p_1, p_2 \le 1, \ \ p_1 + p_2 = 1\}.$$

Because the equation $p_1 + p_2 = 1$ has to be satisfied, Δ is a set of dimension 1 and the set of mixed strategies can be identified to the interval [0, 1]. The set Δ contains the "pure" strategies as particular mixed strategies: a corresponds to $p_1 = 1$ while b corresponds to $p_1 = 0$. In the case of three pure strategies, the set of mixed strategies has dimension 2:

$$S = \{a, b, c\} \quad \rightarrow \quad \Delta = \{p = (p_1, p_2, p_3) | 0 \le p_1, p_2, p_3 \le 1, \ p_1 + p_2 + p_3 = 1\}.$$

We have $P[a] = p_1, \ P[b] = p_2$ and $P[c] = 1 - p_1 - p_2$ where P[A] denotes the probability that the event A realizes. For example, the mixed strategy (1/6, 1/2, 1/3) means that the player will implement strategy a with probability 1/6, strategy b with probability 1/2 and strategy c with probability 1/3.

In general, when there are m pure strategies, a mixed strategy is a *probability distribution* on the set of pure strategies[16]:

$$\Delta = \{p = (p_1, p_2, \ldots, p_m) | 0 \le p_j \le 1 \ \text{ and } \ \sum_{j=1}^{m} p_j = 1\}.$$

[16] In the case of two strategies, Δ is the line segment joining (1, 0) and (0, 1). In the case of three strategies, Δ is the equilateral triangle whose vertices are (1, 0, 0), (0, 1, 0) and (0, 0, 1). In general, Δ is a simplex (see the Mathematical appendix).

A mixed strategy is therefore a lottery that can be seen as a *random machine*. The player programs the machine and then implements the pure strategy suggested by the machine.

In the finite case, a mixed strategy is a *discrete random variable*. Mixed strategies may also be defined on a continuum of pure strategies, in which case they are *continuous random variables*. This case will not be considered in the present book.

To complete the description of the extension of a game to mixed strategies, we have to extend the utility functions under the hypothesis that the preferences over lotteries satisfy the Expected Utility Hypothesis (2.1).

Consider the case of two pure strategies for each player: $S_i = \{a_i, b_i\},\ i = 1, 2$. If p_i denotes the probability that player i attaches to a_i, the expected utility that player i associates to the pair of mixed strategies (p_1, p_2) is given by:

$$\begin{aligned} v_i(p_1, p_2) = {} & p_1 p_2\, u_i(a_1, a_2) + p_1(1 - p_2)\, u_i(a_1, b_2) \\ & + (1 - p_1)p_2\, u_i(b_1, a_2) + (1 - p_1)(1 - p_2)\, u_i(b_1, b_2) \end{aligned}$$

We have used the assumption that players *act independently*, implying a calculation that involves *product* of probabilities. From now on, we shall use the same notation for the utility associated with pure as well as mixed strategies.

Example 2.2 (continued) Consider the simplified version of the battle of the sexes given in Table 2.25 where a_i stands for "Seaside" and b_i stands for "Mountain". A utility equal to 0 is assigned to strategies implying different destinations: separation is costly for both, whatever is the destination.

Table 2.25 Simplified battle of the sexes

	a_2	b_2
	2, 1	0, 0
b_2	0, 0	1, 2

The expected utilities are given by:

$$\begin{aligned} u_1(p_1, p_2) &= 2p_1p_2 + (1 - p_1)(1 - p_2) = 3p_1p_2 - p_1 - p_2 + 1 \\ u_2(p_1, p_2) &= p_1p_2 + 2(1 - p_1)(1 - p_2) = 3p_1p_2 - 2p_1 - 2p_2 + 2 \end{aligned} \tag{2.3}$$

Allowing for mixed strategies enlarges the set of utility levels attainable ex-ante, as illustrated for the battle of the sexes by Fig. 2.15. The outcome (3/4, 3/4) corresponds to the probabilities $p_1 = p_2 = 1/2$ while the outcome (2/3, 2/3) corresponds to $p_1 = 2/3$ and $p_2 = 1/3$.

Moving from pure to mixed strategies in a zero-sum game produces a zero-sum game: the sum of the expected utilities is indeed zero for all probability combinations.

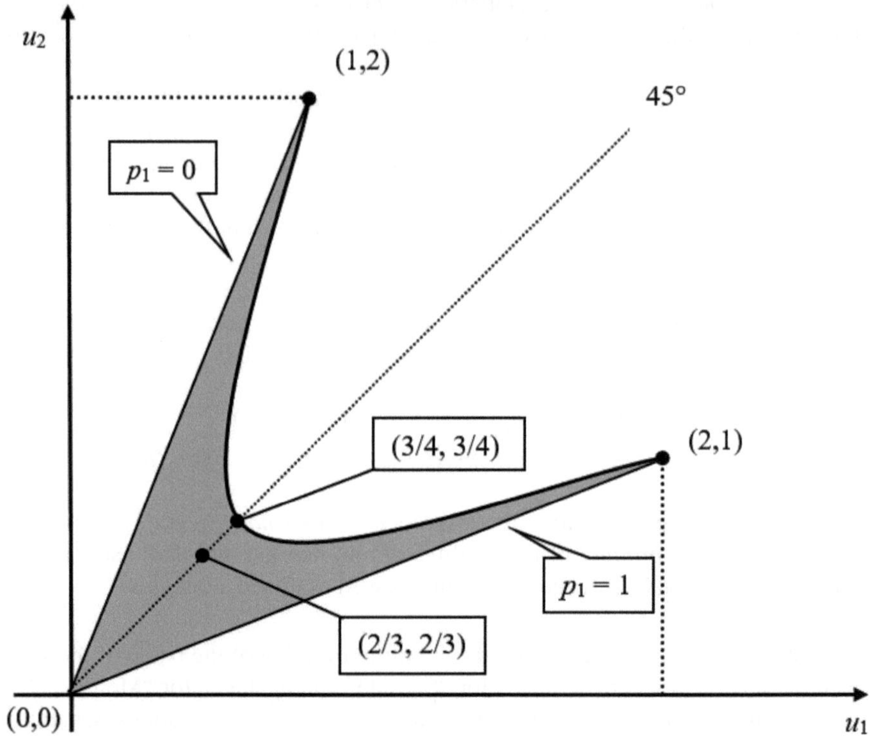

Fig. 2.15 Battle of the sexes: attainable expected outcomes in mixed strategies

Example 2.11 (continued) The game matching pennies offers an illustration. The expected utility of the first player is given by:

$$\begin{aligned} u_1(p_1, p_2) &= p_1 p_2 - p_1(1 - p_2) - p_2(1 - p_1) + (1 - p_1)(1 - p_2) \\ &= -u_2(p_1, p_2). \end{aligned}$$

From now on, we will consider 2-player games in strategic form defined by strategy spaces S_1 and S_2 and utility functions u_1 and u_2 whether strategies and pure or mixed. The concepts will then be defined in this general framework. We must only keep in mind that, in a probabilistic framework, we deal with expected utilities and utility representations are then cardinal, not ordinal.

Behavioral strategies*

Mixed strategies can be introduced in a game in extensive form, in which case probabilities apply to combinations of actions. Why not consider probabilities on the actions of a player? This is the concept of *behavioral strategies*. More precisely, a behavioral strategy for a player associates to each of his information sets a probability distribution over the available actions. This is illustrated in Fig. 2.16 where actions and outcomes have been replaced by the corresponding probabilities. For example, if player 1 chooses b_1 with probability $1 - \alpha_1$ and player 2 chooses a_2 with probability γ_2, the game ends with probability $(1 - \alpha_1)\gamma_2$ and with the payoffs associated with the sequence $b_1 - a_2$.

Behavioral strategies induce mixed strategies:

$$\begin{array}{llll} p_1 = \alpha_1\beta_1 \ \leftrightarrow \ a_1c_1, & & \\ p_2 = \alpha_1(1-\beta_1) \ \leftrightarrow \ a_1d_1, & & q_1 = \gamma_2 \ \leftrightarrow \ a_2, \\ p_3 = (1-\alpha_1)\beta_1 \ \leftrightarrow \ b_1c_1, & & q_2 = 1-\gamma_2 \ \leftrightarrow \ b_2. \\ p_4 = (1-\alpha_1)(1-\beta_1) \ \leftrightarrow \ b_1d_1, & & \end{array}$$

Kuhn (1953) has proven that the reverse is actually true *under perfect recall.*

Proposition 2.4 *For a player, behavioral strategies and mixed strategies are equivalent in the sense that, for all strategy of his opponent, both produce the same probability distribution over the outcomes.*

We verify this proposition for the example given in Fig. 2.16.

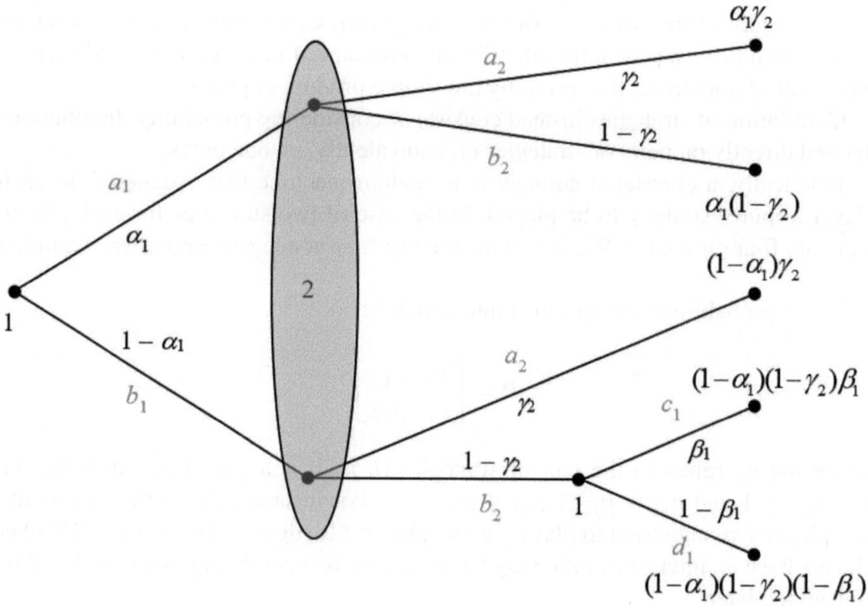

Fig. 2.16 Behavioral strategies

Equalizing the probability distribution on the outcomes resulting from the behavioral strategies with the probability distribution on the outcomes resulting from the mixed strategies in the above example, we obtain the following equations:

$$\alpha_1\gamma_2 = (p_1 + p_2)q_2, \qquad \alpha_1(1-\gamma_2) = (p_1 + p_2)(1-q_2),$$
$$(1-\alpha_1)\gamma_2 = (p_3 + p_4)q_2, \qquad (1-\alpha_1)(1-\gamma_2)\beta_1 = p_3 q_2.$$
$$(1-\alpha_1)(1-\gamma_2)(1-\beta_1) = p_4(1-q_2),$$

This system of equations has a unique solution:

$$\alpha_1 = p_1 + p_2,$$
$$\beta_1 = \frac{p_3}{p_3 + p_4}\frac{q_2}{1-q_2},$$
$$\gamma_2 = q_2.$$

For instance, the mixed strategies (0.2, 0.2, 0.2, 0.4) and (0.4, 0.6) induce the behavioral strategies defined by $\alpha_1 = 4/10$, $\beta_1 = 2/9$ et $\gamma_2 = 4/10$.

Correlated strategies

Mixed strategies are probability distributions on the set of pure strategies of a player, *independently* of the strategies of the other player. Consequently, a pair of mixed strategies induces a probability distribution on pairs of pure strategies and thereby on the set of outcomes. It is given by the simple product of probabilities.

Correlation of strategies instead consists of considering probability distributions defined directly on pairs of strategies or, equivalently, on outcomes.

Practically, a correlated strategy is a random machine that "suggests" to each player a (pure) strategy to be played. In the case of two strategies for each player, there are four outcomes. We then must specify four nonnegative numbers summing to one.

These probabilities are grouped into a matrix:

$$P = \begin{bmatrix} p_{11} & p_{12} \\ p_{21} & p_{22} \end{bmatrix}$$

where the p_{ij} refers to the pair of strategies (i, j). It is a probability distribution: $0 \leq p_{ij} \leq 1$ and $p_{11} + p_{12} + p_{21} + p_{22} = 1$. For instance, p_{12} is the probability that player 1 is suggested to play a_1 while player 2 is suggested to play b_2. Whether players have an interest in following the suggestions is another question that will be considered later.

It is important to realize that suggestions are made *individually*. When receiving a suggestion, each player is able to revise his belief about the suggestion made to his opponent. For instance, if player 1 is suggested to play a_1, he knows that the machine has "fired" in the first line. In general, if the players have respectively m_1 and m_2 pure strategies, there are $m = m_1 \times m_2$ pairs of strategies and a correlated strategy is defined by a matrix of dimension $m_1 \times m_2$.

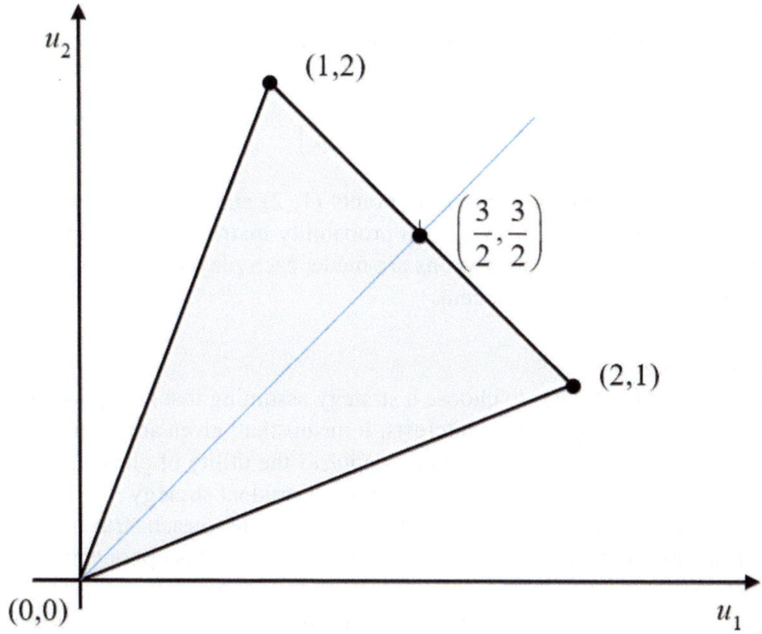

Fig. 2.17 Battle of the sexes: attainable expected outcomes in correlated strategies

Allowing for correlated strategies enlarges further the set of attainable *expected* utilities. Graphically, we obtain the set formed by the points corresponding to the expected utility levels associated with the pure strategies.[17]

Example 2.2 (continued) In the simplified version of the battle of the sexes as described in Table 2.25, we end up with the triangle whose vertices are the points (0, 0), (2, 1) and (1, 2) as illustrated in Fig. 2.17, to be compared to Fig. 2.15.

There, the utility levels on the segment joining the points (1, 2) and (2, 1) are optimal in the sense of Pareto: the expected utility of one player cannot be increased without reducing the expected utility of the other. Recall that a utility pair $(\overline{u}_1, \overline{u}_2)$ *Pareto-dominates* the utility pair (u_1, u_2) if and only if $\overline{u}_1 \geq u_1$ and $\overline{u}_2 \geq u_2$ *with at least one strict inequality.* Put differently, no player is in a worse situation and at least one is in a better situation.

[17] This is the concept of *convex hull*. Formally, the convex hull (or envelope) of a set of points is the smallest convex set that contains the set. Recall that a set is *convex* if it contains all possible segments joining any two of its points (see the Mathematical appendix).

Undominated utility pairs are called optimal (or efficient) in the sense of Pareto. Varying p between 0 and 1 in the probability matrix

$$P = \begin{bmatrix} p & 0 \\ 0 & 1-p \end{bmatrix}$$

generates the line segment joining the points (1, 2) and (2, 1). The middle point (3/2, 3/2) corresponds to $p = 1/2$. Such probability matrices amount to *public suggestions.* Indeed, once the suggestions are made, each player knows the suggestion that has been made to his opponent.

Prudent strategies

Consider player 1, who has to choose a strategy assuming that his opponent will be acting systematically against his interests. It means that, given any strategy $s_1 \in S_1$, player 2 would reply by a strategy that *minimizes* the utility of player 1. This is the worst-case scenario that underlies the concept of prudent strategy.

Formally we proceed in two steps. We first associate to each strategy $s_1 \in S_1$ of player 1 his minimal utility with respect to the strategy of his opponent:

$$Min_{s_2 \in S_2} u_1(s_1, s_2).$$

We then pick up a strategy for player 1 that maximizes his payoff:

$$Max_{s_1 \in S_1}\left[Min_{s_2 \in S_2} u_1(s_1, s_2)\right] = v_1.$$

This defines *prudent strategies*, also called *maximin strategies*.

The level of utility v_1 that is obtained in this way is the *security level* of player 1: it is the minimal gain that player 1 is certain to obtain whatever does his opponent. In case there are several prudent strategies, the player is indifferent between them: they all produce the same security level. Similarly, the security level of player 2 is given by:

$$Max_{s_2 \in S_2}\left[Min_{s_1 \in S_1} u_2(s_1, s_2)\right] = v_2.$$

The identification of the security levels and prudent strategies is easy for games with finite strategy spaces.

For the first player, we identify the minimal utility level along each row and then retain the row corresponding to the maximum of these levels:

$$v_1 = Max_i\left[Min_j\ a_{ij}\right] \text{ where } a_{ij} = u_1(i, j).$$

Similarly, for the second player, by reasoning along columns:

$$v_2 = Max_j\left[Min_i\ b_{ij}\right] \text{ where } b_{ij} = u_2(i, j).$$

Consider the game described by Table 2.26 where we have indicated the minimal levels associated to each strategy. The prudent strategies are then b_1 and b_2 to which are associated with the security levels $v_1 = 1$ and $v_2 = 1$. If both players are prudent, the resulting outcome is (2, 1). It differs from the outcome (2, 3) resulting from the equilibrium (a_1, c_2). There is indeed no reason for a pair of prudent strategies to be an equilibrium.

Table 2.26 Prudent strategies

	a_2	b_2	c_2	
a_1	1, 1	0, 2	2, 3	0
b_1	2 0	2, 1	1, 0	**1**
c_1	0, 3	3, 1	0, 0	0
	0	**1**	0	

In the prisoners' dilemma (Table 2.1), the prudent strategy consists in pleading guilty. In the original formulation of the battle of the sexes (Table 2.2), the preferred destination is the unique prudent strategy. At worst, the partners are separated, each in his or her preferred destination.

Example 2.9 (continued) In the location of a sales outlet game, "*laisser faire*" (*L*) is the prudent strategy for the incumbent while "*no entry*" (*NE*) is the prudent strategy of the potential entrant. This last example shows that, if a player believes that his opponent will adopt a prudent strategy, he has not necessarily an interest in being himself prudent.

Using mixed strategies may improve the security levels because players have then access to a greater set of strategies. In the simplified version of the battle of the sexes given by Table 2.25, the security of each player is zero if we only consider pure strategies. Allowing for mixed strategies, the security levels increase up to 2/3. Indeed, the utility function of the first player is given by:

$$u_1(p_1, p_2) = 3p_2\left(p_1 - \frac{1}{3}\right) - p_1 + 1$$

For $p_1 > 1/3$, the worst for player 1 is $p_2 = 0$ and his utility is equal to $1 - p_1$. In contrast, for $p_1 < 1/3$, the worst is $p_2 = 1$ and his utility is equal to $2p_1$. We have constructed in this way a relation between p_1 and $Min_{p_2}\, u_1(p_1, p_2)$ as illustrated in Fig. 2.18. The prudent strategy of player 1 is given by $p_1 = 1/3$ with a security level equal to 2/3.

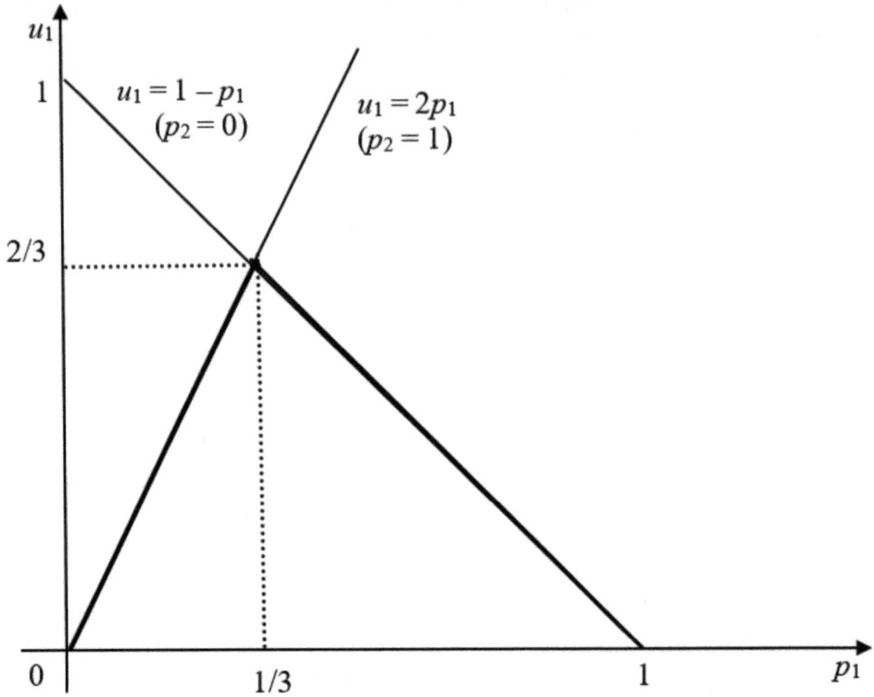

Fig. 2.18 Prudent strategies in the battle of the sexes: graph of $Min_{p_2}\ u_1(p_1, p_2)$

Example 2.11 (continued) In matching pennies, the two strategies are prudent and the security is equal to –1. Here too, using mixed strategies leads to higher utility levels ex-ante: the equilibrium defined by the probabilities (1/2, 1/2) is associated with a zero expected utility. Considering Fig. 2.19, we observe that if $p_1 > 1/2$, the worst for player 1 is $p_2 = 0$ and his utility is equal to $1 - 2p_1$. If instead $p_1 < 1/2$, the worst is $p_2 = 1$ and his utility is equal to $2p_1 - 1$: the prudent strategy consists in flipping a coin. It happens to be an equilibrium as we shall see later. This coincidence between equilibrium strategies and prudent strategies is actually a characteristic of zero-sum games.

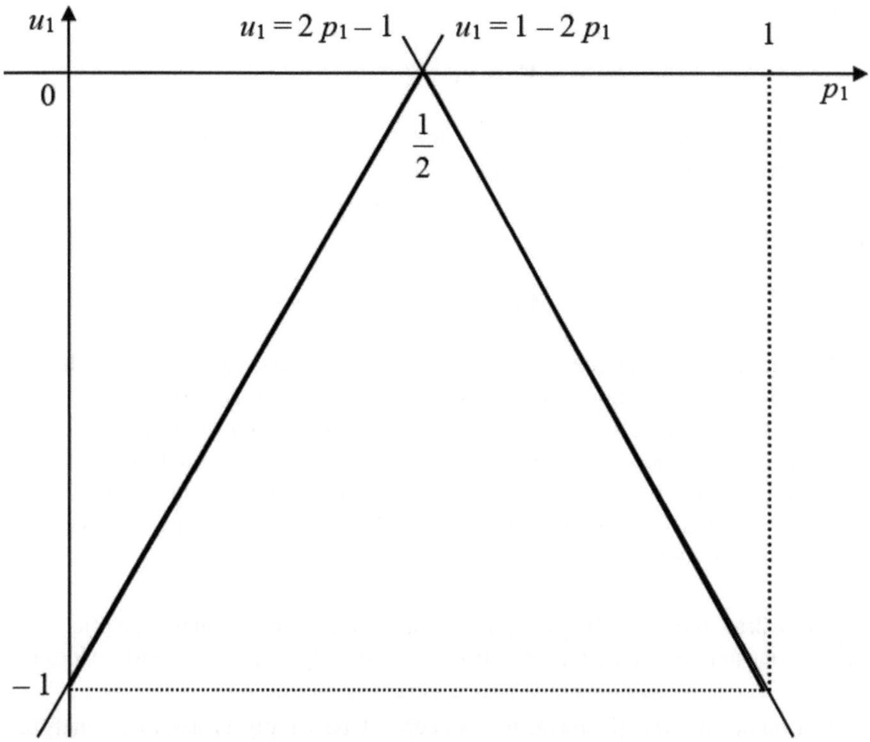

Fig. 2.19 Prudent strategies in matching pennies: graph of $Min_{p_2}\, u_1(p_1, p_2)$

2.5 Dominant and Weakly Dominant Strategies

Best replies
Dominant strategy and dominated strategy
Iterated elimination of dominated strategies
Rationalizability
Weakly dominant strategies and weakly dominated strategies.

We continue to work with 2-player games in strategic form defined by strategy sets S_1 and S_2, and utility functions u_1 and u_2.

Best replies

Conditionally to any given strategy of his opponent, a player is able to select the strategies that bring him the largest utility. This is the concept of *best reply* that amounts to a Gedankenexperiment, a thought experiment. Several strategies may be best replies to a given opponent's strategy, in which case the player is indifferent between them. Formally, in reply to the strategy $a_2 \in S_2$ of player 2, the problem of player 1 is to maximize his utility with respect to his own strategies:

$$Max_{s_1 \in S_1}\ u_1(s_1, a_2).$$

The solutions to this problem define the *set* $\varphi_1(a_2)$ of best replies to the strategy a_2. The best replies of the second player are determined in the same way: $\varphi_2(a_1)$ denotes the set of his best replies to the strategy $a_1 \in S_1$, solutions of the following maximization problem:

$$Max_{s_2 \in S_2}\ u_2(a_1, s_2).$$

This defines two applications: $\varphi_1 : S_2 \to S_1$ and $\varphi_2 : S_1 \to S_2$. In the case where best replies are uniquely defined, they are *reaction functions.*

When there may be several best replies, they are *reaction correspondences.*[18]

In the battle of the sexes, the best reply to the preferred destination of the other is to follow. In the prisoners' dilemma, the best reply is to plead guilty *whatever the other one does*. This is the characteristic of a dominant strategy, a concept that will be formally defined later.

Example 2.13 (continued) In the price competition game, announcing a price lower than the one announced by the other firm is a best reply, except if it leads to losses.[19]

In a game in strategic form, the concept of best reply is useful to analyze a game. In contrast, when players play *sequentially*, the concept of best reply may be operational when they are uniquely defined by a reaction function.

Consider a two-step game. The player playing first is in an advantageous position because he may *anticipate* the choice of his opponent.[20] By incorporating the reaction function of his opponent, his maximization problem is given by:

$$Max_{s_1 \in S_1}\ u_1(s_1,\ \varphi_2(s_1)).$$

This is a well-defined problem because it is a function of s_1 only. This corresponds exactly to the backward induction used in the framework of extensive form games.

[18] A correspondence (or point-to-set mapping) is an application $\varphi : S \to T$ that associates a *subset* of T to each element of the set S. See the Mathematical appendix.

[19] This is formally correct in the discrete case and not in the continuum case where price are real numbers: best replies are then not well-defined.

[20] The idea of a *leader* (player 1) and a *follower* (player 2) can be found in the duopoly model proposed by von Stackelberg (1934).

Dominant strategies and dominated strategies

Consider a player. A strategy dominates another strategy if it leads to a *better* outcome, for *all* the strategies of his opponent. Formally, a_1 *dominates* b_1 if

$$u_1(a_1, s_2) > u_1(b_1, s_2) \text{ for all } s_2 \in S_2.$$

A dominant strategy is a strategy that dominates *all* the other strategies. Formally, a_1 is *dominant* if

$$u_1(a_1, s_2) > u_1(s_1, s_2) \text{ for all } s_1 \in S_1, \ s_1 \neq a_1, \text{ and all } s_2 \in S_2.$$

Hence, a strategy is dominant for a player if it is the *unique* best reply to *all* strategies of his opponent. Due to the presence of a strict inequality in the definition, if a strategy is dominant, it must be *unique.* A weaker notion of domination where the inequality is not strict will be proposed later. In the examples reviewed until now, only the prisoners' dilemma has a dominant strategy: "plead guilty" is dominant for both players.

A strategy is *dominated* if it is dominated by another strategy. In a finite 2-player game, a strategy is dominated if *and only if* it is a never-best reply.[21]

Interestingly, it is possible for a pure strategy to be dominated by a mixed strategy, as the following example shows.

Example 2.14 A Pure Strategy that Dominates a Mixed Strategy. Table 2.27 represents the utility level of player 1. The mixed strategy $(p_1, p_2, p_3) = (0.5, \ 0.5, \ 0)$ dominates the pure strategy c_1. The expected utility associated with the mixed strategy is equal to 3/2, while the utility associated with the pure strategy c_1 is equal to 1. This is indeed so for all $(p_1, p_2, 0)$ such that: $p_1 + p_2 = 1$.

Table 2.27 A pure strategy that dominates a mixed strategy

	a_2	b_2
a_1	3	0
b_1	0	3
c_1	1	1

It is important to avoid confusing the concept of dominance that applies to individual strategies with the concept of dominance in the sense of Pareto that applies to outcomes. For instance, in the prisoners' dilemma, the equilibrium outcome is dominated by the outcome that would have resulted had they both pleaded non-guilty.

[21] See Lemma 60.1 in Osborne and Rubinstein (1994). This does not apply to games with more than 2 players.

Iterated elimination of dominated strategies
Under the assumption of rationality, a player is able to identify the strategies of his opponent that are dominated and guess that he will never implement it. So, when facing a game, the first step is to reduce the game by eliminating all dominated strategies. A strategy may appear dominated only after another one has been eliminated. This may lead to a sequence of eliminations.

Example 2.15 Here is a sequence of eliminations that ends up with the pair of strategies (c_1, c_2).

	a_2	b_2	c_2
a_1	2, 1	6, 0	1, 5
b_1	2, 2	1, 1	2, 0
c_1	3, 1	3, 0	4, 2

	a_2	c_2
a_1	2, 1	1, 5
b_1	2, 2	2, 0
c_1	3, 1	4, 2

	a_2	c_2
c_1	3, 1	4, 2

	c_2
c_1	4, 2

We observe the successive dominance relations $a_2 \succ b_2, c_1 \succ a_1, c_1 \succ b_1$ and $c_2 \succ a_2$ to which is associated the sequence of eliminations (b_2, a_1, b_1, a_2). The pair of strategies (c_1, c_2) defines the unique equilibrium. Alternatively, we could have eliminated b_1 before a_1. Both sequences end up with the pair of strategies (c_1, c_2) to which the outcome (4, 2) is associated.

For a given a game, proceeding to a sequence of eliminations does not necessarily end up with a single pair of strategies. At least it simplifies the game. And, as the above example shows, there may be different sequences of eliminations.

Rationalizability
Identifying the best replies is an exercise that every player can perform, but ideally it should be complemented by beliefs about the opponent's strategies. Quoting Bernheim (1984), "*When a (player) reaches a decision in ignorance of the strategies adopted by the other players, rationality consists of making a choice which is justifiable by an internally consistent system of beliefs*". The concept of rationalizability introduced independently by Bernheim (1984) and Pearce (1984) is an example: a strategy is *rationalizable* if it survives a process of iterated elimination of strategies that are inconsistent with a player's beliefs about the other players' strategies. Interestingly, in finite games, the set of rationalizable strategies coincides with set of strategies that survive after an iterated elimination of dominated strategies.[22]

Weakly dominant strategies and weakly dominated strategies
The definition of dominance requires that a dominant strategy must be *strictly better* than any other strategy, for all strategies of the opponent. This may be too demanding.

[22] See Proposition 61.2 in Osborne and Rubinstein (1994).

A strategy $a_1 \in S_1$ of player 1 is *weakly dominant* if

$$u_1(a_1, s_2) \geq u_1(s_1, s_2) \text{ for all } s_1 \in S_1 \textit{ and } \text{all } s_2 \in S_2$$

with a strict inequality *for at least one* strategy combination. The concept of weakly *dominated strategy* is defined accordingly. Formally, a strategy $b_1 \in S_1$ is weakly dominated if there exists a strategy $a_1 \in S_1$ such that $u_1(a_1, s_2) \geq u_1(b_1, s_2)$ for all $s_2 \in S_2$ with a *strict inequality* for at least one strategy s_2. We may eliminate sequentially weakly dominated strategies, as in the case of dominated strategies. However, this procedure has its limitations because different sequences may lead to different simplified games, unlike the elimination of dominated strategies.

Example 2.9 (continued) In the location of a sales outlet game, "Fight" is weakly dominated by "Laissez-faire" for the incumbent firm.

Example 2.12 (continued) Consider the second price sealed-bid auction where the winner pays the price announced by the loser. The interest of this type of auction is that announcing a price equal to the valuation of the object is a weakly dominant strategy. To illustrate this proposition due to Vickrey (1961), consider buyer 1. We have to verify that the following inequalities are satisfied:

$$u_1(v_1, p_2) \geq u_1(p_1, p_2) \text{ for all } p_1 \in [0, v_1] \textit{ and } \text{all } p_2 \in [0, v_2]$$

with a strict inequality for at least one price combination. Recall that the utility function of the first buyer is given by:

$$u_1(p_1, p_2) = \begin{cases} v_1 - p_2 & \text{if } p_1 > p_2, \\ 0 & \text{if } p_1 < p_2, \\ (v_1 - p_1)/2 & \text{if } p_1 = p_2. \end{cases}$$

Let's first suppose that $v_1 < v_2$. There are three possibilities depending on the value of p_2.

- If $v_1 < p_2 \leq v_2$, the first buyer loses:

$$u_1(v_1, p_2) = 0 = u_1(p_1, p_2) \text{ for all } p_1 \text{ such that } 0 \leq p_1 \leq v_1.$$

- If $p_2 = v_1$, either the first buyer loses or the two buyers divide the object:

$$u_1(v_1, p_2) = 0 = u_1(p_1, p_2) \text{ for all } p_1 \text{ such that } 0 \leq p_1 \leq v_1.$$

- If $0 \le p_2 < v_1$, we have $u_1(v_1, p_2) = v_1 - p_2 > 0$ and:

$$u_1(p_1, p_2) = \begin{cases} v_1 - p_2 & \text{for all } p_1 \text{ such that } p_2 < p_1 \le v_1, \\ \frac{v_1 - p_2}{2} & \text{for } p_1 = p_2, \\ 0 & \text{for all } p_1 \text{ such that } 0 \le p_1 < p_2. \end{cases}$$

In the first two cases, the buyer is indifferent between the prices in the interval $[0, v_1]$. The same applies to the third case for prices above p_2. In this third case, announcing v_1 is more interesting than announcing a price between 0 and p_2 :

$$u_1(v_1, p_2) > u_1(p_1, p_2) \text{ for all } p_1 \text{ such that } 0 \le p_1 \le p_2.$$

Suppose now that $v_1 \ge v_2$. Knowing that $p_2 \le v_2$, we fall back in the case where $0 \le p_2 \le v_1$. Hence, $p_1 = v_1$ is a weakly dominant strategy.

We observe that the conclusion applies independently of v_2. This proposition remains therefore valid when player 1 ignores the value that player 2 attributes to the object, a situation of *incomplete* information.

John Maynard Keynes, whose name is attached to economic recovery policies, was comparing the stock market to a beauty contest. For him, what is important for an investor is not so much to understand the fundamentals of the economy but rather to guess the choices made by the other investors. He writes:

> It is not a case of choosing those that, to the best of one's judgment, are really the prettiest, nor even those that average opinion genuinely thinks the prettiest. We have reached the third degree where we devote our intelligences to anticipating what average opinion expects the average opinion to be. And there are some, I believe, who practice the fourth, fifth and higher degrees. (General Theory of Employment, Interest and Money, 1936).

The following example due to Moulin (1986) illustrates this idea.

Example 2.16 Beauty Contest. Consider a group of n persons ($n \ge 3$). Each must figure out a number between 0 and 100, and register it in an envelope. Envelopes are then open and the mean number μ is computed. The person whose number is *closest to but below* 2/3 of the mean wins 50$. If several persons are concerned, the winner is drawn at random. The choice of the upper bound (100) and the gain (50) are arbitrary. Given that $n = 30$, suppose that the numbers proposed are given in Table 2.28.

Table 2.28 Beauty contest

Registered number	1	3	8	18	25	28	30	37
Number of propositions	2	4	3	5	7	3	4	2

The mean is given by $\mu = (2 \times 1 + 4 \times 3 + \cdots + 2 \times 37)/30 = 581/30 \simeq 19.37$ and 2/3 of it equals 12.9. Therefore, there are nine potential winners.

Actually, if we proceed to an iterated elimination of *weakly* dominated strategies, we end up with an optimal proposal equal to 0. Consider a player. In the first step, he will realize that it is useless to propose a number exceeding 66. Indeed, at best, all other players propose 100 in which case he cannot win by proposing a number superior to 2/3 of 100. This is a fortiori true if other players propose numbers below 100. Each player following the same reasoning acts as if the largest number was 66. Reproducing the same reasoning leads to a maximum number equal to 44, and so on, until reaching 0 after an infinite number of eliminations. Experimentations show that players tend to proceed to a maximum of three successive elimination with a winning proposal around 25.

2.6 Equilibrium

Nash equilibrium
Equilibrium and domination
Equilibria in zero-sum games
Existence of an equilibrium
Risk-dominance in 2 × 2 games *
Introducing a mediator
Equilibria in correlated strategies.

We continue to work with 2-player games in strategic form defined by sets of strategies (pure or mixed) S_1 and S_2, and utility functions u_1 and u_2. In case of mixed strategies, u_1 and u_2 are expected utilities.

Nash equilibrium

In a given game, one may identify pairs of strategies that stand out. This is the case of strategies that lead to an outcome that Pareto-dominates the other outcomes. However, we have seen that there is no guarantee that the players will act accordingly. Players are indeed not bound by possible agreements made before playing a game. This is an essential characteristic of non-cooperative games. If a strategy of one of the players appears to be dominant, the other player could identify it and play a best reply. And if the best reply is unique or if both players have a dominant strategy, the outcome is totally predictable.

In the absence of dominant strategies, one may retain the pairs of strategies that are best replies to each other: they are *stable* in the sense that no player could gain by deviating *unilaterally*. This is the concept of *Nash equilibrium* (equilibrium for short) introduced by Nash (1950, 1951).

Formally, a pair of strategies (a_1, a_2) defines an equilibrium if the following two conditions are simultaneously met:

$$a_1 \in S_1 \text{ and } u_1(a_1, a_2) \geq u_1(s_1, a_2) \text{ for all } s_1 \in S_1,$$
$$a_2 \in S_2 \text{ and } u_2(a_1, a_2) \geq u_2(a_1, s_2) \text{ for all } s_2 \in S_2. \tag{2.4}$$

An equilibrium is defined by a pair of strategies such that each one is a best reply to the other. Quoting Myerson (1999, p. 1070), "*If we can predict the behavior of all players ... our prediction must be* a *Nash equilibrium, or else it would violate (our) assumption of rational individual behavior*".

Notice that equilibrium strategies are not defined independently of one of the others, except for the particular case of zero-sum games, as we shall see later. Notice also that (2.4) applies whether strategies are mixed or not.

An equilibrium (a_1, a_2) is said to be *strict* if it involves strategies that are *unique* best replies to each other. In other words, any deviation from the equilibrium strategy implies a loss:

$$u_1(a_1, a_2) > u_1(s_1, a_2) \text{ for all } s_1 \in S_1,$$
$$u_2(a_1, a_2) > u_2(a_1, s_2) \text{ for all } s_2 \in S_2.$$

An equilibrium (a_1, a_2) is said to be *strong* if the players have no incentive to *jointly* deviate[23]: there is no pair of strategies $(b_1, b_2) \in S_1 \times S_2$ such that:

$$u_i(b_1, b_2) > u_i(a_1, a_2) \;\; i = 1, 2.$$

We have seen that the prisoners' dilemma has a unique equilibrium. It is a strict equilibrium that is, however, not strong: both players have a clear incentive to jointly plead non-guilty.

In the case where best replies are given by reaction functions, an equilibrium is defined by a feasible pair of strategies (a_1, a_2) such that: $a_1 = \varphi_1(a_2)$ and $a_2 = \varphi_2(a_1)$. As a consequence, we have $a_1 = \varphi_1(\varphi_2(a_1))$ meaning that a_1 is a *fixed point* of the function $\varphi_1(\varphi_2(s_1))$.[24]

Alternatively, a_2 is a *fixed point* of the function $\varphi_2(\varphi_1(s_2))$, i.e., $a_2 = \varphi_2(\varphi_1(a_2))$.

In general, when best replies are not unique, one relies on reaction correspondences. An equilibrium is then a fixed point defined by a pair of feasible strategies (a_1, a_2) such that $a_1 \in \varphi_1(a_2)$ and $a_2 \in \varphi_2(a_1)$.

Two games that are strategically equivalent have the same set of equilibria. Indeed, applying increasing transformations to the inequalities (2.4) leaves these inequalities unchanged. However, this only applies to the case of pure strategies: we are then in an ordinal framework where the transformed utilities represent the same preferences. If instead mixed strategies are considered, only linear increasing transformations of

[23] The notion of strong equilibrium was introduced by Aumann (1959). With more than two players, an equilibrium is said to be strong if no *coalition* of players has an incentive to deviate.
[24] Given a function from a set X into itself, a *fixed point* is a point $x \in X$ such that $f(x) = x$.

utilities will leave the equilibrium probabilities unchanged. We will come back to this question when considering equilibria in mixed strategies.

We know that the combination (*G*, *G*) defines an equilibrium in the prisoners' dilemma. It is the unique equilibrium. In contrast, the battle of the sexes has two equilibria (in pure strategies). They correspond to identical destinations: (*S*, *S*) and (*M*, *M*). The coordination problem remains because there is no reason to privilege one equilibrium over the other. We will see that this game also has an equilibrium in mixed strategies.

Example 2.9 (continued) The strategic form of the location of a sales outlet game reveals two equilibria, namely (*E*, *L*) and (*NE*, *F*). We have already seen that the second one covers an irrational behavior. It cannot be detected by reasoning on the strategic form because moving from the extensive form to the strategic form entails a loss of information on the sequential nature of the game.

Example 2.11 (continued) Matching pennies has no equilibrium in pure strategies. We will see that it has a unique equilibrium in mixed strategies that, as may be easily guessed, consists for each player to flip a coin, so that each strategy is played with the same probability.

Example 2.13 (continued) The price competition game has a unique equilibrium, $p_1 = p_2 =$ c: both firms charge the lowest possible price. Their profit is zero and they share the market equally. To show this, let's consider all possible situations.[25]

$p_1 > p_2 > c$	Firm 1 is out of the market and would gain by announcing a price slightly below p_2 in order to obtain the whole market while still making a positive profit. The same argument applies to the situation where $p_2 > p_1 > c$.
$p_1 > p_2 = c$	Both firms make a zero profit. The first one because it is out of the market and the second one because its margin is zero. The second firm could, however, make a positive profit by increasing its price so as to make a positive profit while still getting the whole market. The same argument applies to the situation where $p_2 > p_1 = c$.
$p_1 = p_2 > c$	The firms equally share the market and make a positive profit. This is a cooperative solution. It is, however, not stable: each firm would gain by decreasing slightly its price and obtain the whole market

It only remains one situation: $p_1 = p_2 = c$. It defines the unique equilibrium because no firm could gain by modifying its price: lowering the price would result in losses and increasing it would result in losing the market.

The situation is quite different in the discrete case described in Table 2.29.

[25] Here, the *p*'s are prices, not probabilities.

Table 2.29 Bertrand duopoly: equilibria

	c	$c+1$	$c+2$
c	$\underline{0}, \underline{0}$	$0, \underline{0}$	$0, \underline{0}$
$c+1$	$\underline{0}, 0$	$\underline{D(c+1)/2}, \underline{D(c+1)/2}$	$\underline{D(c+1)}, 0$
$c+2$	$\underline{0}, 0$	$0, \underline{D(c+1)}$	$D(c+2), D(c+2)$

Because we have $D(c+2) < D(c+1)$, there are two equilibria, given, respectively, by $p_1 = p_2 = c$ and $p_1 = p_2 = c + 1$. Clearly, one equilibrium Pareto-dominates the other: (c, c) is not a strong equilibrium. And in case of a price war, firms would eventually end up in the equilibrium where they both make profit. Furthermore, choosing the price just above the unit cost is weakly dominant. Adding prices, $c + 3, c + 4, \ldots$ does not modify the conclusion.

Example 2.17 Contribution to a Public Good *. Economic analysis distinguishes two extreme categories of commodities, private goods and public goods. The quantity consumed by an agent of a private good, like bread or water, cannot be consumed by another one. Public goods instead are not consumed. They are available for all, like public television or national defense. Roads are public goods as well when not subjected to congestion. Toll roads instead are private goods.

The problem with public goods is their financing. Consider the simple case of two commodities, a private good and a public good, and two agents. Each owns a quantity $w > 0$ of the private good. Quantities of private good are denoted x and quantities of public good are denoted y. We suppose that the public good is produced using a technology described by the linear production $y = \alpha x$ where α is some positive real number.

Players are supposed to have the same preferences represented by the utility function $u(x, y) = xy$. The strategic variable is the quantity of private good that a player decides to give up for producing the public good. If x_i denotes the quantity given up by player i, the quantity of public good that is produced is given by $y = \alpha(x_1 + x_2)$. The associated game in strategic form is defined by the strategy spaces $S_1 = S_2 = \{x \in \mathbb{R} | 0 \leq x \leq w\}$ and the utility functions

$$u_i(x_1, x_2) = \alpha(w - x_i)(x_1 + x_2) \quad i = 1, 2.$$

The fact that the game is symmetric simplifies the calculations. It is indeed sufficient to evaluate the best replies of one player. Maximizing the utility of the first player with respect to x_1 leads to the first order condition $w - 2x_1 - x_2 = 0$. It is obtained by zeroing the first derivative of the utility function $u_1(x_1, x_2)$ with respect to x_1. The reaction function of the first player is therefore given by:

$$x_1 = \varphi_1(x_2) = \frac{w - x_2}{2}.$$

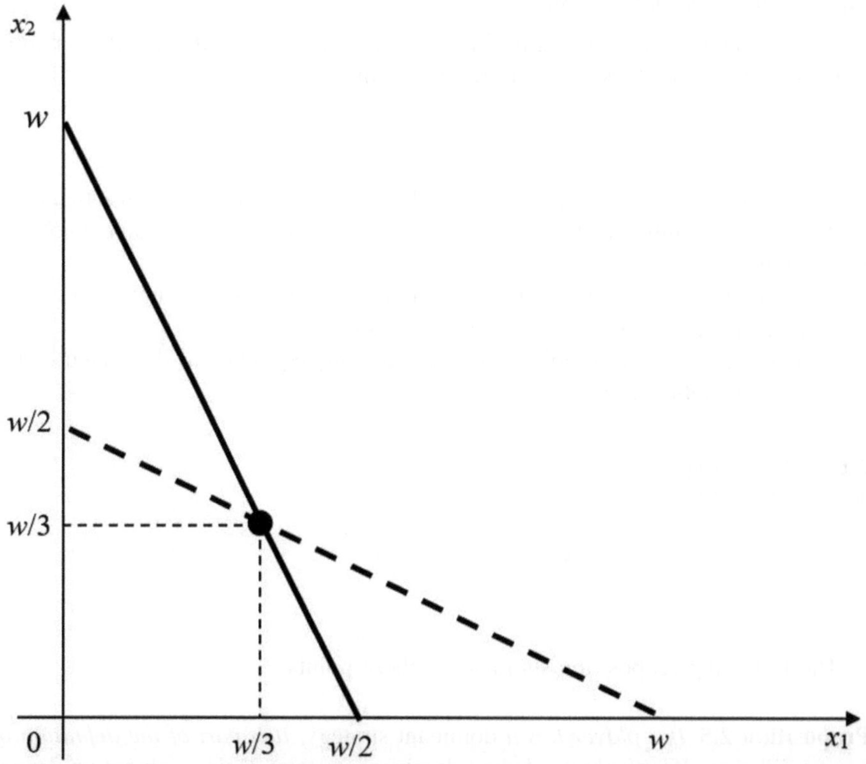

Fig. 2.20 Contribution to a public good

By symmetry, we know that $x_1 = x_2$ at an equilibrium. Solving the equation $x_1 = (w - x_1)/2$, we obtain the solution $\bar{x}_1 = \bar{x}_2 = w/3$. This is illustrated at Fig. 2.20 where the equilibrium is at the intersection between the graphs of the two reaction functions (the dotted line refers to player 2). At equilibrium, each agent sacrifices *one third* of his resources for the production of the public good. This non-cooperative solution is suboptimal from a collective point of view. It is indeed Pareto-dominated by the solution obtained by maximizing the *total* utility[26]:

$$u_1(x_1, x_2) + u_2(x_1, x_2) = (2w - x_1 - x_2)(x_1 + x_2).$$

Zeroing the first derivative with respect to x_1, we get $2w - 2x_1 - 2x_2 = 0$. By symmetry, we obtain $x_1 = x_2 = w/2$ as a unique solution: collective rationality calls for players to devote *half* of their resources for the production of the public good. This example has a prisoners' dilemma flavor. It highlights a phenomenon that is often observed, namely the underproduction of public goods in a non-cooperative framework.

[26] The assumption that individual utilities can be added is a strong assumption that goes beyond a cardinal representation. This question will be discussed in Chap. 3 dealing with bargaining.

Equilibrium and domination

A strategy that is part of an equilibrium cannot be dominated. Indeed, if the pair of strategies (a_1, a_2) defines an equilibrium, we have:

$$u_1(a_1, a_2) \geq u_1(s_1, a_2) \text{ for all } s_1 \in S_1.$$

If each player has a dominant strategy, the game is solved in the sense that these strategies will be implemented for sure if players are rational. This is an *equilibrium in dominant strategies*.

If only one of the two players has a dominant strategy, his opponent knows it and implements his best reply (or one of his best replies).

If there are several best replies, there are as many equilibria as illustrated by the game given in Table 2.30.

Table 2.30 Two equilibria involving a dominant strategy

	a_2	b_2
a_1	3, 2	2, 2
b_1	1, 1	0, 0

The following proposition summarizes these points.

Proposition 2.5 *If a player has a* dominant strategy, *it is part of the definition of any equilibrium. If both players have a* dominant strategy, *their* combination *defines the unique equilibrium.*

The prisoners' dilemma offers an example: "plead guilty" is indeed the dominant strategy for both players and the strategy combination (*G*, *G*) is the unique equilibrium. Here is another example.

Example 2.18 King Solomon Arbitration (Brams, 1980, 2003) Two women who live under the same roof gave birth at the same time. Shortly after the births, one night, one of the two babies dies. Her mother decides to exchange the babies. The two women find themselves facing King Solomon, each claiming that the living baby is theirs. The king decides to have the live baby cut in half! The two mothers reacted differently: one begged the king not to kill the baby, even if she had to leave it to the other, while the other insisted, preferring that the baby should not belong to either of them.

Assuming that the true mother is player 1, Brams suggests that the players' preferences can summarized in Table 2.31 where *P* stands for protesting against the judgment. We see that protesting against the judgment is a dominant strategy for the true mother while accepting it is dominant for the other.

Considering games resulting from an iterated elimination of dominated strategies, we have the following proposition.

Table 2.31 Solomon arbitration

	P	A
P	4, 2	3, 4
A	2, 1	1, 3

Proposition 2.6 *For games defined by* finite *strategy spaces, all sequences of successive eliminations of* dominated strategies *end up at the* same *reduced game. If they end up with a unique pair of strategies, it defines the unique equilibrium.*

In terms of method, one should proceed in two steps: first, eliminate the dominated strategies, following possibly a sequence, and then identify the equilibria, if any, in the resulting reduced game. This result does not extend to games defined by infinite strategy spaces, as shown by Dufwenberg and Stegeman (2002).

We have seen that, for finite games, iterated eliminations of dominated strategies result in rationalizable outcomes. Equilibrium outcomes are rationalizable but rationalizable outcomes do not necessarily define equilibrium. Referring to the battle of the sexes, there are two equilibria but all four outcomes are rationalizable.

Example 2.15 (continued) This a 3×3 game where different sequences of eliminations result in a unique pair of strategies that defines the unique equilibrium. It is therefore also rationalizable.

Example 2.12 (continued) Consider the finite sealed-bid auctions where the players' values are $v_1 = 32$ and $v_2 = 52$. They are represented in Table 2.21 (first price) and Table 2.22 (second price). In the first price auction, there is a unique equilibrium where player 2 bids a price just above player 1 evaluation and wins the auction. In the second price auction, there are several equilibria among which one involves weakly dominant strategies.

It is important to realize that, in situations where there are multiple equilibria, an equilibrium may involve weakly dominated strategies.

Example 2.13 (continued) In the price competition described in Table 2.29, there are two equilibria (c, c) and $(c+1, c+1)$ but choosing a price equal to the unit cost is weakly dominated.

Equilibria in zero-sum games

Consider a zero-sum game defined by the strategy spaces S_1 and S_2 and by the utility function u of the first player. The definition of an equilibrium is simplified in this framework. Indeed, referring to the definition of an equilibrium (2.4), where the utility of the second player is given by $-u$, a pair of strategies (a_1, a_2) defines an equilibrium if and only if:

$$u(a_1, a_2) \geq u(s_1, a_2) \quad \text{for all } s_1 \in S_1,$$
$$-u(a_1, a_2) \geq -u(a_1, s_2) \quad \text{for all } s_2 \in S_2.$$

Combining these two inequalities, we get:

$$u(s_1, a_2) \leq u(a_1, a_2) \leq u(a_1, s_2) \text{ for all } s_1 \in S_1 \textit{ and } \text{ for all } s_2 \in S_2. \quad (2.5)$$

At the point (a_1, a_2), the function u is at a *maximum* with respect to s_1 (in the direction of the s_1-axis) given a_2 and at a *minimum* with respect to s_2 (in the direction of the s_2-axis) given a_1.

The equilibrium of a zero-sum game is therefore a *saddle point* of the function u. The inequalities in (2.5) indeed correspond to the geometric representation of a saddle: maximum in one direction and minimum in the other direction.

If the strategy spaces are finite, we work with a matrix $A = [a_{ij}]$ whose entries are the utility levels of the first player, the utility levels of player 2 being given by $b_{ij} = -a_{ij}$.[27] An equilibrium is then defined by a pair row–column (i_0, j_0) such that the element $a_{i_0j_0}$ is *simultaneously* minimal along row i_0 *and* maximal along column j_0:

$$a_{i_0 j_0} = Max_i a_{i j_0} \text{ or } a_{i_0 j_0} \geq a_{i j_0} \text{ for all row } i,$$
$$a_{i_0 j_0} = Min_j a_{i_0 j} \text{ or } a_{i_0 j_0} \leq a_{i_0 j} \text{ for all columns } j.$$

In the game represented in Table 2.32, (b_1, a_2) is the unique equilibrium.

Table 2.32 Equilibrium in a zero-sum game

	a_2	b_2	c_2
a_1	−3	0	2
b_1	$\underline{1}$	1	2
c_1	−1	3	−2

We define the following two utility levels:

$$\underline{v} = Max_{s_1 \in S_1}[Min_{s_2 \in S_2} u(s_1, s_2)],$$
$$\overline{v} = Min_{s_2 \in S_2}[Max_{s_1 \in S_1} u(s_1, s_2)] = -Max_{s_2 \in S_2}[Min_{s_1 \in S_1} - u(s_1, s_2)].$$

The first one is the *maximin* value that was defined along with prudent strategies: $\underline{v}$ is the *minimum gain* that player 1 can guarantee, i.e., $\underline{v}$ is the security level of player 1. The second one is the *minimax* value: $\overline{v}$ is the *maximal loss* that player 2 can incur, i.e., $-\overline{v}$ is the security level of player 2. Following the definition of prudent strategies, the *maximin strategy* for the first player and the *minimax strategy* for the second are prudent strategies:

$$a_1 \text{ is a prudent strategy for player 1 if } Min_{s_2 \in S_2} u(a_1, s_2) = \underline{v},$$
$$a_2 \text{ is a prudent strategy for player 2 if } Max_{s_1 \in S_1} u(s_1, a_2) = \overline{v}.$$

In the game represented in Table 2.32, the maximin and minimax values coincide, $\underline{v} = \overline{v} = 1$, and define the unique equilibrium, while in the game represented in Table 2.33, the two values differ and there is no equilibrium.

[27] The element a_{ij} of a matrix A is the element located in row i and column j.

Table 2.33 A zero-sum game with no equilibrium

	a_2	b_2	c_2
a_1	1	0	−1
b_1	−2	1	2
c_1	0	3	0

We have indeed $\underline{v} = 0$ and $\overline{v} = 1$. The associated prudent strategies are c_1 and a_2. Actually, an equilibrium exists *if and only if* the two values coincide, in which case the common value $v = \underline{v} = \overline{v}$ is called the *value of the game.*

Proposition 2.7 *In a zero-sum game, an equilibrium exists* if and only if *it has a value.*

Proof We first observe that the minimal gain of player 1 never exceeds the maximal loss of player 2, $\underline{v} \leq \overline{v}$. This is an immediate consequence of the definition of the security levels:

$$\underline{v} = Max_{s_1 \in S_1}\left[Min_{s_2 \in S_2} u(s_1, s_2)\right] = Min_{s_2 \in S_2} u(a_1, s_2) \leq u(a_1, a_2),$$
$$\overline{v} = Min_{s_2 \in S_2}\left[Max_{s_1 \in S_1} u(s_1, s_2)\right] = Max_{s_1 \in S_1} u(s_1, a_2) \geq u(a_1, a_2).$$

where a_1 and a_2 are prudent strategies. Suppose now that the pair of strategies (a_1, a_2) defines an equilibrium. It satisfies the equilibrium conditions (2.5) and we have:

$$Max_{s_1 \in S_1} u(s_1, a_2) = u(a_1, a_2) = Min_{s_2 \in S_2} u(a_1, s_2).$$

By definition of the maximin and minimax values, we have

$$\underline{v} = Max_{s_1 \in S_1}\left[Min_{s_2 \in S_2} u(s_1, s_2)\right] \geq Min_{s_2 \in S_2} u(a_1, s_2),$$
$$\overline{v} = Min_{s_2 \in S_2}\left[Max_{s_1 \in S_1} u(s_1, s_2)\right] \leq Max_{s_1 \in S_1} u(s_1, a_2).$$

Hence, $\underline{v} = \overline{v} = u(a_1, a_2)$. It remains to verify that a game with a value has an equilibrium. If $\underline{v} = \overline{v}$ and if (a_1, a_2) is a pair of prudent strategies, we have

$$u(a_1, \overline{s}_2) \leq Max_{s_1 \in S_1} u(s_1, a_2) = \overline{v} = \underline{v}$$
$$= Min_{s_2 \in S_2} u(a_1, s_2) \leq u(a_1, a_2) \Rightarrow \overline{v} = \underline{v} = u(\overline{s}_1, \overline{s}_2).$$

Hence, (a_1, a_2) is a *saddle point*: $u(s_1, a_2) \leq u(a_1, a_2) \leq u(a_1, s_2)$ for all $s_1 \in S_1$ and $s_2 \in S_2$. ◆

Hence, for zero-sum games with a value, stability in the sense of Nash coincides with prudence. But there is more. When there are several equilibria, the strategies that are part of an equilibrium pair can be *interchanged* without affecting the utility levels of the players.

Proposition 2.8 *Consider a zero-sum game* (S_1, S_2, u). *If the pairs of strategies* (a_1, a_2) *and* (b_1, b_2) *define equilibria, then the pairs* (a_1, b_2) *and* (b_1, a_2) *also define equilibria, and the utility levels are all equal:* $u(a_1, a_2) = u(a_1, b_2) = u(b_1, b_2) = u(b_1, a_2)$.

Proof By definition of an equilibrium, we have:

$$u(a_1, a_2) \geq u(b_1, a_2) \geq u(b_1, b_2),$$
$$u(b_1, b_2) \geq u(a_1, b_2) \geq u(a_1, a_2),$$

from which we deduce the equalities $u(a_1, a_2) = u(a_1, b_2) = u(b_1, b_2) = u(b_1, a_2)$. We also have:

$$u(s_1, a_2) \leq u(a_1, a_2) = u(b_1, a_2) \text{ for all } s_1 \in S_1,$$
$$u(b_1, s_2) \geq u(b_1, b_2) = u(b_1, a_2) \text{ for all } s_2 \in S_2.$$

As a consequence, the pair (b_1, a_2) defines an equilibrium. We proceed in a similar way for (a_1, b_2).◆

As a consequence, in the case of zero-sum games, we may talk about *individual* equilibrium strategies. Prudent strategies are *optimal strategies* and there is no need for coordination between players. This is a fundamental characteristic of zero-sum games.

A zero-sum game is *symmetric* if $S_1 = S_2 = S$ and $u(s_1, s_2) = -u(s_2, s_1)$ for all $s_1, s_2 \in S$. The value of a *symmetric* game, if it exists, is then necessarily equal to zero. Furthermore, if s is an optimal strategy for a player, the pair (s, s) defines an equilibrium. Such zero-sum games are called *fair games.*

Zero-sum games have been used to analyze military decisions, in particular by Haywood (1954). He writes "*The doctrine of decision of the arms forces of the United States is a doctrine based on enemy capabilities. A commander is enjoined to select the course of action which offers the greatest promise of success in view of the enemy capabilities*" (pp. 365–366). This doctrine can be translated in terms of zero-sum games as illustrated by the following episode.

Example 2.19 Battle of the Bismarck Sea. South Pacific, 1943. At the head of a naval convoy, the Japanese Admiral Imamura is heading towards Lae in New Guinea. He has the choice between two routes, either North (N) of New Britain with a bad visibility, or South (S) with a clear weather. In both cases, the journey would take 3 days. The American General Kenney has to decide on which route to concentrate his reconnaissance airplanes. A map is provided in Fig. 2.21.

A simplified version of this situation can be described by a zero-sum game with four outcomes, where the utility for Kenney (and the disutility for Imamura) are measured by the number of days of bombing.

Table 2.34 describes the corresponding game where Kenney is player 1.

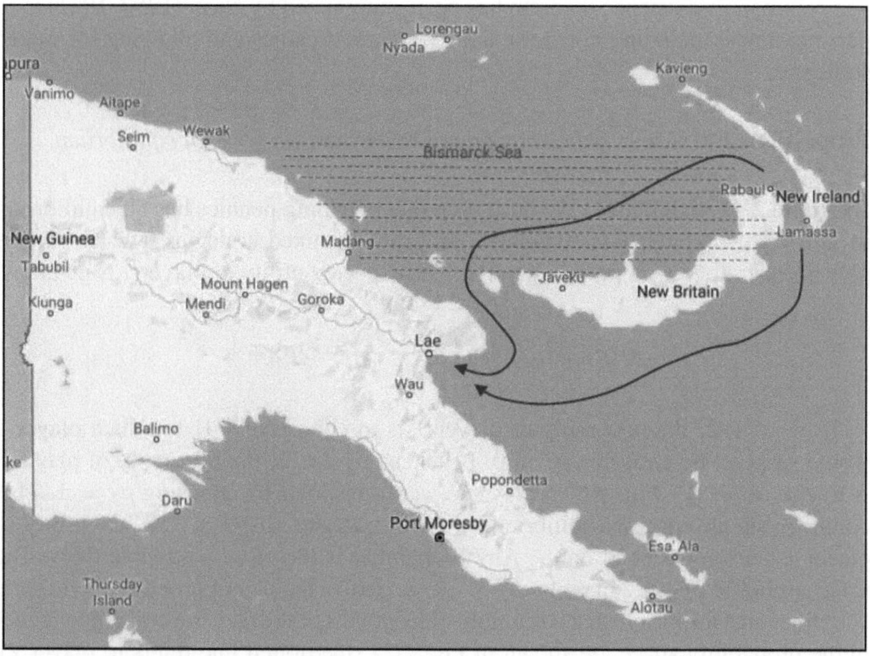

Fig. 2.21 Battle of the Bismarck Sea

Table 2.34 Battle of the Bismarck Sea

	N	S
N	$\underline{2}$	2
S	1	3

(N, N) is the unique equilibrium and it corresponds to what really happened: Kenney was sure that he could bomb for two days while Imamura was sure that he would not be bombed for more than 2 days. The Japanese were sighted after a day of reconnaissance and suffered significant losses.

Notice that "South" is weakly dominated by "North" for Imamura. If Kenney eliminates it (mentally), his choice is clear: he must choose "North". And that's what he did.

Existence of an equilibrium

The first existing result known as the *Minimax Theorem* is due to von Neumann (1928). It applies to finite zero-sum games where mixed strategies are allowed.

Notice that, at an equilibrium, some pure strategy may be assigned a zero probability and nothing excludes the case where the equilibrium involves only pure strategies.

von Neumann's existence theorem has been generalized by Nash (1950, 1951) to *n*-person games, including non-zero sum two-person games and allowing for mixed strategies.

Proposition 2.9 *Games defined by finite strategy spaces have an equilibrium.*

Example 2.11 (continued) We have seen that matching pennies has no equilibrium in pure strategies but it has a (unique) equilibrium in mixed strategies at which players play each strategy with probability 1/2. The expected utility of player 1 is given by:

$$u_1(p_1, p_2) = 4p_1\left(p_2 - \frac{1}{2}\right) - 2p_2 + 1$$

If $p_2 > 1/2$, the best reply of player 1 is to choose $p_1 = 1$, to which player 2 would respond by choosing $p_2 = 0$. If instead $p_2 < 1/2$, the best reply of player 1 is to choose $p_1 = 0$, to which player 2 would respond by choosing $p_2 = 1$. This confirms the absence of equilibrium in pure strategies. If $p_2 = 1/2$, the utility of player 1 does not depend on p_1. Any probability is therefore a possible reply. The same applies to player 2 in reply to $p_1 = 1/2$. Hence, the pair of probabilities (1/2, 1/2) defines an equilibrium and it is unique. The graphs of the reaction correspondences in the probability space are shown in Fig. 2.22 (the dotted line refers to player 2), confirming the existence of a unique equilibrium.

No surprise, the expected utility at equilibrium is equal to zero for both players: matching pennies is a *fair game*. We have seen that it can be applied to penalty kicks in football. Palacios-Huerta (2003) has shown that the kicker and the goal-keeper tend indeed to adopt the strategy that consists of flipping (mentally) a coin.

Example 2.2 (continued) Consider the simplified version of the *battle of the sexes* as given by Table 2.25. Extending it to mixed strategies, the utility functions are given by (2.3). Placing p_1 in evidence in u_1 and p_2 in evidence in u_2, we have:

$$u_1(p_1, p_2) = 2p_1p_2 + (1 - p_1)(1 - p_2) = 3p_1\left(p_2 - \frac{1}{3}\right) - p_2 + 1,$$

$$u_2(p_1, p_2) = p_1p_2 + 2(1 - p_1)(1 - p_2) = 3p_2\left(p_1 - \frac{2}{3}\right) - 2p_1 + 2.$$

In terms of best reply, if $p_2 > 1/3$, player 1 gains by maximizing p_1 and will therefore opt for S that corresponds to $p_1 = 1$, to which player 2 would respond by choosing $p_2 = 1$. If instead $p_2 < 1/3$, the best reply of player 1 is $p_1 = 0$ to which player 2 would respond by choosing $p_2 = 0$. We retrieve in this way the two equilibria in pure strategies previously identified. They are defined by $p_1 = p_2 = 1$ and $p_1 = p_2 = 0$, respectively.

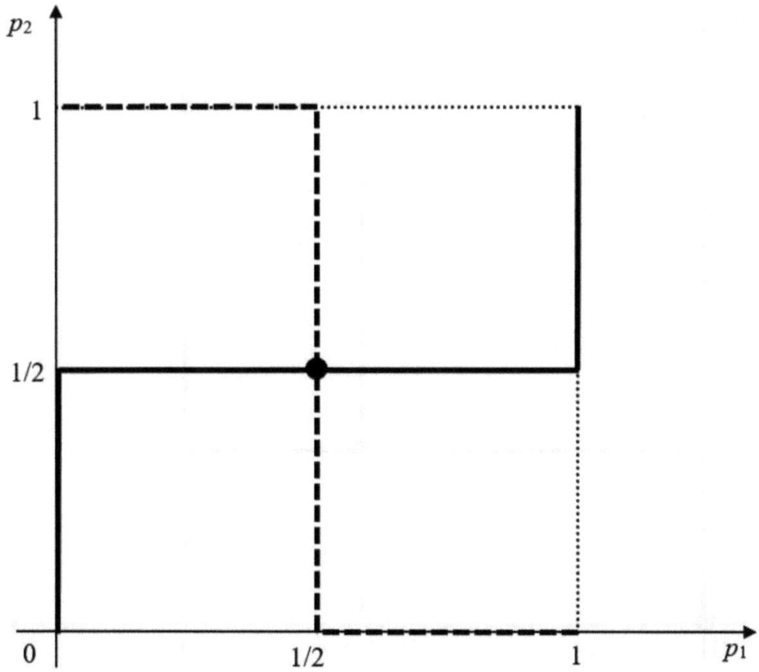

Fig. 2.22 Matching pennies in mixed strategies

The probabilities $p_1 = 2/3$ and $p_2 = 1/3$ define the equilibrium in mixed strategy. We have indeed:

$$u_1(p_1, 1/3) = 2/3 \text{ for all } p_1 \in [0, 1],$$
$$u_2(2/3, p_2) = 2/3 \text{ for all } p_2 \in [0, 1],$$

i.e., any probability is a possible reply to $p_2 = 1/3$ and, similarly, any probability is a possible reply to $p_1 = 2/3$. The graphs of the reaction correspondences are reproduced in Fig. 2.23 (the dotted line refers to player 2).

The three equilibria correspond to the intersections of the graphs of the reaction correspondences. The difference between the two probabilities that define the mixed strategy equilibrium is easily explained: both players play their preferred destination with the same probability, $p_1 = 2/3 = 1 - p_2$, and their expected utility are equal:

$$u_1\left(\frac{2}{3}, \frac{1}{3}\right) = u_2\left(\frac{2}{3}, \frac{1}{3}\right) = \frac{2}{3}.$$

Referring to Fig. 2.15, we observe that the equilibrium outcome (2/3, 2/3) is Pareto-dominated by the outcomes associated with the equilibria in pure strategies, (2, 1) or (1, 2). It is also Pareto-dominated by the outcome resulting from playing

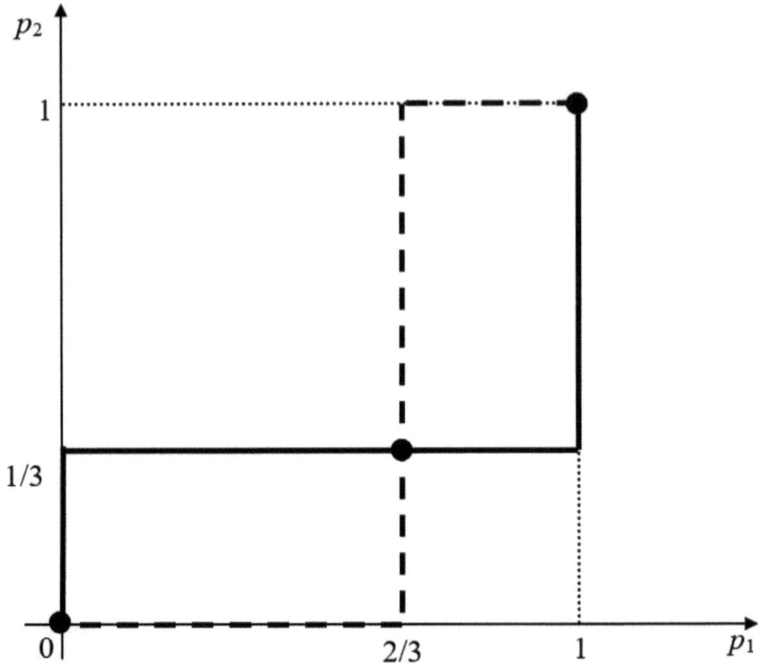

Fig. 2.23 Battle of the sexes in mixed strategies

the preferred destination by the flip of a coin. If the couple decides to rely on equilibrium mixed strategies, they will end up separated with probability of 5/9. It is definitely not a solution to the problem. Coordination is needed, using for instance correlated strategies based on a single random trial that allows reaching points on the segment joining the points (2, 1) or (1, 2), as shown in Fig. 2.17.

In an equilibrium in mixed strategies, dominated strategies have a zero probability. In the preceding example, there is only one equilibrium in pure strategies and no equilibrium in mixed strategies. The game given in Table 2.35 has no equilibrium in pure strategies.

Table 2.35 Game with no equilibrium in pure strategies

	a_2	b_2	c_2
a_1	0, $\underline{2}$	$\underline{2}$, 1	$\underline{2}$, 0
b_1	$\underline{2}$, 0	1, $\underline{2}$	1, 0
c_1	1, $\underline{2}$	0, $\underline{2}$	0, 1

We observe that c_1 and c_2 are dominated. We may therefore reason within the reduced games to identify possible equilibria in mixed strategies. There is one equilibrium. It is defined by the probabilities $p_1 = 2/3$ and $p_2 = 1/3$, leading to the expected utility levels $u_1 = u_2 = 4/3$.

The resolution in mixed strategies of the battle of the sexes illustrates the following proposition.

Proposition 2.10 *At an equilibrium in mixed strategies, each player is indifferent between the pure strategies to which he assigns a positive probability, given the strategy of his opponent.*

This proposition can be used to compute the equilibrium probabilities.

Example 2.11 (continued) In matching pennies, the expected utilities associated with the pure strategies R ($p_1 = 1$) and L ($p_1 = 0$), as functions of the probability p_2, are given by

$$u_1(1, p_2) = 4(p_2 - \frac{1}{2}) - 2p_2 + 1,$$
$$u_2(0, p_2) = -2p_2 + 1.$$

They coincide for $p_2 = 1/2$. Player 1 is then indifferent between R and L. Actually, for $p_2 = 1/2$, the expected utility is independent of p_1 and the following identity is satisfied:

$$u_1\left(p_1, \frac{1}{2}\right) = 0 \text{ for all } p_1 \in [0, 1].$$

Example 2.4 (continued) We have seen that the game of chicken has two equilibria in pure strategies, (S, C) and (C, S). There exists also an equilibrium in mixed strategies. Consider Table 2.36. It is a modified version of the game of chicken initially given in Table 2.6.

Table 2.36 Modified game of chicken

	C	S
C	$-3, -3$	$\underline{2}, \underline{0}$
S	$\underline{0}, \underline{2}$	$1, 1$

The game being symmetric, we have to compute the probability p with which a player decides to continue. On the basis of Proposition 2.10, this probability must be such that the player is indifferent between continuing (C) and swerving (S), given that his opponent makes a choice according to the same probability p. The levels of utility corresponding to the two strategies are given by:

$$u_1(1, p) = 2(1 - p) - 3p,$$
$$u_1(0, p) = 1 - p.$$

They coincide for $p = 1/4$. The equilibrium in mixed strategies is therefore given by the probability pair $(p_1, p_2) = (1/4, 1/4)$. The expected utility is equal 3/4 for each player and the probability of survival is given by $1 - p^2 \simeq 0.9375$.

Notice that, as a consequence of Proposition 2.4, an equilibrium in mixed strategies found within the strategic form associated with a game in extensive form may be written as an equilibrium in behavioral strategies, and vice versa.

Reminder We are in a cardinal setting and therefore the probabilities that define an equilibrium in mixed strategies depend on the utility levels. In this framework, two strategically equivalent games have the same set of equilibria: equilibrium probabilities are invariant if we apply *linear* transformations to payoffs.

Risk-dominance in 2 × 2 games *

When there are several equilibria, it may be possible to identify a *focal* equilibrium outcome, for instance, the Pareto-dominant one, if it exists. It is the case of the stag hunt game which is an example of a coordination problem. But how much can you trust the other? Each player is uncertain about the behavior of the other and choosing to hunt the deer may indeed be risky. It may be safer to catch the hare.

Example 2.6 (continued) The game described in Table 2.37 is a symmetric game that corresponds to the stag hunt.

Table 2.37 Modified stag hunt game

	a_2	b_2
a_1	$\underline{10}, \underline{10}$	0, 5
b_1	5, 0	$\underline{8}, \underline{8}$

There are two strict equilibria and the equilibrium (a_1, a_2) is Pareto-dominant and thereby strong. It is the "cooperative" equilibrium.

Is it likely that the players will choose to cooperate? The answer is no. Indeed, player 2 observes that player 1 would lose more by deviating from (b_1, b_2) than by deviating from (a_1, a_2), 8 compared to 5. He may then expect that player 1 will play b_1. By symmetry, the same is true for player 1 who will expect player 2 to play b_2. Hence, we may expect that players will prefer to play *non-cooperatively*. This reasoning makes sense in a *cardinal framework* where utility differences can be compared. It underlies the concept of risk-dominance introduced by Harsanyi and Selten (1988) and based on subjective probabilities.

Consider the parametrized game given in Table 2.38 where $\alpha_i > \lambda_i$ and $\beta_i > \delta_i,\ i = 1, 2$.

Table 2.38 Parametrized 2 × 2 game

	a_2	b_2
a_1	$\underline{\alpha_1}, \underline{\alpha_2}$	δ_1, λ_2
b_1	λ_1, δ_2	$\underline{\beta_1}, \underline{\beta_2}$

There are two strict equilibria in pure strategies, (a_1, a_2) and (b_1, b_2). The expected utility for player 1 of playing a_1, assuming that player 2 plays a_2 with probability p is given by:

$$u_1(a_1, p) = p\alpha_1 + (1 - p)\delta_1.$$

Similarly, the expected utility of playing b_1 given the probability p is given by:

$$u_1(b_1, p) = p\lambda_1 + (1 - p)\beta_1.$$

Player 1 is then *indifferent* between a_1 and b_1 for a probability p given by:

$$\overline{p}_2 = \frac{\beta_1 - \delta_1}{(\beta_1 - \delta_1) + (\alpha_1 - \lambda_1)}. \tag{2.6}$$

The threshold probability $\overline{p}_2$ is well defined. It is the relative loss associated to a deviation from the equilibrium (b_1, b_2). Similarly, the probability for which player 2 is *indifferent* between a_2 and b_2 is given by

$$\overline{p}_1 = \frac{\beta_2 - \delta_2}{(\beta_2 - \delta_2) + (\alpha_2 - \lambda_2)}. \tag{2.7}$$

Consider the following example used by Harsanyi and Selten to introduce the concept of risk-dominance.

Example 2.20 The Harsanyi–Selten Game (1988, p. 82). The game given in Table 2.39 has two strong equilibria. Which one is most likely?

Table 2.39 Harsanyi–Selten game

	a_2	b_2
a_1	<u>99</u>, <u>49</u>	0, 0
b_1	0, 0	<u>1</u>, <u>51</u>

Here, following the Eqs. (2.6) and (2.7), $\overline{p}_1 = 51/100 = 0.51$ and $\overline{p}_2 = 1/100 = 0.01$. If player 1 expects player 2 to play a_2 with a probability greater than 0.01, he will opt for a_1. Equivalently, if he expects that player 2 to play b_2 with a probability greater than $1 - \overline{p}_2 = 0.99$, he will opt for b_1. Hence, from the point of view of player 1, a_1 is *much less risky* than b_1. Player 2 will be indifferent between a_2 and b_2 for the probability $\overline{p}_2 = 51/100 = 0.51$. Playing a_2 is preferable if he expects player 1 to play a_1 with a probability greater that 0.51. Equivalently, b_2 is preferable if he expects player 1 to play b_1 with a probability greater than 0.49. Hence, from the point of view of player 2, b_2 is *slightly less risky* than a_2. Player 1 has a good reason to play a_1 while player 2 has a weaker reason to play b_2. Considering the fact that player 1 will choose a_1 with a high probability, player 2 will naturally choose a_2. The equilibrium (a_1, a_2) is then said to be *risk-dominant*.

Notice that the pair of probabilities $(\overline{p}_1, \overline{p}_2)$ defines the (unique) equilibrium in mixed strategies. Indeed, referring to Table 2.38, if p_i is the probability assigned to the strategy a_i, the expected utility of player 1 is the function of (p_1, p_2) given by:

$$u_1(p_1, p_2) = p_1(p_2(\alpha_1 - \lambda_1 + \beta_1 - \delta_1) + \delta_1 - \beta_1) + p_2(\lambda_1 - \beta_1) + \beta_1.$$

It is independent of p_1 for $p_2 = \overline{p}_2$. It goes identically for player 2.

The threshold probability $\overline{p}_i$ defined by the Eqs. (2.6) and (2.7) is a measure of the risk associated with the strategy a_i from player i's point of view. Therefore, the risk associated to (a_1, a_2) is the sum of the threshold probabilities $\overline{p}_1 + \overline{p}_2$. In the Harsanyi-Selten game, we have $\overline{p}_1 + \overline{p}_2 = 0.52 < 1$, i.e., the riskiness of (a_1, a_2) is smaller than the riskiness of (b_1, b_2).

It is easily verified that the inequality $\overline{p}_1 + \overline{p}_2 < 1$ is equivalent to:

$$(\beta_1 - \delta_1)(\beta_2 - \delta_2) < (\alpha_1 - \lambda_1)(\alpha_2 - \lambda_2).$$

Hence, the risk-dominant equilibrium is associated to the *largest product of deviations*.[28] In case of equality, there is no domination.

Example 2.6 (continued) Applied to the modified stag hunt game given by Table 2.37, the largest product is associated to the non-cooperative equilibrium, 64 compared to 25. In the Harsanyi–Selten game, the largest product is associated to (a_1, a_2), 4851 compared to 51.

Comparing the product of the deviations is not arbitrary. Harsanyi and Selten actually provide a simple and natural axiomatization of the risk-dominance relation on the class of 2×2 games with two strong equilibria.

Introducing a mediator

In conflicting situations, introducing a mediator may turn to be beneficial for all players. This is the idea introduced by Monderer and Tennenholtz (2009). A mediator is an outsider that can act on behalf of the players, knowing that each player remains free to act without the intervention of the mediator. It means that an additional strategy is available, namely the possibility to call for the intervention of the mediator.

Example 2.21 Prisoners' Dilemma with a Mediator. Consider the prisoners' dilemma and assume that a lawyer proposes to the suspects to serve as a mediator, knowing that if both accept the mediation, the lawyer will plead non-guilty (*NG*) on behalf of them, while if only one does, he will plead guilty (*G*) on behalf of that

[28] This is the *Nash product*, a concept that will play a central role in Chap. 3 devoted to bargaining.

player. His presence then gives rise to the game described by Table 2.40 where M stands for relying on the mediator.

Table 2.40 Prisoners' dilemma with a mediator

	M	G	NG
M	3, 3	2, 2	4, 1
G	2, 2	2, 2	4, 1
NG	1, 4	1, 4	3, 3

We observe that there are two equilibria, one of which involves the mediator that is a strong equilibrium: the players cannot do better by jointly deviating. Monderer and Tennenholtz prove the following proposition.

Proposition 2.11 *Every two-person game has a strong mediated equilibrium.*

Equilibria in correlated strategies

Along with the idea of relying on a mediator, what if the players agree on programming a random machine that will *privately* suggest to each of them a strategy to play? The programming should be such that no player could gain by *not* following the suggestion he receives, exactly like at a Nash equilibrium. If it is the case, the resulting outcome defines a *correlated equilibrium.* Correlation has the advantage that it gives access to a much greater set of outcomes some of which may Pareto-dominate existing Nash equilibria.[29] We have seen this in the battle of the sexes, as illustrated in Fig. 2.17.

A *correlated strategy* is a probability distribution defined on the Cartesian product $S_1 \times S_2$. It associates to each pair of strategies (s_1, s_2) the probability $p(s_1, s_2)$ that s_1 will be suggested to player 1 and s_2 to player 2. In the case of a finite strategy spaces, a correlated strategy can be represented by a probability matrix $P = [p_{ij}]$ where i refers to player 1 and j refers to player 2. In the case of two strategies for each player, the matrix

$$P' = \begin{bmatrix} 1/5 & 3/5 \\ 1/10 & 1/10 \end{bmatrix}$$

says that the machine will suggest a_1 to player 1 and b_2 to player 2 with probability 3/5. Notice that a pair of mixed strategies induces a correlated strategy but the inverse is not true. For instance, it is not possible to reproduce the matrix

$$P'' = \begin{bmatrix} 1/2 & 1/4 \\ 1/4 & 0 \end{bmatrix}$$

[29] This is, however, not the case for zero-sum games. See Moulin and Vial (1978).

using mixed strategies. Once suggestions are made, players have an additional information and they may then revise the probability distribution over the strategies of the opponent, following a simple normalization.[30]

On the basis of the correlated strategy given by the matrix P', if a_1 is suggested to player 1, he knows that a_2 has been suggested to his opponent with probability 1/4: summing the probabilities gives 4/5 and dividing 1/5 by 4/5 gives 1/4. If instead b_1 is the suggestion, he knows that a_2 has been suggested with probability 1/2. On the basis of the correlated strategy given by the matrix P'', if a_1 is the suggestion made to player 1, he knows that a_2 has been suggested with probability 2/3. If instead b_1 is the suggestion, he knows *with certainty* (with probability 1) that a_2 has been suggested to his opponent.

Formally, consider the probability distribution $P = [p(s_1, s_2)]$. If there is a positive probability that the strategy $s_1 = a$ could be suggested to player 1, we have

$$p_1(a) = \sum_{s_2 \in S_2} p(a, s_2) > 0.$$

The *conditional* probability distribution on S_2 is then given by:

$$q_1(a, s_2) = \frac{p(a, s_2)}{p_1(a)}.$$

This is a probability distribution on the suggestions that could be made to his opponent. If instead $p_1(a) = 0$, we may ignore that strategy. Similarly, we define the probability distribution on S_1 associated with a strategy $s_2 = a$ by:

$$q_2(s_1, a) = \frac{p(s_1, a)}{p_2(a)},$$

assuming that $p_2(a) = \sum_{s_1 \in S_1} p(s_1, a) > 0$.

A *correlated equilibrium* is defined by a probability distribution $P = [p(s_1, s_2)]$ such that no player could gain by deviating (unilaterally) from any suggestion that can be made, given these probabilities. This translates into the following two conditions.

- For all strategy $a_1 \in S_1$ such that $p_1(a_1) > 0$,

$$\sum_{s_2 \in S_2} q_1(a_1, s_2)\, u_1(a_1, s_2) \geq \sum_{s_2 \in S_2} q_1(a_1, s_2)\, u_1(s_1, s_2) \quad \text{for all } s_1 \in S_1.$$

30 Formally speaking, we refer here to the definition of a *conditional probability*.

- For all strategy $a_2 \in S_2$ such that $p_2(a_2) > 0$,

$$\sum_{s_1 \in S_1} q_2(s_1, a_2)\, u_2(s_1, a_2) \geq \sum_{s_1 \in S_1} q_2(s_1, a_2)\, u_2(s_1, s_2) \quad \text{for all } s_2 \in S_2.$$

It is important to realize that the same probabilities are used to evaluate the expected gain to deviate.

Consider the simplified version of the battle of the sexes given in Table 2.25:

	a_2	b_2
a_1	2, 1	0, 0
b_1	0, 0	1, 2

The probability matrix P' is not a correlated equilibrium. If a_1 is suggested to player 1, he knows that a_2 has been suggested to player 2 with probability 1/4. If he follows the suggestion to play a_1, his expected utility is given by:

$$\frac{1}{4}2 + \frac{3}{4}0 = \frac{1}{2}.$$

It turns out that he would gain by deviating and playing b_1, giving him a greater expected utility:

$$\frac{1}{4}0 + \frac{3}{4}1 = \frac{3}{4} \; > \; \frac{1}{2}.$$

Similarly, if b_1 is suggested, player 1 knows that a_2 has been suggested to player 2 with probability 1/2. If he follows the suggestion, his expected utility is equal to 1/2 while if he deviates and plays a_1, his expected utility is equal to 1.

The probability matrix

$$P = \begin{bmatrix} 1/2 & 0 \\ 0 & 1/2 \end{bmatrix}$$

defines a correlated equilibrium. If player 1 is suggested to play a_1, he knows that a_2 has been suggested to player 2 (with probability 1) and he has therefore no interest in playing b_1. The same applies to player 2.

This equilibrium corresponds to the natural "solution" of this dilemma that consists in choosing a destination by flipping a coin.

Actually, all probability matrices of the form:

$$P = \begin{bmatrix} p & 0 \\ 0 & 1-p \end{bmatrix}$$

where p is set arbitrarily between 0 and 1 define a correlated equilibrium for the battle of the sexes. Once the suggestions are made, players can guess what has been suggested to the other. By varying p in the interval [0, 1], we generate the line segment joining the points (2, 1) and (1, 2) in the expected utility space, as illustrated in Fig. 2.17.

A point on that segment corresponds to a correlated equilibrium offering to both players an expected utility greater than the one associated with the mixed strategies equilibrium. Because of symmetry, we naturally retain the mid-point (3/2, 3/2) that corresponds to $p = 1/2$. Recall that these probability matrices are akin to public suggestions.

Example 2.4 (continued) Consider the chicken game given by Table 2.6. Here again, correlation is naturally done between the two equilibria in pure strategies (C, S) and (S, C). Indeed, the probability matrix.

$$P = \begin{bmatrix} 0 & p \\ 1 - p & 0 \end{bmatrix}$$

defines a correlated equilibrium for all $p \in [0, 1]$: once a suggestion is made, each player knows what is the suggestion that has been made to the other. Considering player 1, if C is suggested and he accepts it, his expected utility is equal to 2, instead of 1 if he does not accept it. If on the contrary, S is suggested and he accepts it, his expected utility is equal to 0, instead of a loss of 3 if he does not accept it. The following probability matrix also defines a correlated equilibrium:

$$P = \begin{bmatrix} 0 & 1/3 \\ 1/3 & 1/3 \end{bmatrix}.$$

If C is suggested and he accepts it, the expected utility of player 1 is equal to 2, instead of 1 if he does not accept it. If S is suggested and he accepts it, his expected utility is equal to 1/2, instead of – 1/2.

Example 1.22 Game with a Unique Correlated Equilibrium. The game given in Table 2.41 has a unique correlated equilibrium.

Table 2.41 Game with a unique correlated equilibrium

	a_2	b_2
a_1	$\underline{2}, 0$	$0, \underline{1}$
b_1	$0, \underline{1}$	$\underline{1}, 0$

The following four inequalities must indeed be simultaneously satisfied:

$$2p_{11} \geq p_{12},\ p_{22} \geq 2p_{21},\ p_{21} \geq p_{11} \text{ and } p_{12} \geq p_{22}.$$

Imposing the identity $p_{11} + p_{12} + p_{21} + p_{22} = 1$, there is a unique solution: $p_{11} = p_{21} = 1/6$ and $p_{12} = p_{22} = 1/3$. The equilibrium outcome is given by (2/3, 1/2). This game has a unique Nash equilibrium, defined by the mixed strategies (1/2, 1/2) and (1/3, 2/3). It happens to lead to the same expected utilities.

Example 2.23 Moulin-Vial Game. Moulin and Vial (1978) have analyzed the game given in Table 2.42.

Table 2.42 Moulin-Vial game

0, 0	1, $\underline{2}$	$\underline{2}$, 1
$\underline{2}$, 1	0, 0	1, $\underline{2}$
1, $\underline{2}$	$\underline{2}$, 1	0, 0

It has no equilibrium in pure strategies but a unique equilibrium in mixed strategies, defined by the probabilities (1/3, 1/3, 1/3) for both players giving an expected utility equal to 1. The correlated strategy that consists of relying on the throw of a die to choose among the six results with positive payoffs defines an equilibrium with a better outcome. The expected utility is indeed equal to 3/2 for both players.

Mixed or correlated strategies are random mechanisms based on objective and (commonly) known probabilities like throwing a die or spinning a roulette. What happens if strategies were based on subjective probabilities like horse races or elections, about which players typically hold diverging probabilities. This idea to introduce *subjectivity* in correlated strategy choices is due to Robert Aumann (1974). He shows that divergence of opinion between players may result in surprising conclusions. In particular, it may be possible to attain expected utility outcomes falling *outside* the convex hull of the outcomes associated with pure strategies. Furthermore, zero-sum games may lose their competitive character in the sense that cooperation may become interesting.

Example 2.11 (continued) Consider the game matching pennies as given by Table 2.17:

	R	*L*
R	1, −1	−1, 1
L	−1, 1	1, −1

Let B be an event to which player 1 attributes a probability 2/3 and player 2 attributes a probability 1/3. Assume that player 2 plays a_2 with probability 1 while player 1 plays a_1 if B comes true and b_1 if not. The expected utilities associated with these strategies are then positive and equal to 1/3 for both players! Table 2.43 offers another example.

Table 2.43 Subjective correlated equilibrium

	a_2	b_2
a_1	$\underline{1}, 0$	$\underline{3}, \underline{2}$
b_1	0, 1	$2, \underline{3}$

Using the same event, the same subjective probabilities and the same strategies, the expected utilities for both players are equal to 8/3, and the point (8/3, 8/3) falls outside the convex hull of the points (1, 0), (0, 1), (3, 2) and (2, 3).

In these examples, we have generated points that do not dominate *all* attainable outcomes in the absence of divergence: in the first example, the point (1/3, 1/3) does not Pareto-dominate the point (1, −1) and, in the second example, the point (8/3, 8/3) does not Pareto-dominate the point (2, 3). Actually, Aumann shows that there must be at least three players for constructing examples where subjectivity leads to outcomes that dominate *all* the outcomes associated with objective correlated strategies.

2.7 Subgame Perfect Equilibria

Subgame perfection
Ultimatum game
Dictator game
Trust game.

We return to games in extensive form, looking for some simple selection criteria when the associated strategic form reveals multiple equilibria.

Subgame perfection

In a game in extensive form, a subgame is a portion of the game tree starting at an information set containing a *single node* and such that all nodes that follow are included. In particular, the game itself is a subgame. Figure 2.24 illustrates a game that contains only one proper subgame. It starts at the node assigned to player 2. This subgame has a unique equilibrium, (c_1, a_2). The whole game has three equilibria. We retain the first, (b_1c_1, a_2) because it is the only one that includes the equilibrium of the subgame. This is the idea behind the notion of subgame perfection introduced by Selten (1975).[31]

[31] This concept was originally introduced by Selten (1965).

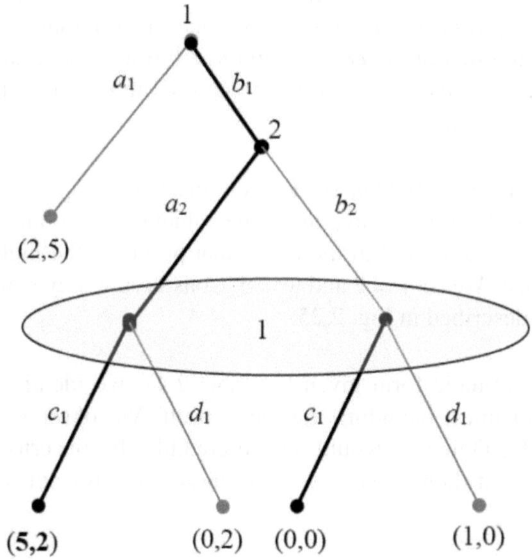

	a_2	b_2
a_1c_1	2, $\underline{5}$	$\underline{2}$, $\underline{5}$
a_1d_1	2, $\underline{5}$	$\underline{2}$, $\underline{5}$
b_1c_1	$\underline{5}$, $\underline{2}$	0, 0
b_1d_1	0, $\underline{2}$	1, 0

	a_2	b_2
c_1	$\underline{5}$, $\underline{2}$	0, 0
d_1	0, $\underline{2}$	$\underline{1}$, 0

Fig. 2.24 A subgame perfect equilibrium

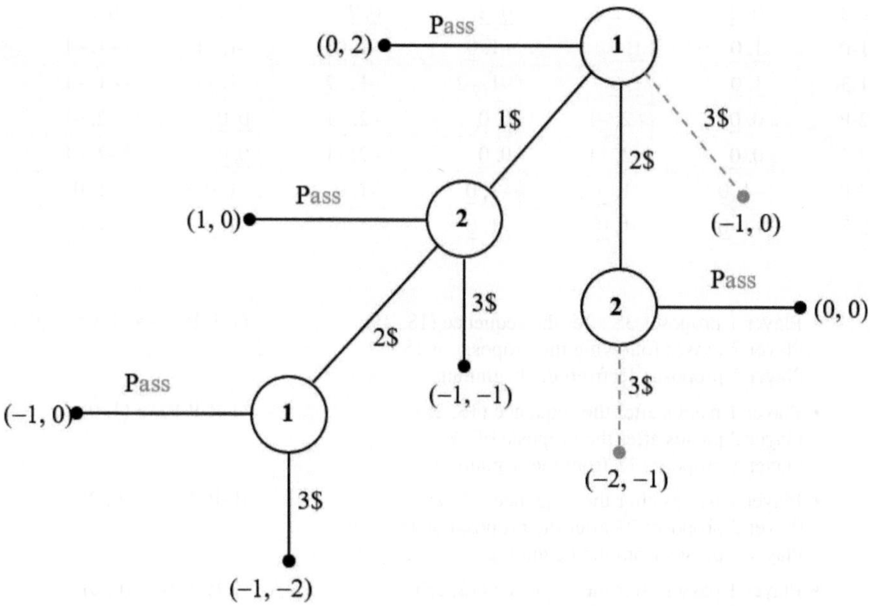

Fig. 2.25 Sequential auction

Formally, an equilibrium is *subgame perfect* if it defines an equilibrium in *all* subgames. We know that an equilibrium defines actions that are optimal in the whole game and in the subgame that are *effectively attained* through the equilibrium strategies. Perfection requires that these actions be optimal in *all* subgames, *including the* subgames *that are not attained.*

Example 2.24 Sequential Auction (Osborne, 2004). An object is put up for sale. There are two potential buyers. They both have the same valuation $v > 0$ and the same budget $w > v$. The object is allocated to the buyer that proposes the highest price but they *both* pay that price! We set $v = 2$ and $w = 3$. Considering only natural numbers, we obtain the game described in Fig. 2.25.

Looking at the associated strategic form given by Table 2.44, we identify 16 equilibria. There are four subgames, including the game itself. We observe that player 2 will never propose 3$. Doing so would not be credible. It concerns the strategies P-3, 2-3, 3-3 and 3-P. It then remains six equilibria. Only four of them pass the test of perfection.

Table 2.44 Sequential auction in strategic form

	P-P	P-3	2-P	2-3	3-P	3-3
P-P	0, 2	0, 2	0, 2	0, 2	0, 2	0, 2
P-3	0, 2	0, 2	0, 2	0, 2	0, 2	0, 2
1-P	1, 0	1, 0	−1, 0	−1, 0	−1, −1	−1, −1
1-3	1, 0	1, 0	−1, −2	−1, −2	−1, −1	−1, −1
2-P	0, 0	−2, −1	0, 0	−2, −1	0, 0	−2, −1
2-3	0, 0	−2, −1	0, 0	−2, −1	0, 0	−2, −1
3-P	−1, 0	−1, 0	−1, 0	−1, 0	−1, 0	−1, 0
3-3	−1, 0	−1, 0	−1, 0	−1, 0	−1, 0	−1, 0

- Player 1 proposes 3$ after the sequence (1$, 2$) (1-3, P-P) → (1, 0)
  Player 2 passes following the proposal of 1$
  Player 1 proposes 1$ from the beginning
- Player 1 passes after the sequence (1$, 2$) (1-P, P-P) → (1, 0)
  Player 2 passes after the proposal of 1$
  Player 1 proposes 1$ from the beginning
- Player 1 passes after the sequence (1$, 2$) (P-P, 2-P) → (0, 2)
  Player 2 proposes 2$ after the proposal of 1$
  Player 1 passes from the beginning
- Player 1 passes after the sequence (1$, 2$) (2-P, 2-P) → (0, 0)
  Player 2 proposes 2$ after the proposal of 1$
  Player 1 proposes 2$ from the beginning

If it was common knowledge that buyers, not only do maximize their gain, but make the *smallest* proposal systematically in case they are indifferent ("Pass" being assimilated to a zero proposal), we finally retain only one equilibrium, namely the second, (1-P, P-P), to which the outcome (1, 0) is associated. The first player proposes 1$ and the second passes, knowing that a player would pass if the other proposed 2$.

Backward induction, when it works, retains only one equilibrium and that equilibrium is automatically subgame perfect because, by definition, *at every node*, the player concerned implements an optimal action. Backward induction cannot be applied when information is imperfect (except in some particular cases) and it is defeated if a player happens to be indifferent between several actions at some node. In that case, subgame perfect equilibria are identified by considering *all* the actions between which a player is indifferent.

This extended backward induction method under perfect information was already considered by Kuhn (1950). It is then equivalent to subgame perfection and ensures the existence of at least one subgame perfect equilibrium.

Example 2.7 (continued) In the modified game tree described at Fig. 2.9, player 2 is indifferent between c_2 and d_2. There are three proper subgames. If the action c_2 is retained, we retrieve the equilibrium (a_1c_1, a_2c_2) to which is associated the outcome (3, 3). Retaining instead the action d_2, we retrieve the equilibrium (b_1c_1, a_2d_2) to which is associated the outcome (5, 2). Hence, there are two subgame perfect equilibria.

Example 2.25 The game described in Fig. 2.26 has six subgame perfect equilibria. The associated strategic form is given in Table 2.45. It reveals a total of nine equilibria. There are three proper subgames and all concern player 2. He is indifferent between *L* and *R* in the first two and prefers *R* in the third. Hence, there are four possibilities: *LLR*, *LRR*, *RRR* and *RLR*. The optimal choice of player 1 is *T* in the first two cases and *M* in the third. In the last case *RLR*, he is indifferent between all three actions. Hence, there are six subgame perfect equilibria: (*T*, *LLR*), (*T*, *LRR*), (*M*, *RRR*), (*T*, *RLR*), (*M*, *RLR*) and (*B*, *RLR*). We could, however, go further and assume that player 1 will never opt for *B* that gives him a maximum payoff of 1.

Table 2.45 Game with six subgame perfect equilibria: the strategic form

	LLL	*LLR*	*LRR*	*LRL*	*RRR*	*RLR*	*RLL*	*RRL*
T	3, 0	3, 0	3, 0	3, 0	1, 0	1, 0	1, 0	1, 0
M	1, 1	1, 1	2, 1	2, 1	2, 1	1, 1	1, 1	2, 1
B	2, 2	1, 3	1, 3	2,2	1, 3	1, 3	2, 2	2, 2

Example 2.26 Consider the game described in Fig. 2.27. After having identified the optimal actions at each node, we observe that player 2 is indifferent between c_2 and d_2. As far as player 1 is concerned, he has no interest in choosing a_1 which is dominated.

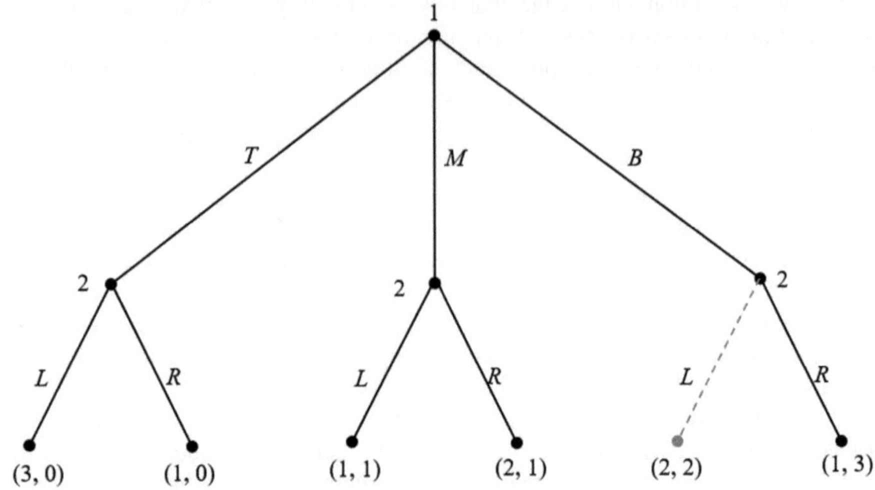

Fig. 2.26 Game tree with six subgame perfect equilibria

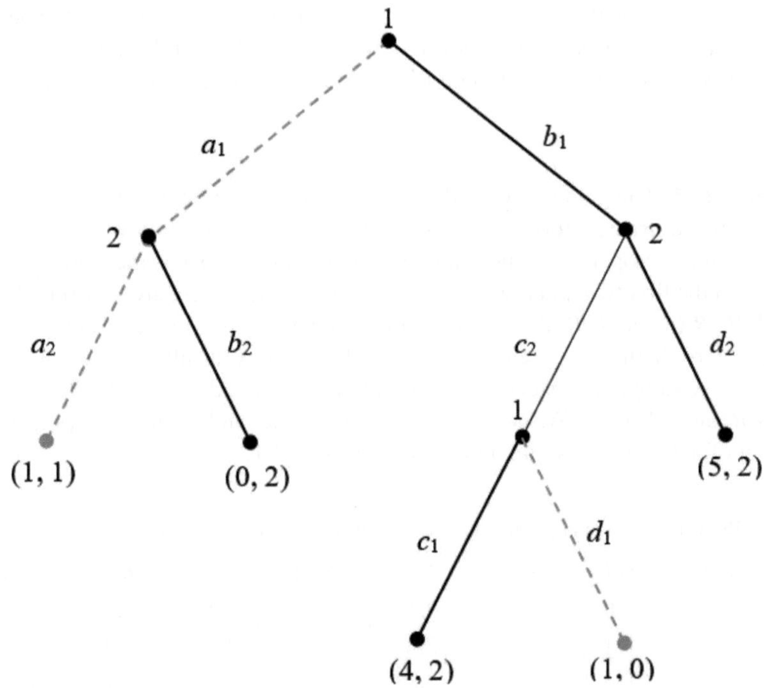

Fig. 2.27 Game tree with two subgame perfect equilibria

This is confirmed by the analysis of the associated strategic form given in Table 2.46. It reveals six equilibria. After elimination of those that involves non-optimal actions, we are left with two subgame perfect equilibria to which are associated with the outcomes (4, 2) and (5, 2). Both involve the weakly dominant strategy b_1c_1 and exclude the actions a_1, d_1 and a_2. The strategy b_2d_2 being weakly dominant, we may only retain the equilibrium (b_1c_1, b_2d_2).

Table 2.46 Game with two subgame perfect equilibria: the strategic form

	a_2c_2	a_2d_2	b_2c_2	b_2d_2
a_1c_1	1, 1	1, 1	0, $\underline{2}$	0, $\underline{2}$
a_1d_1	1, 1	1, 1	0, $\underline{2}$	0, $\underline{2}$
b_1c_1	$\underline{4}$, $\underline{2}$	$\underline{5}$, $\underline{2}$	$\underline{4}$, $\underline{2}$	$\underline{5}$, $\underline{2}$
b_1d_1	1, 0	$\underline{5}$, $\underline{2}$	1, 0	$\underline{5}$, $\underline{2}$

Example 2.10 (continued) In the centipede game, there is a unique subgame perfect equilibrium and it coincides with the solution obtained by backward induction: players stop at each node, resulting in the payoffs (20, 0). Experiments show that this is exceptionally observed. Cooperation is indeed often observed, although cooperation till the end of the game rarely occurs.[32]

Ultimatum Game

Example 2.27 The *ultimatum game* concerns the division of a sum of money, say 20$, between two persons, the first one making a proposal that the second one may accept or reject. If the proposal is accepted, the sum is divided accordingly. If it is rejected, the sum is lost for both. Consider first the case where the sum is infinitely divisible. We denote by $x \in [0, 20]$ the amount that the first player proposes to the second. The resulting extensive form game is given in Fig. 2.28. It includes an infinity of nodes to which player 2 is associated.

In all the subgames that follow a positive offer, the rational choice of player 2 is clear: he will accept the proposal, whatever is the amount being proposed. In the subgame that follows a zero proposal, he is indifferent between accepting or rejecting. Hence, player 2 accepts all offers, including zero, or he only accepts positive offers. In the first case, the choice of the first payer is clear: he keeps the whole sum for himself. In the second case, *no offer is optimal*: for any amount, however small, it is always more advantageous to offer less. As a consequence, there is only one subgame perfect equilibrium: player 2 accepts all offer, including zero, and player 1 keeps the 20$. This conclusion is directly linked to that fact that x is a *real number*. If instead, we consider a *finite division*, there is a second subgame perfect equilibrium at which player 2 accepts only positive offers and player 1 offers the *smallest positive* amount.

[32] See McKelvey and Palfrey (1992), and Nagel and Tang (1998).

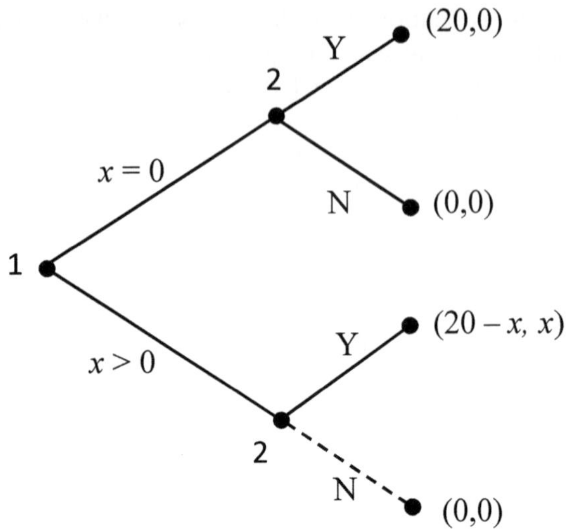

Fig. 2.28 Ultimatum game

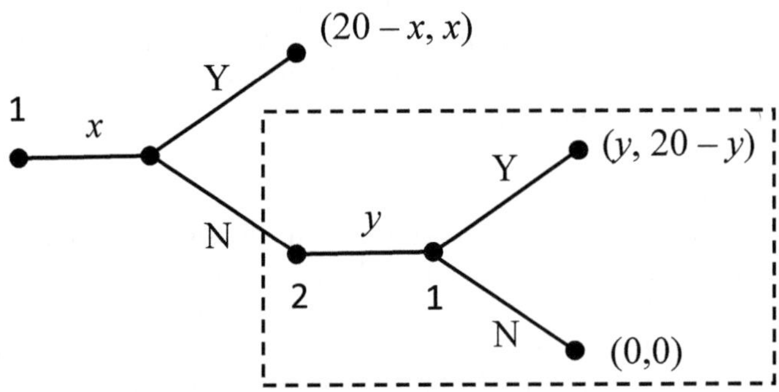

Fig. 2.29 Ultimatum game with a counteroffer

What happens if player 2 can make a counteroffer?

The corresponding extensive form is then given in Fig. 2.29. There is a new subgame that is a standard ultimatum game where the roles have been reversed. There is now an infinity of subgame perfect equilibria and they all end up with the same result, namely (0, 20). Indeed, either $0 \leq x < 20$ and the equilibrium is given by the sequence of actions $(x, N, 0, Y)$. Or else, $x = 20$ and the equilibrium is given by the sequence $(20, Y)$. The first player has no power and it is the second player that takes the lead.

What happens if we consider the time it takes to reach a division?

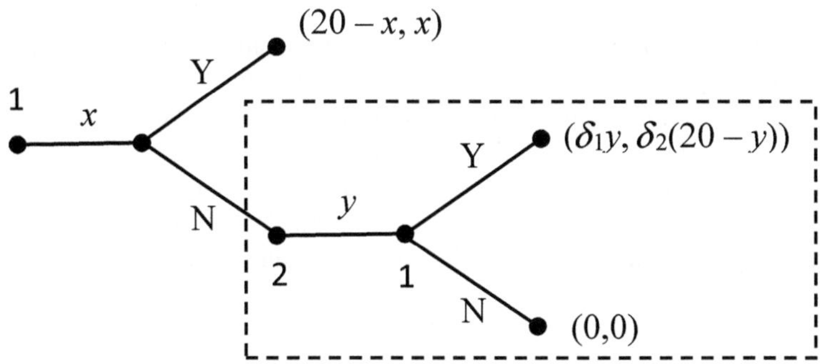

Fig. 2.30 Ultimatum game with impatience

The idea is to introduce a discount factor to represent the impatience of the players. Figure 2.30 illustrates the corresponding game where δ_i $(0 < \delta_i \leq 1)$ is the discount factor of player *i*. The smaller is δ_i, the more impatient is player *i*. We then end up with a unique subgame perfect equilibrium with $((1 - \delta_2)20,\ \delta_2 20))$ as an outcome: player 1 offers δ_2, player 2 only accepts the offers greater or equal to δ_2 and player 1 accepts all offers. We observe that only the discount factor of the last player affects the final result, confirming that impatience may be costly…

The ultimatum game was introduced by Güth et al. (1982) in a paper that has been the starting point of a large literature on experimental games. The ultimatum game has been the object of many experiments and variations everywhere in the world with similar results: players in the second position tend to reject offers that are significantly inferior to the half and players in the first position tend to offer an amount close to the half. The majority of the proposals are indeed propositions between 40 and 50% while the majority of the rejections are observed below 20%.

These experimental results contradict the assumption of rationality according to which players are exclusively guided by the maximization of the amount of money. One must account for players' sense of equity, as discussed for instance by Selten (1978) using a variety of examples. Furthermore, beyond the fact that players have a limited foresight, psychology and neuroscience may help us to understand these observations.[33] In particular, emotions play an important role in the decision processes of individuals in interaction, as shown convincingly by Camerer (2003), a text mostly based on results from experimental research.[34] The rejection of a small offer could indeed be explained by the anger triggered by the insult felt, a reaction that the first player can anticipate. These explanations have, however, their limits as shown by the experimental results obtained in the dictator game.

[33] See the review by Battigalli and Dufwenberg (2022)

[34] See also Winter (2014) and Eric Van Damme et al. (2014).

Dictator Game

Example 2.28 The *dictator game* is an ultimatum game where the second player is *passive*: the proposed division is implemented whether he accepts or not the offer. It is not properly speaking a game. The only rational decision of the first player is to keep the whole amount for himself. However, what is actually observed differs drastically: players in the first position generally propose a positive amount, generally below the average amount observed in the ultimatum game. More precisely, we observe a positive proposal in about 60% of the cases with an average of about 20% of the amount at stake.

There may be several reasons for such a behavior. It could reveal a preference for some form of equality linked to an idea of fairness. More simply, it could be linked to a sense of empathy whereby the utility of a person also depends on the utility of the other.

Trust Game

Example 2.29 Beyond the ultimatum game and dictator game, another game has been the object of many experiments, the *trust game*. A person is endowed with an amount of money, say 20$, with the possibility of transferring part (or all) of this amount to another person, in which case the amount transferred is tripled. That person has then the possibility to send back part of the resulting amount. The game is played in total anonymity as in the ultimatum game. It is described in Fig. 2.31 where the second stage is a dictator game. There is a unique subgame perfect equilibrium: the first player transfers zero while the second returns zero. Again, this is not what is actually observed in experiments. Most players in the first position do transfer part of their endowment while most of the players in the second position do refund part of the returns. More precisely, about 10% of the players in the first position decide not to invest while less than 20% of the players in the second position who have benefited from a transfer decide not to refund anything. Moreover, and perhaps surprisingly, the amount refunded exceeds on average the amount received.

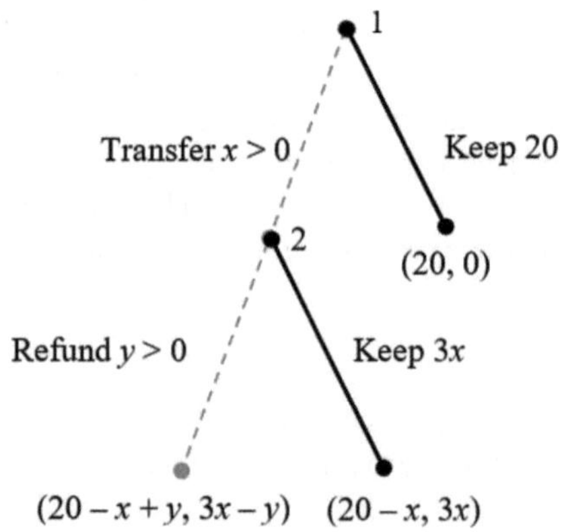

Fig. 2.31 Trust game

2.8 Concluding Remarks

The concept of Nash equilibrium is central in the theory of non-cooperative games.[35] From a normative point of view, if you want to advise players how to play a game, you should suggest equilibrium strategies. Recommending non-equilibrium strategies would indeed be self-defeating: at least one player could gain by deviating, assuming that the other will follow the recommendation. As a result, no player will follow the recommendation. The picture is clear if there is a unique equilibrium or if one of the two players has a dominant strategy (possibly obtained through a sequence of eliminations). But we have seen many examples where there are several equilibria. How to differentiate them and which one to recommend if we cannot rely on the existence of an equilibrium that strictly dominates the others in terms of Pareto or in terms of risk.

The literature on equilibrium refinement tries to narrow down the set of Nash equilibria by exploring their rational choice foundations given the players' beliefs on their opponent's strategies.[36] Within an extensive form game, an analysis of the sequences of actions that underlie the various equilibria may help to eliminate some equilibria. xSubgame perfectness is such an approach. Equilibrium selection aims at retaining a single equilibrium. It is akin to the search for the Holy Grail. The book of Harsanyi and Selten (1988) is such an attempt based on comparing equilibria in various terms, including Pareto-dominance and risk-dominance.

Equilibrium refinement and equilibrium selection are conceptually and technically difficult, and go beyond the framework of the present introductory text. This applies as well to two important topics that have been left aside, *incomplete information* and *repeated games*. Readers willing to investigate these topics are invited to refer to the textbooks listed at the end of the book.

In this chapter, we have limited our analysis to non-cooperative situations involving two players. It can easily be extended to three players or more, except if we take into account the possibility that coalitions form. In the 2-player situation, we have defined the notion of strong equilibrium: the players cannot gain by jointly deviating. This definition can be extended to a n-player situation, $n \geq 3$: an equilibrium is strong if no *coalition* of players can gain by jointly deviating.

References

Allais, M. (1953). Le comportement de l'homme rationnel devant le risque: Critique des postulats and axioms de l'école américaine. *Econometrica, 21*, 503–546.

[35] Myerson (1999) explains how Nash's contribution "*was a turning point in the history of economic thought*".

[36] See Selten (1975), Kohlberg and Mertens (1986), Mertens (1989, 1991), van Damme (1991) and the synthesis by Govindan and Wilson (2008).

Aumann, R. J. (1959). Acceptable points in general cooperative n-person games. In A. W. Tucker & R. Luce (eds.), *Contribution to the theory of games*, vol. IV, Annals of mathematics studies, vol. 40, pp. 287–324.
Aumann, R. J. (1974). Subjectivity and correlation in randomized strategies. *Journal of Mathematical Economics, 1*, 67–96.
Axelrod, R. (1984). *The evolution of cooperation.* Basic Books.
Battigalli, P., & Dufwenberg, M. (2022). Belief-dependent motivations and psychological game theory. *Journal of Economic Literature, 60*, 833–882.
Bernheim, B. D. (1984). Rationalizable strategic behavior. *Econometrica, 52*, 1007–1028.
Bernoulli, D. (1738). Specimen theoriae novae de mensura sortis. *Commentarii Academiae Scientiarum Imperialis Petropolitanae, 5*, 175–192. English translation by J. W. Friedman (1954) in *Econometrica, 22*, 22–36.
Bertrand, J. (1883), Revue des ouvrages *Théorie mathématique de la richesse sociale* d'Augustin Cournot and *Recherches sur les principles mathématiques de la théorie des richesses* de Léon Walras, *Journal des Savants, 67*, 499–508. English translation by J. W. Friedman (1988) in *Cournot oligopoly*, A. F. Daughety (ed.). Cambridge University Press, Cambridge.
Brams, S. J. (1975). *Game theory and politics.* The Free Press (republished in 2003 by Dover).
Brams, S. J. (1980). *Biblical games.* The MIT Press.
Brams, S.J. (1985a). *Rational politics.* Decision, games and strategy, Congressional Quarterly, Washington.
Brams, S.J. (1985b). *Superpower games.* Yale University Press, New Haven.
Brams, S. J. (2003). *Negotiation games. Applying game theory to bargaining and arbitration,* Revised edition, Routledge.
Camerer, C. F. (2003). *Behavioral game theory: Experiments in strategic interaction.* Princeton University Press.
Cournot, A. (1838). *Recherches sur les principes mathématiques de la théorie des richesses,* Hachette, Paris. English translation by N. T. Bacon (1927). *Researches into the mathematical principles of the theory of wealth,* MacMillan, New York.
Debreu, G., et al. (1954). Representation of a preference ordering by a numerical function. In M. Thrall (Ed.), *Decision processes* (pp. 159–165). Wiley.
Dufwenberg, M., & Stegeman, M. (2002). Existence and uniqueness of maximal reductions under iterated strict dominance. *Econometrica, 70*, 2007–2023.
Govindan, S., & Wilson, R. (2008). Refinements of Nash equilibrium. In S. N. Durlauf & L. E. Blume (eds.), *The new Palgrave dictionary of economics* (2nd edn.). MacMillan.
Güth, W., Schmittberger, R., & Schwarze, B. (1982). An experimental analysis of ultimatum bargaining. *Journal of Economic Behavior and Organization, 3*, 367–388.
Harsanyi, J., & Selten, R. (1988). *A general theory of equilibrium selection in games.* The MIT Press.
Haywood, O. G. (1954). Military decisions and game theory. *Journal of the Operations Research Society, 2*, 365–385.
Huygens, C. (1657). De ratiociniis in ludo aleae, *Exercitationum Mathematicarum*, Liber V.
Keynes, J. M. (1936). *General theory of employment Interest and money.* The Macmillan Press.
Kolhberg, E., & Mertens, J.-F. (1986). On the strategic stability of equilibria. *Econometrica, 54*, 1003–1037.
Kuhn, H. W. (1950). Extensive games. *Proceedings of the National Academy of Sciences, 36*, 570–576.
Kuhn, H. W. (1953). Extensive games and the problem of information. In H. W. Kuhn & A. W. Tucker (eds.) (pp. 245–266).
Mc Kelvey, R., & Palfrey, T. (1992). An experimental study of the centipede game. *Econometrica, 69*, 803–836.
Mertens, J.-F. (1989). Stable equilibria, a reformulation. Part I. Definition and basic properties. *Mathematics of Operations Research, 14*, 575–625.
Mertens, J.-F. (1991). Stable equilibria, a reformulation. Part II. Discussion of the definition and further results. *Mathematics of Operations Research, 16*, 694–753.

Monderer, D., & Tennenholtz, M. (2009). Strong mediated equilibrium. *Artificial Intelligence, 173*, 180–195.
Moulin, H. (1986). *Game theory for the social sciences* (2nd ed.). NYU Press.
Moulin, H., & Vial, J. Ph. (1978). Strategically equivalent games: the class of games whose completely mixed equilibria cannot be improved upon. *International Journal of Game Theory, 7*, 201–221.
Myerson, R. B. (1999). Nash equilibrium and the history of economic theory. *Journal of Economic Literature, 37*, 1067–1082.
Nagel, R., & Tang, F. F. (1998). Experimental results on the centipede game in normal form: An investigation on learning. *Journal of Mathematical Psychology, 42*, 356–384.
Nash, J. F. (1950). Equilibrium points in *N*-person games. *Proceedings of the National Academy of Sciences of USA, 36*, 48–49.
Nash, J. F. (1951). Non-cooperative games. *Annals of Mathematics, 54*, 286–295.
Osborne, M. (2004). *An introduction to game theory*. Oxford University Press.
Osborne, M., & Rubinstein, A. (1994). *A course in game theory*. The MIT Press.
Palacios-Huerta, I. (2003). Professionals play minimax. *Review of Economic Studies, 70*, 395–415.
Pearce, D. G. (1984). Rationalizable strategic behavior and the problem of perfection. *Econometrica, 52*, 1029–1050.
Rosenthal, R. (1981). Games of perfect information, predatory pricing and the chain-store paradox. *Journal of Economic Theory, 25*, 92–100.
Schelling, T. (1960). *The strategy of conflict*. Harvard University Press.
Selten, R. (1965). Spieltheoretische Behandlung eines Oligopolmodells mit Nachfrage-trägheit. *Zeitschrift für die gesamte Staatswissenschaft / Journal of Institutional and Theoretical Economics, 121*, 301–324 and 667–689.
Selten, R. (1975). A reexamination of the perfectness concept for equilibrium points in extensive games. *International Journal of Game Theory, 4*, 25–55.
Selten, R. (1978). The Equity Principle in Economic Behavior. In Gottinger H.W. and W. Leinfellner (eds.), *Decision Theory Social Ethics*, Issues in Social Choice, D. Reidel Publishing Company, Dordrecht, 289–301.
Taylor, A. D., & Pacelli, A. M. (2008). *Mathematics and politics. Strategy, voting, power and proof*. Springer.
van Damme, E. (1991). Refinements of Nash equilibrium, CentER discussion paper 1991–7, University of Tilburg, The Netherlands
van Damme, E., et al. (2014). How Werner Güth's Ultimatum game shaped our understanding of social behavior. *Journal of Economic Behavior and Organization, 108*, 292–313.
Varian, H. R. (1992). *Microeconomic analysis* (3rd ed.). Norton.
Vickrey, W. (1961). Counterspeculation, auctions, and competitive sealed tenders. *Journal of Finance, 16*, 8–37.
von Neumann, J. (1928). Zur Theorie der Gesellschaftspiel, *Mathematische Annalen, 100*, 295–320. English translation in Tucker, A. W. & Luce, R. D. (eds.) (1959). Contributions to the theory of games IV. *Annals of mathematical studies* (pp. 13–42). Princeton University Press.
von Neumann, J., & Morgenstern, O. (1944). *Theory of games and economic behavior*. Princeton University Press (latest edition dated 1953).
von Stackelberg, H. (1934), *Marktform und Gleichgewicht*, (translated into Englisg in 2011 under the title *Market structure and equilibrium*, Springer).
Winter, E. (2014). *Feeling smart*. Public Affairs.

Bargaining and Consensus

3

The preceding chapter was concerned with non-cooperative situations although cooperation was not excluded. Introducing a mediator or correlated strategies were steps towards cooperation. However, binding agreements were excluded. Behind the intervention of a mediator or the use of correlated strategies, there was no formal contract that the players agreed upon and signed: players could avoid relying on the mediator or deviate from the suggestion that they receive from a random mechanism.

In the present chapter instead, binding agreements between players will be allowed: the search for a consensus is the object of the present chapter.

In general, a bargaining problem faced by two players is defined by a set of outcomes among which one is identified as the *disagreement outcome*, also called *status quo*. While their preferences are conflicting, they know that an agreement is desirable as long as there are outcomes better than the status quo—better in the sense of Pareto. As a consequence, they have an interest in bargaining. Either the bargaining leads to a consensus on a particular outcome, or it fails and they fall back to the disagreement outcome. The status quo plays the role of a threat. If they eventually reach a consensus, it necessarily results from a *compromise*: each player could get more at the expense of the other.

Here, we will not describe an actual bargaining process nor attempt to predict the result of a bargaining. We will instead adopt a normative point of view. The idea is to propose a *rule* that results from the combination of a number of desirable properties (axioms) that can be applied to any bargaining problem to produce a solution. In this way, the solution to a bargaining problem is directly associated with the relevance of the axioms underlying the rule. This is the approach initiated by Nash (1950).

P. Dehez, *Game Theory for the Social Sciences*, Springer Series in Game Theory,
https://doi.org/10.1007/978-3-031-58241-7_3

3.1 Two-person Bargaining Problems

Bargaining problems derived from non-cooperative games
Free disposal
Transferable utility
In case of a disagreement
Beyond non-cooperative games
Definition of a bargaining problem.

We will first start from a non-cooperative game, before giving a general bargaining problem.

Bargaining Problems Derived from a Non-cooperative Game
Starting from a game in strategic form with two players and finite strategy spaces, we construct the set of attainable outcomes expressed *in expected utility terms.* They are the outcomes that result from the implementation of correlated strategies which are lotteries on the outcomes associated to the combinations of pure strategies. Geometrically, it coincides with the convex hull of the outcomes associated to the pure strategies, as illustrated in Fig. 2.17 for the battle of the sexes. Similarly, Fig. 3.1 illustrates the set associated to an arbitrary game.

Each point in the set corresponds to the implementation of a *contract* between the players that specifies a particular lottery on the combinations of strategies. This is the *bargaining space*. Here, the maximal utility for player 1 is equal to 4 and it is equal to 3 for player 2. However, the utility pair (4, 3), called the *utopia point*, is not feasible. Players should find an agreement somewhere on the upper boundary. It would indeed be absurd to pick up a point in the interior.

The simplified version of the battle of the sexes offers another example. The bargaining space is the triangle represented in Fig. 2.17, with vertices (2, 1), (1, 2) and (0, 0). We have seen that the natural solution is to throw a dice. In terms of expected utility, it leads to the utility pair. This solution is *ex-ante* fair for it offers

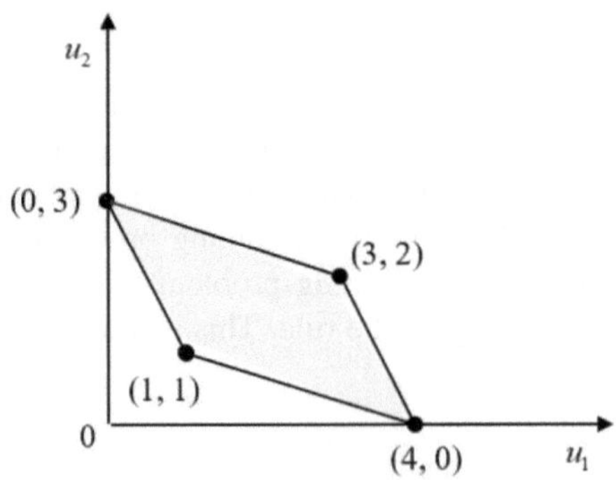

	a_2	b_2
a_1	4 0	1 1
b_1	3 2	0 3

Fig. 3.1 A game in the expected utility space

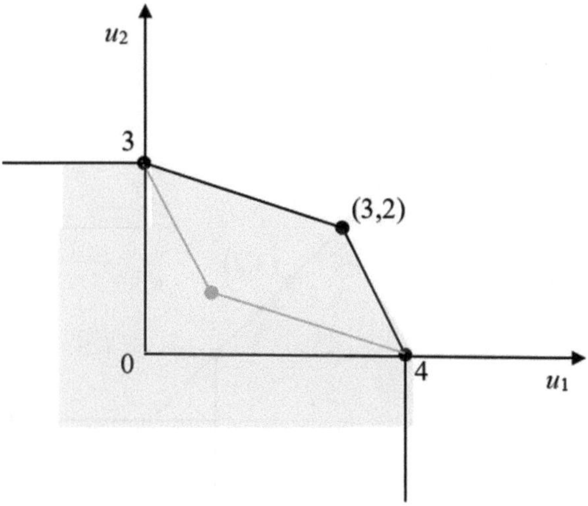

Fig. 3.2 Introducing free disposal

the same expected utility to both players. It is located in the middle of the segment joining the points (2, 1) and (1, 2).

Two assumptions allow for an enlargement of the bargaining space, free disposal and transferable utility. The first one is innocuous. The second one will actually *not* be made in the present chapter.

Free Disposal of Utility

Free disposal simply means that players always have the option to forego a payoff, as illustrated in Fig. 3.2. This should not affect the solution of a bargaining simply because no player has an interest to do so. Hence, there is no loss of generality in assuming free disposal, as illustrated in Fig. 3.2 that expands the feasible set shown in Fig. 3.1.

Assuming free disposal means that the bargaining space is a *comprehensive* set:

$$x \in A \text{ and } x' \leq x \Rightarrow x' \in A$$

i.e., all points "below" the feasible points are included in the set.

Transferable Utility

Unlike free disposal, the assumption of transferable utility is restrictive because it assumes that utilities are expressed in terms of a common and infinitely divisible good, a "money". Referring to Fig. 3.2, it means that the points located on the line segment joining the points (5, 0) and (0, 5) are attainable, as illustrated in Fig. 3.3. For instance, the outcome (2, 3) is feasible via a contract stipulating that the strategies b_1 and a_2 will be implemented, with a transfer of 1 monetary unit from player 1 to player 2.

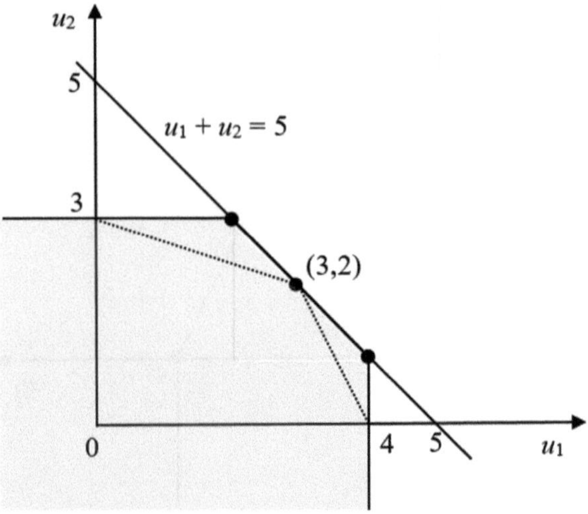

Fig. 3.3 Assuming transferable utility

This assumption makes sense only if the players are *risk neutral* and payoffs are expressed in terms of some commodity money. When utility is assumed to be transferable, we are no longer in a cardinal utility framework. We will come back to this point when discussing the *utilitarian solution*. If not otherwise mentioned, utility will not be assumed transferable. Transferable utility is the object of Chap. 4 where cooperation among any number of players will be considered.

In case of a Disagreement

To complete the description of a bargaining problem, it is necessary to specify what happens in case of a disagreement. We assume that there is an outcome in the bargaining space, called the disagreement point. It may be the initial outcome—the status quo—or the outcome corresponding to the security levels of each player, the *maximin* utility levels. In the case of the above example, we observe that (a_1, b_2) is the unique Nash equilibrium (in pure strategies). Moreover, it implies a dominant strategy for the first player and turns out to result from a prudent behavior. The utility 1 is indeed the security level of both players. Hence $(1, 1)$ is the natural disagreement point. Notice that it is also the outcome associated to the equilibrium.

Once the disagreement point is identified, all outcomes corresponding to lower utility levels can be ignored: we only have to retain the points located North-East of the disagreement point.

Beyond Non-cooperative Games

Bargaining problems need not be associated to non-cooperative games. The following example is the simplest bargaining problem we could think of. It concerns the division of an amount of money, say 100 dollars.

Example 3.1 Divide 100 Dollars Hundred dollars is offered to two players provided they agree on its division. In the non-cooperative version, the players express *simultaneously* a demand. If the sum of the requests does not exceed 100 dollars, they get what they asked for. If not, they get nothing. There is a multiplicity of equilibria among which we may retain the point (50, 50) that appears as the point focal.

The cooperative version is described by the bargaining problem where (0, 0) is the disagreement point. In case there is agreement, the result is of the form $u = (x, 100 - x)$ with $x \in [0, 100]$.

It is illustrated by Fig. 3.4, under the assumption of free disposal while retaining only the points that have nonnegative coordinates. Starting from an arbitrary division $(x, 100-x)$ on the boundary, we observe that any increase in favor of one player is in the disadvantage of the other. Which division to choose?

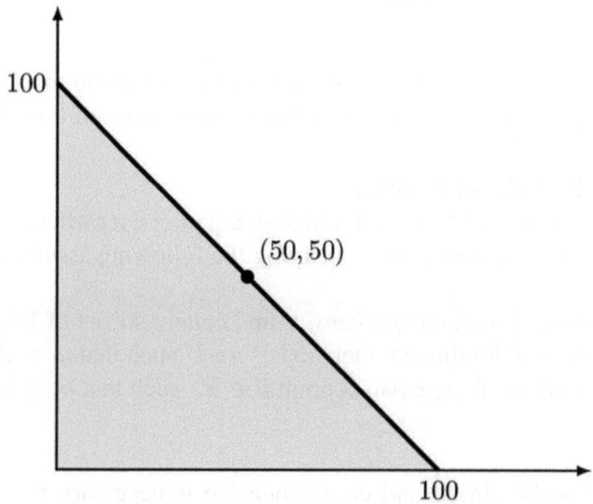

Fig. 3.4 Divide 100 dollars

As nothing differentiates the players, only the equal division (50, 50) is justified. However, the implicit assumption is that the players are both risk neutral and that utility is transferable.

What happens if one player is risk-averse? We then leave the transferable utility framework and the concavity of the utility function leads to a different representation.

Assume for instance that player 1 is risk-neural while player 2 is risk-averse, their preferences being represented by the utility functions $u_1(x) = x$ and $u_2(x) = 10\sqrt{x}$. The points along the boundary are given by $(u_1(x),\ u_2(100 - x))$ where x varies in the interval [0, 100]. Figure 3.5 illustrates the resulting modification. For $u_1 = 50$, we have $u_2 = 10\sqrt{50} \simeq 70$. The solution is no longer immediate and we

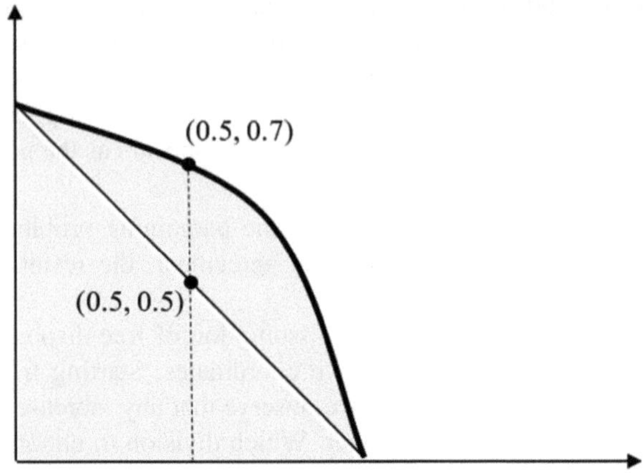

Fig. 3.5 Divide 100 dollars with risk aversion

will see that risk aversion is a handicap that is reflected in the solution. Notice that the bargaining space is convex, as a result of the concavity of the utility functions.

Definition of a Bargaining Problem
Formally, a *bargaining problem* is defined by a pair (U, d) where U is a subset of $\mathbb{R}^2$ and d is the disagreement point, satisfying the following assumptions:

- U is a *nonempty*, *closed*, *comprehensive* and *convex* subset of $\mathbb{R}^2$,
- $d \in U$ and is Pareto-dominated: there exists $u \in U$ such that $u_i > d_i$ $(i = 1, 2)$,
- U is *bounded above*: there exists a point $\overline{u} \in \mathbb{R}^2$ such that $u_i \leq \overline{u}_i$ $(i = 1, 2)$ for all $u \in U$.

Requiring U to be closed and comprehensive is necessary but not restrictive: U contains its boundary points and utility is freely disposable: $u \in U$ and $u' \leq u$ imply $u' \in U$. In case of a noncooperative underlying game, convexity reflects the fact that U is derived from the implementation of correlated strategies or that the set of alternatives is a continuum and players are not risk lovers. The disagreement point must naturally be a feasible utility pair and players should have an incentive to bargain while potential gains are bounded.

Figure 3.6 describes an arbitrary bargaining problem where the point $b = (b_1, b_2)$ is the *utopia point* defined by the maximum utility levels for each player. The point b does not belong to U. If it was the case, the bargaining question would just not exist: the two players would agree on choosing b as a solution.

The three examples that follow are bargaining problems that are not derived from non-cooperative games.

Example 3.2 Bankruptcy Problem A company goes bankrupt. Its market value L falls short of the sum of its debts. Let's assume that there are two creditors. We

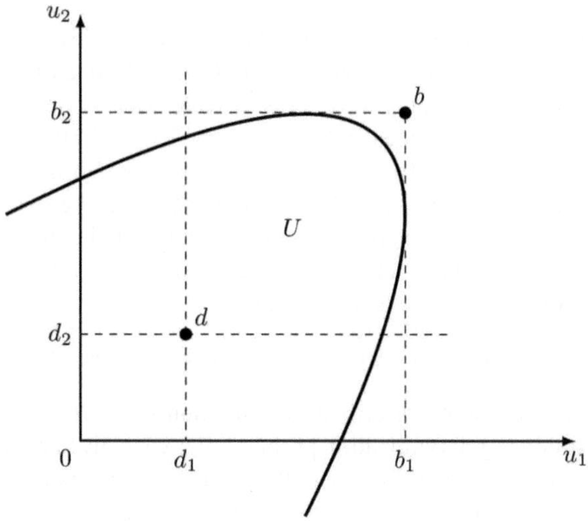

Fig. 3.6 A bargaining problem

denote by b_1 and b_2 their claims. They are such that $b_1 + b_2 > L$. We assume that the creditors are *risk-neutral*. The problem is then illustrated by Fig. 3.7 where u_i denotes the amount received by creditor i. The point b is the utopia point.

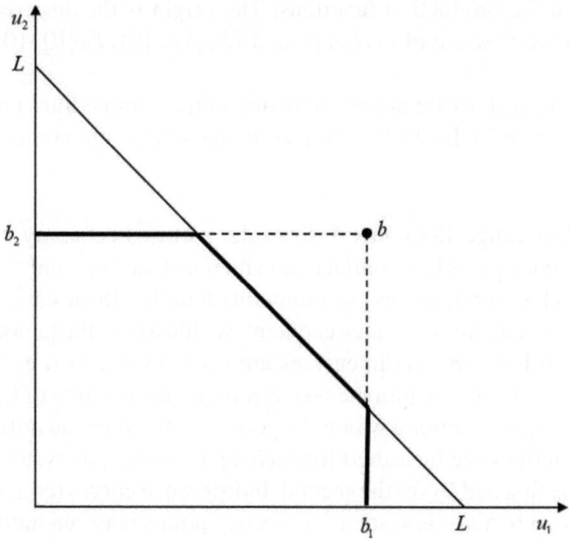

Fig. 3.7 Bankruptcy problem

Example 3.3 International Trade * Two countries ($i = 1, 2$) have a technology that uses two factors of production (inputs). These technologies are described by the production functions $z_i = F_i(x_i, y_i)$ where x_i and y_i are the quantities of inputs used to produce the quantity z_i of output. Returns to scale are assumed to be decreasing: the production functions are concave. Each country detains 10 units of the input that bears its number: $\omega_1 = (10, 0)$ and $\omega_2 = (0, 10)$. The two inputs are necessary to produce: $F_i(0, y_i) = F_i(x_i, 0) = 0$. As a consequence, the two countries must exchange. We assume that both countries are only interested in the commodity they produce. Hence, their utility functions can then be written as $u_i(z_1, z_2) = z_i$ and the corresponding bargaining space is then given by:

$$U = \left\{z \in \mathbb{R}^2 | z_1 \leq F_1(x_1, y_1),\ z_2 \leq F_2(x_2, y_2),\ x_1 + x_2 = 10,\ y_1 + y_2 = 10\right\}.$$

The boundary of U can be described by a function $z_2 = G(z_1)$ obtained from the solution of the following maximization problem. For each given z_1, we associate the input combination (x_1, y_1) that maximizes the production of the second country while keeping the production in the first equal to z_1: $G(z_1) = Max_{(x_1,y_1)} F_2(10-x_1, 10-y_1)$ subject to

$$\begin{aligned} &0 \leq x_1 \leq 10, \\ &0 \leq y_1 \leq 10, \\ &F_1(x_1, y_1) = z_1. \end{aligned}$$

In this way, we generate a curve made of the points $(z_1, G(z_1))$ obtained by varying z_1 in the interval $[0, F_1(10, 10)]$. The convexity of the bargaining space results from the concavity of the production functions. The origin is the disagreement point. It corresponds to the absence of exchange and $(F_1(10, 10), F_2(10, 10))$ is the utopia point.

Notice that the utilities are expressed in unit of the commodities produced. Utility is, however, not transferable because the exchange of the commodities produced has been excluded.

Example 3.4 Exchange Economy * Consider a closed economy without production. The economic agents have initial endowments of various commodities that they may trade. They have preferences on commodity bundles. In the case of two agents, it is possible to represent this exchange economy within a box, the famous Edgeworth's box illustrated in Fig. 3.8. Its dimensions are given by the total endowment of the two commodities. A point within the box specifies a distribution of the commodities between the two agents, among which the point ω defined by the initial endowments ω_1 and ω_2. Quantities are measured for each agent in the axis system defined by its origin, 0_1 for the first and 0_2 for the second. Indifference curves (equivalence classes) of an agent belong to his axis system.[1] Tangency points between indifference curves

[1] Usual assumptions are made on preferences (monotonicity, convexity, ...). They can be found in any manual of microeconomics, for instance Varian (1992).

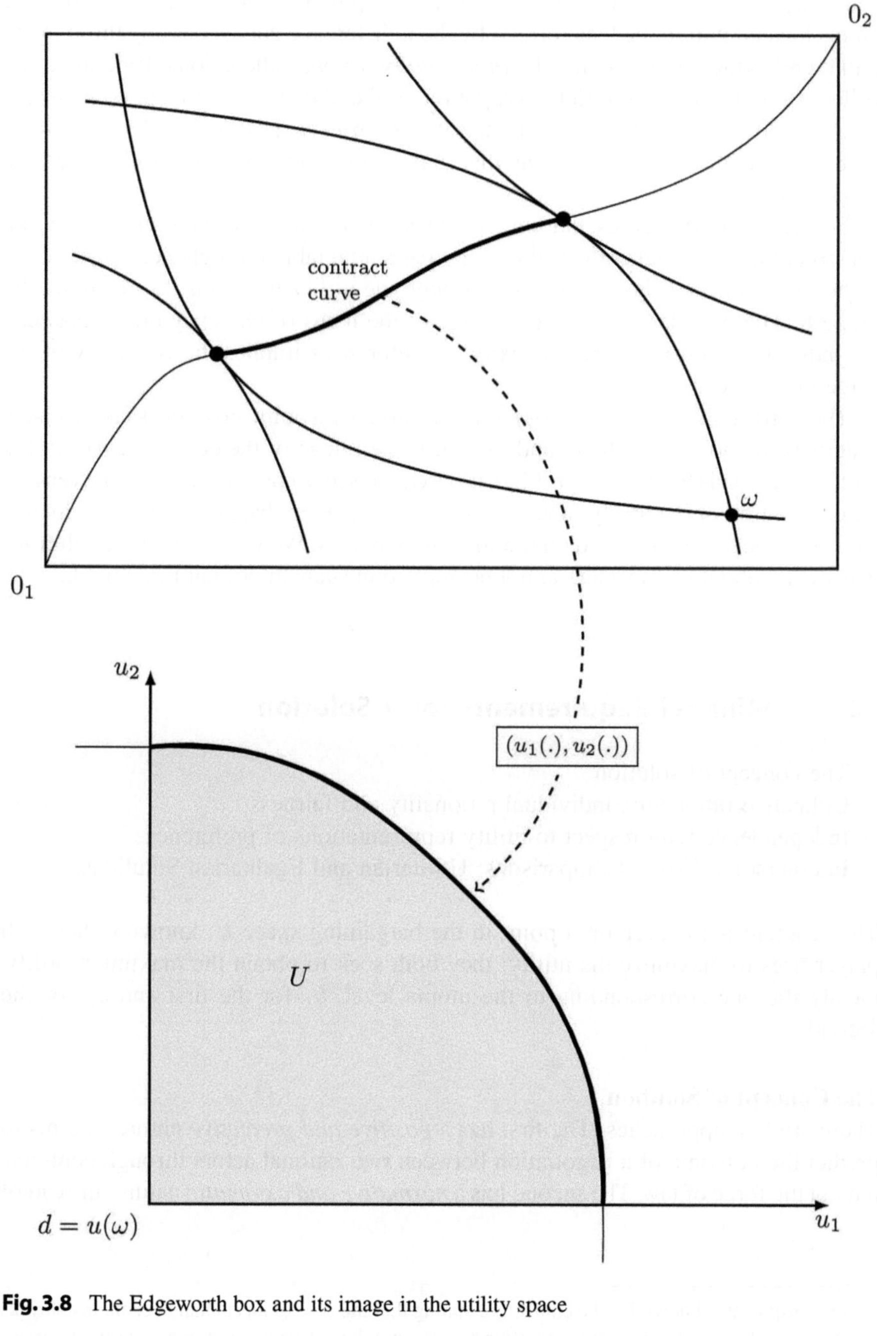

Fig. 3.8 The Edgeworth box and its image in the utility space

define the allocations (redistributions) that are optimal in the sense of Pareto. The points located within the lens formed by the indifference curves passing through the initial endowment point define the *individually rational* allocations. By combining collective and individual rationality, we retain the allocations corresponding to the tangency point within the lens. It defines the *contract curve* imagined by Edgeworth (1881) that collects the allocations that may result from a bargaining between the two agents.[2]

For given utility representation u_1 and u_2 of the agents' preferences, we can construct the set U that collects the utility pairs attainable through exchange, i.e., U is the *image* of the Edgeworth's box through the utility functions, as illustrated by Fig. 3.8. The boundary of U is the image of the locus of tangency points between the indifference curves. The convexity of preferences implies the convexity of the bargaining space.[3]

The utility pair $(u_1(\omega_1), u_2(\omega_2))$ is the disagreement point: no trade is taking place. It defines the portion of the boundary that is the image of the contract curve in the utility space. This bargaining problem is based on *ordinal* preferences: *any* increasing transformation of the utility functions leads to a different bargaining space which is equivalent because it is based on the *same preferences*. We will see that the solutions that we are about to consider cannot be applied in such an ordinal framework.

3.2 Minimal Requirements for a Solution

The concept of solution
Collective rationality, individual rationality and fairness
Independence with respect to utility representations of preferences
Interpersonal Utility Comparisons: Utilitarian and Egalitarian Solutions.

The problem is to agree on a point in the bargaining space U, knowing that each player tries to maximize his utility: they both seek to obtain the maximum utility, ideally the one corresponding to the utopia level, b_1 for the first and b_2 for the second.

The Concept of Solution

There are two approaches. The first has a *positive and predictive* nature. It aims to predict the outcome of a negotiation between two rational actors through contracts having the force of law. The second has a *normative and axiomatic* nature: instead of

[2] Edgeworth is also known for the conjecture stating that the core of an exchange economy shrinks and tends to the set of competitive equilibria as the number of agents in the economy increases. That conjecture has been proven by Debreu and Scarf (1963). For more details, see Hildenbrand and Kirman (1988).

[3] Preferences are convex if the indifference curves are convex: $x \sim y \Rightarrow \lambda x + (1-\lambda)y \succcurlyeq x$.

trying to determine a solution to a particular bargaining problem, it aims at building a *rule* that can be applied to any bargaining problem, a rule that is fair in the sense that it leads to a solution that a neutral and benevolent arbitrator could suggest. It is that second approach that will be followed here. It consists in outlining a number of desirable properties that a rule should satisfy and to show that *only one rule* satisfies these properties together. The relevance of the induced rule can then be judged by the properties that underlie it, avoiding to judge the relevance of particular solutions. It is the axiomatic approach that was initiated by Nash (1950) and extended to cooperative games with transferable utility by Shapley (1951). This extension is the object of Chap. 4.

Formally, we look for a function φ that associates to each bargaining problem (U, d) point $\varphi(U, d) = (\varphi_1(U, d), \varphi_2(U, d)) \in U$: the rule φ specifies a utility level for each player and defines a *feasible* utility pair.

Efficiency, Individual Rationality and Fairness

If we want solutions to get a unanimous support, there are three fundamental properties that any rule ought to satisfy. A rule φ will be considered as acceptable only if it satisfies the following three basic axioms: collective rationality, individual rationality, and symmetry.

B1 *Collective rationality*[4]

For any given bargaining problem (U, d), $(u_1, u_2) > \varphi(U, d) \Rightarrow (u_1, u_2) \notin U$.

This is *Pareto optimality* or *efficiency*: there can be no feasible outcome that offers more to one player and not less to the other. Consequently, a solution must be on the boundary of the set U that corresponds to utility levels not exceeding the utopia levels b_1 and b_2.

The second axiom requires incentive compatibility: a player would refuse a contract that gives him less than his disagreement level.

B2 *Individual rationality*

For any given bargaining problem (U, d), $\varphi_i(U, d) \geq d_i$ $(i = 1, 2)$.

This requirement stems from the definition of the disagreement point: only the outcomes located North-East of the disagreement point matter, i.e., only the subset is $U_d = \{u \in U | u \geq d\}$ matters.

For a given feasible utility combination $u = (u_1, u_2)$, we are interested in the players' *gains* that are measures relatively to the disagreement point. They are given by the utility differences $(u_1 - d_1)$ and $(u_2 - d_2)$ respectively. Individual rationality (B2) imposes that, at a solution, the players' gains must be nonnegative.

---

[4] When comparing vectors, we adopt the following conventions: $x \geq y$ means $x_h \geq y_h$ for all h, $x > y$ means $x_h \geq y_h$ for all h with a strict inequality for *at least one h*, and $x \gg y$ means $x_h > y_h$ for *all h*.

A bargaining problem (U, d) is *symmetric* if we can permute the players without modifying the structure of the bargaining space. It means that the 45° line is an axis of symmetry of U:

$$(u_1, u_2) \in U \Leftrightarrow (u_2, u_1) \in U.$$

In particular, $d_1 = d_2$. Dividing 100 dollars and the battle of the sexes are symmetric bargaining problems. No solution should benefit a player if there are no elements that make it possible to distinguish them.

B3 *Symmetry*
For any given symmetric bargaining problem (U, d), $\varphi_1(U, d) = \varphi_2(U, d)$.

This is a fairness property that echoes a fundamental principle of distributive justice, that is, *equal treatment of equals*. The same solution obtains if the identities of the players are exchanged.

It is important to realize that the description of a bargaining problem must be *exhaustive* in the sense that it must include all relevant elements. Hence, if a problem is symmetric, we may conclude that the players are perfectly substitutable, i.e., equal.

If we limit ourselves to symmetric bargaining problems, we observe that collective rationality (B1) and symmetry (B3) determine *one and only one* solution: it is defined by the intersection between the boundary and the 45° line. Individual rationality (B2) is then automatically satisfied.

Independence with Respect to the Utility Representations of Preferences
The players' preferences are the fundamental data of a bargaining problem and solutions should depend exclusively on them. The expected utility assumption allows the representation of preferences by a utility function that is defined up to a linear and increasing transformation. Hence, in this cardinal framework, solutions should not depend on the choice of a particular utility representation. This is the object of the following property that requires that any linear and increasing transformation of the utility function of a player translates into the same transformation of the solution.

B4 *Independence with respect to utility representations of preferences*
For any given bargaining problem (U, d) and real numbers $\alpha_i > 0$ and β_i $(i = 1, 2)$, the solution of the transformed problem (U', d') defined by $u_i' = \alpha_i u_i + \beta_i$ and $d_i' = \alpha_i d_i + \beta_i$ is such that $\varphi_i(U', d') = \alpha_i \varphi_i(U, d) + \beta_i$ $(i = 1, 2)$.

This is a property of *covariance*: the solution of the transformed problem is the transformation of the initial solution. B4 allows an arbitrary bargaining problem to be transformed into a *normalized* bargaining problem whose disagreement point is the origin (0, 0). This indeed corresponds to a simple translation. As a consequence, there would be no loss of generality in considering bargaining problems whose disagreement point is the origin. Considering bargaining problems whose boundary is a line segment, B4 allows symmetrizing and normalizing it.[5] That amounts to move the disagreement point to the origin and to modify the utility scales of each player so as to end up with the triangular bargaining space whose vertices are the points (0, 0), (1, 0) and (0, 1).

All these bargaining problems are therefore equivalent. Figure 3.9 illustrates the successive transformations of an arbitrary bargaining problem. The disagreement point is first moved to the origin by subtracting d_i. The intersections with the axis become $b_i - d_i$ and it then remains to divide by $b_i - d_i$. That amounts to the following transformation:

$$v_i = \frac{u_i - d_i}{b_i - d_i} \quad (i = 1, 2).$$

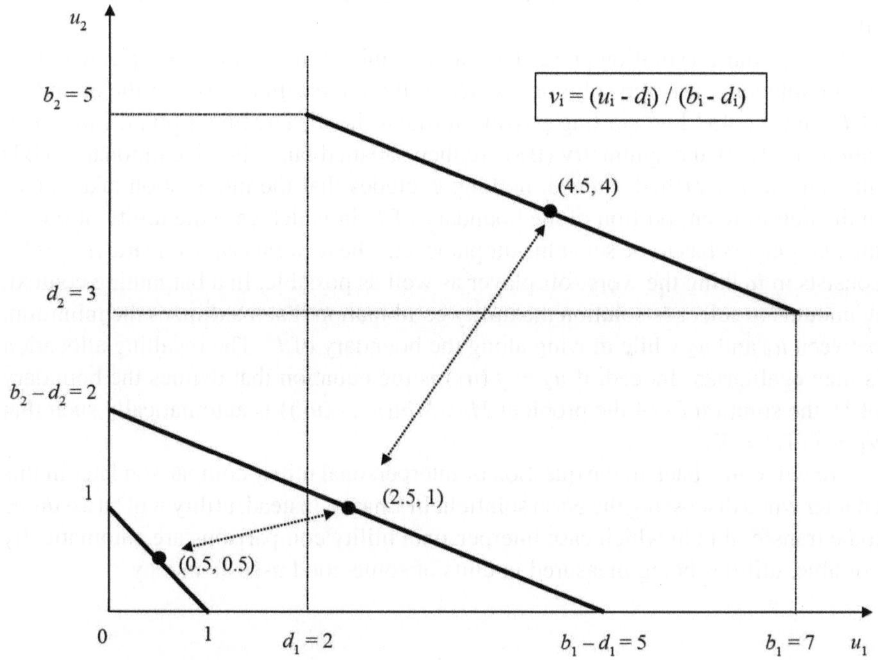

Fig. 3.9 Normalized bargaining problem

The axioms B1, B3 and B4 then determine a unique solution, namely the point in the middle of the line segment, as illustrated in Fig. 3.9.

[5] Actually, that applies to any bargaining problem whose Pareto frontier limited by the disagreement point is a straight line.

Interpersonal Utility Comparisons: Utilitarian and Egalitarian Solutions
What is an equitable solution? This is a philosophical question that belongs to the realm of normative theories of justice and opens the delicate question of interpersonal utility comparison as the following citation from Hammond (1991) indicates: "*Although we all make interpersonal* utility *comparisons, many economists and philosophers argue that our limited* information *about other people's minds renders them meaningless*". The axiom B4 excludes such comparisons: individual utilities can be manipulated *independently* (but linearly) without affecting the outcome: it is not possible to compare players' utilities nor to add them.

However, in the literature, interpersonal comparisons of utilities underlie several solutions. We shall mention two of them: the utilitarian solution and the egalitarian solutions.

The utilitarian solution retains the outcome that maximizes the *sum* of utilities $u_1 + u_2$ on the set U.[6] It implies that utilities are measured in a common unit. This solution satisfies collective rationality (B1), individual rationality (B2) and symmetry (B3).

The egalitarian solution prescribes the maximization of utilities subject to equality. Graphically, it is the solution located at the intersection between the boundary of U and the 45° line starting passing through the disagreement point. Individual rationality (B2) and symmetry (B3) are then satisfied but collective rationality (B1) may fail to be satisfied. Indeed, nothing excludes that the intersection takes place in the non-efficient portion of the boundary of U in which case the utility of one of the two players has to be set at his utopia level. The *leximin criterion* (Rawls, 1971) consists in making the worst-off player as well as possible. In a bargaining context, it amounts to select as solution the utility combination that maximizes the minimum between u_1 and u_2 while moving along the boundary of U. The resulting allocation is then egalitarian. Indeed, if $u_2 = f(u_1)$ is the equation that defines the boundary of U, the solution $\overline{u}_1$ of the problem $Max\ Min(u_1, f(u_1))$ is automatically such that $\overline{u}_1 = f(\overline{u}_1) = \overline{u}_2$.

We will come back to the question of interpersonal utility comparison later in this chapter when discussing the Nash solution. In Chap. 4 instead, utility will be assumed to be transferable in which case interpersonal utility comparisons are automatically possible, utilities being measured in units of some good used as money.

3.3 Nash Solution

Independence with respect to irrelevant alternatives
Construction of the Nash solution
Generalized Nash solution *
Nash solution: a compromise between utilitarianism and egalitarianism *

[6] It is equivalent to the maximization of the sum of the gains $(u_1 - d_1) + (u_2 - d_2)$ on U.

Limits of the Nash solution
Nash solution and sequential bargaining.

While the utilitarian solution prescribes the maximization of the sum of gains, we will see that the Nash solution consists in maximizing the *product of gains* $(u_1 - d_1) \times (u_2 - d_2)$ on the set U. What is remarkable is that this rule results from a single additional axiom.

Independence with Respect to Irrelevant Alternatives
Players may face different bargaining situations. If in a particular situation, they agree on a utility combination u while the combination u' is accessible, it would be natural to exclude that, in another situation, they agree on u' while u is accessible.[7] This is the idea behind the following axiom illustrated in Fig. 3.10.

B5 *Independence with respect to irrelevant alternatives*
Given two bargaining problems (U, d) and (V, d), if $U \subset V$ and $\varphi(V, d) \in U$, then $\varphi(U, d) = \varphi(V, d)$.

There are two ways to read this axiom. If the problem (U, d) is obtained from the problem (V, d) by *eliminating* some outcomes while keeping the solution of the initial problem, the solution of the reduced problem should not change: the disappearance of some outcomes should not affect the solution as far as this solution

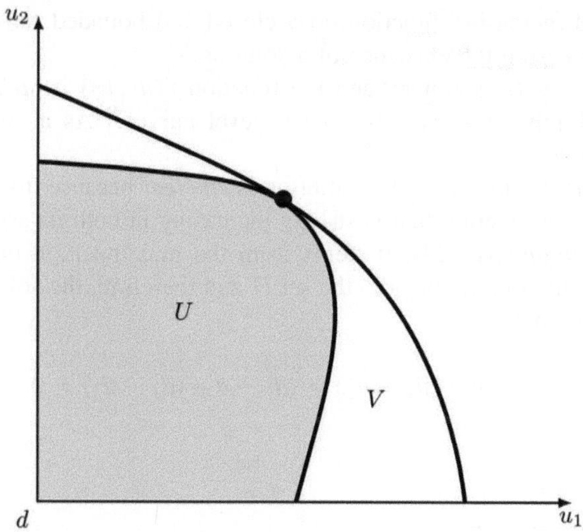

Fig. 3.10 Independence with respect to irrelevant alternatives

[7] There is a parallel with the *weak axiom of revealed preference* in individual choice theory, the difference being that here we consider collective choices.

remains accessible. Alternatively, if the problem (V, d) is obtained from the problem (U, d) by *adding* new outcomes and if the solution of the enlarged problem differs, it must be one of the new outcomes.

The axiom B5 implies that the solution actually depends on the disagreement point and on the boundary of the bargaining space U within the neighborhood of the solution itself.

Notice that B5 it is satisfied by the solution of the maximization of an arbitrary increasing function $f(u_1, u_2)$ on the set U. The nature of this function is defined by the other axioms. Indeed, combined with efficiency, symmetry and independence with respect to utility representations of preferences, B5 allows the univocal characterization of the rule proposed by Nash (1950, 1953). This is the object of the following proposition.

Proposition 3.1 *The axioms B1 to B5 define* one and only one *rule* φ. *Furthermore, the solution corresponds to the maximization on U of the function* $f(u_1, u_2) = (u_1 - d_1)(u_2 - d_2)$ *with respect to* u_1 and u_2.

Equivalently, the Nash solution maximizes the *product* of gains. It is the point on the boundary that maximizes the area of the rectangle defined by the disagreement point and the boundary.

To prove Nash's proposition, we will first check that the Nash solution exists, is unique and satisfies all five axioms. We will then build the solution from the axioms, confirming its unicity.

Existence. The solution is well defined as the result of the maximization of a continuous and increasing function on a closed and bounded (above) set. These two conditions ensure the existence of a solution.[8]

Unicity The set U is convex and the function $f(u_1, u_2)$ is *strictly* concave, a property that implies that strictly convex level curves.[9] As a consequence, the solution is unique.

Collective *rationality* (B1). The solution is *efficient* because it is defined by the maximization of a function that is strictly increasing in both its arguments.

Individual rationality (B2). It stems from the maximization under constraint. The disagreement point belongs to the set U and therefore, the solution $(\overline{u}_1, \overline{u}_2)$ is necessarily such that:

$$(\overline{u}_1 - d_1)(\overline{u}_2 - d_2) \geq (d_1 - d_1)(d_2 - d_2) = 0.$$

[8] This is known as the Bolzano–Weierstrass Theorem.

[9] A level curve associated to a function $f(x, y)$ is the locus of points (x, y) corresponding to a given value of the function, $f(x, y) = k$. For instance, the level curves in maps or the indifference curves in consumer choice.

Hence, the differences $(\overline{u}_1 - d_1)$ and $(\overline{u}_2 - d_2)$ must have the same sign. As efficiency excludes the case where the solution is dominated by the disagreement point, only one possibility remains, namely $\overline{u}_1 \geq d_1$ and $\overline{u}_2 \geq d_2$.

Symmetry (B3). In the case of a symmetric bargaining problem, the function to maximize is symmetric and, as a consequence, the solution $(\overline{u}_1, \overline{u}_2)$ must be such that $\overline{u}_1 = \overline{u}_2$.

Independence with respect to utility representations of preferences (B4). Applying the linear transformations of utilities $u_i' = \alpha_i u_i + \beta_i$, we get:

$$(u_1' - d_1')(u_2' - d_2') = \alpha_1 \alpha_2 (u_1 - d_1)(u_2 - d_2)$$

where the constant $\alpha_1 \alpha_2$ is positive and does not affect the solution of the maximization. Hence, the solution of the transformed problem coincides with the solution of the initial problem. Notice that the value at the solution has no interest in itself.

Independence with respect to irrelevant alternatives (B5). This property is satisfied because the solution results from the maximization of a function. Withdrawing utility pairs different from the solution does not affect the solution.

Notice that the axiom of Individual rationality is actually redundant: the four axioms B1, B3, B4 and B5 actually suffice to characterize uniquely the Nash solution. Apparently, Nash had not realized it.

Construction of the Nash Solution

For a given bargaining problem (U, d), there exists *one and only one line segment*—bordered by the axis whose origin is the disagreement point—that is tangent to the boundary of *U at its middle point*. This segment defines the problem (V, d).[10]

We have seen that the axioms B1 to B4 determine a unique solution in the case of a bargaining problem whose boundary is a line segment, namely its middle point. It then suffices to apply B5 to conclude that this point is the unique solution.

The level curves of the function $f(u_1, u_2) = (u_1 - d_1)(u_2 - d_2)$ are *rectangular hyperbolas* in the axis system whose origin is the disagreement point.[11] One of the characteristics of rectangular hyperbolas is that the point of contact of any tangent is located in the middle of the line segment limited by the axis.

The Nash solution is then located at the tangency point between the highest-level curve and the boundary of the set U. It amounts to say that the Nash solution maximizes the function $f(u_1, u_2)$ on the set U. Figure 3.11 illustrates the construction of the Nash solution for $d = (0, 0)$.

Example 3.1 (continued) The Nash solution of divide 100 dollars is given by (50, 50) when players are risk neutral. The problem is indeed symmetric. If instead players are

[10] Intuitively, this is obvious. In the case where U is strictly convex, it stems from the intermediary value theorem. If the Pareto efficient boundary contains line segments, the proof is less simple but the idea remains the same.

[11] The function f is the "*Nash product*" that appeared in the section on risk-dominance (Chap. 2).

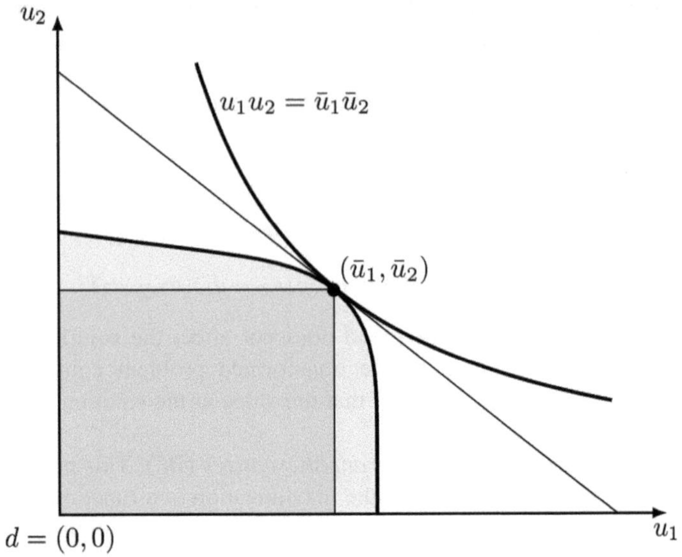

Fig. 3.11 Nash solution

risk-averse, the solution differs and is disadvantageous for the player that is most risk-averse. Referring to the example illustrated by Fig. 3.5 where $u_1(x) = x$ and $u_2(x) = 10\sqrt{x}$, the Nash solution is given by $(\overline{u}_1, \overline{u}_2) = (200/3,\ 100/\sqrt{3}) \simeq (66.66, 57.74)$, to which is associated the division (66.7, 33.3). Indeed, the equation of the boundary of the bargaining space is given by $u_2 = 10\sqrt{100 - u_1}$. Maximizing the product of gains is then equivalent to maximizing the function $u_1\sqrt{100 - u_1}$. Setting to zero its first derivative, we get $\overline{u}_1 = 200/3$. The fact that the division is disadvantageous for the player who is averse to risk is a general observation in bargaining solutions.

Example 3.2 (continued) In the bankruptcy problem, what is prescribed by the Nash solution depends on the debt levels compared to half the value of the firm. Figure 3.12 illustrates the case where the two debts are greater than *L*/2. The solution then consists in dividing the value equally: $\overline{u}_1 = \overline{u}_2 = L/2$. Figure 3.13 instead illustrates the case where only one of the debts is smaller than *L*/2, in which case the other must be greater than *L*/2. The Nash solution then consists in allocating the maximum to the creditor with the smallest debt and what is left to the other.

Generalized Nash solution *

The Nash solution may be adjusted to account for differences between players. The resulting solution then breaks with the symmetry axiom.

Example 3.1 (continued) Divisions of 100$ of the form (α 100, $(1 - \alpha)$ 100) are possible for some $\alpha \in [0, 1]$. They are obtained as solutions of the maximization of the *weighted* Nash product $u_1^{\alpha}u_2^{1-\alpha}$ on the set $\{(u_1, u_2) \in \mathbb{R}_+^2 \,|\, u_1 + u_2 = 100\}$.

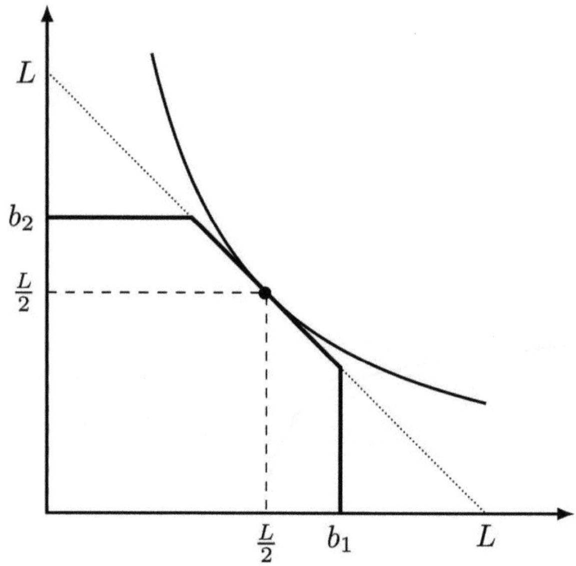

Fig. 3.12 Nash solutions of the bankruptcy problem assuming $b_1, b_2 \geq \frac{L}{2}$

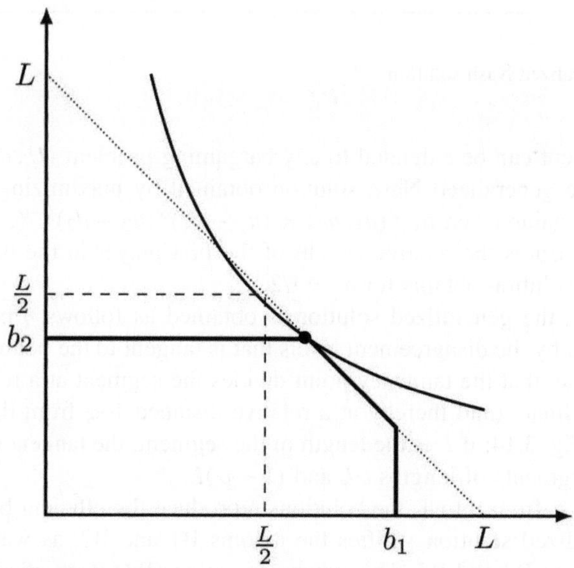

Fig. 3.13 Nash solutions of the bankruptcy problem assuming $b_2 < \frac{L}{2}$

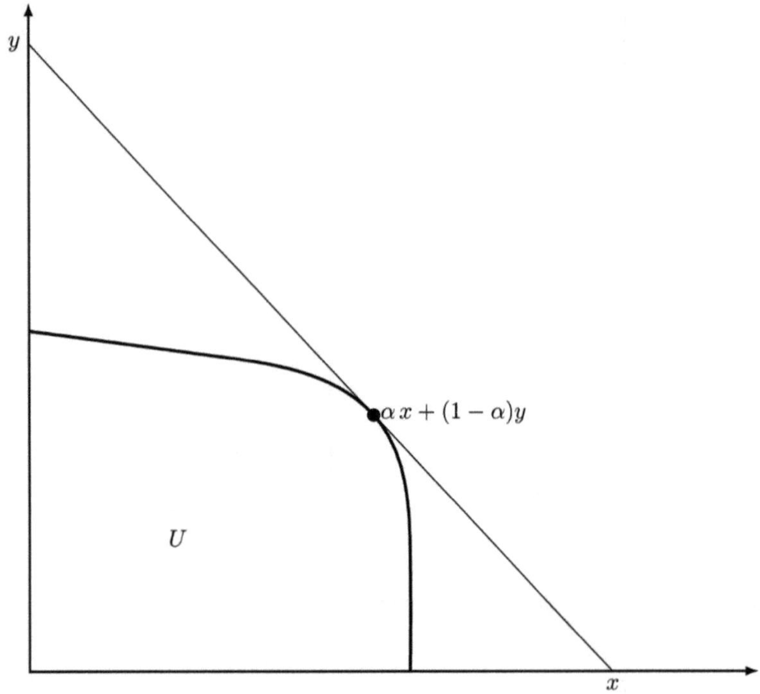

Fig. 3.14 Generalized Nash solution

This argument can be extended to any bargaining problem (U, d): given some $\alpha \in [0, 1]$, the generalized Nash solution obtained by maximizing the weighted average of the gains given by $f(u_1, u_2) = (u_1 - d_1)^{\alpha}(u_2 - d_2)^{1-\alpha}$.

Here, α measures the relative weight of the first player in the bargaining. The original Nash solution obtains for $\alpha = 1/2$.[12]

Graphically, the generalized solution is obtained as follows. Fix the line segment delimited by the disagreement levels that is tangent to the boundary of the set U in such a way that the tangency point divides the segment at a relative distance α from the ordinate (and thereby at a relative distance $1–\alpha$ from the abscissa) as illustrated in Fig. 3.14: if L is the length of the segment, the tangency point divides into two subsegments of lengths αL and $(1 - \alpha)L$.

By varying α from 0 to 1, the solutions reproduce the efficient boundary.

The generalized solution verifies the axioms B1 and B2, as well as the independence axioms B4 and B5. The symmetry axiom (B3) is satisfied only for $\alpha = 1/2$.

[12] There is an equivalence between the identification of the points where a function attains a maximum and the points where any increasing transformation of this function attains a maximum.

Nash solution: a compromise between utilitarianism and egalitarianism*

The Nash solution excludes interpersonal comparisons of utility, in contrast to the utilitarian and egalitarian rules, two rules that are dependent on the utility representations of preferences. Nash solution actually offers a compromise between these two rules in the following sense. Given a bargaining problem (U, d), there exists a rescaling of the utility scales such that the Nash solution of the transformed problem equalizes the gains *and* maximizes their sum: Nash solution combines equality of (rescaled) gains and their maximization. This remarkable characterization is due to Shapley (1969).

Proposition 3.2 *If* $(\overline{u}_1, \overline{u}_2)$ *is the* Nash solution *of the problem* (U, d)*, there exist positive reals* λ_1 *and* λ_2 *such that:*

- $\lambda_1(\overline{u}_1 - d_1) = \lambda_2(\overline{u}_2 - d_2)$,
- $(\overline{u}_1, \overline{u}_2)$ *maximizes the weighted sum* $\lambda_1(u_1 - d_1) + \lambda_2(u_2 - d_2)$ *on U.*

Proof Without loss of generality, let's consider the case where the disagreement point is the origin (0, 0). There is no change if we divide by $\lambda_1 + \lambda_2$. Hence, we can set $\lambda_1 = \lambda$ and $\lambda_2 = 1 - \lambda$. and the coefficient λ is given by the equality of gains:

$$\overline{\lambda} = \frac{\overline{u}_2}{\overline{u}_1 + \overline{u}_2}.$$

By construction, the solution of the problem $(\overline{U}, 0)$, obtained through the transformations $v_1 = \overline{\lambda} u_1$ and $v_2 = (1 - \overline{\lambda})\, u_2$ is the egalitarian solution. To see this, it suffices to apply the same transformations to the Nash solution:

$$\begin{array}{l}\overline{v}_1 = \overline{\lambda}\overline{u}_1 \\ \overline{v}_2 = (1 - \overline{\lambda})\overline{u}_1\end{array} \Rightarrow \overline{v}_1 = \overline{v}_2 = \frac{\overline{u}_1\overline{u}_2}{\overline{u}_1 + \overline{u}_2}.$$

It remains to verify that the second condition is satisfied for $\lambda = \overline{\lambda}$, i.e., $(\overline{u}_1, \overline{u}_2)$ maximizes $\overline{u}_2 u_1 + \overline{u}_1 u_2$ on the set U.

We know that the Nash solution results from the maximization of the product of utilities. The equation of the hyperbola that is tangent to U at $(\overline{u}_1, \overline{u}_2)$ is given by $u_1\, u_2 = \overline{u}_1\, \overline{u}_2 \Rightarrow u_2 = \overline{u}_1\overline{u}_2/u_1$. Its derivative at the tangency point is given by:

$$\frac{du_2}{du_1}\Big|_{u_1=\overline{u}_1} = -\frac{\overline{u}_1\overline{u}_2}{\overline{u}_1^2} = -\frac{\overline{u}_2}{\overline{u}_1}.$$

The equation of the tangent line is therefore given by $u_2 = 2\overline{u}_2 - (\overline{u}_2/\overline{u}_1)u_1$. Hence, we can conclude that $(\overline{u}_1, \overline{u}_2)$ maximizes $\overline{u}_2 u_1 + \overline{u}_1 u_2$ on the set U, as illustrated by Fig. 3.15. ♦

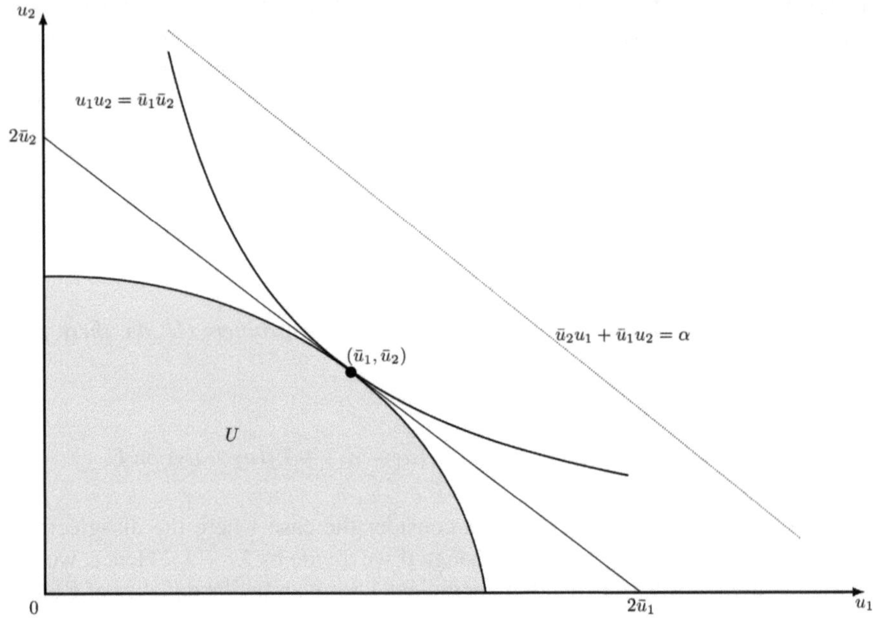

Fig. 3.15 Proposition 3.2

Actually, Myerson (1991, p. 383) proves that it is a necessary and sufficient condition: a utility pair is the Nash solution of a bargaining problem *if and only if* there exists a rescaling of utilities such that the Nash solution of the transformed problem is egalitarian and utilitarian.

Looking at the definition of $\overline{\lambda}$ given in the proof of Proposition 3.2, we observe that the gain of one player is weighted by the relative gain of the other. The proof of the above proposition reveals that when gains are equal (egalitarian solution), the slope of the tangent at the solution is equal to –1: the sum of the gains is therefore maximal (utilitarian solution). Hence, the following corollary.

Proposition 3.3 *If the Nash solution is egalitarian, it coincides with the utilitarian solution.*

Limits of the Nash Solution

Consider two bargaining problems, the first one being obtained by truncating the second one while keeping the solution of the first. Nash solution then does not change, as illustrated by Fig. 3.16: it remains in the middle of the line segment.

That means that the Nash solution only depends on the disagreement point and the neighborhood of the solution itself, with the consequence that the same point is the solution of a large variety of bargaining problems.

The problem is the lack of monotonicity of the Nash solution. Considering two bargaining problems (U, d) and (V, d) such that $U \subset V$, we would expect a solution

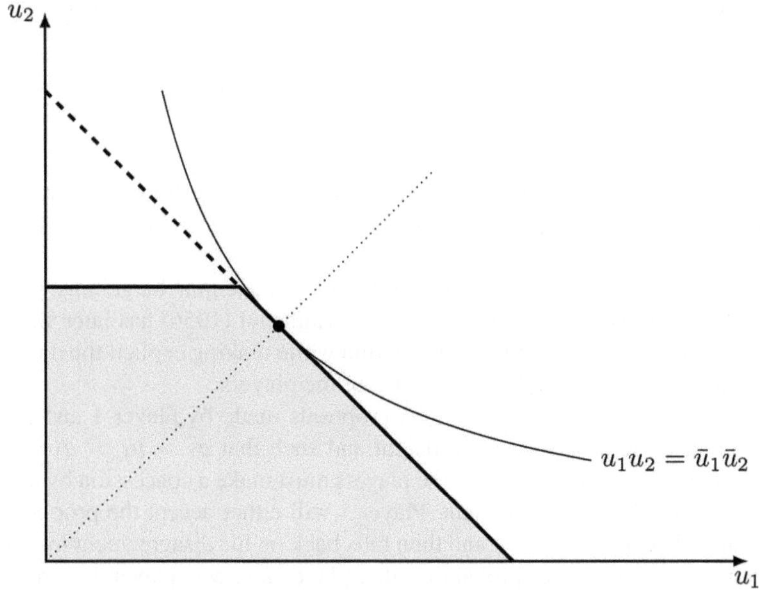

Fig. 3.16 Truncated bargaining problem

φ to reflect the fact that V contains more opportunities than U by not allocating less to any player:

$$U \subset V \;\Rightarrow\; \varphi(V,d) \geq \varphi(U,d).$$

This property is known as *strong monotonicity*. Comparing the Nash solution to the bankruptcy problems illustrated in Figs. 3.12 and 3.13 shows that the Nash solution fails to satisfy this property. Kalai (1977) showed that the egalitarian solution is the *only* solution that satisfies B1 (efficiency) and B3 (symmetry) together with strong monotonicity.

In the next section, we will consider a weaker monotonicity requirement that takes the utopia point into account and leads to a simple solution.

Nash Solution and Sequential Bargaining

Nash solution is an axiomatic solution. We may think of an arbitrator whose role is to convince the players of the relevance of the axioms: if the players accept the axioms, they must agree with the proposal.

Nash (1953) has proposed to associate to a bargaining problem a non-cooperative game where the players formulate *simultaneously* a demand. They are accepted whenever they are jointly feasible. If not, players end up at the disagreement point. Divide 100 dollars (Example 3.1) illustrates such a game.

In general, the game is described by the strategy sets $S_i = [d_i, b_i]$ and the utility functions

$$u_i(s_1, s_2) = \begin{cases} s_i \text{ if } (s_1, s_2) \in U, \\ d_i \text{ otherwise.} \end{cases}$$

This is a one-shot game that has an infinite number of equilibria all corresponding to efficient strategy pairs (s_1, s_2) such that $s_i \geq d_i$ $(i = 1, 2)$. The Nash solution is therefore one of these equilibria.

Before Nash, Zeuthen (1930) has proposed a *sequential* bargaining procedure implying successive concessions by players. Harsanyi (1956) has later shown that this procedure converges to the Nash solution while making explicit the dependence of the solution on the attitude towards risk of the players.

Let (a_1, a_2) and (b_1, b_2) be the last proposals made by player 1 and player 2. Assume that these proposals are efficient and such that $a_1 > b_1 > d_1$ and $b_2 > a_2 > d_2$. In such a situation, one of the players must make a concession by accepting the proposal made by his opponent. Player 1 will either accept the proposal of his opponent and get a_2 or reject it and then falls back on his disagreement level d_1. Let p_2 denotes the (subjective) probability that player 2 rejects player 1's proposal. If player 1 insists on refusing to make a concession, his expected utility is then equal to $p_2 d_1 + (1 - p_2) a_1$ to be compared to a_2. Player 1 maximizes his expected utility and will therefore reject b_1 if $p_2\, d_1 + (1 - p_2)\, a_1 > b_1$, i.e., if $p_2 < \overline{p}_1$ where $\overline{p}_1$ is defined by:

$$\overline{p}_1 = \frac{a_1 - b_1}{a_1 - d_1}.$$

Similarly, if p_1 denotes the probability that player 1 rejects player 2's proposal, player 2 will reject a_2 if $p_1\, d_2 + (1 - p_1)\, a_2 > b_2$, i.e., if $p_1 < \overline{p}_2$ where $\overline{p}_2$ is defined by:

$$\overline{p}_2 = \frac{b_2 - a_2}{b_2 - d_2}.$$

The bound $\overline{p}_1$ is the maximum probability of conflict that player 1 is prepared to face in order to obtain a_1 instead of accepting the less favorable proposal b_1 of his opponent. Similarly, $\overline{p}_2$ is the maximum probability of conflict that player 2 is prepared to face in order to obtain b_2 instead of accepting the less favorable proposal a_2 of his opponent. Harsanyi calls these bounds the players' *risk limits*. Zeuthen idea is that a concession will come from the player with the *smaller* risk limit.

To quote Harsanyi (1956, p. 148), a player "*will make a concession to his opponent once he finds that the latter's determination is firmer (i.e., the latter's readiness to risk a conflict is greater) than his own*". Player 1 will make a concession if $\overline{p}_1 < \overline{p}_2$ and "*a concession need not be the complete acceptance of the other party's last offer, but it must be large enough to reverse the inequality sign*".

It is easily verified that $\overline{p}_1 \leq \overline{p}_2$ is equivalent to $(a_1-d_1)(a_2-d_2) \leq (b_1-d_1)(b_2-d_2)$. Hence, the concession will come from the player whose proposal is associated with the smallest Nash product. If $\overline{p}_1 < \overline{p}_2$, player 1 will make a concession and make a new proposal associated to a higher utility product. In case of equality, both players will make a concession by expressing each demand associated with a higher utility product. Hence, the utility product keeps growing through successive concessions until it reaches a maximum, the Nash solution. "*Zeuthen's approach... supplements Nash's more abstract treatment... by supplying a plausible psychological model for the actual bargaining process*" (Harsanyi, 1956, p. 144).

3.4 Kalai–Smorodinsky Solution

Correct identification of the utopia levels
Proportionality: the Kalai and Smorodinsky solution
Individual monotonicity.

We have seen that imposing the Independence with respect to irrelevant alternatives (B5) has for consequence that the resulting solution is not very sensitive to modifications of the bargaining space. Several alternative rules have been proposed to overcome this insensitivity. We will retain only one, the simplest and most elegant one, suggested by Raiffa (1953) and axiomatized by Kalai and Smorodinsky (1975).[13] It considers the players' aspirations as measured by the utopia levels.[14]

Correct Evaluation of the Utopia Levels

There are two critical points in a bargaining problem, the disagreement point $d = (d_1, d_2)$ and the utopia point $b = (b_1, b_2)$. It seems logical that the aspiration levels represented by the utility levels b_1 and b_2 play a role in the solution. Aspirations must, however, be correctly evaluated by considering the disagreement point. To do so, the correct utopia point is obtained from the subset of individually rational outcomes $U_d = \{u \in U | u \geq d\}$:

$$b_1(U, d) = Max\{x_1 \in \mathbb{R} | \text{there exists } x_2 \in \mathbb{R} \text{ such that } (x_1, x_2) \in U_d\},$$
$$b_2(U, d) = Max\{x_2 \in \mathbb{R} | \text{there exists } x_1 \in \mathbb{R} \text{ such that } (x_1, x_2) \in U_d\}.$$

Proportionality: The Kalai–Smorodinsky Solution

The solution proposed by Kalai and Smorodinsky (1975) consists of satisfying the players *in proportion to their aspirations* as defined by $b_1(U, d)$ and $b_2(U, d)$. Under efficiency (B1), the solution is given by the intersection between the boundary of

[13] See also Luca and Raiffa (1957, p. 134).

[14] In Raiffa (2002), the author formalizes various negotiation analyses in a decision-making prespective.

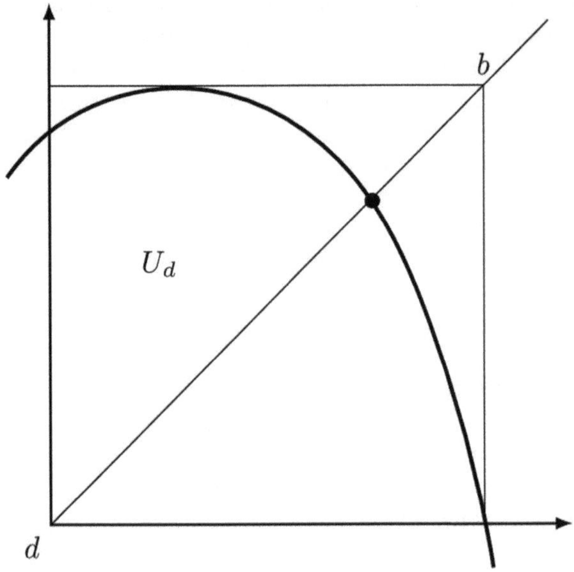

Fig. 3.17 KS solution

the U and the line segment joining the disagreement point and the utopia point. Figure 3.17 illustrates this rule for two different situations.

Geometrically, we move within the rectangle whose vertices are (d_1, d_2), (d_1, b_2), (b_1, d_2) and (b_1, b_2). The equation of the line joining the disagreement point to the utopia point is given by:

$$u_2 = \frac{1}{b_1 - d_1}((d_2 b_1 - d_1 b_2) + (b_2 - d_2)\, u_1).$$

Proportionality appears more clearly in the case where $d = (0, 0)$. Indeed, in this case, the ratio of the utilities is equal to the ratio of the utopia levels:

$$\frac{\overline{u}_2}{\overline{u}_1} = \frac{b_2}{b_1}.$$

Example 3.2 (continued) The solution of the bankruptcy problem prescribed by the KS solution is illustrated by Figs. 3.18 and 3.19, depending on the importance of the debts relatively to $L/2$. In both situations, it simply consists in redistributing *proportionally* the value of the firm:

$$\overline{u}_i = \frac{b_i}{b_1 + b_2} L \ (i = 1, 2).$$

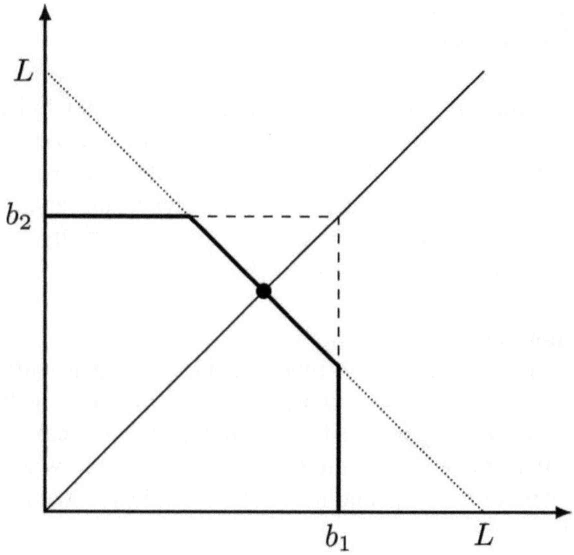

Fig. 3.18 KS solution of the bankruptcy problem, assuming $b_1, b_2 \geq \frac{L}{2}$

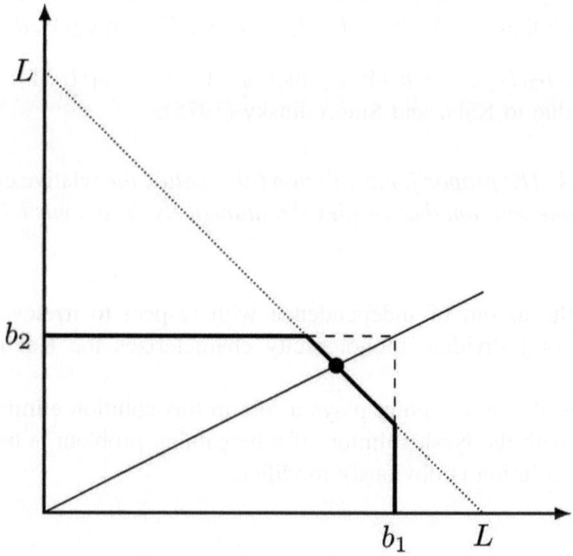

Fig. 3.19 KS solution of the bankruptcy problem, assuming $b_2 < \frac{L}{2}$

Notice that this proportional solution corresponds to the decision usually taken by a judge, in the absence of a priority clause.

Example 3.1 (continued) The solution of the division of 100 dollars when one of the players is risk-averse differs slightly from the Nash solution. Referring to the example illustrated by Fig. 3.5, the proportional solution is given by (61.8, 38.2). Indeed, proportionality requires equality $u_1 = u_2$. Hence, the amount x received by player 1 is solution of the equation $x = \sqrt{100 - x}$ or, alternatively, $x^2 + x - 100 = 0$. The admissible solution is given by $x = 61.8$.

Individual Monotonicity
Strong monotonicity requires that for two bargaining problems with a common disagreement point d, $U \subset V \Rightarrow \varphi(V, d) \geq \varphi(U, d)$. The egalitarian solution satisfies strong monotonicity but Nash solution does not. A weaker form of monotonicity requires that, if new opportunities were made available, without affecting the disagreement point nor the utopia utility level of one player, then it cannot penalize the other player.

B6 *Individual monotonicity*
Consider two bargaining problems with a common disagreement point, (U, d) and (V, d), such that $U \subset V$. If $b_1(U, d) = b_1(V, d)$ then $\varphi_2(V, d) \geq \varphi_2(U, d)$.

Similarly, if $b_2(U, d) = b_2(V, d)$ then $\varphi_1(V, d) \geq \varphi_1(U, d)$. The following proposition is due to Kalai and Smorodinsky (1975).

Proposition 3.4 *The proportional solution (also called the* relative egalitarian solution*) is the unique solution that verifies simultaneously the axioms B1 to B4 together with B6.*

Replacing the axiom of independence with respect to irrelevant alternatives by the axiom of individual monotonicity characterizes the Kalai–Smorodinsky solution.

The fact that the utopia point plays a role in this solution eliminates the problem identified with the Nash solution: if a bargaining problem is truncated—as in Fig. 3.16—the solution is obviously modified.

3.5 Concluding Remarks

The axiomatic approach to bargaining problems faced by two players says nothing on the way bargaining is actually conducted. We have indeed adopted the point of view of a mediator who is willing to guide the choice of the players. If he succeeds in convincing the players of the validity of the properties that underlie a particular rule, the players must logically accept the solution resulting from their application.

Being based on the maximization of the product of gains, the Nash and Kalai–Smorodinsky solutions can easily be extended to an arbitrary number of players. Limiting the analysis to two players allows for an easy geometric treatment. There is, however, another reason: when there are more than two players, the possibility of coalition formation should be accounted for. This is precisely what will be done in Chap. 4 although in a different framework, assuming that utility is transferable.

Nash bargaining belongs to the field of social choice where the *axiom of independence of irrelevant alternative* plays a central role. It is indeed the key axiom in the famous *Arrow's Impossibility Theorem.*[15]

We have seen the bargaining procedure proposed by Zeuthen. Another bargaining procedure based on noncooperative game was sketched in Chap. 2, in the framework of the *Ultimatum game.* More generally, a procedure can be modeled as a game in extensive form where at each step a player expresses a demand that the other may accept or refuse. If players are impatient, backward induction leads to a unique equilibrium where the player who is the first to play expresses a demand that the other accepts.[16]

References

Arrow, K. J. (1951). *Social choice and individual values* (2nd edn., 1963). Wiley.

Debreu, G. and Scarf, H. (1963). A limit theorem on the core of an economy, *International Economic Review, 4*, 235–246.

Edgeworth, F. Y. (1881). *Mathematical psychics: An essay on the application of mathematics to the moral sciences.* Kegan and co.

Hammond, P. J. (1991). Interpersonal comparisons of utility: Why and how they are and should be. In J. Elster & J. E. Roemer (Eds.), *Interpersonal comparisons of well-being* (pp. 200–254). Cambridge University Press.

Harsanyi, J. C. (1956). Approaches to the bargaining problem before and after the theory of games. *Econometrica, 24*, 144–157.

Hildenbrand, W. and Kirman, A. (1988). *Equilibrium analysis*, North-Holland.

Kalai, E. (1977). Proportional solutions to bargaining situations: Interpersonal utility comparisons. *Econometrica, 45*, 1623–1630.

Kalai, E., & Smorodinsky, M. (1975). Other solutions to Nash's bargaining problem. *Econometrica, 43*, 513–518.

Luce, D., & Raiffa, H. (1957). *Games and decisions.* Wiley.

Myerson, R. (1991). *Game theory, analysis of conflict.* Harvard University Press.

[15] See Arrow (1951).

[16] See Rubinstein (1982).

Nash, J. F. (1950). The bargaining problem. *Econometrica, 18*, 155–162.
Nash, J. F. (1953). Two-person cooperative games. *Econometrica, 21*, 141–154.
Raiffa, H. (1953). Arbitration schemes for generalized two-person games. In H. W. Kuhn & A. W. Tucker (Eds.), *Contributions to the theory of games II*, Annals of Mathematical Studies 28 (pp. 361–387), Princeton University Press.
Raiffa, H. (2002). *Negotiation analysis.* Harvard University Press.
Rawls, J. (1971). *Theory of justice.* Harvard University Press.
Rubinstein, A. (1982). Perfect equilibrium in a bargaining model. *Econometrica, 50*, 97–109.
Shapley, L. S. (1951). Notes on the *n*-person game II: The value of an *n*-person game, *Research memoreandum* 670, The Rand Corporation, Santa Monica.
Shapley, L. S. (1969). Utility comparison and the theory of games. *La Decision: Agregation and Dynamique Des Ordres De Preference, 171*, 251–263.
Varian, H. R. (1992). *Microeconomic analysis* (3rd edn.). Norton.
Zeuthen, F. (1930). *Problems of monopoly and economic warfare.* Routledge and Sons.

4 Cooperation and Fair Division

When two players are facing each other, the question of cooperation is simple: either they cooperate or they do not cooperate. When instead, there are three players or more, players can form coalitions. This enriches considerably the analysis. The concept of coalition is indeed central in the analysis of games involving more than two players. If a group of players decides to form a coalition, it means that they dissociate themselves from the set of all players (called the "grand coalition") in order to cooperate between themselves. However, the question that is being addressed concerns the cooperation between *all* players and the allocation among them of the resulting "social" outcome. Hence, the role played by coalitions remains *potential*. Beyond the maximum gain that the players can generate altogether by cooperating, we need to know the gain that each coalition of players could obtain through the cooperation of its members, independently of the actions of the players outside the coalition. When a coalition forms, what matters is the outcome it can achieve, without specifying the organizational details. Quoting Shapley, cooperative game theory "*is concerned with things like* cooperation, *coalition, organizational structure, commitment, trust, compromise, threat, enforceability and indeed the whole legal/social/cultural environment. It deemphasizes questions of tactical optimization, the detailed spelling out of rules and the numerical calculation of outcomes and payoffs*".[1] The possibility of binding and enforceable agreements is an element that further differentiates cooperative games from non-cooperative games. In Aumann's words, "*A game is called cooperative if*

[1] Shapley (1968).

P. Dehez, *Game Theory for the Social Sciences*, Springer Series in Game Theory,
https://doi.org/10.1007/978-3-031-58241-7_4

there is available a mechanism, such as a court, to enforce agreements. In a cooperative game, any feasible outcome may be achieved if the players subscribe to the appropriate agreement".[2]

Cooperative games, also called *coalitional games*, are of two types, depending on the possibility of transfers between players. Here we will assume that transfers are feasible by assuming that utilities are specified in terms of some commodity-money. These are *games with transferable utility*, also called *games with side payments.*

One particularity of cooperative games is the existence of many solution concepts. This is due to the fact that the study of cooperative games naturally invites a normative reflection. In this chapter, we will analyze three concepts: the *core*, the *Shapley value* and the *nucleolus*. The core specifies allocations of the social outcome that are immune from deviations by coalitions of players. It may be empty or contain many distributions. The Shapley value and the nucleolus are allocation *rules* that specify a unique allocation of the social outcome. These rules are based on desirable properties, axioms, exactly like the Nash solution to the bargaining problem.

4.1 Transferable Utility Games

Games in coalitional form
Superadditive games
Marginal contributions
Some emblematic examples.
Monotonic games and symmetric games
Convex game
Normalized and equivalent games.
Simple games
Harsanyi dividends *
Imputations: collective and individual rationality

We consider a set $N = \{1, 2, \ldots, n\}$ of n players, $n \geq 2$. Coalitions are subsets of N and we assume that all coalitions are a priori possible.[3] Hence, there are as many coalitions as there are subsets of N, minus one because the empty set is also a subset of N. In the case where $n = 3$, the set of players is $N = \{1, 2, 3\}$ and there are three coalitions of size 2: $\{1, 2\}$, $\{1, 3\}$ and $\{2, 3\}$. The three singletons are also considered as coalitions, as well as the "grand coalition N". Hence, there are seven coalitions altogether. In general, for n players, there are $2^n - 1$ possible coalitions, a number that becomes very large as the number of players increases:

[2] Aumann's foreword to the book of Harsanyi and Selten (1988).

[3] Restrictions on coalition formation have been introduced by Aumann and Drèze (1974). See also Myerson (1977) who models coalition structures using graphs that describe the links that exist between players.

3, 7, 15, 31, ... In what follows, most examples will concern games with three or four players.

We denote by $v(N)$, a real number, the total gain that the grand coalition can generate if the players coordinate their actions, with the realization of the maximum collective gain in mind. It is expressed in some commodity-money, like wheat, gold or dollars.

We have seen in the first chapter many examples of games where the rational behavior of the players leads to a suboptimal outcome.

Example 2.10 (continued) In the centipede game, the cooperative solution consists of pursuing the game till the end, allowing for a total gain equal to 140. This is the maximum that the players can hope to obtain together if they accept to make choices that are not optimal *from their individual point of view*. It then remains to agree on the division of this collective gain.

The division of the collective gain is precisely the question that is the object of the present chapter: how to divide $v(N)$ among the players? How can they be compensated for their participation in the collective endeavor? Which reasonable restrictions can we impose on possible divisions? Can we construct rules based on some desirable properties that can be applied to various situations?

Games in coalitional form

We place ourselves in situations where gains (and losses) can be expressed in terms of some commodity-money. It is then possible to add individual gains implying that we fall outside of the ordinal or even cardinal frameworks. We are in a framework where *utility is transferable* and utilities are definitely comparable.

To answer the question of the players' compensations within a given game, we need to know how they contribute to the outcome resulting from their cooperation. We will see that knowing what a player contributes to the grand coalition does generally not give a correct picture of his contributions. To get an overall measure of the contribution of a player to a game, we need to know his contributions to all coalitions. This requires knowing the gain that each coalition may expect to obtain if it forms. More precisely, what a coalition is worth is defined as the maximum gain it can get *whatever the player outside the coalition can do.* Starting from a game in strategic form, possibly obtained from an extensive form game, we proceed to an additional reduction by computing what each coalition can obtain when their members coordinate their strategies with the best collective outcome in mind. The concepts of maximin strategy and security level can be used to give a formal content to the notion of worth of a coalition within the 2-player non-cooperative game opposing the coalition to the coalition formed by the outsiders, assuming that the latter coordinate their strategies to the detriment of the dissident coalition. To quote Shapley (1968), it is assumed "*that each coalition will experience the most damaging countermove by the rest of the players*".

Formally, given a set of players N, we define a function v that associates a real number to each subset of N. For all $S \neq N$, the number $v(S)$ represents the minimum gain that coalition S is sure to obtain if it forms and players act jointly. In particular, $v(i)$ represents the minimum gain that player i alone can ensure. $v(N)$ instead is the maximum gain that the grand coalition can realize. This is the notion of *characteristic function* introduced by von Neumann (1928).[4] The pair (N, v) defines a *cooperative game with transferable utility* (or *side payments*) with, by convention, we set $v(\emptyset) = 0$.

For n players, there are $2^n - 1$ coalitions and the transferable utility game (N, v) involving can alternatively be defined by a vector $v \in \mathbb{R}^{2^n-1}$. The following notation will sometimes be used: $v = (v(1), v(2), v(3) | v(1, 2), v(1, 3), v(2, 3) | v(1, 2, 3))$, similarly for 4-player games.

The question that is addressed concerns the division between players of the worth of the grand coalition. More precisely, given a game (N, v), one has to find n numbers $x_1, x_2, \ldots, x_n$ such that their sum equal $v(N)$. Imposing equality is associated with collective rationality or *efficiency*: it is not possible to distribute more and it would be inefficient to distribute less.[5]

We denote by $X(N, v)$ the set of *efficient allocations* associated to the game (N, v) :

$$X(N, v) = \left\{ x \in \mathbb{R}^n \,\middle|\, \sum_{i=1}^{n} x_i = v(N) \right\}. \tag{4.1}$$

Notation Inclusion of sets is denoted by $S \subset T$ while *strict* inclusion is denoted by $\subseteq$ The lowercase letters *n, s, t, …* correspond to the size of the finite sets *N, S, T,…* For all vectors, $x = (x_1, \ldots, x_n)$, we denote by $x(S)$ the sum of its coordinates:

$$x(S) = \sum_{i \in S} x_i$$

with the convention $x(\emptyset) = 0$. We denote by $S \cup i$ and $S \backslash i$ the coalitions resulting from the addition of player i or its subtraction. In the absence of ambiguity, braces will be dropped in the definition of sets. The *restriction* of a game (N, v) to a subset $T \subset N$ is denoted by (T, v_T) where $v_T(S) = v(S)$ for all $S \subset T$.

Superadditive games

Cooperation generates gains by exploiting the complementarities that exist between players. At the very least, cooperation should not entail losses: no coalition should be worth less than the sum of the worth realized by any of its partitions. Put differently, if two coalitions having no player in common merge, the worth of the coalition resulting from their union should not fall below the sum of their worth:

$$S \cap T = \emptyset \;\Rightarrow\; v(S \cup T) \geq v(S) + v(T). \tag{4.2}$$

[4] In the 1928 paper, von Neumann has introduced the concept of characteristic function in a zero-sum framework. The general definition was later given in the 1944 book.

[5] Efficiency and collective rationality are synonymous.

This is *superadditivity*, an assumption that will be made throughout the chapter. We denote by $SG(N)$ the set of all *superadditive* characteristic functions defined on a given set N of players.

Superadditivity implies that the sum of the individual worth never exceeds the worth of the grand coalition:

$$\sum_{i=1}^{n} v(i) \leq v(N).$$

A game is said to be *essential* if this inequality is strict. In an essential game, it is possible to reward all players *above* their individual worth: players have a potential interest in joining the grand coalition.

Under superadditivity, an inessential game is *additive*:

$$v(S) = \sum_{i \in S} v(i) \quad \text{for all } S \subset N.$$

Indeed, superadditivity implies that

$$\sum_{i \in S} v(i) \leq v(S) \quad \text{for all } S \subset N.$$

Assuming a strict inequality sign for a coalition T, we end up with a contradiction:

$$\sum_{i \in N} v(i) < v(T) + v(N \backslash T) \leq v(N).$$

Inessential games are without interest simply because there is no incentive to form the grand coalition. Players will prefer to settle for their individual worth: $(v(1), \ldots, v(n))$ is indeed the only acceptable allocation. The status quo is the only efficient allocation.

Marginal contributions

How to measure the contribution of a player to a game?

Let's consider player i. The difference $v(N) - v(N \backslash i)$ cannot be used *alone* to measure his contribution to the game (N, v) because, as we shall see, it may be null. We must consider his potential contributions to all coalitions of which he is a member. These are the *marginal contributions.* The marginal contribution of player i to a coalition S is given by:

$$Cm_i(S) = v(S) - v(S \backslash i).$$

They include the marginal contribution to the grand coalition as well as the individual worth. Indeed, we have $Cm_i(\{i\}) = v(\emptyset) - v(i) = v(i)$.

Player i is *null* if his marginal contributions are *all* null: $Cm_i(S) = 0$ for all $S \subset N$. Player i is *dummy* if his marginal contributions coincide with his individual worth: $Cm_i(S) = v(i)$ for all $S \subset N,\ i \in S$.

Two players i and j are said to be *substitutable* in a game (N, v) if their marginal contributions to the coalitions to which they both belong are equal:

$$Cm_i(S) = Cm_j(S) \text{ for all } S \subset N \text{ such that } i, j \in S.$$

Hence, the players i and j are substitutable if:

$$v(S \backslash i) = v(S \backslash j) \quad \text{for all } S \subset N \text{ such that } i, j \in S,$$

or

$$v(S \cup i) = v(S \cup j) \quad \text{for all } S \subset N \backslash \{i, j\}.$$

By superadditivity, marginal contributions never fall below individual worth:

$$v(S \backslash i) + v(i) \leq v(S) \quad \Rightarrow \quad Cm_i(S) \geq v(i).$$

Some emblematic examples
The following examples describe situations that will be used to illustrate the various solution concepts that will be defined in this chapter. Other examples will be introduced in subsequent sections.[6]

Example 2.10 (continued) The cooperative version of the centipede game can be described by the following characteristic function

$$\begin{aligned} v(1) &= 20, \\ v(2) &= 0, \\ v(1, 2) &= 140. \end{aligned}$$

Indeed, if they agree to let the game go until the end, they end up with a total of 140. Alone, player 2 cannot hope to get anything while player 1 is sure to gain 20.

In most cases, the number of players will be assumed to be greater than two.

Example 4.1 Luggage Handlers. A traveler arrives at a train station. He has four suitcases. A team of three luggage handlers appear, each being able to carry two suitcases. The cost is 1.5$ per suitcase and the four suitcases must be carried. Because

[6] These examples and many others can be found for instance in Moulin (1986, 1988) and in Shubik (1982).

the luggage handlers form a team, this situation can be described by a 3-player cooperative game with transferable utility. Its characteristic function is given by:

$$\begin{aligned} v(1) &= v(2) = v(3) = 0, \\ v(1,2) &= v(1,3) = v(2,3) = 6, \\ v(1,2,3) &= 6. \end{aligned}$$

i.e., $v = (0, 0, 0|6, 6, 6|6)$. Two luggage handlers could do the job, although the way they distribute the four suitcases among them does not matter. We just have to specify how to distribute the 6$ between the three luggage handlers. The difficulty comes from the fact that there is one luggage handler too much and nothing tells us which one.

Example 4.2 *Sale of a land* (Shubik, 1982; von Neumann & Morgenstern, 1944)
Consider a situation that includes a farmer, a real estate developer and an oil company. The farmer (player 1) owns the land that brings him a revenue r_1. The real estate developer and the oil company (players 2 and 3) hope to get a revenue equal to r_2 and r_3 respectively. These three numbers are *reservation prices*: the farmer will not sell at a price below r_1, the real estate developer will not buy at a price higher than r_2 and an oil company will not buy at a price higher than r_3. We assume that the following inequalities hold: $0 \leq r_1 \leq r_2 \leq r_3$.

This situation can be described by a cooperative game with transferable utility. The worth of the farmer alone is equal to r_1 while the worth of the grand coalition is equal to r_3. It is indeed the maximum gain that the three players together may hope to obtain within that situation: it is in the collective interest for the farmer to sell its land to the oil company. That does not mean that the real estate developer is excluded.

If the farmer decides to form a coalition with the oil company, their worth will also be equal to r_3. Similarly, if the farmer decides to form a coalition with the real estate developer, the worth of the coalition $\{1, 2\}$ is equal to r_2. All other coalitions have a zero worth. Hence, the characteristic function is given by:

$$\begin{aligned} v(1) &= r_1, \\ v(2) &= v(3) = v(2,3) = 0, \\ v(1,2) &= r_2, \\ v(1,3) &= v(1,2,3) = r_3. \end{aligned}$$

An allocation of r_3 between the three players defines the price that the oil company pays to the farmer and the compensation given to the real estate developer. But how could the latter claim a compensation? This is a surprising question at first sight but it makes sense because the real estate developer plays a role once $r_2 < r_3$.

The problem would be quite different if the game only involved the farmer and the oil company. Indeed, the presence of the real estate developer ensures to the farmer a price at least equal to r_2. Later, in computations, we will assume that the revenues are given by $r = (100, 200, 300)$.

Example 4.3 Voting. Consider a three-member committee. If a simple majority wins, any two-member coalition can impose its choice. The associated characteristic function is then given by:

$$v(1) = v(2) = v(3) = 0,$$
$$v(1, 2) = v(1, 3) = v(2, 3) = 1,$$
$$v(1, 2, 3) = 1.$$

A coalition whose worth is equal to 1 is said to be "winning". In such a situation, all players are "equal", a symmetry that is lost once a player holds a *veto right*. If this is the case of player 1, $v(2, 3) = 0$. And the symmetry is definitely lost if player 1 is a *dictator*. He can decide alone: $v(1) = 1$ and the corresponding game is inessential. If instead unanimity is required, $v(S) = 1$ *if and only if* $S = N$.

In general, a voting *game* is defined by the set W of winning coalitions, the coalitions that, given the decision rules, may take a decision. The associated characteristic function v is a function that takes two possible values, 0 or 1, with $v(S) = 1$ *if and only if* the coalition $S \in W$. Voting games are the object of Chap. 5.

Notice that under simple majority, the 3-player voting game is equivalent to the luggage game (Example 4.1) where the gain to share is equal to 1 instead of 6.

Example 4.4 Crop Sharing (Shubik, 1984; Shapley & Shubik, 1967). In a feudal village, there are m agricultural workers and a landowner. This small society can be analyzed through a cooperative game with $n = m + 1$ players. The production conditions are described by a production function $y = F(z)$ that gives the amount of wheat produced when there are z workers on the fields. At this stage, we only assume that F is an increasing function $F(0) = 0$. Further assumptions on the type of returns to scale will be considered later.

Given that the landowner (say player 1) does not work on the fields, the maximum crop is $F(m)$ and the characteristic function is given by:

$$v(S) = \begin{cases} F(s-1) & \text{if } 1 \in S, \\ 0 & \text{if } 1 \notin S, \end{cases}$$

where the variable s denotes the size of coalition S. How to divide the crop? If workers receive an equal amount of w as a wage, the accounting identity $r+mw = F(m)$ must be satisfied where r denotes the rent allocated to the landowner.

We have seen that, starting from a non-cooperative game, the construction of the associated characteristic function is a reduction, a "*presolution*" to use the word of von Neumann. In this formulation, the strategic aspects are implicit. It is, however, not always possible to separate the strategic aspects of a game from its cooperative aspects, as illustrated by the example of blackmail discussed by Shubik (1982, p. 131). A worker tells his employer "*Since you make profits thanks to my work, I ask you to share them with me. If you refuse, I'm gonna mutilate myself so that I can't work anymore, thereby depriving you of profits*".

This situation is illustrated in Fig. 4.1, where the employer is the first to move and the threat of the worker is not credible. In the worst case, the worker ends up with 0 while the employer is sure to make at least 50, which means that he takes seriously the threat of the worker. Together, they can make 100. In this reduced form, the weakness of the worker does not appear, a weakness linked to the dramatic consequences of the implementation of its threat. Using the strategic form, the characteristic function is given by:

$$
\begin{aligned}
v(1) &= 50,\\
v(2) &= 0,\\
v(1,2) &= 100.
\end{aligned}
$$

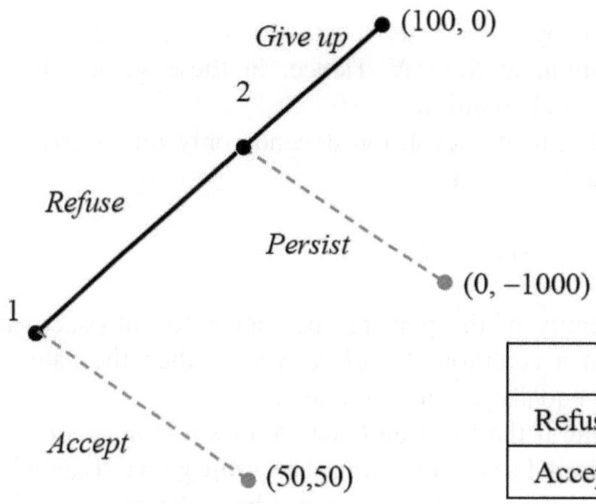

	Give up	Persist
Refuse	100, 0	0, − 1000
Accept	50, 50	50,50

Fig. 4.1 Blackmail game

Monotonic games and symmetric games

A game is *monotonic* if enlarging a coalition does not reduce its worth:

$$S \subset T \;\Rightarrow\; v(S) \leq v(T).$$

As a consequence, the characteristic function is maximal at the grand coalition.

In all previous examples, games are monotonic. In a monotonic game, marginal contributions are nonnegative:

$$v(S\backslash i) \leq v(S) \quad \Rightarrow \quad Cm_i(S) \geq 0.$$

Superadditivity alone does not guarantee that the characteristic function is maximal at the grand coalition. It is however the case of games that have nonnegative individual worth.

Proposition 4.1 *For all games* (N, v) *such that* $v(i) \geq 0$ *for all* $i \in N$*, superadditivity implies that the* characteristic function v *is positive-valued and monotonic.*

Proof Consider a nonempty coalition S and a player $i \notin S$. By superadditivity, we have:

$$v(S \cup i) \geq v(S) + v(i).$$

Hence, if $v(i) \geq 0$ for all $i \in N$, adding a player to a coalition does not reduce its worth, i.e., v is monotonic. Non-negativity of the $v(S)$ is an immediate consequence of the above inequalities, starting with $S = \{i\}$ for any i. ◆

In superadditive games defined by a characteristic function whose values are nonnegative, it attains its maximum at $S = N$. Hence, in these games, it is collectively rational to form the grand coalition.

A game is *symmetric* if the worth of a coalition depends only on its size. It means that there exists a function f such that

$$v(S) = f(s) \text{ for all } S \subset N.$$

In a symmetric game, the identity of the players does not enter into account in the evaluation of the worth of a coalition. *Equal division* is then the natural solution: the total gain is divided equally among the players.

A symmetric game is monotonic if the function f that defines it is *nondecreasing*. The luggage game (Example 4.1) is symmetric. The crop game (Example 4.4) instead is not: two coalitions of the same size do not have the same worth, depending on the presence of the landowner.

Here is an example of a symmetric and superadditive game that fails to be monotonic because it does not satisfy the non-negativity condition.

Example 4.5 Garbage Game (Shapley & Shubik, 1969; Shubik, 1982). An isolated community on n families faces the problem of managing their waste. Each family tries to get rid of his garbage bag by leaving it in a neighbor's backyard …

The disutility for a family is proportional to the number of garbage bags found in its garden. The corresponding characteristic function is then given by:

$$v(S) = \begin{cases} -(n-s) & \text{for all } S \neq N, \\ -n & \text{for all } S = N. \end{cases}$$

It defines a symmetric non-monotonic game, as shown by Fig. 4.2.

It is however superadditive: take two disjoint coalitions S and T. Either $S \cup T \neq N$, in which case we have:

$$v(S) + v(T) = (s+t) - 2n < s + t - n = v(S \cup T),$$

or $S \cup T = N$, in which case we have:

$$v(S) + v(T) = (s+t) - 2n = -n = v(N).$$

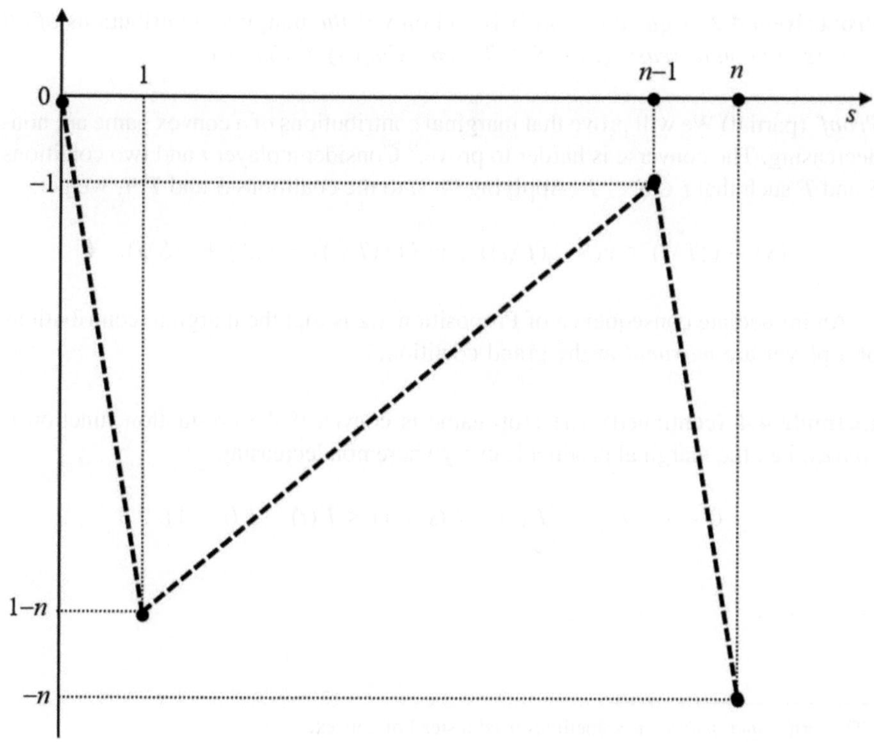

Fig. 4.2 Garbage game

Convex games

Convex games form an important class of games with interesting properties. A game (N, v) is *convex* if for all coalitions $S, T \subset N$, we have:

$$v(S \cup T) \geq v(S) + v(T) - v(S \cap T). \tag{4.3}$$

In words, the worth resulting from the merger of any two coalitions is never smaller than the sum of the worth of the coalitions, net of the worth of the coalition made of the players who belong to the two coalitions.[7] Applied to disjoint coalitions, we retrieve the definition of superadditivity (4.2): convex games are superadditive.

Example 4.1 (continued) The luggage game is not convex. For the coalitions $S = \{1, 2\}$ and $T = \{1, 3\}$, the reverse inequality applies: $v(S) + v(T) = 12 > 6 = v(S \cup T)$.

Example 4.2 (continued) For the coalitions $S = \{1, 2\}$ and $T = \{1, 3\}$, we verify that the land game is also not convex.

The following proposition gives an equivalent characterization of convex games: the greater the coalition you belong to, the more you contribute.[8]

Proposition 4.2 *A game is convex* if and only if *the* marginal contributions *of all players are nondecreasing:* $i \in S \subset T \Rightarrow Cm_i(S) \leq Cm_i(T)$.

Proof (partial) We will prove that marginal contributions of a convex game are nondecreasing. The converse is harder to prove.[9] Consider a player i and two coalitions S and T such that $i \in S \subset T$. Applying (4.2) to the coalitions S and $T \backslash i$, we get:

$$v(S) + v(T\backslash i) \leq v(S \cup (T\backslash i)) + v(S \cap (T\backslash i)) = v(T) + v(S\backslash i). \quad \blacklozenge$$

An immediate consequence of Proposition 4.2 is that the marginal contributions of a player are *maximal* at the grand coalition.

Example 4.4 (continued) The crop game is convex if the production function is *convex,* i.e., the marginal product is everywhere nondecreasing:

$$0 < s < t \Rightarrow F(s) - F(s-1) \leq F(t) - F(t-1).$$

[7] The term *supermodular* is sometimes used instead of convex.

[8] This characterization is due to Shapley (1971).

[9] See for instance Maschler et al. (2020, p. 717).

To prove this assertion, consider a player i and two coalitions S and T such that $i \in S \subset T$. There are several cases to consider. Assume first that player i is a worker. Then, if the landowner belongs to S, we have $v(S) - v(S\backslash i) = F(s-1) - F(s-2) \leq F(t-1) - F(t-2) = v(T) - v(T\backslash i)$ as a consequence a nondecreasing marginal product.

If the landowner belongs to the coalition $T\backslash S$ we have:

$$\begin{aligned} v(S) &= v(S\backslash i) = 0, \\ v(T) - v(T\backslash i) &= F(t-1) - F(t-2) > 0, \end{aligned}$$

since the production function is increasing. If the landowner does not belong to T, we have:

$$v(S) = v(S\backslash i) = v(T) = v(T\backslash i) = 0.$$

Finally, if player i is the landowner, i.e., $i = 1$, we have:

$$\begin{aligned} v(S) - v(S\backslash 1) &= F(s-1), \\ v(T) - v(T\backslash 1) &= F(t-1) > F(s-1). \end{aligned}$$

In all cases, the convexity condition is verified.

Notice that the proof reveals that the converse is true: convexity implies a nondecreasing marginal product.

Normalized and equivalent games

The 0-*normalization* of a game (N, v) is obtained by the following transformation:

$$v_0(S) = v(S) - \sum_{i \in S} v(i) \quad \text{for all } S \subset N.$$

By definition, $v_0(i) = 0$ for all $i \in N$. For instance, the 0-normalization of the game defined by the vector $v = (-1, 0, 2|1, 3, 3|\, 5)$ is given by the vector $v_0 = (0, 0, 0|2, 2, 1|\, 4)$.

If we start from an *essential* game, we can go further. The 01-*normalization* of a game (N, v) is the game (N, v_{01}) defined by:

$$v_{01}(S) = \frac{1}{v(N) - \sum_{i \in N} v(i)} \left(v(S) - \sum_{i \in S} v(i) \right) = \frac{v_0(S)}{v_0(N)}.$$

For instance, the 01-normalized version of the game $v = (-1, 0, 2|1, 3, 3|\, 5)$ is given by $v_{01} = (0, 0, 0|0.5, 0.5, 0.25|\, 1)$.

Example 4.2 (continued) In the land game where $r = (100, 200, 300)$, the 0-normalized game is obtained by subtracting 100 from the worth of the coalitions including player 1. Being essential, the game can be normalized by dividing all worth by 200. We then have:

$$v_{01}(1,2) = \frac{100}{200} = \frac{1}{2},$$
$$v_{01}(1,3) = \frac{200}{200} = 1,$$
$$v_{01}(2,3) = 0.$$

There is actually no loss of generality in normalizing games. Indeed, the allocations $(x_1, ..., x_n)$ and $(y_1, ..., y_n)$ of a game (N, v) and its normalization (N, v_{01}) are linked by the following equations:

$$x_i = v(i) + \left(v(N) - \sum_{j \in N} v(j) \right) y_i \Leftrightarrow y_i = \frac{x_i - v(i)}{v(N) - \sum_{j \in N} v(j)}.$$

Superadditivity is preserved under normalization: we remain within the set $SG(N)$ of games.

Two games (N, v) and (N, w) are *strategically equivalent* if there exists $a > 0$ and $b \in \mathbb{R}^n$ such that $w(S) = a\, v(S) + b(S)$. A normalized game and the original game are strategically equivalent. So are the luggage game and the voting game under simple majority (Examples 4.1 and 4.3).

Simple games

Considering a given property, a coalition is said to be *winning* if it has that property. A *simple game* is defined by a set of players N and a binary characteristic function v on N that takes the value 1 or 0 whether a coalition is winning or not. The characteristic function defining a simple game is assumed to be superadditive with $v(N) = 1$. Superadditivity implies monotonicity, according to Proposition 4.1, and two disjoint coalitions cannot be simultaneously winning:

$$S \subset T \text{ and } v(S) = 1 \Rightarrow v(T) = 1,$$
$$S \cap T = \emptyset \text{ and } v(S) = 1 \Rightarrow v(T) = 0.$$

Voting games are simple games. In simple games, marginal contributions are equal to 0 or 1. The marginal contribution of player i to the coalition S is equal to 1 *if and only if* $v(S) = 1$ and $v(S \backslash i) = 0$. In all other cases, his marginal contribution is null.

Simple games are generally not convex: if two winning coalitions S and T have nonempty *and* non-winning intersection we have

$$v(S) + v(T) = 2,$$
$$v(S \cup T) + v(S \cap T) = 1.$$

Harsanyi dividends *

For any given subset $T \subset N$, consider the games (N, u_T) defined by:

$$u_T(S) = 1 \quad \text{if } T \subset S,$$
$$= 0 \text{ otherwise.}$$

These games are called *T-unanimity* games. They are convex and play a central role in proving the unicity of the Shapley value.

The T-unanimity games form a basis of the space $\mathbb{R}^{2^n-1}$ of n player games: for any given characteristic function v on N, there exists a *unique* collection $(\alpha_T | \ T \subset N)$ of $2^n - 1$ real numbers such that:

$$v(S) = \sum_{T \subset N} \alpha_T u_T(S) = \sum_{T \subset S} \alpha_T. \tag{4.4}$$

The coefficients α_T's are known as *Harsanyi dividends*. They were introduced by Harsanyi (1959, 1963). They can be defined recursively, starting with $\alpha_\emptyset = 0$, as follows:

$$\alpha_T = v(T) \ - \sum_{S \subsetneq T} \alpha_S \quad \text{for all } T \subset N. \tag{4.5}$$

Hence, we have:

$$\alpha_{\{i\}} = v(i),$$
$$\alpha_{\{i,j\}} = v(i,j) - v(i) - v(j),$$
$$\alpha_{\{i,j,k\}} = v(i,j,k) - v(i,j) - v(i,k) - v(j,k) + v(i) + v(j) + v(k), \ldots$$

Example 4.2 (continued) The Harsanyi dividends of the land game where $r = (100, 200, 300)$ are given by:

$$\alpha_{\{1\}} = 100,$$
$$\alpha_{\{2\}} = \alpha_{\{3\}} = \alpha_{\{2,3\}} = 0,$$
$$\alpha_{\{1,2\}} = 200 - 100 = 100,$$
$$\alpha_{\{1,3\}} = 300 - 100 = 200,$$
$$\alpha_{\{1,2,3\}} = 300 - 200 - 300 + 100 = -100.$$

Example 4.4 (continued) The Harsanyi dividends of the crop game depend on the production function. If $F(z) = z$ or $F(z) = z^2$, they are all nonnegative. They are given respectively by (0, 0, 0 | 1, 1, 0 | 0) and (0, 0, 0 | 1, 1, 0 | 2). If instead $F(z) = \sqrt{z}, \alpha_{\{1,2,3\}} = \sqrt{2} - 2 < 0$.

We observe that Harsanyi dividends may be negative. *Positive games* are games whose dividends are all nonnegative. Referring to (4.4), positive games are convex. Indeed, T-unanimity games are convex and a positive game is a linear combination of T-unanimity games whose coefficients are nonnegative. Positive games form an interesting class of games on which solution concepts tend to converge: the core coincides with the set of weighted Shapley values as well as the Harsanyi set, the set of all distributions of Harsanyi dividends.[10]

Imputations: collective and individual rationality

Remember that the question addressed by the theory of cooperative games is the allocation of the outcome resulting from the cooperation of all players. In the context of a game with transferable utility (N, v), the outcome to be divided is the amount $v(N)$.

What would be the *minimal restrictions* that should be imposed on allocations? The very first has been anticipated: it is not feasible to distribute more than $v(N)$ and it would be irrational to distribute less. Allocations must belong to $X(N)$, this is a question of *collective rationality* or *efficiency*.

Because $v(i)$ is the minimal amount that player i can ensure himself in all circumstances, it is natural to exclude the allocations that would give less to that player. It means that we reject any allocation x that would violate the inequalities $x_i \geq v(i)$. This defines the allocations that are *individually rational*: no player is in a position to object, at least individually. The possibility that a coalition of players may object is another question. It underlies the notion of core that will be discussed in the next section.

An *imputation* is an allocation that is both efficient *and* individually rational.[11] The imputation set associated to the game (N, v) is given by:

$$I(N, v) = \{x \in \mathbb{R}^n | x(N) = v(N) \text{ and } x_i \geq v(i) \text{ for all } i \in N\}. \tag{4.6}$$

By superadditivity, the inequality $\sum v(i) \leq v(N)$ is verified. As a consequence, the imputation set $I(N, v)$ is a nonempty subset of $X(N, v)$. The two sets coincide and reduce to the singleton $(v(1), v(2), \ldots, v(n))$ in the case of an inessential game.

---

[10] See Dehez (2017) for an extensive study of Harsanyi dividends and related concepts.

[11] The term “pre-imputation” is sometimes used instead of imputation.

For an essential game, it is a simplex of dimension $n - 1$.[12] Its center of gravity defines the *equal division of the surplus*:

$$ES_i(N, v) = v(i) + \frac{1}{n}\left(v(N) - \sum_{j=1}^{n} v(j)\right) \quad i = 1, \ldots, n. \tag{4.7}$$

Players obtain their individual worth plus an equal share in the resulting surplus, a nonnegative amount by superadditivity. Notice that equal division of the surplus coincides with the egalitarian allocation when the $v(i)$'s are all zero.

Figure 4.3 represents the imputations set of a 3-player game, an equilateral triangle whose sides are division between any two players of the amount $v(N)$ net of the individual worth of the third player. More generally, if we fix the amount allocated to a given player, say $x_2 = a$, we obtain a line segment that collects the distribution of what is left between the other two players. Because the imputation set has dimension 2, it can be represented in the plane, as illustrated in Fig. 4.4.

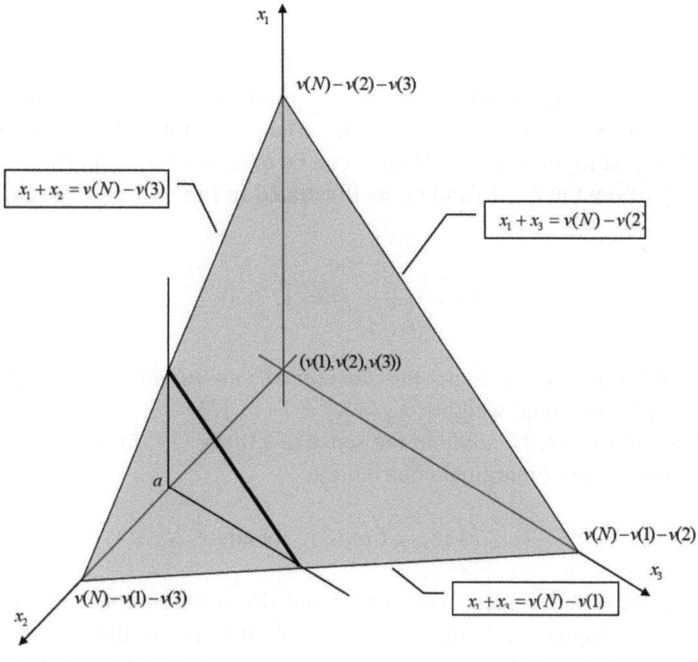

Fig. 4.3 3-player imputation set in $\mathbb{R}^3$

[12] It is an equilateral triangle ($n = 3$), a regular tetrahedron ($n = 4$),… More in the Mathematical appendix.

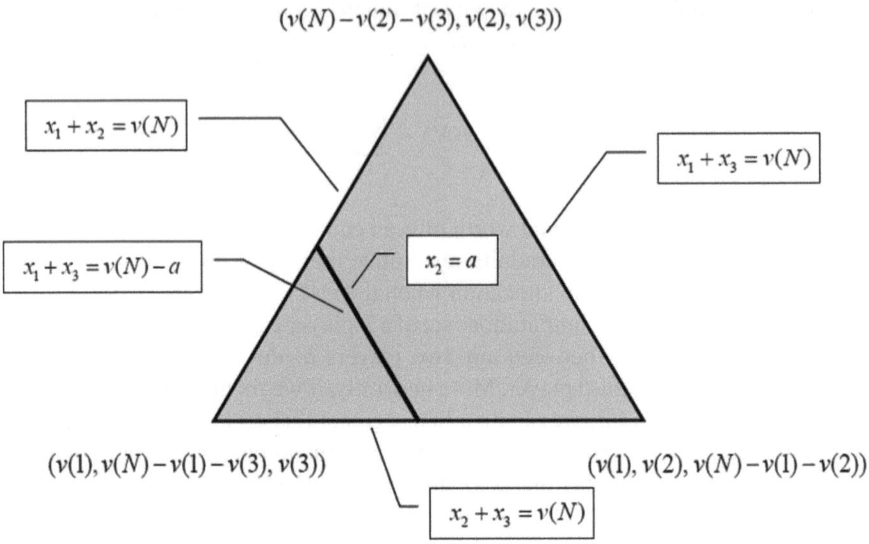

Fig. 4.4 3-player imputation set in $\mathbb{R}^2$

Equilateral triangles have the following property: the sum of the distances ℓ_1, ℓ_2 and ℓ_3 between any point x inside the triangle and its sides is a constant that is therefore equal to its height.[13] Then, x can be obtained by placing weights λ_1, λ_2 and λ_3 proportional to ℓ_1, ℓ_2 and ℓ_3, as illustrated in Fig. 4.5: $x = (\lambda_1 a, \lambda_2 a, \lambda_3 a)$ where:

$$\lambda_i = \frac{\ell_i}{\sum \ell_j} \quad (i = 1, 2, 3).$$

The weights $(\lambda_1, \lambda_2, \lambda_3)$ are the *barycentric coordinates*. Equal division is obtained by placing equal weights, $\lambda_1 = \lambda_2 = \lambda_3 = 1/3$.

An allocation x is *reasonable* in the sense of Milnor (1952) if no player obtains more than his *maximal* marginal contribution:

$$x_i \leq Max_{S \subset N} Cm_i(S) \quad \text{for all } i \in N.$$

This requirement is indeed reasonable and the solution concepts that will be studied in this chapter all define reasonable imputations. In the case of a convex game, the marginal contribution of a player being maximal at the grand coalition, an allocation is reasonable if $x_i \leq Cm_i(N)$ for all $i \in N$.

[13] This property, known as Viviani's Theorem, actually defines equilateral triangles.

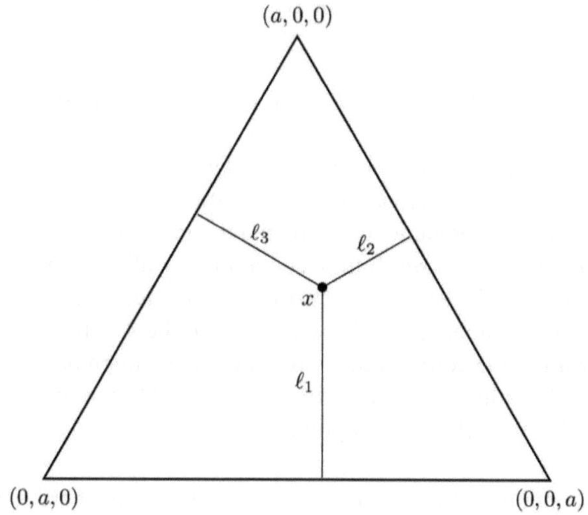

Fig. 4.5 Barycentric coordinates

4.2 Stability: The Core

The core
Competitive forces and the core
Non-emptiness of the core
Geometric characterization of the core of a convex game
Justified objections: the bargaining set *.

Which additional restrictions could we impose on allocations, beyond individual and collective rationality? Individual rationality is a natural restriction, so why not extend it to coalitions? We could indeed require that an allocation gives *to any coalition* not less than what it could obtain if it decided to form instead of joining the grand coalition. This is the argument that underlies the definition of core, a concept introduced by Shapley (1955).[14]

The core
By definition, $v(S)$ measures what coalition S is sure to obtain in the worst case. It would then be natural to only retain the allocations x such that:

$$\sum_{i \in S} x_i \geq v(S) \text{ for all } S \subset N.$$

[14] Gillies (1953, 1959) has introduced the term "core" in relation to the concept of *stable set* introduced by von Neumann and Morgenstern. It is Shapley (1955) who was the first to formally give the definition of the core as a solution concept. See Zhao (2018) for more details.

This defines the core of a game as the set of allocations that give to all coalitions at least their worth:

$$C(N, v) = \{x \in \mathbb{R}^n | x(N) = v(N) \text{ and } x(S) \geq v(S) \text{ for all } S \subset N\}. \quad (4.8)$$

The core is a subset of the set of imputations defined by (4.6): $C(N, v) \subset I(N, v)$. Indeed, when applied to singletons, core inequalities cover individual rationality.

Notice that in a 2-player game, the core and the imputation set coincide.

Observe that the core is *a set.* It may contain many allocations or be *empty.* In a n-player game, the core is defined by 2^n–1 *linear inequalities.* While some of them may be redundant, it is no surprise that they may not be satisfied simultaneously.

In 3-player games, the core can be represented in the imputation triangle as illustrated in Fig. 4.6 for a hypothetical game, assuming $v(1) > 0$ and $v(2) = v(3) = 0$. The slightly shaded triangle is the imputation set.

Example 4.1 (continued) No hope for the luggage handlers: there is no nonnegative allocation (x_1, x_2, x_3) such that:

$$x_1 + x_2 + x_3 = 6,$$
$$x_1 + x_2 \geq 6,$$

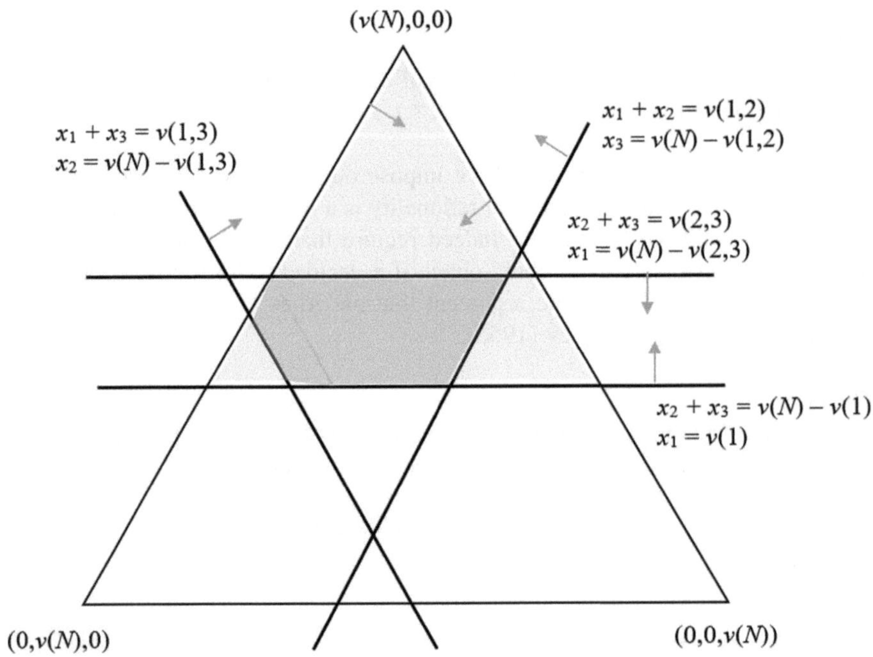

Fig. 4.6 Core of a hypothetical game

$$x_1 + x_3 \geq 6,$$
$$x_2 + x_3 \geq 6.$$

Indeed, any of the three inequalities including two components implies that the third component must be equal to zero.

Example 2.1 (continued) The core of the divide 100 dollars game is the set of nonnegative allocations (x_1, x_2) such that $x_1 + x_2 = 100$: core allocations are of the form $x = (y, 100 - y)$ where y is a real number in the interval [0, 100].

Looking at the definition of the core given in (4.8), if we combine the equation $x(N) = v(N)$ and the inequalities $x(N \backslash S) \geq v(N \backslash S)$, we obtain that core allocations satisfy the following *equivalent* inequalities $x(S) \leq v(N) - v(N \backslash S)$ for all $S \subset N$. They say that no coalition can obtain more than its marginal contribution to the grand coalition. In other terms, no coalition can obtain more than what is left, once the coalition formed by the outsiders has obtained the minimum to which they are entitled. Hence, x is a core allocation if $x(N) = v(N)$ and

$$v(S) \leq x(S) \leq v(N) - v(N \backslash S) \text{ for all } S \subset N. \tag{4.9}$$

In particular, no player can obtain more than his marginal contribution to the grand coalition: $v(i) \leq x_i \leq v(N) - v(N \backslash i)$ for all $i \in N$. It turns out that, together with efficiency, these inequalities completely define the core in the 3-player case.

Proposition 4.3 *The* core of *a 3-player game* (N, v) *is defined by the efficient allocations* x *verifying the following three inequalities:*

$$\begin{aligned} v(1) &\leq x_1 \leq v(1, 2, 3) - v(2, 3) \\ v(2) &\leq x_2 \leq v(1, 2, 3) - v(1, 3) \\ v(3) &\leq x_3 \leq v(1, 2, 3) - v(1, 2) \end{aligned} \tag{4.10}$$

Proof By individual rationality, we have $x_i \geq v(i)$. Using the equation $x_1 + x_2 + x_3 = v(1, 2, 3)$, we have $x_2 + x_3 \geq v(2, 3) \Leftrightarrow x_1 \leq v(1, 2, 3) - v(2, 3)$ for player 1, and similarly for player 2 and player 3. ♦

Example 4.2 (continued) The core of the land game for $r = (100, 200, 300)$ is defined by

$$\begin{aligned} x_1 + x_2 + x_3 &= 300, \\ 100 \leq x_1 &\leq 300, \\ 0 \leq x_2 &\leq 0, \\ 0 \leq x_3 &\leq 100. \end{aligned} \Rightarrow \begin{aligned} 200 \leq x_1 &\leq 300, \\ x_2 &= 0, \\ x_1 + x_3 &= 300. \end{aligned}$$

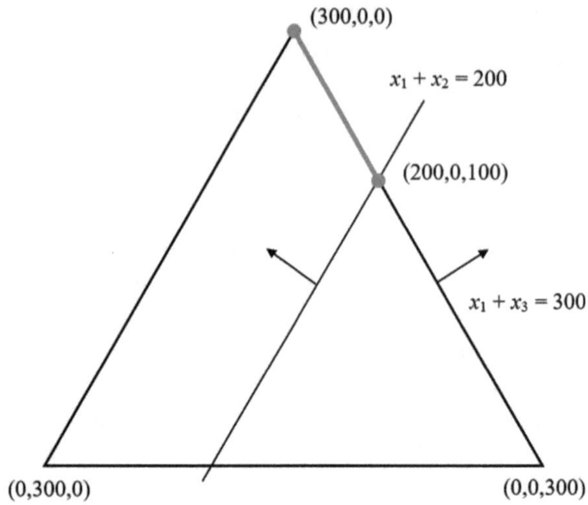

Fig. 4.7 Core of the land game

Hence, core allocations are of the form (p, 0, 300–p) where p, the price at which the land is sold, lies between 200 and 300, as illustrated in Fig. 4.7. The real estate developer is not compensated even if he plays a role. Indeed, his reservation price is the *minimum* price at which the farmer will sell his land. As a consequence, the inequality $x_1 \geq 100$ is redundant.

In the case where the two buyers have the same reservation price, say $r_2 = r_3 = 300$, it is easily verified that the core reduces to the single allocation (300, 0, 0): the seller exploits the competition between the two buyers up to the limit. When instead the reservation prices differ, the seller's ability to exploit the competition between the two buyers is limited by the price difference. However, the allocation (0,0,300) remains a core allocation.

A word of caution: the inequalities (4.10) contained in Proposition 4.3 may give the impression any player may actually end up with his individual worth in the core. This is not necessarily so. Consider the game $v = (0, 0, 2|\ 3, 4, 5|\ 7)$. The inequalities (4.10) are given by:

$$0 \leq x_1 \leq 2,$$
$$0 \leq x_2 \leq 3,$$
$$2 \leq x_3 \leq 4,$$

but player 2 is actually sure to receive at least 1. Indeed, player 1 cannot receive more than 2 and player 3 cannot receive more than 4, while the amount to be divided is equal to 7.

Here is an alternative way to look at the core. A coalition may oppose an allocation if it does not offer to its members more than what they are being proposed. Formally, a coalition S is able to *object* to an allocation x if there exists an alternative allocation y such that:

$$y(S) \leq v(S) \text{ and } y_i > x_i \text{ for all } i \in S.$$

We observe that nothing is said about the players outside S. It is a situation where the coalition is disengaging itself from the grand coalition. It corresponds to the popular expression "make game by itself". The pair (S, y) formed by the coalition S and the alternative y is called an *objection* to the imputation x. The core can then be defined as the set of allocations against which there is no objection.

Instead of the term "objection", reference is sometimes made to "blocking". That point of view is not correct according to Shapley (1973) who prefers to use the terms "*improve upon*": an allocation is in the core of a game if no coalition is able to do better for its members. Edgeworth uses the term "*recontracting*" in the framework of an exchange economy as described in Example 3.4.

Example 4.3 (continued) The voting game where decisions are taken by simple majority and player 1 has a veto right illustrates the limits of a definition in terms of blocking. The game is defined by $v = (0, 0, 0|1, 1, 0|1)$. Its core reduces to the allocation $(1, 0, 0)$ that gives the entire worth of the game to the veto player. However, players 2 and 3 are both in a position to block because player 1 needs at least one of them, while they cannot object.

Notice that the above voting game is strategically equivalent to the land game (Example 4.2) obtained when the reservation prices of the two buyers are equal. If $r_2 = r_3 = 300$, the allocation (220, 0, 80) is an objection to the allocation (200, 50, 50), but the allocation (280, 20, 0) is an objection to the allocation (220, 0, 80), and so on. This sequence eventually ends up with the unique core allocation (300, 0, 0).

Core allocations are "*socially stable*" in the sense that no coalition can object. The fact that the core of a game is empty is not properly speaking a negative result. It tells us that the game describes a situation in which it is impossible to satisfy all coalitions. If the core is empty or contains several allocations, a compromise is needed if we wish to single out a particular allocation, as the *Shapley value* or the *nucleolus* that will be studied later in this chapter. Alternatively, we could limit in one way or another the conditions in which coalitions can object. This is what the concept of *bargaining set* does. It will be the object of a subsequent section.

The core does not remunerate null players but it does not necessarily allocate equal amounts to substitutable players. There are, however, allocations that grant them the same amount. This is the object of the following two propositions.

Proposition 4.4 *In a* core *allocation, a* null player *obtains a zero amount and a* dummy player *obtains his worth.*

Proof Consider a game (N, v), an allocation $x \in C(N, v)$ and a player $i \in N$. We know that

$$v(i) \leq x_i \leq v(N) - v(N \backslash i).$$

If player i is null, $v(i) = v(N) - v(N\backslash i) = 0$. Hence, using (4.10) $x_i = 0$. If player i is dummy, $v(i) = v(N) - v(N\backslash i)$. Hence, $x_i = v(i)$. ◆

Proposition 4.5 *If two players are substitutable in a game* (N, v) *whose* core *is nonempty, the* core *allocations obtained by exchanging their coordinates are also* core *allocations. Moreover, the* core *contains allocations that allocate equal amounts to* substitutable players.

Proof Assume that players 1 and 2 are substitutable in a game (N, v) and fix an allocation $x' \in C(N, v)$, i.e., $x'(S) \geq v(S)$ for all $S \subset N$. Construct the allocation x'' as follows:

$$x''_1 = x'_2 \text{ and } x''_2 = x'_1,$$
$$x''_i = x'_i \text{ for all } i \neq 1, 2.$$

Fix a coalition $S \subset N$. If $\{1, 2\} \subset S$ or if $1, 2 \notin S$, we have $x''(S) = x'(S) \geq v(S)$. If instead $1 \in S$ and $2 \notin S$, we have:

$$x''(S) = x'(S\backslash 1) + x'_2 = x'((S \cup 2)\backslash 1) \geq v((S \cup 2)\backslash 1).$$

The last inequality follows from the fact that $x' \in C(N, v)$. Player 1 and 2 being substitutable players, we have $v((S \cup 2)\backslash 1) = v((S \cup 2)\backslash 2) = v(S)$. Hence $x''(S) \geq v(S)$ for all $S \subset N$.

To prove the second part of the proposition, we use the fact that the core is a convex set: it contains the line segment joining x' and x'' and in particular its mid-point $x = (x' + x'')/2$. By construction, $x_1 = x_2$. ◆

Last but not least, the core is a *covariant* solution concept: if the games (N, v) and (N, w) are strategically equivalent, i.e., $w(S) = a\, v(S) + b(S)$ for some $a > 0$ and $b \in \mathbb{R}^n$, we have:

$$x \in C(N, v) \text{ and } y_i = a\, x_i + b_i \ (i = 1, \ldots, n) \Rightarrow y \in C(N, w).$$

Indeed, if $x(S) \geq v(S)$ for all $S \subset N$, we have:

$$y(S) = a\, x(S) + b(S) \geq a\, v(S) + b(S) = w(S) \text{ for all } S \subset N.$$

The covariance property of the core is an immediate consequence of the fact that the core is defined by linear inequalities.

Competitive forces and the core

Shubik (1959) was the first to point out that the notion of core had been anticipated by Edgeworth (1881), in the *non*-transferable utility framework of an exchange economy as defined in Example 2.4. Edgeworth has indeed shown that the allocation that is associated to a price equilibrium between demand and supply belongs to the core:

competitive equilibria are core allocations. The ability of the core to highlight the competitive forces that are underlying a given situation is confirmed by the land game (Example 4.2), especially in the case where the two buyers have the same reservation price. The following game offers another example based on perfectly complementary goods.

Example 4.6 Gloves Market (Shapley, 1955). Consider four players. The first two own one left-hand glove each, the third owns one right-hand glove while the last one owns *two* right-hand gloves: (*L, L, R, RR*). Assuming that players can trade, the worth of a coalition is given by the number of pairs it is able to form. Hence, together, they have two pairs to share and the characteristic function is given by:

$$v(1) = v(2) = v(3) = v(4) = v(1,2) = v(3,4) = 0,$$
$$v(1,3) = v(1,4) = v(2,3) = v(2,4) = v(1,2,3) = v(1,3,4) = v(2,3,4) = 1,$$
$$v(1,2,4) = v(1,2,3,4) = 2.$$

Core allocations (x_1, x_2, x_3, x_4) are such that $x_1 + x_2 + x_3 + x_4 = 2$ and

$$x_1 + x_3 \geq 1, \ x_1 + x_4 \geq 1,$$
$$x_2 + x_3 \geq 1, \ x_2 + x_4 \geq 1,$$
$$x_1 + x_2 + x_4 \geq 2.$$

Redundant inequalities have been omitted. It is easily verified that, together, these conditions define a *unique* allocation, namely $x = (1, 1, 0, 0)$. This is the *competitive allocation*: the excess supply of right-hand gloves drives their price down to zero. It is a situation of a *disadvantageous endowment*.

What happens if the first two players form a syndicate and act as a single player? The game associated to the gloves' distribution (*LL, RR, R*) is defined by the vector $v = (0, 0, 0 \mid 2, 1, 0 \mid 2)$ and core allocations are of the form $(1+\alpha, 1-\alpha, 0)$ where $0 \leq \alpha \leq 1$. The owner of a single glove is still excluded from the market. In the absence of transfers, the core contains only two allocations, (2, 0, 0) and (1, 1, 0), two solutions that account for indivisibility. The second player is necessarily penalized by the excess supply of right-hand gloves at the advantage of the left-hand owner.

However, player 2 does not have an interest in collusion.

Consider a different situation where each player owns only one type of glove, with ℓ left-hand glove owners and r left-hand glove owners. Hence there are $n = \ell + r$ players. If $r = \ell$, the total number of pairs is equal to ℓ and the core allocates α to each left-hand owner and $1-\alpha$ to each right-hand owner, where α is an arbitrary real number between 0 and 1. Indeed, considering two players of different types, they are entitled to at least one pair. But they cannot be given more than one pair at the risk of upsetting the coalition of the other players who are entitled to at least $\ell - 1$ pairs. Finally, two players of the same type cannot be given different amounts. Indeed, if i and j are left-hand owners while k is the right-hand owner, we have $x_i + x_k = 1$ and $x_j + x_k = 1$, implying $x_i = x_j$. If transfers between players were excluded, there would be only two core allocations: one that allocates one pair to each left-hand owner and one that allocates one pair to each right-hand owner. If instead $r < \ell$, the core allocates one pair to each right-hand glove owner and nothing to the others. Indeed, if i is a left-hand owner, we have $v(N) = v(N \backslash i) = r$ implying $x_i = 0$.

Non-emptiness of the core

Superadditivity is definitely not sufficient to guarantee the existence of core allocations. Superadditivity is not even a necessary condition. The non-emptiness of the core of a game (N, v) implies that we have[15]:

$$\sum_{h=1}^{m} v(S_h) \leq v(N) \text{ for all } \textit{partitions } (S_1, \ldots, S_m) \text{ of } N.$$

Indeed, we have: $v(N) = x(N) = \sum_{h=1}^{m} x(S_h) \geq \sum_{h=1}^{m} v(S_h)$.

There is a general theorem that provides *necessary and sufficient* conditions for the existence of core allocations. It was obtained independently by Bondareva (1963) and Shapley (1967). These conditions define the class of games that have nonempty core, called *balanced games*.

In the case of three players, balancedness boils down to the following five conditions:

$$\begin{aligned}
v(1, 2, 3) &\geq v(1) + v(2) + v(3), \\
v(1, 2, 3) &\geq v(1, 2) + v(3), \\
v(1, 2, 3) &\geq v(1, 3) + v(2), \\
v(1, 2, 3) &\geq v(2, 3) + v(1), \\
v(1, 2) + v(1, 3) + v(2, 3) &\leq 2\, v(1, 2, 3).
\end{aligned}$$

Superadditivity covers the first four inequalities. Hence, we are left with a single condition for superadditive games, namely:

$$v(1, 2) + v(1, 3) + v(2, 3) \leq 2\, v(1, 2, 3). \tag{4.11}$$

It is obtained by adding the three core inequalities

$$\begin{aligned}
x_1 + x_2 &\geq v(1, 2), \\
x_1 + x_3 &\geq v(1, 3), \\
x_2 + x_3 &\geq v(2, 3).
\end{aligned}$$

[15] This is a property known as *cohesiveness*. It results from superadditivity.

Hence, the core is nonempty if coalitions of intermediary size are not too powerful. For instance, in the luggage game (Example 4.1) or the equivalent simple majority voting game (Example 4.4), the coalitions of size 2 are too powerful: the sum of their values exceeds 2. In the land game (Example 4.2) instead, the inequality is verified. The role of intermediary size coalitions appears clearly in symmetric games. If f is the function of coalition size that defines the characteristic function v on N, we have $v(S) = f(s)$ and the core conditions read:

$$x(N) = f(n) \text{ and } x(S) \geq f(s) \text{ for all } S \subset N.$$

Clearly, if the core is nonempty, it contains the equal division allocation. Equal division belongs to the core if the following inequalities are satisfied

$$s\frac{f(n)}{n} \geq f(s) \Leftrightarrow \frac{f(s)}{s} \leq \frac{f(n)}{n}. \quad \text{for all } s = 1, 2, \ldots, n-1.$$

Graphically, it means that the point $(n, f(n))$ is visible from the origin, as shown in Fig. 4.8.

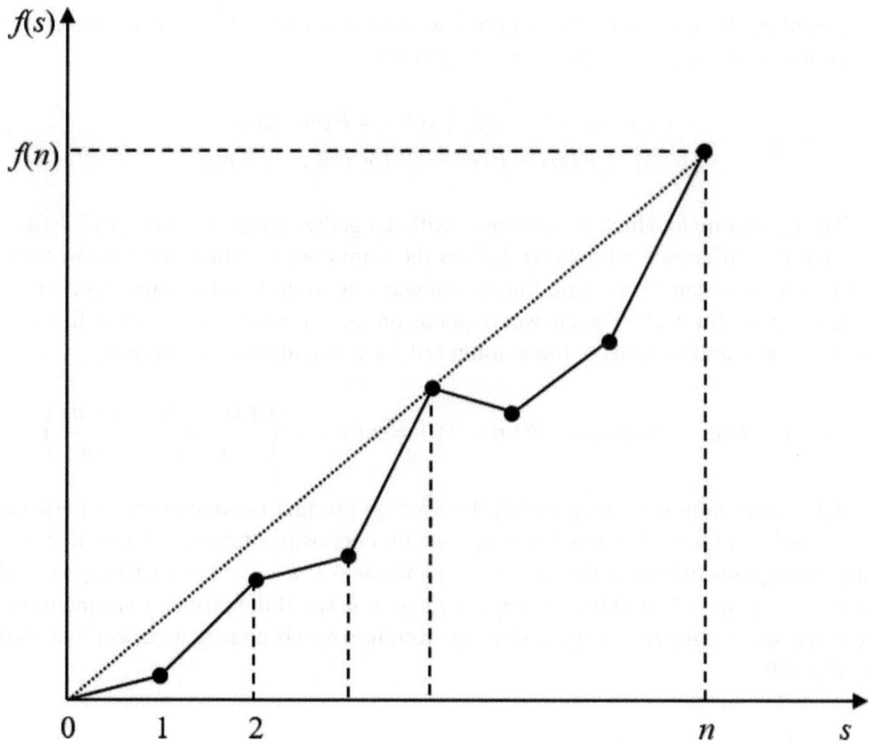

Fig. 4.8 Visibility of the point $(n, f(n))$

To quote Shubik (1982, p. 150), this illustrates "*how the existence of a* core *depends on the relative weakness of coalitions of intermediary size*". This condition is not met in the garbage game once $n \geq 3$.

Some subclasses of game have a nonempty core. The following proposition due to Shapley (1971) tells us that convex games are balanced.

Proposition 4.6 *Convex games have a nonempty* core.

Example 4.4 (continued) We have seen that the crop game is convex when returns to scale are increasing or constant. Actually, its core is always nonempty: the allocation $x = (F(m), 0, \ldots, 0)$ that gives to the landowner the totality of the crop is indeed always a core allocation. Workers have no way to object. Its core can be defined by the maximum wage a worker can hope to obtain. Let x be a core allocation and consider the coalition $T = N\backslash 2$. Its worth is $F(m-1)$, the minimum it is entitled to. Hence, we have:

$$x(T) \geq F(m-1),$$
$$x(T) + x_2 = x(N) = F(m).$$

Together, these two elements imply that the marginal product $F(m) - F(m-1)$ is the maximum wage and the core can be written as:

$$C(N, v) = \{x \in \mathbb{R}^n_+ \mid x(N) = F(m) \text{ and } x_i \leq F(m) - F(m-1) \text{ for } i = 2, \ldots, n\}.$$

The maximum to which workers are entitled together is equal to $m(F(m) - F(m-1))$ and the difference with $F(m)$ defines the minimum to which the landowner is entitled to. But can we be sure that it is always possible to remunerate workers at their marginal product? The answer depends on the form of the production function between m–1 and m. Indeed, the amount left for the landowner is given by:

$$b(m) = F(m) - m(F(m) - F(m-1)\,) = m(m-1)\left(\frac{F(m-1)}{m-1} - \frac{F(m)}{m}\right)$$

This expression is nonnegative if the average product is nonincreasing between m – 1 and m. Figures 4.9 and 4.10 illustrate two opposite situations.[16] Consider the line passing through the points $(m, F(m))$ and $(m-1, F(m-1))$. Its slope is equal to $F(m) - F(m-1)$ and its intercept is equal to $b(m)$. If the production function is concave (decreasing returns to scale), the minimum rent is nonnegative, as illustrated by Fig. 4.9.

[16] The scale has been deliberately overstretched.

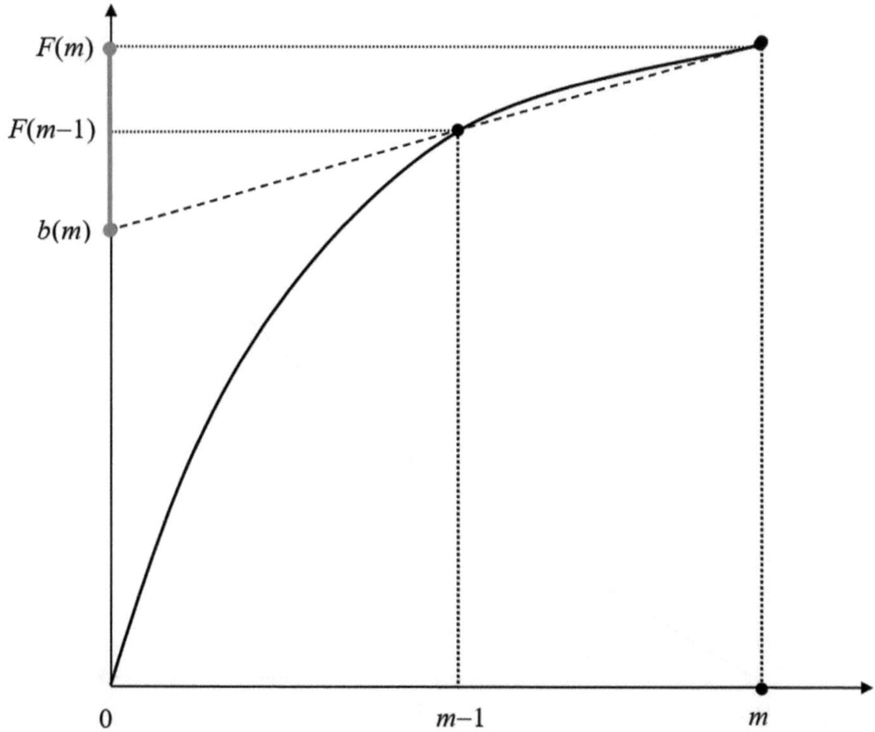

Fig. 4.9 Core of the crop game with decreasing returns

If instead the production function is convex, returns are increasing and $b(m) < 0$. It is then not possible to remunerate all workers at their marginal product and the minimum rent is equal to zero, as illustrated by Fig. 4.10. In this situation, the allocation that gives the total crop to the workers also belongs to the core. Actually, here the core coincides with the imputations set.

Symmetric core allocations are of the form $(r, w, \ldots, w)$ where $r = F(m) - m\,w$ is the landowner rent and the maximum wage is given by:

$$\overline{w} = Min\left(F(m) - F(m-1),\ \frac{F(m)}{m}\right).$$

Some classes of games have an empty core. This is the case of essential and constant sum games. A game is a *constant sum* if $v(S) + v(N\backslash S) = v(N)$ for all $S \subset N$. For instance, the luggage game (Example 4.1) is a constant sum game.

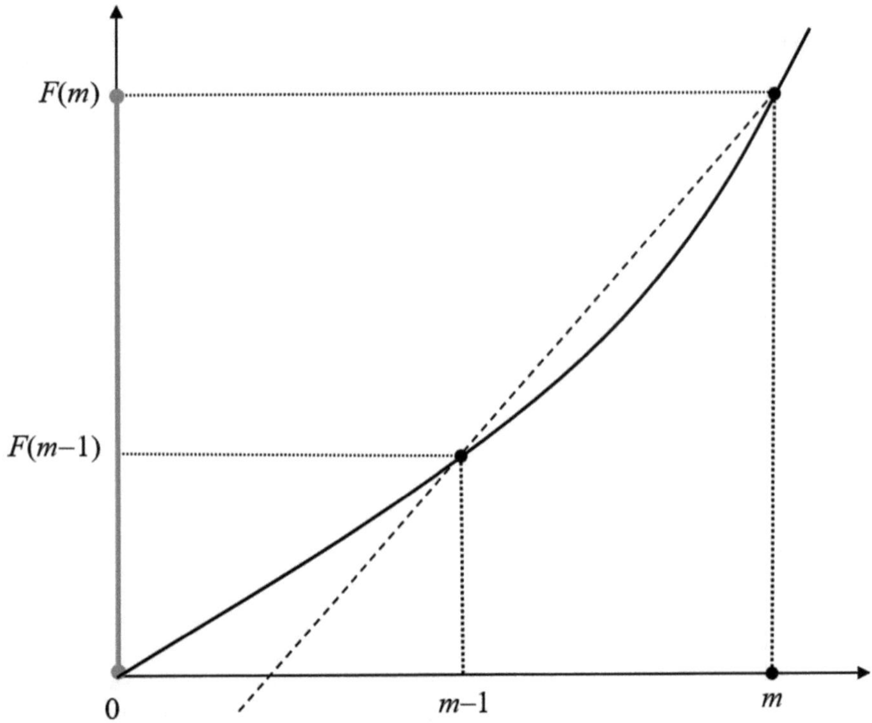

Fig. 4.10 Core of the crop game with increasing returns

Proposition 4.7 *A constant sum game has a nonempty* core if and only if *it is inessential.*

Proof Consider a constant sum game (N, v). If x is a core allocation, we have $x(S) \geq v(S)$ and $x(N \backslash S) \geq v(N \backslash S)$ for all $S \subset N$. Adding these two inequalities, we get:

$$v(N) = x(N) \geq v(S) + v(N \backslash S) = v(N) \quad \text{for all } S \subset N.$$

Hence, we must have equality: $x(S) = v(S)$ for all $S \subset N$. In particular, $x(i) = v(i)$ for all $i \in N$, i.e., the game (N, v) is inessential. The reverse is trivially true: an inessential game is a constant sum. ◆

Alternative proof

We know that in core allocations, no player can obtain more than his marginal contribution to the grand coalition. Hence, if x is a core allocation, we have:

$$v(i) \leq x_i \leq v(N) - v(N \backslash i) \quad \text{for all } i \in N.$$

The game being constant sum, we have $v(N\backslash i) + v(i) = v(N)$. Hence, $x_i = v(i)$. ◆

In this chapter, we will see that the core of a simple game is always empty except if at least one player has a *veto right*: there exists a player i such that $v(S) = 0$ for all S not containing i.

Geometric characterization of the core of a convex game
When nonempty, the core has an interesting geometric structure as can be observed by looking at the core represented in Fig. 4.6.

Proposition 4.8 *The* core *of a balanced n player game is a* bounded *and* convex set *whose maximal dimension is equal to n –1.*

Proof Applied to individual players, the inequalities (4.9) reduces to $v(i) \leq x_i \leq v(N) - v(i)$ for all i. Core allocations are therefore bounded. Because the core is defined by *linear* inequalities, convexity follows. Indeed, considering two core allocations x^1, $x^2 \in C(N, v)$, their convex combination $x = \lambda x^1 + (1 - \lambda)x^2$ where $\lambda \in [0, 1]$ verifies the core inequalities:

$$x^k(S) \geq v(S),\ k = 1, 2 \ \Rightarrow\ x(S) \geq \lambda v(S) + (1 - \lambda)v(S) = v(S).$$

Finally, because the equation $x(N) = v(N)$ must be satisfied, one dimension is lost and, as a consequence, the core dimension cannot exceed $n - 1$. ◆

Core allocations satisfy the following inequalities that define half-spaces:

$$\sum_{i \in S} x_i \geq v(S) \text{ for all } S \subsetneq N.$$

As a consequence, the core is an intersection, possibly empty, of half-spaces: it is a *polyhedral set*. Because it is also bounded, it is actually a *polytope.*[17] This is well illustrated by Fig. 4.6.

When applied to a convex game, we know that the core is nonempty (Proposition 4.6). It turns out that its vertices can be characterized.

Let's denote by Π_N the set of all orderings (permutations) $\sigma = (i_1, ..., i_n)$ of the n players. To each ordering $\sigma \in \Pi_N$, we associate the vector of marginal contributions $\mu^\sigma(N, v)$ defined by:

$$\begin{aligned}
&\mu^\sigma_{i_1}(N, v) = v(i_1) - v(\emptyset) = v(i_1),\\
&\mu^\sigma_{i_k}(N, v) = v(i_1, ..., i_k) - v(i_1, ..., i_{k-1}) \quad (k = 2, ..., n - 1),\\
&\mu^\sigma_{i_n}(N, v) = v(N) - v(N\backslash i_n).
\end{aligned} \tag{4.12}$$

[17] See the Mathematical appendix for more details.

The idea is to follow the order $(i_1, \ldots, i_n)$, allocating successively the marginal contribution of the next player. There are $n!$ orderings and therefore $n!$ vectors although not necessarily distinct.

First observation: the marginal contribution vectors are allocations:

$$\mu^{\sigma}(N, v) \in X(N, v) \quad \text{for all} \quad \sigma \in \Pi_N.$$

Indeed, $\sum_{i \in N} \mu_i^{\sigma}(N, v) = v(N)$ for all $\pi \in \Pi_N$ by construction.

Second observation: marginal contribution vectors are imputations:

$$\mu^{\sigma}(N, v) \in I(N, v) \text{ for all } \sigma \in \Pi_N.$$

Indeed, by superadditivity, the marginal contributions of a player cannot exceed his individual worth.

Example 4.2 (continued) Table 4.1 contains the marginal contribution vectors of the land game. There are four distinct vectors.

Example 4.3 (continued) Table 4.2 contains the marginal contribution vectors of the voting game where simple majority applies and player 1 has a veto right. There are three distinct marginal contribution vectors.

We already know that the core is a convex polyhedral set, actually a polytope. The following remarkable result is due to Shapley (1971).

Table 4.1 Marginal contribution vectors of the land game

π	1	2	3
123	100	100	100
132	100	0	200
213	200	0	100
231	300	0	0
312	300	0	0
321	300	0	0

Table 4.2 Marginal contribution vectors of the simple majority game with veto

π	1	2	3
123	0	1	0
132	0	0	1
213	1	0	0
231	1	0	0
312	1	0	0
321	1	0	0

Proposition 4.9 *The vertices of the* core *of a convex game are precisely the marginal contribution vectors.*

Ichiishi (1981) has shown that the converse is also true, hence the following proposition.

Proposition 4.10 *A game is convex* if and only if *its* core *is the* convex polyhedral set *whose* vertices *are the* marginal contribution vectors.

The convex hull of the marginal contribution vectors defines what is called the *Weber set*, a concept introduced by Weber (1988) who proved that it always contains the core. Both sets coincide when applied to convex games. Hence, a game is convex if (and only if) all marginal contribution vectors are core allocation. Once such a vector is not a core allocation, we can conclude that the underlying game is not convex.

Example 4.4 (continued) Table 4.3 gives the marginal contribution vectors of the crop games with two workers. There are five distinct vectors. Figure 4.11 shows the

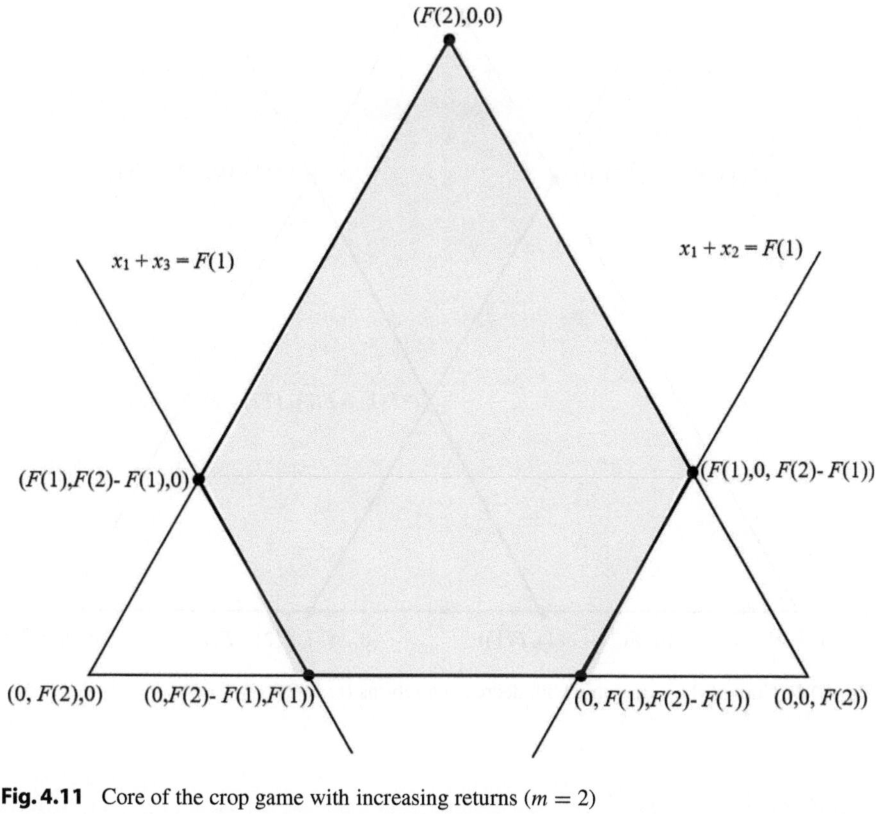

Fig. 4.11 Core of the crop game with increasing returns ($m = 2$)

Table 4.3 Marginal contribution vectors of the crop game

π	1	2	3
123	0	$F(1)$	$F(2) - F(1)$
132	0	$F(2) - F(1)$	$F(1)$
213	$F(1)$	0	$F(2) - F(1)$
231	$F(2)$	0	0
312	$F(1)$	$F(2) - F(1)$	0
321	$F(2)$	0	0

core of the crop game under the assumption of increasing returns, $F(2) > 2F(1)$. The five vertices correspond to the five distinct marginal contribution vectors. They all belong to the core, confirming the convexity.

Figure 4.12 shows the core of the crop game under the assumption of decreasing returns, $F(2) < 2F(1)$. We observe that the core is contained in the Weber set.

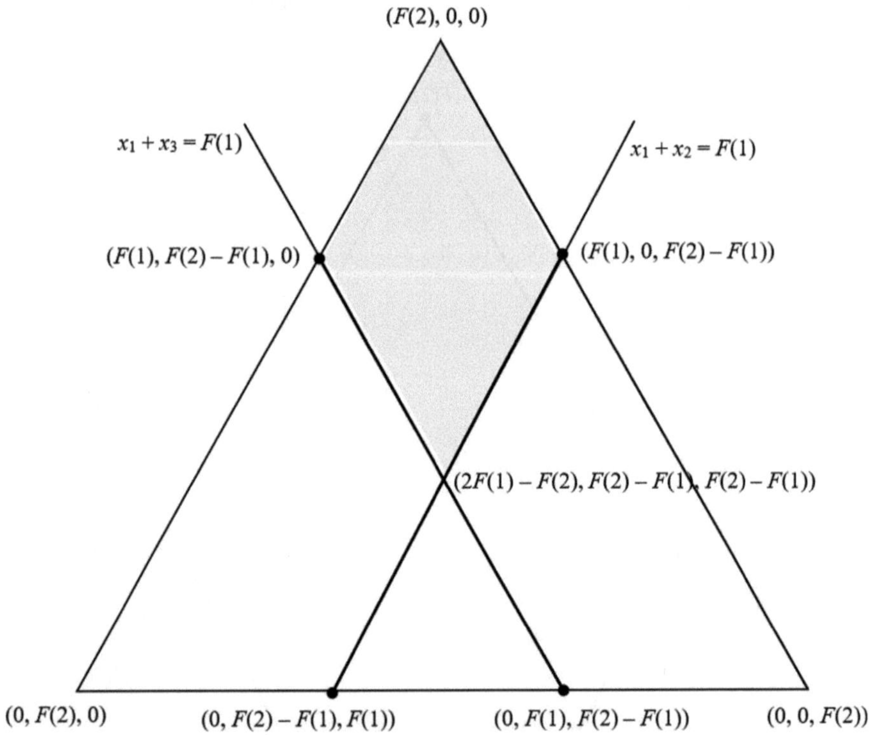

Fig. 4.12 Core of the crop game with decreasing returns ($m = 2$)

Other examples of convex games will be considered later, in particular in the framework of applications, as solving a bankruptcy, computing landing fees or royalties and dividing damage.

Justified objections: the bargaining set *

Consider a game (N, v). We have seen that an objection to an allocation x is defined by a pair (S, y) such that $S \neq \emptyset$, $y(S) \leq v(S)$ and $y_i > x_i$ for all $i \in S$. The core is then the set of allocations against which there is no objection.

The absence of restrictions on objections is one reason for the emptiness of the core. The concept of bargaining set addresses this issue by introducing the possibility of counter-objections.

There are several definitions. The first definition is due to Aumann and Maschler (1964) who use objections between players. Here we shall retain the simpler and more natural definition that has been proposed by Mas-Colell (1989), based on objections between coalitions.

A *counter-objection* formulated against an objection (S, y), itself formulated against an allocation x, is defined by a pair (T, z) where $T \neq S$ and $z \in \mathbb{R}^n$ such that:

$$\begin{aligned} &\text{(a)} \quad z(T) \leq v(T), \\ &\text{(b)} \quad z_i > y_i \quad \text{for all } i \in T \cap S, \\ &\text{(c)} \quad z_i > x_i \quad \text{for all } i \in T \backslash S. \end{aligned} \tag{4.13}$$

A coalition T formulates a counter-objection that is (a) *feasible* for coalition T, (b) *better* than the objection for the players concerned ($i \in T \cap S$) and (c) *better* than the initial allocation for the players joining the coalition ($i \in T \setminus S$).[18] An objection is said to be *justified* if it faces no counter-objection.

Notice that the coalition engaged in the counter-objection may not include members of the coalition engaged in the objection. The case $T \cap S = \emptyset$ is indeed not excluded, in which case a counter-objection is just an alternative objection.[19]

The *bargaining set* is the set of imputations against which there is no justified objection: any objection is the object of a counter-objection. The bargaining set contains the core, because the latter contains all the allocations against which there is no objection. Under superadditivity, the bargaining set is nonempty.[20] We could go further by excluding a counter-objection because it is the object of another counter-objection, and so on, leading to a chain of counter-objections. This idea was used by Dutta et al. (1989) to define what they call the *coherent bargaining set*.

---

[18] Here we have adopted the modification proposed by Shimomura (1997) that consists in requiring *strict* inequalities in objections and counter-objections, a choice that is more appropriate.

[19] The question of the intersection between the coalition formulating an objection and the coalition formulating the counter-objection is not insignificant. Some definition imposes that this intersection be nonempty.

[20] See for instance Vohra (1991) or Einy, Holzman and Monderer (1999).

Example 4.1 (continued) We know that the core of the luggage game is empty. However, there are no justifiable objections against the egalitarian allocation $x = (2, 2, 2)$. No player alone is able to object. What about 2-player coalitions? The objection $y = (3, 3, 0)$ formulated by coalition $S = \{1, 2\}$ is not justified because the coalition $T = \{1, 3\}$ can formulate the counter-objection $z = (3.5, 0, 2.5)$. More generally, using the property of real numbers according to which, however close to 4 is α, there is a real β between α and 4, such that objections of the form $y = (a, 6 - a, 0)$ where $2 < a < 4$ call for counter-objections of the form $z = (b, 0, 6-b)$ where $a < b < 4$.

Actually, the bargaining set is the set of imputations such that no player receives 3 or more, as shown in Fig. 4.13. To prove this statement, let us first consider an allocation x such that $x_i < 3$ for all i. Any 2-player coalition, say $S = \{2, 3\}$, can object by proposing an allocation y such that $y_2 + y_3 = 6 > x_2 + x_3$. Clearly, y_2 and y_3 cannot both exceed 3. Assume $y_2 \leq 3$ so that $x_1 + y_2 < 6$. The coalition $T = \{1, 2\}$ is then in a position to counter-object by proposing an allocation z such that $z_1 + z_2 = 6$, $z_1 > x_1$ and $z_2 > y_2$. Hence, all possible objections face a counter-objection.

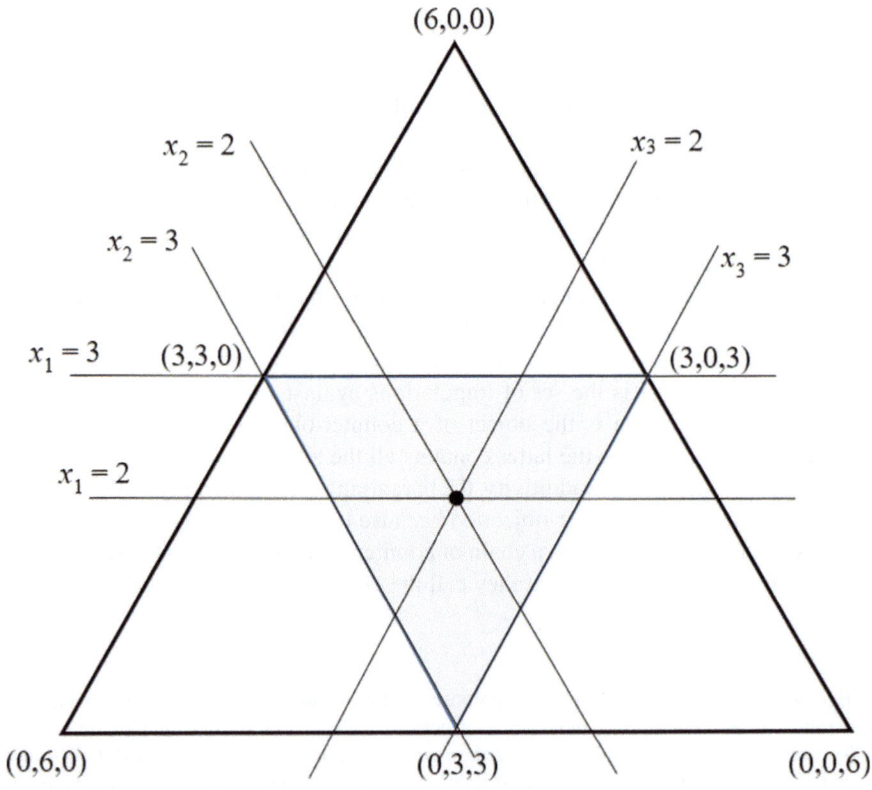

Fig. 4.13 Bargaining set of the luggage game

It remains to show that any allocation that grants 3 or more to a player cannot be in the bargaining set. Consider an allocation x in which player 1 gets $3 + \alpha$ for some $\alpha \geq 0$. The other players then get together $3 - \alpha$ and are in a position to object with $y = (0, 3, 3)$. There is no credible counter-objection against y. Indeed, if player 1 forms a coalition with one of the other two players, say $T = \{1, 2\}$, they cannot achieve a feasible allocation z: it should be such that $z_1 > 3+\alpha$ and $z_2 > 3$, an impossibility.

Dutta et al. (1989) prove that the bargaining set and the core coincide in the convex case. This is true whether strict inequalities are used in (4.13) or not. With strict inequalities, there is a stronger result due to Izquiero and Rafels (2012).

Proposition 4.11 *The* bargaining set *coincides with the* core if and only if *the game is convex.*

4.3 Fairness: The Shapley Value

Fairness and value
The Shapley value
Axiomatic foundations of the Shapley value
Properties of the Shapley value
The Shapley value as a distribution of dividends *.

The approach followed by Shapley in the early 1950s differs from the one we have followed until now. As for the Nash solution to the bargaining problem, it consists of formulating a number of axioms that, taken together, define a *unique allocation rule* φ that associates an allocation $x = \varphi(N, v)$ to any given game (N, v). It is a compromise, known as the Shapley value. It requires that the players adhere to the axioms that underlie the rule. Except for some classes of games, the Shapley value has no link to the core, the latter being a concept that does not involve any value judgment.[21]

Fairness and value

"*At the foundation of the theory of games is the assumption that a player can evaluate in terms of his* utility *scale every situation that can result from a play of a game*", a quotation from Shapley (1951).[22] It confirms that the concept of value was initially intended to measure what a player may reasonably expect from playing a game. That point of view raises the question of efficiency: nothing guarantees that the evaluations of the players are consistent. Here we shall adopt a different point of

[21] The core has been axiomatized by Peleg (1986). See also Chapter 13 of the *Handbook of game theory*, vol. 1.

[22] This is a sentence extracted from a Rand Research Memorandum published in August 1951, anticipating one of the results contained in Shapley's PhD dissertation defended in March 1953 at the Department of Mathematics of the University of Princeton.

view, of a normative nature, with fair division in mind. This implies that efficiency will be assumed to hold from the start.

Fairness is a concept that is not easy to formalize. We may refer to the well-known Aristotelian general principle "*Equals should be treated equally and unequals should be treated unequally in proportion to similarities and differences*". Equal treatment between equals is a clear principle that any reasonable allocation mechanism must obey. The second part of Aristotle's sentence that concerns the unequals is not so clear. Applied to a cooperative framework, it says that participants in a collective enterprise must be compensated according to their contributions, a widely accepted principle. It requires that the contributions can be identified and measured. The sentence uses the term "proportionally" but it is not necessarily to be taken literally.

In the framework of cooperative games with transferable utility, the contributions of a player are measured by his marginal contributions. Two players are then considered to be equal if they are substitutable and there is no external reason to differentiate them. An equal remuneration must then apply to players with identical marginal contributions. This is the *symmetry axiom*. The difficult question concerns the remuneration of the unequals. We will see that it is enough to know how to remunerate null players. Their marginal contributions are null and, therefore, they do not deserve remuneration according to the contribution principle. This is the *null player axiom*.

Beyond these two axioms, there is a "hidden axiom" according to which the outcome resulting from the allocation rule should depend only on the characteristic function, and not on any other elements. The characteristic function is often a reduced form and "*the hidden 'domain' axiom... demands that we shut our eyes to the structural detail that stands behind the* characteristic function" to quote Shapley (1981a, p. 132). It implies that two different game situations, giving rise to identical characteristic functions, should produce identical outcomes. Moreover, there is an implicit requirement of existence and uniqueness: we only consider rules that associate one and only one allocation to any given game.

Many allocation rules do satisfy the efficiency, symmetry and null player axioms. Additional axioms are therefore required to eventually single out a unique allocation rule. Shapley (1953) shows that only one additional (and simple) axiom is actually needed to characterize a unique rule, namely *additivity*. It says that, when confronted to different games on a *common set of players*, a player evaluates them independently of each other. The remuneration of a player in the game obtained by adding the characteristic functions equals the sum of the remunerations obtained in each individual game. It is an independence axiom that makes the value a linear operator. Shapley (1981b, p. 59) insists on the fact that violations of additivity can often result from violation of the hidden axiom.

The contribution principle may be pushed further by imposing that a player's remuneration depends *exclusively* on his contributions, independently of the contributions of the other players. More precisely, a player having equal marginal contributions in two different games should be remunerated equally. This is the *marginalist axiom*. It is an independence axiom, like the additivity axiom. Replacing the additivity axiom with the marginalist axiom produces the Shapley value. *Monotonicity* is an equivalent principle. It requires that if a game is modified in such a way that the marginal contributions of a given player do not decrease, his remuneration should not decrease, independently of the changes affecting the marginal contributions of the other players. These alternative axioms have been proposed by Young (1985a).

Balanced contributions is another axiom that covers the effect of a player leaving a game. It requires that players should gain (or lose) the same amount from cooperating: *what I lose if you leave the game should be equal to what you lose if I leave the game.* Together with efficiency, balanced contributions characterize the Shapley value, a remarkable result due to Myerson (1980).

Other axiomatizations have been proposed. For instance, Béal and Navarro (2020) have replaced the symmetry and the null player axioms by requiring that players without whom a coalition is unproductive be treated equally.

The Shapley value

Consider the following procedure: a players' ordering is picked up at random and each player then obtains his marginal contribution, depending on his position in the ordering. This produces an allocation that corresponds to the marginal contribution vector associated to that ordering, defined in (4.12). To be fair, all orderings must be possible and equiprobable. In *expected terms*, each player obtains his *average* marginal contribution. This procedure defines a rule called the *Shapley value*:

$$SV_i(N, v) = \frac{1}{n!} \sum_{\sigma \in \Pi_N} \mu_i^{\sigma}(N, v) \quad i = 1, \ldots, n. \tag{4.14}$$

Because marginal contribution vectors are imputations, the Shapley value defines an imputation. Notice that the Shapley value generally differs from the simple average of the marginal contribution vectors that we denote by $AV(N, v)$. Coincidence occurs only in the case where the marginal contribution vectors are distinct or all have the same multiplicity.

There is an alternative formulation that consists in allocating to each player his expected marginal contribution to a coalition chosen at random, knowing that coalitions of the same size are equally likely and coalitions' size have the same probability to occur.

The number of coalitions of size s that contain a given player is equal to the number of combinations of s–1 elements taken in a set of n–1 elements:

$$\mu_n(s) = C_{n-1}^{s-1} = \frac{(n-1)!}{(s-1)!(n-s)!}.$$

The probability to pick up a coalition of size s containing a given player is then given by $1/\mu_n(s)$ and all sizes have the same probability, namely $1/n$. The product of these two probabilities is given by:

$$\alpha_n(s) = \frac{(s-1)!(n-s)!}{n!}.$$

It turns out that the Shapley value can equivalently be written as:

$$SV_i(N,v) = \sum_{\substack{S \subset N \\ i \in s}} \alpha_n(s)(v(S) - v(S \backslash i)) \quad (i = 1, ..., n). \tag{4.15}$$

Actually, there is no need to restrict the sum to coalitions including player i since the marginal contributions are zero for coalitions that do not include player i.

Proposition 4.12 *The definitions* (4.14) *and* (4.15) *of the Shapley value are equivalent.*

Proof Let S_i^σ us denote the set of players who precede player i in the ordering σ, i included. The expression (4.14) then becomes.

$$SV_i(N,v) = \frac{1}{n!} \sum_{\sigma \in \Pi_N} \left(v(S_i^\sigma) - v(S_i^\sigma \backslash i)\right).$$

For all coalitions $S \subset N$, there are $(s-1)!(n-s)!$ orderings such that $S_i^\sigma = S$. We then retrieve the second formulation (4.15):

$$SV_i(N,v) = \frac{1}{n!} \sum_{S \subset N} (s-1)!(n-s)!(v(S) - v(S \backslash i)) \quad (i = 1, ..., n). \quad \blacklozenge$$

The coefficients α_n are functions of coalition size. Looking at Table 4.4, we observe that the weighting $\alpha_n(s)$ favors coalitions of small or large sizes against coalitions of intermediate sizes. However, one must consider the number of coalitions containing a given player. These numbers are given by given by $\mu_n(s)$, as given in Table 4.4.

We observe that the weighting is uniform: $\alpha_n(s)\mu_n(s) = 1/n$ for all s.

What the Shapley value allocates to player i can be seen as the average of the average marginal contribution: for each coalition size, compute the average marginal contribution given the number of coalitions of that size that contain player i, and then compute the average of these averages.

Table 4.4 $\alpha_n(s)$, $\mu_n(s)$

	$s = 1$	$s = 2$	$s = 3$	$s = 4$	$s = 5$
$n = 2$	1/2, 1	1/2, 1			
$n = 3$	1/3, 1	1/6, 2	1/3, 1		
$n = 4$	1/4, 1	1/12, 3	1/12, 3	1/4, 1	
$n = 5$	1/5, 1	1/20, 4	1/30, 6	1/20, 4	1/5, 1

Table 4.5 Marginal contributions of the simple majority game with veto

	1	2	3	
$\{1, 2\}$	1	1	0	1/6
$\{1, 3\}$	1	0	1	1/6
$\{1, 2, 3\}$	1	0	0	1/3

For 2-player games, the Shapley value coincides with the equal division of the surplus (4.7):

$$SV_i(\{1, 2\}, v) = v(i) + \frac{1}{2}(v(1, 2) - v(1) - v(2)) \quad i = 1, 2.$$

Example 4.2 (continued) Table 4.1 lists the marginal contribution vectors of the land game. We apply (4.14): adding along columns and dividing the result by $3! = 6$, we obtain its Shapley value $SV(N, v) = (1300/6,\ 100/6,\ 400/6)$, approximately $(216.6,\ 16.7,\ 66.7)$.

We observe that player 2 is compensated by the other two players for his contribution. The compensation is low but recall that the core excludes any compensation in his favor. The Shapley value is not a core allocation: the coalition $\{1, 3\}$ is in a position to object.

Example 4.3 (continued) Table 4.2 lists the marginal contribution vectors of the voting game with simple majority and veto right. Its Shapley value $SV(N, v) = (2/3,\ 1/6,\ 1/6)$, approximately equals $(0.66,\ 0.17, 0.17)$. Table 4.5 lists the marginal contributions to *winning* coalitions. The last column lists the associated weights. It illustrates the alternative formulation (4.15).

Example 4.7 *Collusion of factor owners* (Hansen & Gabszewicz, 1972)
This example is an extension of the crop game (Example 4.4). We consider a technology, freely accessible, that produces a commodity (output) using *two production factors* (inputs). It is described by a production function $y = F(z_1, z_2)$, an increasing function in both arguments, such that $F(0, 0) = 0$.

There are n factor owners and the pair $(a_i, b_i) \in \mathbb{R}^2_+$ denotes the quantities of factors owned by player i. If a coalition forms, the endowments of its members are pooled. The characteristic function is then given by $v(S) = F(a(S), b(S))$ where $a(S)$ and $b(S)$ are the quantities of factors owned by coalition S.

The form of the production function, in particular the type of returns to scale, are important characteristics, as in the crop game. Consider the case of three factor owners and the production function $F(z_1, z_2) = z_1 + z_1 z_2$ that exhibits increasing returns to scale:

$$F(\lambda z_1, \lambda z_2) > \lambda F(z_1, z_2) \text{ for all } \lambda > 1.$$

Table 4.6 Marginal contribution vectors of the factor owners' game

	1	2	3
123	6	36	30
132	6	48	18
213	42	0	30
231	54	0	18
312	18	48	6
321	54	12	6
	180	144	108

If the endowments in inputs are (6, 0), (0, 6) and (2, 2) respectively, the characteristic function is given by:

$$v(1) = 6,\ v(1, 2) = 42,$$
$$v(2) = 0,\ v(1, 3) = 24,$$
$$v(3) = 6,\ v(2, 3) = 18,\ v(1, 2, 3) = 72.$$

The marginal contribution vectors are given in Table 4.6. Summing vertically and dividing by 6, we obtain the Shapley value: $SV(N, v) = (30,\ 24,\ 18)$.

Notice that the marginal contribution vectors are distinct. As a consequence, the Shapley value coincides with the average marginal contribution vector $AV(N, v)$. Using the alternative definition (4.10) contained in Proposition 4.3 that applies to 3-player games, the core is the set of allocations such that:

$$6 \le x_1 \le 54,$$
$$0 \le x_2 \le 48,$$
$$6 \le x_3 \le 30.$$

Referring to Proposition 4.10, Fig. 4.14 confirms that this game is convex: its vertices coincide with the marginal contribution vectors.[23]

[23] Distinct vectors is a characteristic of *strictly* convex games.

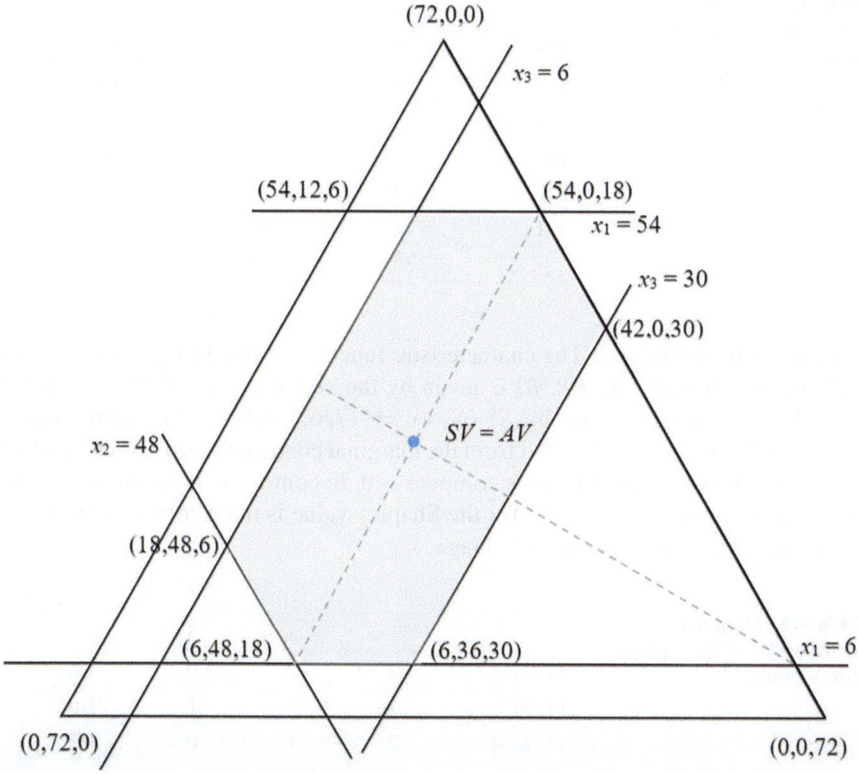

Fig. 4.14 Core of the factor owners' game

Example 4.8 The Square Game (Shapley, 1971) is defined by $v(S) = \left(\sum_{i \in S} i\right)^2$

It is a convex game, actually a *strictly* convex game: its marginal contribution vectors are all distinct. The Shapley value then coincides with the average marginal contribution vector.

In the 3-player case, the game is given by the vector (1, 1, 1 | 9, 16, 25 | 36). The marginal contribution vectors are given by Table 4.7 from which we deduce the Shapley value: $SV(N, v) = AV(N, v) = (6, 12, 18)$.

Table 4.7 Marginal contribution of the square game

	1	2	3
123	1	8	27
132	1	20	15
213	5	4	27
231	11	4	21
312	7	20	9
321	11	16	9
	36	72	108

Example 4.6 (continued) The characteristic function of the 3-player gloves game with the distribution (*LL, RR, R*) is given by the vector $v = (0, 0, 0 \mid 2, 1, 0 \mid 2)$. The Shapley value is given by $SV(N, v) = (7/6, 4/6, 1/6)$, approximately $(1.16, 0.67, 0.17)$. It is obtained from the marginal contributions listed in Table 4.8. We observe that the third player is compensated, in contrast to core allocations that are of the form $(1 + \alpha, 1 - \alpha, 0)$: the Shapley value is not a core allocation. The first players keep, however, an advantage.

Table 4.8 Marginal contributions of the 3-player gloves game

	1	2	3	
$\{1, 2\}$	2	2	0	1/6
$\{1, 3\}$	1	0	1	1/6
$\{1, 2, 3\}$	2	1	0	1/3

Example 4.6 (continued) Let's compute the Shapley value of the 4-player gloves game with the distribution (*L, L, R, RR*). Player 3 contributes 1 to the coalitions $\{1, 3\}$, $\{2, 3\}$ and $\{1, 2, 3\}$, and 0 to all the others. Given that the weight associated to coalitions of sizes 2 and 3 is equal to 1/12, we have $SV_3(N, v) = 1/4$. Player 4 contributes 1 to the coalitions $\{1, 4\}$, $\{2, 4\}$ and $\{1, 2, 3, 4\}$, and 2 to coalition $\{1, 2, 4\}$. Given that the weight associated to the grand coalition is equal to 1/4, we have $SV_4(N, v) = 7/12$.

Knowing that the sum must be equal to 2 and that the first two players are substitutable, the Shapley value is easily obtained: $(7/12, 7/12, 3/12, 7/12)$. We are far from the unique core allocation (1, 1, 0, 0) that does not recognize the role played by the right-hand glove owners. Without them, no pairs could be formed. Remember that monetary transfers between players are allowed.

Example 4.7 (continued) Consider the factor owners game with the production function

$$F(z_1, z_2) = z_1 + Min(0, z_2 - 2)$$

and the input endowments' (6, 0), (0, 6), (2, 2). The characteristic function is then given by

$$\begin{aligned} &v(1) = 6,\ v(1,2) = 10, \\ &v(2) = 4,\ v(1,3) = 8, \\ &v(3) = 2,\ v(2,3) = 8, \quad v(1,2,3) = 14. \end{aligned}$$

The core is defined by the following inequalities:

$$\begin{aligned} &6 \le x_1 \le 6 \Rightarrow x_1 = 6, \\ &4 \le x_2 \le 6, \\ &2 \le x_3 \le 4. \end{aligned}$$

There are two distinct marginal contribution vectors, (6, 4, 4) and (6, 6, 2), each with the same multiplicity, and the core is the line segment joining these two points. As a consequence, the game is convex and the Shapley value is located at the middle of the segment: $SV(N, v) = (6, 5, 3)$. Because marginal contribution vectors have the same multiplicity, it coincides with the average marginal contribution vector.

Example 4.4 (continued) What does the Shapley value prescribe in the crop game? As workers are substitutable, they are each entitled to an identical wage. It then suffices to compute the rent of the landowner.

We will use the formula (4.14) based on marginal contribution vectors. Looking at a particular players' ordering, we only have to look at the *position* of the landowner. If he is in position s, his marginal contribution is equal to $F(s-1)$. There are $n = m + 1$ different positions, all equiprobable. His Shapley value is therefore equal to the average marginal contribution vector computed in terms of his position:

$$SV_1(N, v) = \frac{1}{m+1}(F(0) + F(1) + F(2) + \ldots + F(m)) = \frac{1}{m+1}\sum_{s=1}^{m+1} F(s-1).$$

What remains is then uniformly distributed among the m workers.

This result is remarkable because it is independent of the shape of the production function. We have only required it to be an increasing function such that $F(0) = 0$.

It appears that we can approximate the share of the landowner by the size of the area located under the graph of the production function between 0 and m, the approximation improving with the number of workers. Hence the shape of the production function plays a role.

Figure 4.15 shows that the share of the landowner is greater (resp. smaller) than the share of the workers if returns to scale are everywhere decreasing (resp.

increasing). They are equal if returns to scale are everywhere constant. In the mixed case, it may be greater or smaller. Workers have a clear incentive to form a syndicate in the case where returns to scale are decreasing. Indeed, if the landowner had to face a syndicate, the result would be the equal division of the crop, more than in the absence of a syndicate.

Example 4.9 Sharing a Treasury. You have discovered a treasury. Although you only need the help of one person to extract it, you decide to ask m persons to come and help you. Assuming you are player 1, the associated game is given by:

$$\begin{aligned} v(S) &= 1 \quad \text{if } 1 \in S \text{ and } s \geq 2, \\ &= 0 \quad \text{otherwise.} \end{aligned}$$

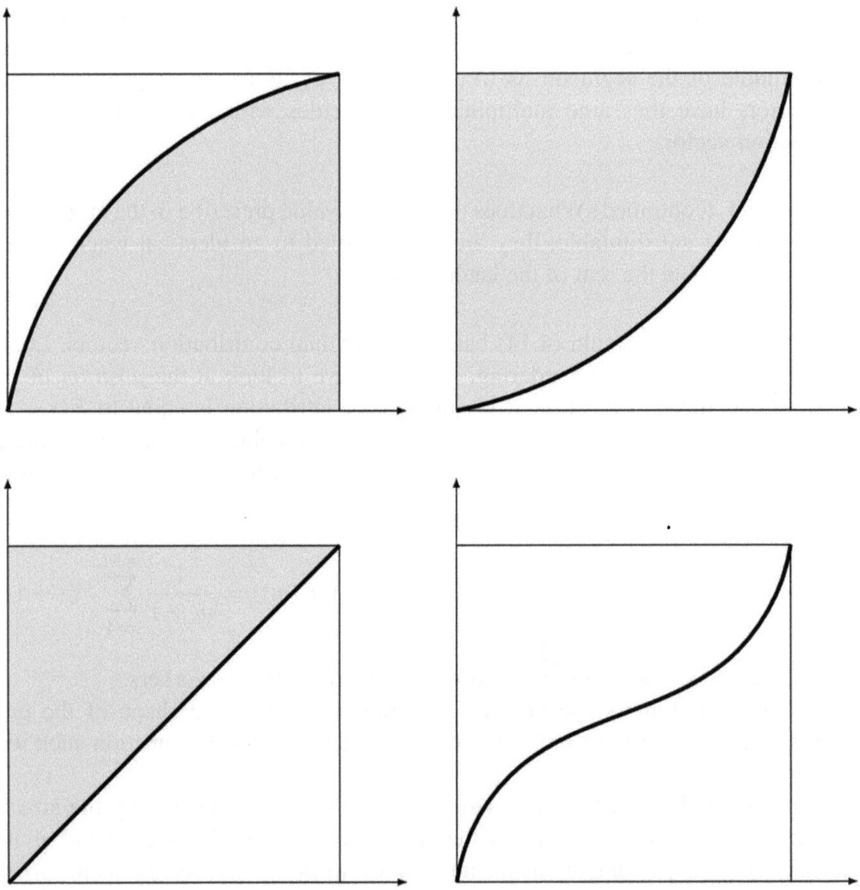

Fig. 4.15 Shapley shares of the landowner and workers in the crop game

In all the orderings in which you are *not* first, you get the total value of the treasury (normalized to 1). You are the first in $(n-1)!$ orderings. Hence, your share according to the Shapley value is given by:

$$1-\frac{(n-1)!}{n!}=1-\frac{1}{n}=1-\frac{1}{m+1}\quad\rightarrow\quad 1 \text{ as } m\rightarrow\infty.$$

You definitely have an interest in asking for help to as many persons as possible! Your share is indeed increasing in m and tends to 1 as m increases. This remains true if you need the help of k persons: if $k \leq m-1$, your share is equal to $1-k(n-1)!/n! = (m+1-k)/m+1$. In contrast, the core allocates you all, in all instances! Indeed, if we consider a player $i \neq 1$, we must have

$$\sum_{j\neq i} x_j \geq 1.$$

Combined with $\sum x_j = 1$, we get that $x_i = 0$. This applies to all $i \neq 1$ and the core then consists of the single allocation (1, 0, 0, ..., 0).

Axiomatic foundations of the Shapley value

Let's now investigate the axiomatic foundations of the Shapley value. An allocation rule is a mapping $\varphi : SG(N) \rightarrow \mathbb{R}^n$ that associates an allocation to any superadditive game. For each of the axiom that follows, we must read "*For all sets of players N* and superadditive games on *N*, *we only retain the allocation rules* φ *satisfying...*".

A1 *Efficiency*: $\sum_{i=1}^{n} \varphi_i(N, v) = v(N)$, i.e., $\varphi(N, v) \in X(N, v)$.

A2 *Symmetry* (equal treatment of substitutable players)[24]:
If i and j are substitutable in a game (N, v), then $\varphi_i(N, v) = \varphi_j(N, v)$.

A3 *Null player*: $\varphi_i(N, v) = 0$ if i is null in the game (N, v).

A4 *Additivity*: For all games $v_1, v_2 \in SG(N)$, $\varphi(N, v_1+v_2) = \varphi(N, v_1)+\varphi(N, v_2)$.

where the "game sum" $(N, v_1 + v_2)$ is simply defined by $v(S) = v_1(S) + v_2(S)$. Remember that adding characteristic functions preserves the property of superadditivity: the characteristic function $v = v_1 + v_2$ remains an element of the set *SG*(*N*).

Efficiency corresponds exactly to the requirement of collective rationality: an allocation rule must distribute the value of the game. Equal treatment of substitutable players and null players stem from the principles of fairness (equal treatment of equal) and contribution: an identical amount is given to substitutable players and null players are not compensated.

[24] Shapley has actually used a different but equivalent axiom, namely *anonymity*: if players' names are permuted, so are the players' payoffs. It simply means that the allocation does not depend on the name of the players.

Additivity is more difficult to interpret. It has to do with independence: a player involved in different games, together with the same players, is assumed to value these games independently. As a consequence, applying the allocation rule to the sum of games must produce an allocation that is the sum of the allocations resulting from the application of the rule to the original games. In Shapley's words "*The third axiom ("law of aggregation") states that when two independent games are combined, their values must be added player by player*" (1953, p. 309).

It is additivity that is responsible for the linear structure of the Shapley formula.

Many allocation rules satisfy the first three axioms. The simplest one consists of dividing equally the value of the game among its non-null players. What is remarkable is that adding the additivity axiom singles out a unique rule. It is the object of the following proposition due to Shapley (1953).

Proposition 4.13 *There is one and only one efficient allocation rule that satisfies* the axioms of symmetry, null player *and* additivity. *It is the* Shapley value.[25]

The Shapley value, as given by (4.15), allocates to each player i a weighted sum of his marginal contributions.[26] Considering its definition in terms of marginal contribution vectors, assume that a players' ordering is chosen randomly. Players then follow the ordering, arriving one after the other to receive their marginal contributions. Ex-ante, each player then obtains his expected marginal contribution as given by (4.14).

Referring to the formulations of the Shapley value, we observe that it is additive as a result of its linear structure. Furthermore, as only the marginal contributions appear, it automatically satisfies the symmetry and null player axioms.

Since the publication of Shapley's result, alternative axiomatizations have been proposed. Some try to avoid relying on additivity. Such an axiomatization, due to Young (1985a), is based on the notion of monotonicity. Among the many definitions of monotonicity, we retain the following one.

A5 *Monotonicity*: Given two games (N, v_1) and (N, v_2), if for some $i \in N$, $v_1(S) - v_1(S\backslash i) \geq v_2(S) - v_2(S\backslash i)$ for all $S \subset N$ then $\varphi_i(N, v_1) \geq \varphi_i(N, v_2)$.

Given two games on a common set of players, if a player never contributes less in the first than in the second, the allocation rule should not grant him less within the first game than in the second. Young proves that, together with the axioms of efficiency and symmetry, monotonicity suffices to characterize uniquely the Shapley value.

[25] The proof is postponed to the end of this section where the Shapley value is defined in terms of the Harsanyi dividends.

[26] Formally the sum is limited to the coalitions containing player i although it makes no difference. Indeed, if a player is not a member of a coalition, his marginal contribution is null.

Proposition 4.14 *There is one and only one efficient allocation rule that satisfies the axioms of* symmetry *and* monotonicity. *It is the* Shapley value.

A5 is a strong requirement: when comparing two games, what is taken into account for a given player are his marginal contributions, independently of the others' contributions. Hence, what the Shapley value allocates to a player depends exclusively on *his* marginal contributions and the relation is increasing. Hence, monotonicity implies the property of marginalism:

A6 *Marginalism:* Given two games (N, v_1) and (N, v_2), if for some $i \in N$, $v_1(S) - v_1(S\backslash i) = v_2(S) - v_2(S\backslash i)$ for all $S \subset N$, then $\varphi_i(N, v_1) = \varphi_i(N, v_2)$.

Given two games on a common set of players, if a player contributes identically in both games, the allocation rule should grant him identical amounts. It is easily seen that marginalism implies the null player axiom. If (N, v_2) is the *null game* defined by $v_2(S) = 0$ for all $S \subset N$, efficiency and symmetry together imply $\varphi_i(N, v_2) = 0$ for all $i \in N$. If now player i is null in the game (N, v_1), marginalism implies $\varphi_i(N, v_1) = 0$: the null player axiom is verified.

Another remarkable axiomatization, due to Myerson (1980), relies on the effect of removing a player. If player j drops out, the difference $\varphi_i(N, v) - \varphi_i(N\backslash j, v_{N\backslash j})$ measures the gain (or the loss) for player i.

A7 *Balanced contributions*: For all games (N, v) and all $i, j \in N$, $\varphi_i(N, v) - \varphi_i(N\backslash j, v_{N\backslash j}) = \varphi_j(N, v) - \varphi_j(N\backslash i, v_{N\backslash i})$.

where v_T is the restriction of v to the subset of players T: *what I lose if you leave the game should be equal to what you lose if I leave the game.*

Proposition 4.15 *There is one and only one efficient allocation rule that satisfies the axiom of* balanced contributions. *It is the* Shapley value.

Proof The proof is simple and proceeds by induction starting with a 2-player game and then adding players successively. Consider an allocation (x_1, x_2) of $v(1, 2)$. Balanced contributions then implies the following equality:

$$x_1 - v(1) = x_2 - v(2) \;\Leftrightarrow\; x_1 - x_2 = v(1) - v(2).$$

Combined with efficiency, it leads to the Shapley value of the game $(\{1, 2\}, v)$ that is given by the equal division of the surplus:

$$x_i = v(i) + \frac{1}{2}(v(1, 2) - v(1) - v(2)) \;\; i = 1, 2.$$

Adding a third player and applying balanced contributions, we obtain the following equalities:

$$x_1 - \left(v(1) + \frac{1}{2}(v(1, 3) - v(1) - v(3))\right)$$

$$= x_2 - \left(v(2) + \frac{1}{2}(v(2,3) - v(2) - v(3)) \right),$$

$$x_1 - \left(v(1) + \frac{1}{2}(v(1,2) - v(1) - v(2)) \right)$$

$$= x_3 - \left(v(3) + \frac{1}{2}(v(2,3) - v(2) - v(3)) \right).$$

Combining them with efficiency leads to the Shapley value of the game of a 3-player game. And so on... ◆

Béal and Navarro (2020) have reformulated the symmetry axiom using the concept of necessary players. Player i in *necessary* (or *veto*) in a game (N, v) if $v(S) = 0$ whenever $i \notin S$.

A8 *Equal treatment of necessary players* If players i and j are necessary in a game (N, v), then $\varphi_i(N, v) = \varphi_j(N, v)$.

Proposition 4.16 *There is one and only one efficient allocation rule that satisfies equal treatment of necessary players and additivity. It is the Shapley value.*

Notice that in games where individual worth is nonnegative, player i is necessary if and only if $v(N \backslash i) = 0$. This follows from Proposition 4.1 according to which these games are monotonic under superadditivity.

Properties of the Shapley value

The Shapley value meets all the properties used to define it. It defines an imputation by superadditivity, but nothing guarantees that it belongs to the core of balanced games, those games with a nonempty core. We have indeed seen a number of examples where the Shapley value could be improved upon by some coalitions.

There are, however, subclasses of balanced games whose Shapley value belongs to the core. This is the case of convex games. Proposition 4.6 tells us that the core of a convex game is nonempty and Proposition 4.10 tells us that the core of a convex game is the convex hull of the marginal contribution vectors. The Shapley value being the average of these vectors, it must belong to the core. Moreover, it occupies a central position, as illustrated in Fig. 4.14.

Necessary and sufficient conditions under which the Shapley value is a core allocation can be found in the literature. They turn out to be simple and interpretable when applied to 3-player games. Moreover, among the 3-player games whose core is nonempty, the Shapley value is a core allocation for 64% of them while only 46.85% are convex (see Dehez & Pacini, 2024).

Marginal contribution vectors are all reasonable in the sense of Milnor:

$$v(i) \leq \mu_i^\pi(N, v) \leq \ Max_{S \subset N} Cm_i(S) \text{ for all } \ \pi \in \Pi_N \text{ and all } i \in N.$$

Hence, the following proposition.

Proposition 4.17 *The* Shapley value *defines* a Milnor-reasonable imputation.

The Shapley value is a *covariant*: if the games (N, v) and (N, w) are strategically equivalent, i.e., $w(S) = a\ v(S) + b(S)$ for some $a > 0$ and $b \in \mathbb{R}^n$, it is easily verified that:

$$SV_i(N, w) = a\ SV_i(N, v) + b_i \quad (i = 1, \ldots, n).$$

In addition, the Shapley value is a *linear operator*

$$SV(N, \alpha\, v + \beta\, w) = \alpha\ SV(N, v) + \beta\ SV(N, w)$$

for all real numbers α and β. And it is a continuous function with respect to the game data.

What about adding or removing players? The axiom of balanced contributions gives a first answer. Starting with a game (N, v), if player i leaves the grand coalition, we are left with the game $(N\backslash i, v_{N\backslash i})$. Superadditivity implies that $v(N) - v(N\backslash i) \geq v(i)$. Hence, $v(N\backslash i) \leq v(N)$ if $v(i) \geq 0$, i.e., the size of the amount to be distributed stays constant or decreases. It should not be beneficial to any of the remaining players. This corresponds to the property of population monotonicity introduced by Thomson (1983). An allocation rule φ is *population monotonic* if, given a game (N, v) and a player $i \in N$, we have:

$$\varphi_j(N\backslash i, v_{N\backslash i}) \leq \varphi_j(N, v) \text{ for all } j \in N,\ j \neq i.$$

In general, the Shapley value is not population monotonic. Here is an example.

Example 4.10 Consider the 4-player game $v = (0, 0, 0, 0 \mid 1, 2, 3, 4, 5, 6 \mid 9, 7, 9, 8 \mid 10)$. It is superadditive but not convex. Its Shapley value is $(1.83,\ 2.17,\ 3.17,\ 2.83)$. The game obtained by removing player 3 is given by $v = (0, 0, 0 \mid 1, 3, 5 \mid 7)$. Its Shapley value is given by the allocation $(2.83, 3.33, 3.83)$, to be compared to the allocation $(1.83,\ 2.17,\ 2.83)$. Population monotonicity is clearly violated: the payoffs of the players 2 and 4 are greater.

However, Sprumont (1990) proves that the Shapley value is population monotonic in the class of convex games.

The Shapley value as a distribution of dividends *

Harsanyi proved that the Shapley value can be obtained by distributing *uniformly* the dividends of each coalition. The argument is simple and underlies Shapley's proof of the unicity of the value. Consider the T-unanimity game (N, u_T) defined for some $T \subset N$ by:

$$u_T(S) = \begin{cases} 1 \text{ if } T \subset S, \\ 0 \text{ if } T \not\subset S. \end{cases}$$

Its Shapley value is given by:

$$SV_i(N, u_T) = \begin{cases} \frac{1}{t} \text{ for all } i \in T, \\ 0 \text{ for all } i \notin T. \end{cases}$$

This follows from efficiency, knowing that players inside T are substitutable and players outside T are null. According to the expression (4.4), a characteristic function can be decomposed as a weighted sum of T-unanimity games:

$$v(S) = \sum_{T \subset N} \alpha_T u_T(S) = \sum_{T \subset S} \alpha_T$$

where the coefficients (α_T) are the Harsanyi dividends. Hence, by linearity, we have a third and equivalent definition of the Shapley value:

$$SV_i(N, v) = \sum_{T \subset N} SV_i(N, \alpha_T u_T) = \sum_{T \subset N} \alpha_T \, SV_i(N, u_T) = \sum_{T \subset N : i \in T} \frac{1}{t} \alpha_T. \quad (4.16)$$

The dividends of each coalition are *uniformly* divided among their members and the Shapley value allocates to each player the sum of his share in the dividends of the coalitions of which he is a member.

Example 4.2 (continued) The dividends of the land game are given by (100, 0, 0 | 100, 200, 0 | –100). The Shapley value is then given by:

$$x_1 = 100 + \frac{100}{2} + \frac{200}{2} - \frac{100}{3} \simeq 216.7,$$
$$x_2 = \frac{100}{2} - \frac{100}{3} \simeq 16.7,$$
$$x_3 = \frac{200}{2} - \frac{100}{3} \simeq 66.7.$$

Example 4.3 (continued) The Harsanyi dividends of the *voting game* where simple majority applies and player 1 has a veto right are given by (0, 0, 0 | 1, 1, 0 | –1). The Shapley value is therefore given by:

$$x_1 = \frac{1}{2} + \frac{1}{2} - \frac{1}{3} = \frac{2}{3}, \quad x_2 = x_3 = \frac{1}{2} - \frac{1}{3} = \frac{1}{6}.$$

Example 4.11 *Cooperative product game* (Dehez, 2024; Rosales, 2014)

Consider a situation where a coefficient is attached to each player, a_i for player i, with $a_i \geq 1$ for all $i \in N$ A product game is defined by the following characteristic function:

$$v(S) = \prod_{i \in S} a_i - 1 \quad \text{for all } S \subset N.$$

Using (4.5), the Harsanyi dividends are given by:

$$\begin{aligned}
\alpha_{\{i\}} &= a_i - 1,\\
\alpha_{\{i,j\}} &= a_i\, a_j - a_i - a_j + 1 = (a_i - 1)(a_j - 1),\\
\alpha_{\{i,j,k\}} &= a_i\, a_j\, a_k - a_i\, a_j - a_i\, a_k - a_j\, a_k + a_i + a_j + a_k - 1\\
&= (a_i - 1)(a_j - 1)(a_k - 1), \ldots
\end{aligned}$$

By extension, the dividend of a coalition is equal to the product of the weights of its members:

$$\alpha_T = \prod_{i \in T} (a_i - 1) \;\Rightarrow\; SV_i(N, v_a) = \sum_{T \subset N:\, i \in T} \frac{1}{t} \prod_{j \in T} (a_j - 1) \quad (i = 1, \ldots, n).$$

Dividends being nonnegative, product games are positive and thereby convex. The 3-player game associated to the coefficient vector $a = (2, 4, 6)$ is defined by $v = (1, 3, 5 \mid 7, 11, 23 \mid 47)$. The dividends are given by (1, 3, 5|3, 5, 15 | 15) hence the Shapley value (10, 17, 20).

4.4 Justice: The Nucleolus *

The ε-core and least-core
The nucleolus
Proprieties of the nucleolus

We have seen that the emptiness of the core may be explained by the absence of restrictions on objections, hence the concept of a bargaining set that retains only the allocations against which there is no justified objection. In the presence of a game whose core is empty, an alternative route consists in minimizing the dissatisfaction of players and coalitions. That is the idea that underlies the notions of least-core and nucleolus.

The ε-core and least-core

Given an allocation, the dissatisfaction of a coalition is measured by the gap between its worth and what it obtains. More precisely, we define the *loss* or *excess* of coalition S at an allocation x by $e(x, S) = v(S) - x(S)$. The coalition which objects most strongly to a given payoff vector is the one that has the greatest loss. For a given ε, the *ε-core* is the set of allocations such that no coalition suffers a loss greater than ε:

$$C_\varepsilon(N, v) = \left\{ x \in \mathbb{R}^n \mid x(N) = v(N),\;\; e(S, x) \le \varepsilon \text{ for all } S \subset N,\; S \ne \emptyset, N \right\}.$$

The ε can be interpreted "*as a threshold, below which the blocking maneuver implicit [in the definition of the core]—the actual exercise of 'group* rationality*'—is not considered worth the trouble*" (Shapley & Shubik, 1966, p. 813). In view of the definition of the core given by (4.8), we have $C_0(N, v) = C(N, v)$: the core is the set of allocations such that no coalition suffers a loss. Notice that the grand coalition is excluded in the definition of the ε-core in order to allow for $\varepsilon < 0$.

Maschler et al. (1979) have introduced the notion of *least-core* defined as the set of allocations that *minimize the largest loss*:

$$LC(N, v) = \left\{x \in \mathbb{R}^n | x(N) = v(N), e(S, x) \leq \varepsilon_{\min} \text{ for all } S \subset N, S \neq \emptyset, N \right\} \tag{4.17}$$

where $\varepsilon_{\min} = Min_{x \in X(N,v)} Max_{\substack{S \subset N \\ S \neq \emptyset, N}} e(x, S)$.

It is the intersection of all nonempty ε-cores. The least-core is always nonempty and its dimension is equal to $n - 2$. It is a subset of the core, if nonempty, in which case A $\varepsilon_{min} \leq 0$. priori, nothing ensures that the elements of the ε-cores and of the least-core are imputations. However, it can be shown that, under superadditivity, the allocations of the least-core are individually rational: $LC(N, v) \subset I(N, v)$. The *symmetric least-core* is the subset of the least-core that allocates identical amounts to substitutable players.

Example 4.3 (continued) We have seen that the core of the simple majority voting game is empty. Let's compute the smallest ε such that $e(x, \{i, j\}) = 1 - (x_i + x_j) \leq \varepsilon$ for all $i \neq j$. Adding these three inequalities and using the identity $x_1 + x_2 + x_3 = 1$, we get $1 \leq 3\varepsilon$. The smallest ε such that $e(S, x) \leq \varepsilon$ for all $S \subset N,\ S \neq \emptyset, N$ is therefore given by $\varepsilon_{min} = 1/3$ and the least-core reduces to the singleton $\{(1/3, 1/3, 1/3)\}$. Figure 4.16 illustrates the ε-core for $\varepsilon = 1/2$.

Example 4.12 MPS Game. Maschler et al. (1979) have analyzed the following game:

$$\begin{aligned} &v(1) = 0,\ v(1, 2) = 20, \\ &v(2) = 0,\ v(1, 3) = 10, \\ &v(3) = 0,\ v(2, 3) = 50,\ v(1, 2, 3) = 60. \end{aligned}$$

This game is not convex but has a nonempty core represented in Fig. 4.17. Let's compute the smallest ε such that $e(S, x) \leq \varepsilon$ for all $S \subset N,\ S \neq \emptyset, N$ The ε-core is the set of allocations x such that $x_1 + x_2 + x_3 = 60$ and

$$\begin{aligned} -\varepsilon &\leq x_1 \leq 10 + \varepsilon, \\ -\varepsilon &\leq x_2 \leq 50 + \varepsilon, \\ -\varepsilon &\leq x_3 \leq 40 + \varepsilon. \end{aligned}$$

The smallest ε for which these three inequalities are satisfied is given by $\varepsilon_{min} = -5$. The least-core is therefore the set of allocations x such that $x_1 + x_2 + x_3 = 60$, $x_1 = 5$, $x_2 = \alpha$ and $x_3 = 55 - \alpha$ where α is in the interval [20, 45]. It is a segment located in the center of the core, as illustrated in Fig. 4.17.

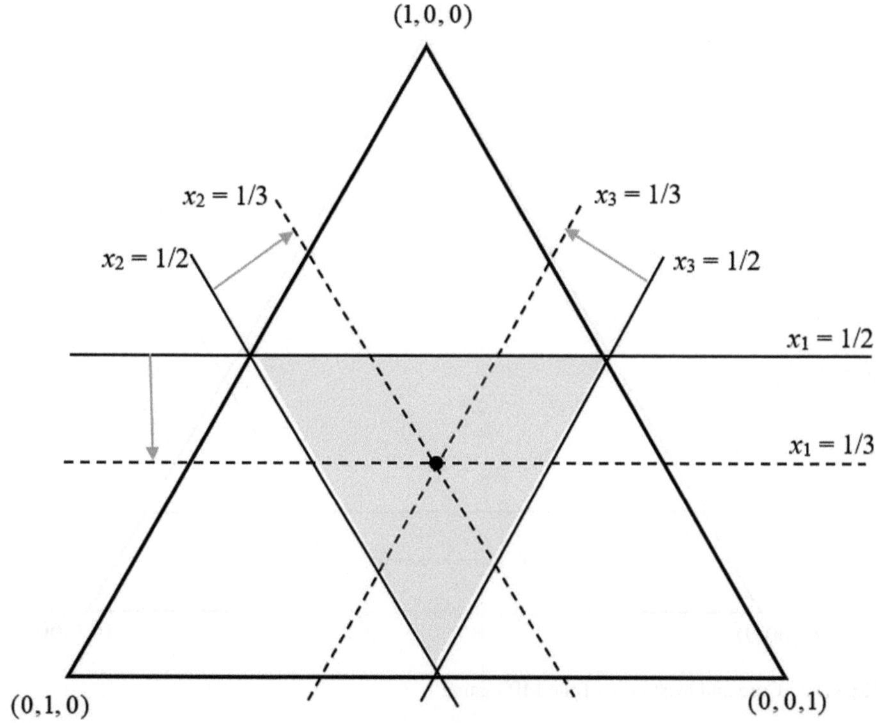

Fig. 4.16 ε-core and least-core of the simple majority voting game

We see in that example that it is still possible to reduce the dissatisfaction of some coalitions while keeping $x_1 = 5$. This is precisely what the nucleolus does.

Example 4.13 Game with an Empty Core The following 3-player game has been studied by Shubik (1982, p. 156):

$$v(i) = 0 \quad (i = 1, 2, 3),$$
$$v(1, 2) = v(1, 3) = 6,$$
$$v(1, 2, 3) = v(2, 3) = 10.$$

The core is indeed empty: the sum of the $v(i, j)$ equals 22, more that twice $v(1, 2, 3)$, violating condition (4.11). Players 2 and 3 are substitutable and the Shapley value is given by (2, 4, 4). The ε-core is the set of allocations x such that $x_1 + x_2 + x_3 = 10$ and

$$-\varepsilon \leq x_1 \leq \varepsilon,$$
$$-\varepsilon \leq x_2 \leq 4 + \varepsilon,$$
$$-\varepsilon \leq x_3 \leq 4 + \varepsilon.$$

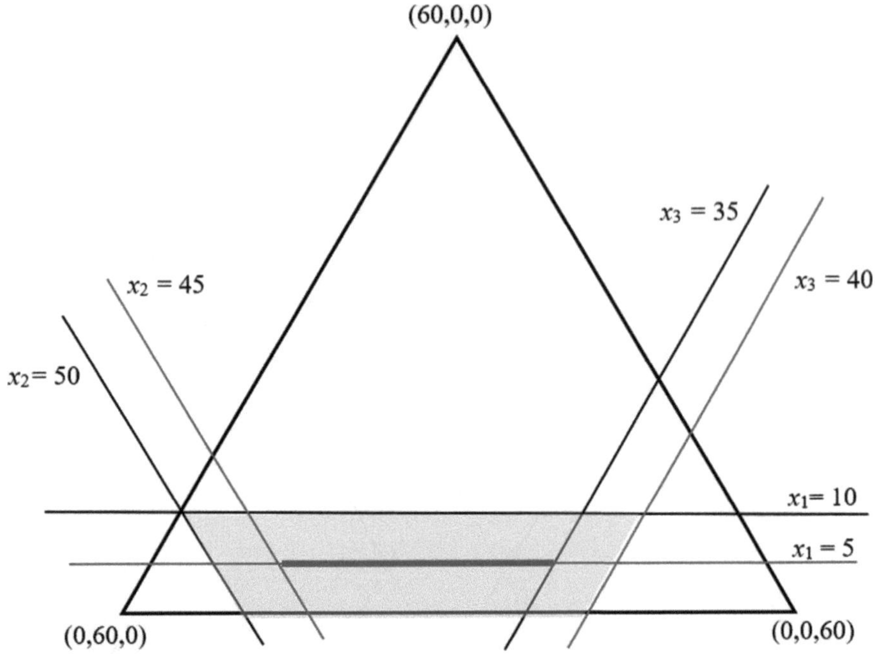

Fig. 4.17 Core and least-core of the MPS game

The core being empty, the least-core implies a positive ε. Adding the three right-hand sides of the above inequalities leads to the following inequality: $10 \leq 8+3\varepsilon$. Hence, the lowest possible value of ε is 2/3 and the least-core is the singleton $\{(2/3, 7/15, 7/15)\}$.

The nucleolus*

The nucleolus goes beyond the least-core defined in (4.17) by comparing losses *lexicographically* to eventually retain a single allocation.[27] The procedure goes as follows.

For any given allocation $x \in X(N, v)$, we form the vector $\theta(x)$ obtained by ordering in a *decreasing way* the $2^n - 2$ numbers $e(x, S)$ corresponding to the nonempty coalitions S, except the grand coalition, i.e., $\theta_h(x) \leq \theta_k(x)$ for $h \leq k$. These vectors are then compared *lexicographically*: $\theta(x) \prec_L \theta(y)$ if and only if:

either $\theta_1(x) < \theta_1(y)$.

or there is a $k \geq 2$ such that $\theta_k(x) < \theta_k(y)$ and $\theta_h(x) = \theta_h(y)$ for all $h < k$.

Hence, by definition, $\theta(x) \sim_L \theta(y)$ if and only if $\theta(x) = \theta(y)$. An allocation x is considered better than an allocation y *if and only if* $\theta(x)$ is lexicographically

[27] The lexicographic order was defined in the Chap. 2.

smaller than $\theta(y)$. This defines a binary relation on the set of allocations. The following proposition, due to Schmeidler (1969), establishes the unicity of the resulting allocation, called the nucleolus.

Proposition 4.18 *There is one and only one allocation* $x \in X(N, v)$ *such that* $\theta(x) \prec_L \theta(y)$ *for all* $y \in X(N, v),\ y \neq x$.

This is actually the definition of the *pre-nucleolus*. Schmeidler defines the nucleolus on the set of imputations instead. It makes no difference under superadditivity: Moulin (1988) shows that the pre-nucleolus is individually rational under superadditivity.

To quote Maschler et al., (1979, p. 303), the nucleolus results "*of an arbitrator's desire to minimize the dissatisfaction of the most dissatisfied coalition*".[28] When the core is nonempty, it is more appropriate to reverse this quotation by saying that the nucleolus is "*the result of an arbitrator's desire to maximize the satisfaction of the least satisfied coalition*".

Proposition 4.18 tells us that the nucleolus is always well-defined and consists of a single allocation. It therefore defines a *rule*, like the Shapley value, that associates to every game (N, v) a unique allocation $NU(N, v)$. In contrast to the Shapley value, there is no formula for the nucleolus, except in particular cases. Its computation requires solving a sequence of linear optimization problems or a single large linear optimization problem.[29] The following sequence of inclusions holds:

$$NU(N, v) \in LC(N, v) \subset C_\varepsilon(N, v)\ \textit{for all}\ \varepsilon \text{ such that } C_\varepsilon(N, v) \neq \emptyset.$$

If the core is nonempty, it contains the nucleolus that can then be viewed as a *core selection*. It occupies a central position. However, it differs from the *center of gravity*, another core-selection introduced by Gonzáles-Díaz and Sánchez-Rodríguez (2007). When the least-core is a singleton, no need for computation: it defines the nucleolus. This is the case of the coreless game given in Example 4.13. Its nucleolus is given by (2/3, 7/15, 7/15).

The nucleolus often differs from the Shapley value, except in the 2-player case where they both coincide with the equal division of the surplus (4.7). Indeed, the ε-core is the set of allocations x such that $x_1 + x_2 = v(1, 2)$ and $-\varepsilon + v(1) \leq x_1 \leq v(1, 2) - v(2) + \varepsilon$. The value of ε such that the two sides of the above inequality coincide is given by *minus* half of the surplus $v(1, 2) - v(1) - v(2)$. It defines the least-core and thereby the nucleolus.

Example 4.3 (continued) To illustrate the lexicographic procedure, consider the 3-player voting game where simple majority applies and the first player has a veto

---

[28] This "leximin" procedure has definitely a Ralwsian flavor. See Rawls (1971).

[29] See Kohlberg (1972).

right. Let's compare the allocations $x = (1/3, 1/3, 1/3)$, $y = (1/2, 1/4, 1/4)$ and $z = (1, 0, 0)$.

The associated losses are given by Table 4.9 and the ordered vectors are given by:

$$\theta(x) = (1/3,\ 1/3,\ -1/3,\ -1/3,\ -1/3,\ -2/3),$$
$$\theta(y) = (1/4,\ 1/4,\ -1/4,\ -1/4,\ -1/2,\ -1/2),$$
$$\theta(z) = (0,\ 0,\ 0,\ 0,\ 0,\ -1).$$

We observe that $\theta(z) \prec_L \theta(x) \prec_L \theta(y)$. Actually, $\theta(z) \prec_L \theta(x)$ for all $x \in X(N, v)$, $x \neq z$. Hence, z is the nucleolus, what we already knew because the core reduces to the allocation z.

Table 4.9 Losses associated to the simple majority voting game with veto

	x	y	z
$\{1\}$	−1/3	−1/2	−1
$\{2\}$	−1/3	−1/4	0
$\{3\}$	−1/3	−1/4	0
$\{1, 2\}$	1/3	1/4	0
$\{1, 3\}$	1/3	1/4	0
$\{2, 3\}$	−2/3	−1/2	0

Example 4.2 (continued) The core of the land game is nonempty. The nucleolus being an element of the core, it must be of the form $NU(N, v) = (p,\ 0,\ 300 - p)$ where p belongs to the interval [200, 300]. As a function of p, the losses associated with the six proper subsets of N are given by:

$$\begin{aligned} &e(a, \{1\}) = 100 - p, && e(a, \{1, 2\}) = 200 - p, \\ &e(a, \{2\}) = 0, && e(a, \{1, 3\}) = 0, \\ &e(a, \{3\}) = p - 300, && e(a, \{2, 3\}) = p - 300. \end{aligned}$$

We can ignore $e(a, \{1\})$ that is always smaller than $e(a, \{1, 2\})$. Moreover, $e(a, \{3\})$ and $e(a, \{2, 3\})$ coincide while $e(a, \{2\})$ and $e(a, \{1, 3\})$ are identically zero. It remains to look at $e(a, \{1, 2\})$ and $e(a, \{2, 3\})$ as illustrated in Fig. 4.18. Their intersection corresponds to $p = 250$ and the nucleolus is given by $NU(N, v) = (250,\ 0,\ 50)$. It is located in the middle of the line segment that defines the core and coincides with the least-core.

In general, if players are ordered in terms of their reservation prices, the nucleolus is given by:

$$NU_1(N, v) = \frac{r_n + r_{n-1}}{2},$$

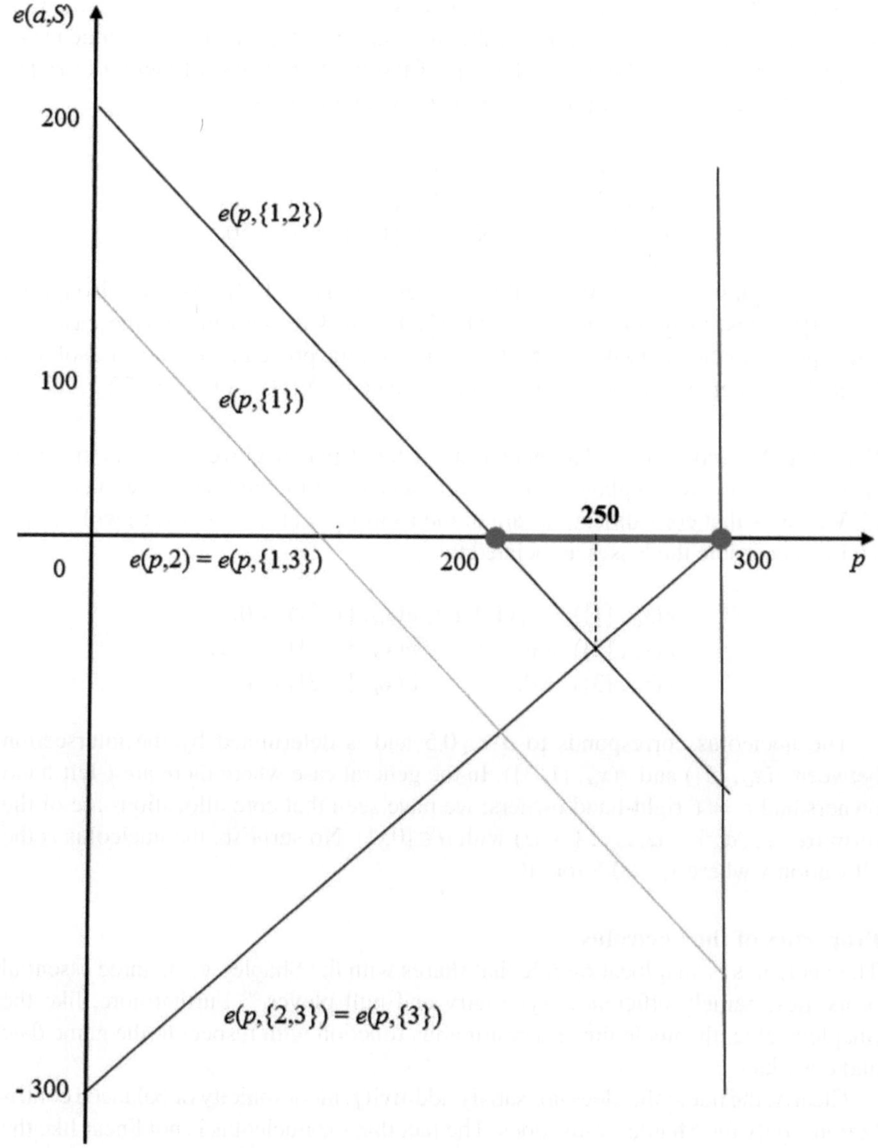

Fig. 4.18 Least-core and nucleolus of the land game

$$NU_i(N, v) = 0 \text{ for } i = 2, \ldots, n-1,$$
$$NU_n(N, v) = \frac{r_n - r_{n-1}}{2}.$$

Notice that the nucleolus exclusively depends on the price difference $r_n - r_{n-1}$.

Example 4.12 (continued) In the MPS game, the nucleolus is of the form $(5,\ a,\ 55-a)$ where the parameter a belongs to the interval [20, 45]. This is a consequence of the fact that the nucleolus is an element of the least-core. As a function of a, the losses associated to the six proper subsets of N are given by:

$$\begin{aligned} &e(a,\{1\}) = -5, &&e(a,\{2,3\}) = -5,\\ &e(a,\{2\}) = -a, &&e(a,\{1,2\}) = 15-a,\\ &e(a,\{3\}) = a-55, &&e(a,\{1,3\}) = a-50. \end{aligned}$$

We can ignore $e(a,\{2\})$ that is always inferior to $e(a,\{1,2\})$. We can also ignore $e(a,\{3\})$ that is always inferior to $e(a,\{1,3\})$. Figure 4.19 confirms that the least-core corresponds to the interval [20, 45] The lexicographic procedure results in a solution located at its center. Hence, the nucleolus is given by $NU(N,v) = (5,\ 32.5,\ 22.5)$.

Example 4.6 (continued) The nucleolus of the 3-player gloves game is given by (1.5, 0.5, 0). It gives to player 1 an amount located in the middle of the interval [1, 2]. We know that core allocations are of the form $x_\alpha = (1+\alpha, 1-\alpha, 0)$ with $\alpha \in [0, 1]$. Let's compute the losses associated to x_α :

$$\begin{aligned} &e(x_\alpha,\{1\}) = -(1+\alpha), &&e(x_\alpha,\{1,2\}) = 0,\\ &e(x_\alpha,\{2\}) = \alpha-1, &&e(x_\alpha,\{1,3\}) = -\alpha,\\ &e(x_\alpha,\{3\}) = 0, &&e(x_\alpha,\{2,3\}) = \alpha. \end{aligned}$$

The nucleolus corresponds to $\alpha = 0.5$ and is determined by the intersection between $e(x_\alpha,\{2\})$ and $e(x_\alpha,\{1,3\})$. In the general case where there are ℓ left-hand owners and $r = \ell$ right-hand owners, we have seen that core allocations are of the form $(\alpha,\ldots,\alpha, 1-\alpha,\ldots, 1-\alpha)$ with $\alpha \in [0, 1]$. No surprise, the nucleolus is the allocation x where $x_i = 0.5$ for all i.

Properties of the nucleolus

The nucleolus is an allocation rule that shares with the Shapley value three essential properties, namely efficiency, symmetry and null player.[30] Furthermore, like the Shapley value, the nucleolus is a continuous function with respect to the game date and covariant.

Clearly, the nucleolus does *not* satisfy additivity, monotonicity or balanced contributions: only the Shapley value does. The fact that the nucleolus is not linear like the Shapley value is not necessarily a problem. The lack of monotonicity is, however, a drawback. Actually, the nucleolus does not even satisfy a much weaker monotonicity property: if only the worth of the grand coalition $v(N)$ increases, leaving unchanged the worth of proper coalitions, the nucleolus may allocate to some players a smaller amount.[31]

[30] See Maschler et al. (2013).

[31] This is a result due to Megiddo (1974).

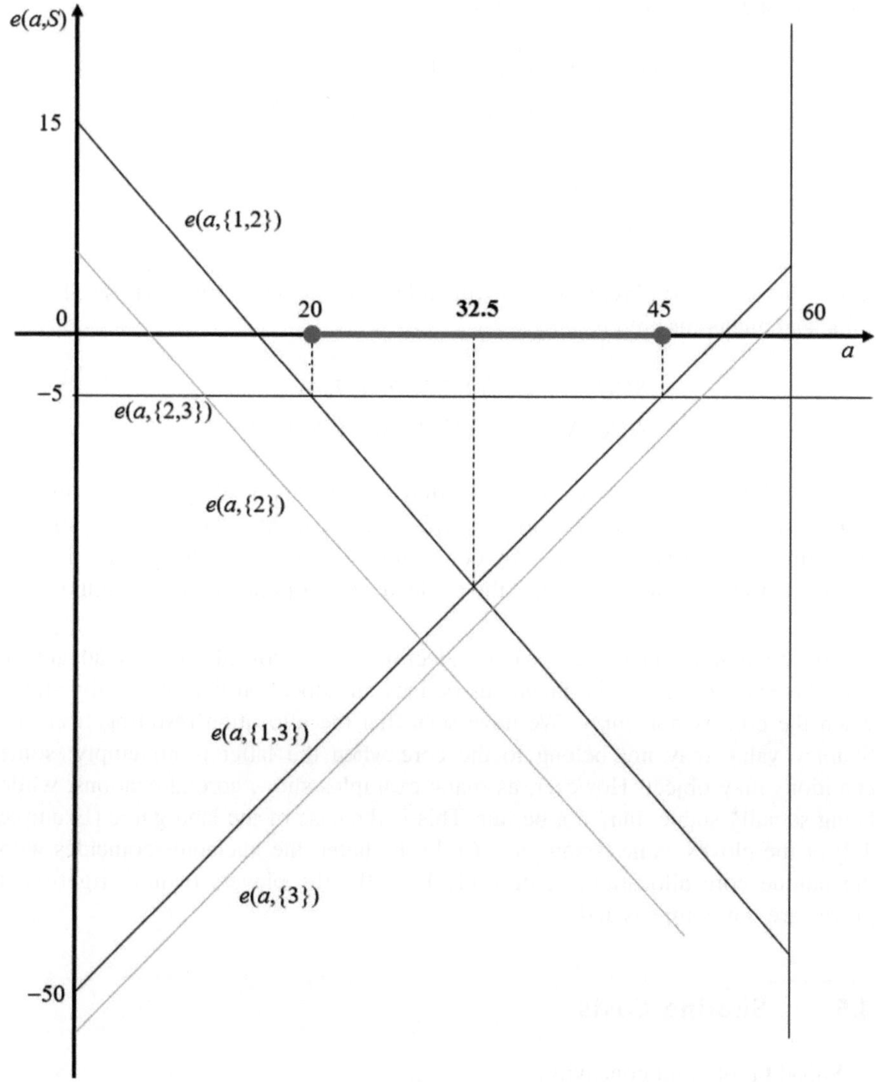

Fig. 4.19 Least-core and nucleolus of the MPS game

The nucleolus has been axiomatized by Sobolev (1975).[32]

[32] For more details, see the discussion by Maschler in the Chapter 18 of the first volume of the *Handbook of Game Theory* (Aumann & Hart, 1992).

Example 4.14 Consider the following 4-player proposed by Sönmez (1993):

$$v(i) = 0 \text{ for all } i = 1, 2, 3, 4,$$
$$v(i, j) = 1 \text{ for all } i, j = 1, 2, 3, 4, \quad i \neq j,$$
$$v(1, i, j) = 2 \text{ for all } i, j = 2, 3, 4, \quad i \neq j,$$
$$v(2, 3, 4) = 2,$$
$$v(1, 2, 3, 4) = 6,$$

where the last three players are substitutable. It is a convex game whose Shapley value and nucleolus are given by:

$$SV(N, v) = (3/4, 7/4, 7/4, 7/4),$$
$$NUC(N, v) = (1/2, 11/6, 11/6, 11/6).$$

Removing player 4 leaves three substitutable players, leading to the following results: $SV(N, v) = NUC(N, v) = (2/3, 2/3, 2/3)$. As expected, they all lose according to the Shapley value—by convexity of the game—while player 1 gains according to the nucleolus. Hence, the nucleolus is not population monotonic.

The fact that the nucleolus is a core selection may be considered as an advantage over the Shapley value: the nucleolus defines an allocation that is socially stable when the core is nonempty. We have seen that the allocation resulting from the Shapley value may not belong to the core when the latter is nonempty: some coalitions may object. However, as many examples show, core allocations, while being socially stable, may not be fair. This is the case of the land game (Example 4.2) or the gloves game (Example 4.6). In the latter, the nucleolus coincides with the unique core allocation, namely (1, 1, 0, 0): the players owning right-hand gloves are not compensated.

4.5 Sharing Costs

Subadditivity and concavity
Cost and surplus sharing
The core of a cost game
The Shapley value of a cost game.

Cooperative games with transferable utility can be used to analyze and solve cost-sharing problems. A set of players have a common project, for instance, the construction of an infrastructure whose cost is known. How to share this cost is the question.

Subadditivity and concavity
Considering transferable utility games that are superadditive is in line with the idea that players have to divide a surplus. If the problem concerns the division of a cost, it would be natural to require that the characteristic function be *subadditive*:

$$c(S) + c(T) \geq c(S \cup T) \text{ for all } S \text{ and } T \subset N \text{ such that } S \cap T = \emptyset. \tag{4.18}$$

The inequalities (4.2) that define superadditivity are reversed. The pair (N, c) where c is a subadditive function, define a cost-sharing game. The cost to be divided is given by $c(N)$. It is the minimum cost of realizing the project while $c(S)$ is the maximum cost that coalition S would have to support if it decided to form and realize the project to the sole benefit of its members. In particular, $c(i)$ is its *stand-alone cost* of player i.

Subadditivity implies that forming the grand coalition is never detrimental when compared to the situation where the players are isolated:

$$\sum_{i \in N} c(i) \geq c(N)$$

A cost game is *essential* if this inequality is strict: there is then a potential gain to participate in the grand coalition. It is *concave* if the following inequalities are satisfied

$$c(S) + c(T) \geq c(S \cup T) + c(S \cap T) \text{ for all } S \text{ and } T \subset N. \tag{4.19}$$

The inequalities (4.3) that define convexity are reversed.[33] Concavity implies subadditivity. In the context of cost-sharing, marginal contributions $c(S) - c(S\backslash i)$ are *marginal costs* and we have the inverse of Proposition 4.2. It confirms that concavity is linked to economies of scales.

Proposition 4.19 *A game* (N, c) *is concave* if and only if marginal costs *are nonincreasing:*

$$i \in S \subset T \;\Rightarrow\; c(T) - c(T\backslash i) \leq c(S) - c(S\backslash i).$$

Example 4.15 Network Game. Consider three towns that have the project of building a communication network that will connect them to a communication node. The connection costs are given by Fig. 4.20. If we ignore the question of capacity, the associated cost game is defined by the following characteristic function:

$$\begin{aligned}
&c(1) = 10, \; c(1,2) = 10 + 10 = 20,\\
&c(2) = 14, \; c(1,3) = 10 + 14 = 24,\\
&c(3) = 16, \; c(2,3) = 14 + 6 = 20, \quad c(1,2,3) = 10 + 10 + 6 = 26.
\end{aligned}$$

[33] A set function f is concave if and only if the function $-f$ is convex.

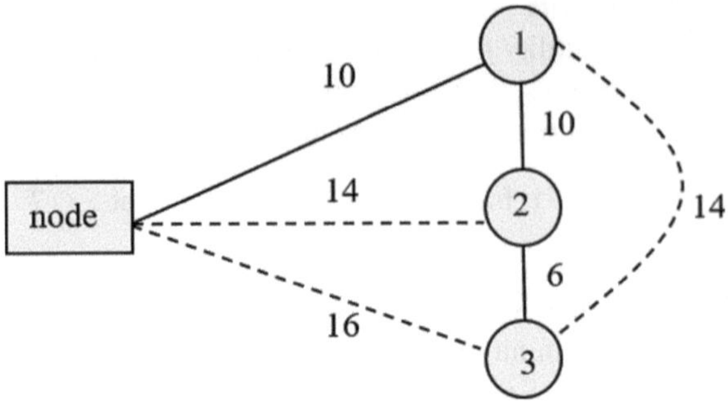

Fig. 4.20 Communication network

Cost and surplus sharing

If the grand coalition forms, it generates a surplus that is equal to the difference between the sum of the individual costs and the cost of the integrated network. In this way, given a cost-sharing game (N, c), we define the associated surplus sharing game (N, v) by:

$$v(S) = \sum_{i \in S} c(i) - c(S). \tag{4.20}$$

Here, $v(S)$ measures what coalition S would gain if it decided to form and $v(i) = 0$ for all i. In particular, $v(N)$ is the total surplus to be divided. We observe that the cost game cannot be retrieved from the surplus game without knowing the stand-alone costs $c(i)$.

The properties of subadditivity and concavity of the cost game (N, c) translate into superadditivity and convexity of the surplus game (N, v) and vice versa.

Example 4.15 (continued) The surplus game associated to the network game is given by:

$$\begin{aligned}
&v(1) = 0,\ v(1,2) = 24 - 20 = 4,\\
&v(2) = 0,\ v(1,3) = 26 - 24 = 2,\\
&v(3) = 0,\ v(2,3) = 30 - 20 = 10,\ v(1,2,3) = 40 - 26 = 14.
\end{aligned}$$

Following (4.20), it is possible to convert a surplus allocation into a cost allocation, and inversely. The surplus and cost allocations $x = (x_1, \ldots, x_n)$ and $y = (y_1, \ldots, y_n)$ are linked by the following identities

$$x_i + y_i = c(i) \quad (i = 1, \ldots, n). \tag{4.21}$$

It says that the share of the total cost borne by player i is equal to his individual cost net of his share in the total surplus: $y_i = c(i) - x_i$. Inversely, the share of player i in the total surplus is equal to his individual cost net of his share in the total cost: $x_i = c(i) - y_i$.

We may therefore work indifferently on the cost game or on the associated surplus game. We could have worked with the characteristic function, $-c$ although this is less convenient and without content. Notice that it is not possible to associate a cost-sharing game to a surplus sharing game without knowing the stand-alone costs $c(i)$.

Using (4.20), marginal contributions of the surplus game (N, v) and marginal costs of the associated cost game (N, c) are related by the following identity:

$$\begin{aligned} c(S) - c(S\backslash i) &= \left(\sum_{j \in S} c(j) - v(S)\right) - \left(\sum_{j \in S\backslash i} c(j) - v(S\backslash i)\right) \\ &= c(i) - (v(S) - v(S\backslash i)). \end{aligned}$$

The core of a cost game

In parallel with (4.6) and (4.8), the imputation set and the core of a cost game (N, c) are naturally defined by:

$$I(N, c) = \{y \in \mathbb{R}^n | y(N) = c(N) \text{ and } y_i \leq c(i) \text{ for all } i \in N\},$$

and

$$C(N, c) = \{y \in \mathbb{R}^n | y(N) = c(N) \text{ and } y(S) \leq c(S) \text{ for all } S \subset N\}.$$

An imputation specifies a division of the total cost in such a way that no player pays more than his stand-alone cost. A core allocation is an imputation such that no coalition pays more than its stand-alone cost. Remembering (4.9), the core can alternatively be defined as

$$C(N, c) = \{y \in \mathbb{R}^n | y(N) = c(N) \text{ and } y(S) \geq c(N) - c(N\backslash S) \text{ for all } S \subset N\}. \tag{4.22}$$

It says that core allocations are exempt of cross subsidies (Faulhaber, 1975): coalitions pay at least their additional cost. Given (4.21), we indeed have the following mirror inequalities:

$$y(S) \leq c(S) \quad \Leftrightarrow \quad x(S) \geq v(S),$$

and

$$y(S) \geq c(N) - c(N\backslash S) \quad \Leftrightarrow \quad x(S) \leq v(N) - v(N\backslash S).$$

Example 4.15 (continued), The surplus and cost allocations x and y of the core of the network game satisfy the following inequalities

$$\begin{array}{lcl} 0 \leq x_1 \leq 4, & & 6 \leq y_1 \leq 10, \\ 0 \leq x_2 \leq 12, & \text{and} & 2 \leq y_2 \leq 14, \\ 0 \leq x_3 \leq 4, & & 6 \leq y_3 \leq 16. \end{array}$$

Figures 4.21 and 4.22 illustrate the two core definitions.

The Shapley value of a cost game

In line with the definition of the Shapley value in terms of marginal contributions given in (4.15), the Shapley value of a cost-sharing game requires each player to pay an amount equal to an average of his marginal costs. Using (4.21), the Shapley of a cost-sharing game (N, c) and the Shapley value of the associated surplus sharing game are related by the following identity:

$$SV_i(N, c) = c(i) - SV_i(N, v) \quad (i = 1, \ldots, n). \tag{4.23}$$

Example 4.15 (continued) Tables 4.10 and 4.11 collect the marginal cost and the marginal contribution vectors of the network game. We observe that the cost game

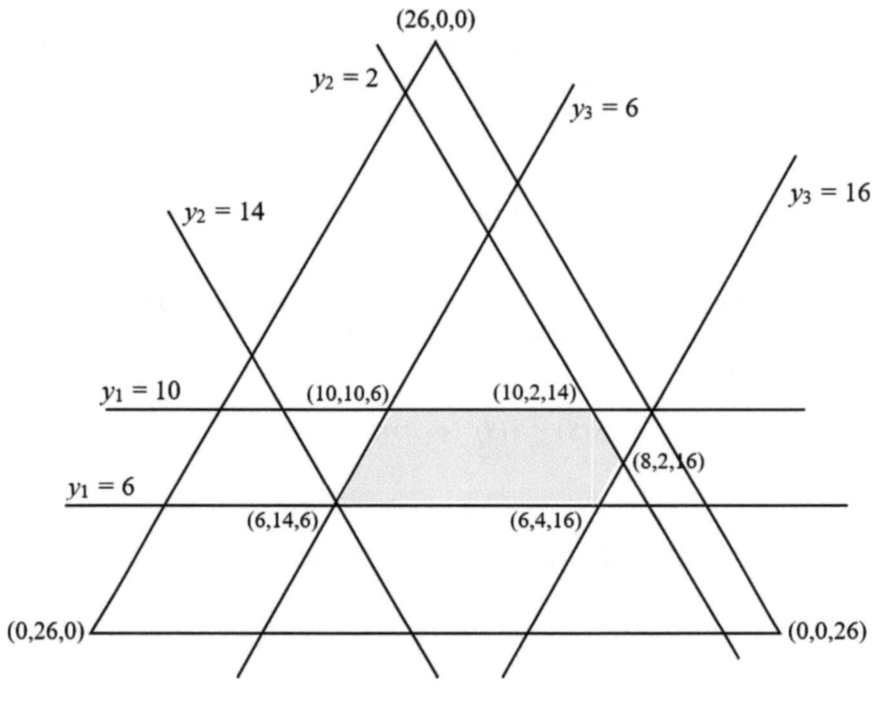

Fig. 4.21 Core of the cost-sharing network game

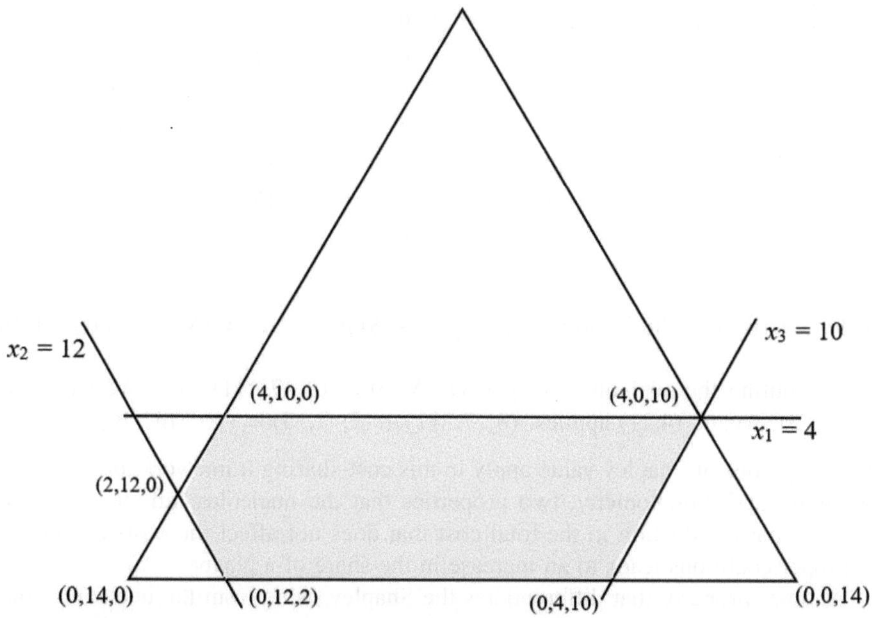

Fig. 4.22 Core of the surplus sharing network game

is concave and that the surplus game is convex. Indeed, as we can see in Fig. 4.21 and Fig. 4.22, the vertices of the core of the cost game correspond to the five distinct vectors identified in Table 4.10 and, likewise, the vertices of the core of the surplus game correspond to the five distinct vectors identified in Table 4.11.

Using these two tables, we get the Shapley values:

$$SV(N, c) = (46/6,\ 46/6,\ 64/6) \simeq (7.66,\ 7.66,\ 10.66),$$
$$SV(N, v) = (14/6,\ 38/6,\ 32/6) \simeq (2.33,\ 6.33,\ 5.33),$$

Table 4.10 Marginal cost vectors of the network cost game

	1	2	3
123	10	10	6
132	10	2	14
213	6	14	6
231	6	14	6
312	8	2	16
321	6	4	16
	46	46	64

Table 4.11 Marginal contribution vectors of the network surplus game

	1	2	3
123	0	4	10
132	0	12	2
213	4	0	10
231	4	0	10
312	2	12	0
321	4	10	0
	14	38	32

and we verify that the identity (4.21) applies: $SV_i(N, c) + SV_i(N, v) = c(i)$ for all i.

Computing the nucleolus, we get $NU(N, c) = (8,\ 7,\ 11)$ and $NU(N, v) = (2,\ 7,\ 5)$. Again, (4.21) applies: $(8,\ 7,\ 11) + (2,\ 7,\ 5) = (10,\ 14,\ 16)$.

The properties of Shapley value apply in this cost-sharing framework, in particular additivity and monotonicity, two properties that the nucleolus fails to satisfy. It may be that a reduction in the total cost that does not affect the costs associated to proper coalitions leads to an increase in the share of a player.

Another property that differentiates the Shapley value from the nucleolus concerns the division of a *fixed cost*. Given a coalition $T \subset N$, a fixed cost that affects the members of a coalition T is an additional amount F that affects all coalition that includes members of T:

$$\begin{aligned} c'(S) &= c(S) + F \quad \text{if } S \cap T \neq \emptyset, \\ &= c(S) \qquad\quad \text{otherwise.} \end{aligned}$$

In Dehez (2011) it is shown that the Shapley value is the unique efficient and symmetric sharing rule that allocates *uniformly* the fixed cost among the members of T:

$$\begin{aligned} SV_i(N, c') &= SV_i(N, c) + \tfrac{1}{t}F \text{ for all } i \in T, \\ &= SV_i(N, c) \qquad\quad \text{for all } i \in N \backslash T. \end{aligned}$$

The nucleolus instead imposes different additional contributions, not only to the payers in T but also to players outside T. This is unfair.

Example 4.16 Fixed Cost Game. Consider the following 4-player cost-sharing game:

$c(1) = 7, c(2) = 9, c(3) = 13, c(4) = 15,$
$c(1, 2) = 15, c(1, 3) = 19, c(1, 4) = 21, c(2, 3) = 20, c(2, 4) = 22, c(3, 4) = 25,$
$c(1, 2, 3) = 27, c(1, 2, 4) = 26, c(1, 3, 4) = 24, c(2, 3, 4) = 26,$
$c(1, 2, 3, 4) = 30.$

The cost allocations derived from the Shapley value and the nucleolus are respectively given by (5.08, 6.75, 8.58, 9.58) and (5.5, 7.5, 8.25, 8.75). Consider adding a fixed cost $F = 2$ that affects only the first two players. Then, $T = \{1, 2\}$ and the cost allocations become (6.08, 7.75, 8.58, 9.58) and (6.33, 8.33, 8.50, 8.83) respectively: the Shapley value divides the fixed cost equally between the players 1 and 2 while the nucleolus imposes additional contributions to all players. Each of the first two players pays 0.83 more while the last two pay respectively 0.25 and 0.08 more.

4.6 Applications

Bankruptcy rules
Landing fees
Sharing data
Patents and royalties
Sharing information
Apportionment of damage
Dividing a collective probability of success
Elections and approval voting

There exists a large number of applications of transferable utility games, mostly using the Shapley value, in many different domains, including, of course, economics, political science and law, but also various fields of engineering.[34] The applications to political science will be the object of Chap. 5. Here, we will consider applications to economic and legal problems.

Bankruptcy rules (Aumann & Maschler, 1985; O'Neill, 1982).
The following problem appears in the Babylonian Talmud.[35] A man dies. His estate appears to be insufficient to cover the promises he had made to his three spouses. A Mishna (Kethubot 93a) considers three different levels of wealth for given promises. The prescriptions are given in Table 4.12 where the rows refer to different estate values and the columns refer to the spouses and the promises that were made. Many religious scholars have worked on this table, trying to find a consistent explanation of the proposed divisions. In vain.

We observe that if the estate value is low (actually equal to the lowest promise), equal division applies. If instead, the estate value is high (actually equal to the highest promise), proportional division applies. But what about the intermediary case?

[34] Many applications use the Shapley value. See for instance the handbook of Algaba et al. (2020).
[35] The Talmud is a text more than 2000 years old that frames the civil, criminal and Jewish religious law.

Barry O'Neill (1982) has been the first to study, in a game theoretical perspective, the solutions proposed in the Talmud to different division problems, including the above problem and the "*contested garment*".

The story is the following. Two persons are fighting over a piece of garment. One claims the whole, while the other claims half. This situation is described in a famous Mishna (Baba Metzia 2a) where it is prescribed to give 3/4 of the garment to the first. The rationale is the following. Since the second only claims half, the first may have half. It then remains to share the remaining half and equal division naturally applies. The resulting solution is then given by:

$$x_1 = \frac{E}{2} + \frac{1}{2}\frac{E}{2} = \frac{3}{4}E,$$
$$x_2 = 0 + \frac{1}{2}\frac{E}{2} = \frac{1}{4}E,$$

where E denotes the size of the garment.

This division can easily be generalized to any pair of claims. If d_1 and d_2 are the claims, the *uncontested* amounts are given by:

$$a_1 = Max(0, E - d_2),$$
$$a_2 = Max(0, E - d_1).$$

The division rule is then given by:

$$x_1 = a_1 + \frac{1}{2}(E - a_1 - a_2) = \frac{1}{2}(E + a_1 - a_2),$$
$$x_2 = a_2 + \frac{1}{2}(E - a_1 - a_2) = \frac{1}{2}(E + a_2 - a_1).$$

It is the solution of the following equation system:

$$x_1 + x_2 = E,$$
$$x_1 - x_2 = a_1 - a_2.$$

It also corresponds to the equal division of the surplus (and to the Shapley value) associated to the 2-player game (N, v) defined by:

$$v(1) = a_1,$$

Table 4.12 Talmudic prescriptions

	100	200	300
100	33.3	33.3	33.3
200	50	75	75
300	50	100	150

$$v(2) = a_2,$$
$$v(1, 2) = E.$$

In the case where the claims are both greater than E, $a_1 = a_2 = 0$ and we obtain $x_1 = x_2 = E/2$. If they are both smaller than E, $a_i = E - d_i$ for $i = 1, 2$ and we obtain:

$$x_1 = (E - d_2) + \frac{1}{2}(d_1 + d_2 - E) = \frac{E + d_1 - d_2}{2},$$
$$x_2 = (E - d_1) + \frac{1}{2}(d_1 + d_2 - E) = \frac{E + d_2 - d_1}{2}.$$

These problems belong to the family of bankruptcy *problems.* Consider a bankrupt firm whose value is equal to E and n creditors. The sum of their claims exceeds the value of the firm:

$$D = \sum_{i=1}^{n} d_i > E$$

where d_i is i's claim. Claims are ordered: $0 < d_1 \leq d_2 \leq ... \leq d_n$. The corresponding bankruptcy problem is denoted by $(E|d_1, ..., d_n)$ and a division of E specifies the amounts assigned to each claimant.

Aumann and Maschler (1985) have used the contested garment solution to define a rule that can be applied to any bankruptcy game. Moreover, they show that it reproduces the divisions proposed by the Talmud and coincides with the nucleolus of a well-defined game.

A solution $(x_1, ..., x_n)$ to the problem $(E|d_1, ..., d_n)$ is *consistent with the* contested garment *solution* if, for all pairs of creditors i and j, the division of the sum $x_i + x_j$ between these two creditors according to the contested garment solution for claims d_i and d_j reproduces x_i and x_j. Aumann and Maschler prove that there is *one and only one* consistent solution.

We easily verify that the prescriptions of the Talmud are all consistent. For instance, if we consider the first two spouses in the situation (200|100, 200, 300), they receive together 125. The uncontested amounts are $a_1 = Max\,(0, 125-200) = 0$ and $a_2 = Max\,(0, 125 - 100) = 25$. The contested garment solution of the problem (125 | 100, 200) is then given by:

$$x_1 = 0 + \frac{100}{2} = 50,$$
$$x_2 = 25 + \frac{100}{2} = 75.$$

Recalling how we have defined the concept of characteristic function, its natural definition in the context of a bankruptcy problem $(E|d_1, ..., d_n)$ is given by:

$$v(S) = \begin{cases} E - d(N\backslash S) & \text{if } d(N\backslash S) < E, \\ 0 & \text{if } d(N\backslash S) \geq E. \end{cases}$$

Indeed, the worst that can happen to a coalition, if it forms, is that those outside the coalition have been reimbursed as much as possible: $v(S)$ is the amount that coalition S may hope to obtain if priority has been given to those outside S. The worth of coalition S is then given by:

$$v(S) = Max\,(0, E - d(N\backslash S)). \tag{4.24}$$

In particular, we have $v(N) - v(N\backslash i) = Min\,(E, d_i)$. Hence, the debts coincide with the marginal contributions to the grand coalition if they do not exceed the value of the estate. The game defined by (4.24) extends the idea of uncontested rights to any number of claimants.

Proposition 4.20 Bankruptcy games *are convex.*

Proof We use the equivalent formulation $v(S) = Max\ [0, d(S) - K]$ where $K = d(N) - E > 0$. We define $\Delta = v(S) + v(T) - v(S \cup T) - v(S \cap T)$ and distinguish three cases:

- $d(S) > K$ and $d(T) > K$, in which case we have:

$$\begin{aligned}\Delta &= (d(S) + d(T) - 2K) - (d(S \cup T) - K) - v(S \cap T)\\ &= (d(S \cap T) - K) - v(S \cap T) \leq 0.\end{aligned}$$

- $d(S) \leq K$ and $d(T) > K$, in which case we have

$$\Delta = (0 + d(T) - K) - (d(S \cup T) - K) - 0 = -d(S\backslash T) \leq 0.$$

- $d(S) \leq K$ and $d(T) \leq K$, in which case we have

$$\Delta = Max(0, d(S \cup T) - K) \leq 0.$$

In all three cases $\Delta \leq 0$, confirming the convexity of the game (N, v). ♦

The core of a bankruptcy game is therefore nonempty and is the convex polyhedral set whose vertices are the marginal contribution vectors. In the core, no claimant can obtain more than his claim:

$$x_i \leq v(N) - v(N\backslash i) = Min(E, d_i).$$

Applying (4.24) to the Talmudic problem (200 |100, 200, 300), we obtain the game v = (0, 0, 0 | 0, 0, 100 | 200).

Its Shapley value is given by $SV(N, v) = (33.3,\ 83.3,\ 83.3)$. It differs from the division prescribed by the Talmud. As a consequence, the Shapley value is not consistent with the contested garment solution.

Aumann and Maschler prove that this unique consistent rule actually coincides with the nucleolus of the above game.

Example 4.17 Bankruptcy Game I. Consider the bankruptcy situation (600 | 150, 300, 450). The corresponding bankruptcy game is then defined by: $v = (0, 0, 150|150, 300, 450|600)$. Alone, the first two creditors cannot expect a reimbursement: once the others have been reimbursed, nothing is left. The last one instead may expect 150. It is what is left once the others have been reimbursed. The coalition $\{1, 3\}$ may expect 300 once creditor 2 has been reimbursed, and so on... Table 4.13 gathers the marginal contribution vectors.

Table 4.13 Marginal contribution vectors of the bankruptcy game I

	1	2	3
123	0	150	450
132	0	300	300
213	150	0	450
231	150	0	450
312	150	300	150
321	150	300	150
	600	1050	1950

There are four distinct vectors and the Shapley value is given by (100, 175, 325). The corresponding losses are (50, 125, 125). The core is the set of allocations (x_1, x_2, x_3) of 600 such that:

$$0 \leq x_1 \leq 150,$$
$$0 \leq x_2 \leq 300,$$
$$150 \leq x_3 \leq 450.$$

It is represented in Fig. 4.23. The four vertices of the core coincident with the four marginal contribution vectors and the Shapley value is in a central position. It happens that the nucleolus coincides with the average of the core vertices that is given by (75, 187.5, 337.5).

This coincidence applies to the three Talmudic situations given in Table 4.12. However, this is not a general characteristic of bankruptcy games. Moreover, using the average of core vertices as a solution may lead to inconsistent allocations as in the following example.

Example 4.18 Bankruptcy Game II. Consider the bankruptcy situation $(400 \mid 200, 300, 400)$. The corresponding bankruptcy game is defined by $v = (0, 0, 0, 0|0, 100, 200|400)$.

The marginal contribution vectors are given in Table 4.14 from which we compute the Shapley value (83.33, 133.33, 183.33). There are five distinct vectors and the allocation (100, 160, 140) is obtained as the simple average. We observe that

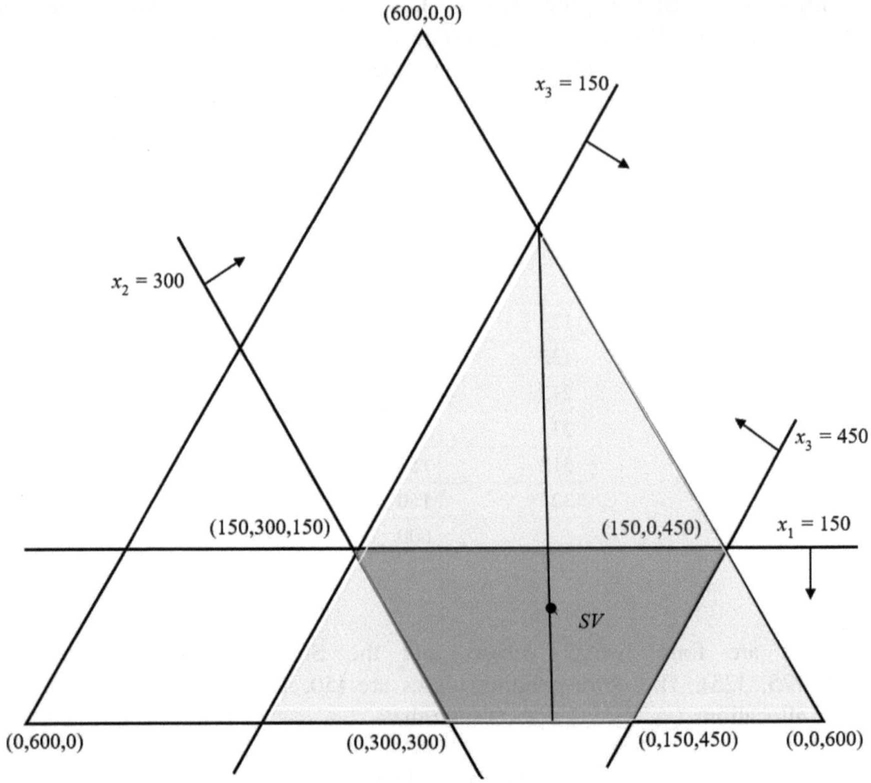

Fig. 4.23 Core of the bankruptcy game II

the last player, who has the highest debt, gets less than the second one! The average of the marginal contribution vectors is definitely not an appropriate solution.

The nucleolus is given by the allocation (100, 150, 150). We observe that the last two creditors obtain the same amount while their claims differ. This was already observed in the Talmudic example with, however, a difference. Here these

Table 4.14 Marginal contribution vectors of the bankruptcy game II

	1	2	3
123	0	0	400
132	0	300	100
213	0	0	400
231	200	0	200
312	100	300	0
321	200	200	0
	500	800	1100

two creditors are not substitutable. This may be a reason to consider that the Shapley value is a more acceptable rule.

In the bankruptcy game (500 | 100, 300, 600), Shapley value and nucleolus coincide, and happen to be equal to the average of the marginal contribution vectors (50, 150, 300).

The *constrained equal award* is another rule. It is of the form by $x_i = Min(\alpha, d_i)$: claimants receive the same amount except those who claim less than α. The parameter α is uniquely determined in such a way that $\sum x_i = E$. Applied to the Talmudic table 4.12, it prescribes equal amounts for all three estate values. For an estate value equal to 400, the prescription becomes (100, 150, 150). Yet another rule will be considered at the end of the next section.

Landing fees (Littlechild & Owen, 1973).

Consider an infrastructure that meets the specific needs of the beneficiaries. A cost is associated to each beneficiary, with the particularity that the needs of one cover the needs of all those with a lower cost. This covers many different situations, like for instance, an elevator in a building, a dam on a river or an airport landing field.

Let $N = \{1,\ldots,n\}$ be the set of beneficiaries. If a_i denotes the cost associated with beneficiary *i*, the total cost of the infrastructure is the maximum of the a_i's. And, if we consider a subset *S* of beneficiaries, the associated cost is the maximum of the a_i's for $i \in S$. This defines a cost game (*N*, *c*), known as *airport game*:

$$c(S) = Max_{i \in S}\, a_i \quad \text{for all } S \subset N. \tag{4.25}$$

In particular, $c(i) = a_i$ and $c(N) = Max\,(a_1, \ldots, a_n)$.

In the airport story, each type of airplane is assimilated to a player and to the minimum length of the airfield necessary for its type. It is convenient to order the costs, from the smallest to the largest: $0 < a_1 < a_2 < \ldots. < a_n$. The total cost to be divided is then given by $c(N) = a_n$.

Example 4.19 In the case of three players, the airport game defined in (4.25) is given by:

$$\begin{aligned} c(1) &= a_1, \\ c(2) &= c(1,2) = a_2, \\ c(3) &= c(1,3) = c(2,3) = c(1,2,3) = a_3. \end{aligned}$$

The following proposal confirms that economies of scale are involved in this problem: marginal costs are decreasing.

Proposition 4.21 *Airport* games are concave.

Proof Let S and T be two coalitions to which are associated the costs $c(S) = a_S$ and $c(T) = a_T$. Without loss of generality, we assume that $a_S \geq a_T$. We therefore have:

$$c(S \cup T) = Max\ (a_T, a_S) = a_S,$$
$$c(S \cap T) \leq Min\ (a_T, a_S) = a_T,$$

and $c(S) + c(T) - c(S \cup T) - c(S \cap T) = a_T - c(S \cap T) \geq 0$. The inequalities (4.19) are therefore satisfied, confirming the concavity of the game (N, a). ♦

There is a natural solution based on the principle that *no one should have to pay for the users associated with a greater cost*. If a company uses airplanes that need a 1 km long airfield, it should not have to pay for the longer airfield necessary for greater airplanes. This "*downstream principle*" leads to a simple triangular formula where additional costs are divided equally. It is given by:

$$\begin{aligned}
y_1 &= \tfrac{a_1}{n}, \\
y_2 &= \tfrac{a_1}{n} + \tfrac{a_2-a_1}{n-1}, \\
&\dots \\
y_k &= \tfrac{a_1}{n} + \tfrac{a_2-a_1}{n-1} + \dots + \tfrac{a_k-a_k-1}{n-k+1}, \\
&\dots \\
y_n &= \tfrac{a_1}{n} + \tfrac{a_2-a_1}{n-1} + \dots + \tfrac{a_{n-2}-a_{n-1}}{2} + a_n - a_{n-1}.
\end{aligned} \tag{4.26}$$

This formula has been proposed by different authors, in particular by Thompson (1971), in his PhD dissertation on airport fees at Birmingham airport. The link with cooperative games has been established later by Littlechild and Owen (1973) and by Littlechild and Thompson (1977) who have shown that this formula corresponds to the Shapley value $SV(N, c)$ of the airport game (4.26).

Example 4.19 (continued) The Shapley value of the 3-player airport game is given by:

$$\begin{aligned}
y_1 &= \frac{a_1}{3}, \\
y_2 &= \frac{a_1}{3} + \frac{a_2 - a_1}{2} = \frac{a_2}{2} - \frac{a_1}{6}, \\
y_3 &= \frac{a_1}{3} + \frac{a_2 - a_1}{2} + a_3 - a_2 = a_3 - \frac{a_2}{2} - \frac{a_1}{6}.
\end{aligned}$$

It can also be obtained from the marginal cost vectors associated to the 3-player airport game given in Table 4.15.

Table 4.15 Marginal cost vectors of the 3-player airport cost game

	1	2	3
123	a_1	$a_2 - a_1$	$a_3 - a_2$
132	a_1	0	$a_3 - a_1$
213	0	a_2	$a_3 - a_2$
231	0	a_2	$a_3 - a_2$
312	0	0	a_3
321	0	0	a_3
	$2a_1$	$3a_2 - a_1$	$6a_3 - 3a_2 - a_1$

Core allocations y satisfy the following inequalities

$$\begin{aligned} &y_i \le a_i \ (i = 1, 2, 3), \\ &y_1 + y_2 \le a_2, \\ &y_1 + y_3 \le a_3, \\ &y_2 + y_3 \le a_3. \end{aligned} \quad \Rightarrow \quad \begin{aligned} &0 \le y_1 \le a_1, \\ &0 \le y_2 \le a_2, \\ &a_3 - a_2 \le y_3 \le a_3. \end{aligned}$$

together with $y_1 + y_2 + y_3 = a_3$. The core is represented in Fig. 4.24 where its vertices are the marginal cost vectors, confirming the concavity of the cost game.

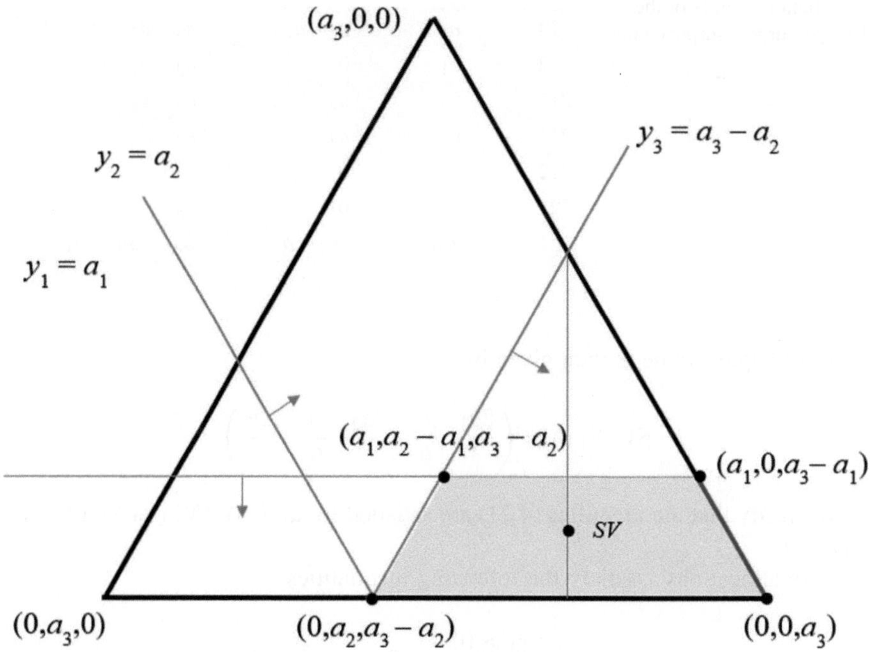

Fig. 4.24 Core of the 3-player cost-sharing airport game

The surplus sharing game associated to the airport game is given by:

$$v(S) = \sum_{i \in S} a_i - Max_{i \in S}\, a_i.$$

We observe that the largest cost a_n does not appear in the formulation of the surplus game. Actually, knowledge of the largest cost a_n suffices for the reconstruction of airport cost game from the airport surplus game.

Example 4.19 (continued) The 3-player surplus sharing game associated to the airport game is given by:

$$\begin{aligned} &v(1) = v(2) = v(3) = 0,\\ &v(1, 2) = v(1, 3) = a_1,\\ &v(2, 3) = a_2,\\ &v(1, 2, 3) = a_1 + a_2. \end{aligned}$$

Furthermore, the last two players are substitutable, a feature that is independent of the number of players. The marginal contribution vectors of the surplus game are given in Table 4.16.

Table 4.16 Marginal contribution vectors of the 3-player airport surplus game

	1	2	3
123	a_1	$a_2 - a_1$	$a_3 - a_2$
132	a_1	0	$a_3 - a_1$
213	0	a_2	$a_3 - a_2$
231	0	a_2	$a_3 - a_2$
312	0	0	a_3
321	0	0	a_3
	$2a_1$	$3a_2 - a_1$	$6a_3 - 3a_2 - a_1$

The Shapley value is then given by

$$SV(N, v) = \left(\frac{2a_1}{3}, \frac{a_1}{6} + \frac{a_2}{2}, \frac{a_1}{6} + \frac{a_2}{2}\right).$$

We verify that the identities (4.21) are satisfied for all i: $SV_i(N, v) + SV_i(N, c) = c(i) = a_i$.

Core allocations x satisfy the following inequalities

$$\begin{aligned} &x_1, x_2, x_3 \geq 0,\\ &x_1 + x_2 \geq a_1,\\ &x_1 + x_3 \geq a_1,\\ &x_2 + x_3 \geq a_2. \end{aligned} \Rightarrow \begin{aligned} &0 \leq x_1 \leq a_1,\\ &0 \leq x_2 \leq a_2,\\ &0 \leq x_3 \leq a_2. \end{aligned}$$

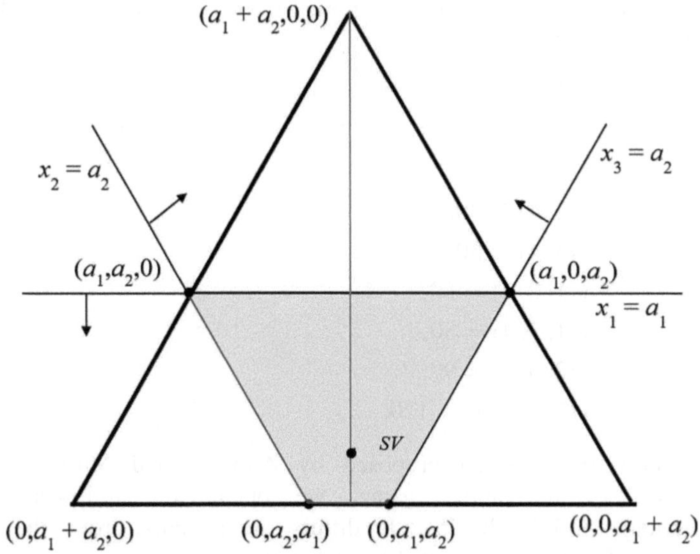

Fig. 4.25 Core of the 3-player surplus sharing airport game

together with $x_1 + x_2 + x_3 = a_1 + a_2$. The core is represented in Fig. 4.25 where its vertices are the marginal contribution vectors, confirming the convexity of the surplus game.

What about the nucleolus of an airport game? There actually exists a formula due to Sönmez (1993). Applied to the 3-players case, it is given by:

$$NU(N,c) = \begin{cases} \left(\frac{a_2}{3},\, \frac{a_2}{3},\, a_3 - \frac{2a_2}{3}\right) & \text{if } 3a_1 \geq 2a_2 \\ \left(\frac{a_1}{2},\, \frac{a_2}{2} - \frac{a_1}{4},\, a_3 - \frac{a_2}{2} - \frac{a_1}{4}\right) & \text{if } 3a_1 \leq 2a_2 \end{cases}$$

We observe that the allocation obtained when $3a_1 \leq 2a_2$ coincides with the average of the core vertices $AV(N, c)$.

We have already cited O'Neill (1982) in the framework of bankruptcy. He has studied another heritage problem from the Talmud, credited to Rabin Ibn Ezra and dated 1140. The story is the following.

Example 4.20 Rabin Ibn Ezra Method. Jacob dies. He has four sons, Reuben, Simeon, Levi and Judah ranked in terms of age. Reuben produces a deed that gives him the whole heritage whose value is 120. Simeon produces a deed that gives him half of it while Levi produces a deed that gives him one third and Judah produces a deed that gives him one fourth.

This is the bankruptcy problem $(120 \mid 30, 40, 60, 120)$. The associated game is defined by:

$$\begin{aligned}
&v(1) = v(2) = v(3) = v(4) = 0,\\
&v(1,2) = v(1,3) = v(2,3) = v(1,2,3) = 0,\\
&v(1,4) = 20,\\
&v(2,4) = 30,\\
&v(3,4) = 50,\\
&v(1,2,4) = 60,\\
&v(1,3,4) = 80,\\
&v(2,3,4) = 90,\\
&v(1,2,3,4) = 120.
\end{aligned}$$

If we apply the solution proposed by Aumann and Maschler, namely the nucleolus of the above game, we obtain the following division of the heritage $(15, 20, 30, 55)$. It differs significantly from the division (7.50, 10.83, 20.83, 80.83) proposed by Rabin Ibn Ezra whose reasoning goes as follows.

The three oldest sons tell to Judah "You are entitled to 30 and so do we. Hence, you get one fourth of 30". The two oldest then tell to Levi "You have got your share of 30 and you are entitled to one third of the difference between 40 and 30". Finally, Reuben tell to Simeon "You have got your share of 40 and you are entitled to half of the difference between 60 and 40". What remains then goes to him.

This corresponds to the division principle of the airport game as defined by (4.26) when creditors are ordered in terms of debts. It turns out that the division proposed by Rabin Ibn Erza corresponds indeed to the Shapley value of the game whose characteristic function is given by $v(S) = Max_{i \in S} d_i$.[36]

Sharing data (Dehez & Tellone, 2013)

REACH is a large program of the European Commission aimed at regulating the production, import and utilization of chemical substances (for instance, benzene, tungsten or titan) within the European Union.[37] It was started in 2008 and was supposed to be completed by the end of 2018. Firms had to submit a complete synthesis for each of the substances they produce, import and utilize, resulting in a huge data set. There are indeed about 30,000 substances and a hundred parameters for each substance! Some of the parameters are known, being either publicly available or detained by some firms. Others require specific and costly analysis.

In order to avoid the duplication of analysis, the Commission has encouraged firms to exchange information within consortia, one consortium for each substance,

[36] Applied to the contested garment problem, the method proposed by Rabbin Ibn Ezra reproduces the division (1/4, 3/4) proposed by the Talmud.

[37] See https://echa.europa.eu/regulations/reach/understanding-reach.

together with a system of compensation between its members. While the Commission was suggesting a system of compensations based on some accounting examples, it has been recognized that transferable utility games were offering the right framework to construct a coherent compensation system. The Shapley value has been proposed and experimented. However, at the end, it was never adopted, with some major firms preferring to negotiate compensations directly with other firms (and competitors…).

To formalize the problem, consider a particular substance and the associated consortium formed by a set $N = \{1,\ldots,n\}$ of firms. The set of data associated to that substance is denoted by $M_0 = \{1, \ldots, m\}$ and the subset of data owned by firm i is denoted by M_i. The *present* cost of reproducing data h is assumed to be known and given by $d_h > 0$: it is the value of data h. We denote by M_S the data set detained by coalition S:

$$M_S = \bigcup_{i \in S} M_i,$$

and we suppose that every data is detained by at least one firm: $M_N = M_0$. The value of the complete data set is denoted by v_0 :

$$v_0 = \sum_{h \in M_0} d_h.$$

No other restrictions are needed: a firm may detain no data at all while another may detain the complete data set, and the same data may be owned by several firms. If a coalition forms, the cost of acquiring the missing data is given by:

$$c(S) = \sum_{h \in M_0 \backslash M_S} d_h = v_0 - \sum_{h \in M_S} d_h \quad \text{for all } S \subset N,\ S \neq \emptyset.$$

This defines a cost game (N, c), called *data game*. Because $c(N) = 0$, it belongs to the class of *compensation games*: an allocation is an allocation $(y_1, y_2, \ldots, y_n)$ such that:

$$\sum_{i \in N} y_i = 0.$$

Example 4.21 Data Game. Consider the case of three firms and three data, with $M_1 = \emptyset$, $M_2 = \{1, 3\}$ and $M_3 = \{2, 3\}$, $d = (6, 9, 12)$. The data game and the associated surplus game are given by

$$\begin{aligned}
&c(1) = d_1 + d_2 + d_3 = 27, && v(1) = v(2) = v(3) = 0,\\
&c(2) = c(1, 2) = d_3 = 9, && v(1, 2) = v(1, 3) = 27,\\
&c(3) = c(1, 3) = d_1 = 6, && v(2, 3) = 15,\\
&c(2, 3) = c(1, 2, 3) = 0. && v(1, 2, 3) = 42.
\end{aligned}$$

Proposition 4.22 Data games *are subadditive and monotonic decreasing.* Data games *where at least one player does not detain the entire data set are essential.*

Proof If $M_0 \neq M_i$ for at least one i, we have

$$\sum_{i\in N} c(i) = nv_0 - \sum_{i\in N}\sum_{h\in M_i} d_h > 0.$$

Because $c(N) = 0$, the game is essential.

To check subadditivity, consider two coalitions S and T such that $S \cap T = \emptyset$. We then have:

$$\begin{aligned} c(S) + c(T) &= 2v_0 - \sum_{h\in M_S} d_h - \sum_{h\in M_T} d_h \\ &= c(S\cup T) + v_0 - \sum_{h\in M_S\cap M_T} d_h \geq c(S\cup T). \end{aligned}$$

Now, consider two coalitions S and T such that $S \subset T,\ S \neq \emptyset$. We then have $M_S \subset M_T$ and

$$c(T) - c(S) = \sum_{h\in M_S} d_h - \sum_{h\in M_T} d_h \leq 0.$$

Consequently, $c(T) \leq c(S)$: the characteristic function is decreasing with respect to set inclusion. ◆

A data game can be written as a sum of elementary games. Consider the game (N, c_h) associated to data h given by:

$$c_h(S) = \begin{cases} 0 & \text{if } S\cap T_h \neq \emptyset, \\ d_h & \text{if } S\cap T_h = \emptyset, \end{cases}$$

where $T_h = \{i \in N | h \in M_i\}$ is the set of players that detain data h. We then have:

$$\sum_{h\in M_0} c_h(S) = \sum_{h\in M_0\setminus M_S} d_h = c(S).$$

The core of a data game is nonempty: it contains the allocation (0, 0,…, 0). Indeed $c(N) = 0$ and $c(S) \geq 0$ for all $S \subset N$. The core has a particular geometric structure and it *only depends upon the cost of the data that are detained by single players.* We denote by $\overline{M}_0 \subset M_0$ the set of data that are detained by single players and by $\overline{M}_i = M_i \cap \overline{M}_0$ the set of data that player i is alone to detain. Alongside, we define successively the value of the data in $\overline{M}_0$ and the value of the data in $\overline{M}_i$:

$$\overline{v}_0 = \sum_{h \in \overline{M}_0} d_h \quad \text{and} \quad \overline{v}_i = \sum_{h \in \overline{M}_i} d_h$$

In particular, we have $\overline{v}_i = c(N \backslash i)$.

Proposition 4.23 *The* core *of a* data game (N, c) *is a regular simplex given by:*

$$C(N, c) = \{y \in \mathbb{R}^n | y(N) = 0 \text{ and } y_i \geq -\overline{v}_i \text{ for all } i = 1, ..., n\}.$$

Proof If $y \in C(N, c)$, we have $y(N \backslash i) \leq c(N \backslash i) = \overline{v}_i$. As $y(N) = 0$, we then have $y_i \geq -\overline{v}_i$. If instead y satisfies the above definition of the core, we have:

$$y(S) = -y(N \backslash S) \leq \sum_{i \in N \backslash S} \overline{v}_i \leq \sum_{h \in M_0 \backslash M_S} d_h = c(S) \text{ for all } S \subset N.$$

If $\overline{M}_0 \neq \emptyset$, we have $\overline{v}_0 > 0$ and the core is the simplex whose vertices are given by:

$$a^1 = (\overline{v}_0 - \overline{v}_1, -\overline{v}_2, ..., -\overline{v}_n),$$
$$a^2 = (-\overline{v}_1, \overline{v}_0 - \overline{v}_2, ..., -\overline{v}_n), ...,$$
$$a^n = (-\overline{v}_1, -\overline{v}_2, ..., \overline{v}_0 - \overline{v}_n).$$

Indeed, translating the core by adding the vector $\overline{v} = (\overline{v}_1, ..., \overline{v}_n)$, we obtain the set $\{y \in \mathbb{R}^n_+ | y(N) = \overline{v}_0\}$. It is the regular simplex whose n vertices are $(\overline{v}_0, 0, ..., 0)$, $(0, \overline{v}_0, 0, ..., 0)$,..., $(0, ..., 0, \overline{v}_0)$. The vertices of the core are then obtained by subtracting the vector$\overline{v}$.

If instead $\overline{M}_0 = \emptyset$, we have $\overline{v}_i = 0$ for all i and $C(N, c) = \{0\}$: once *each* data is detained by more than one firm, the core reduces to the allocation that excludes compensations. ◆

The proof is illustrated by Fig. 4.26. Notice that the core allocates zero to firms without data. The fact that the core is a simplex is a characteristic of the so-called 1-*convex games*, a concept introduced by Driessen (1985).[38] The symmetric structure of the simplex implies that the nucleolus of a 1-convex game is the center of gravity of the core.

[38] See Dehez (2021) for a survey on 1-convex games.

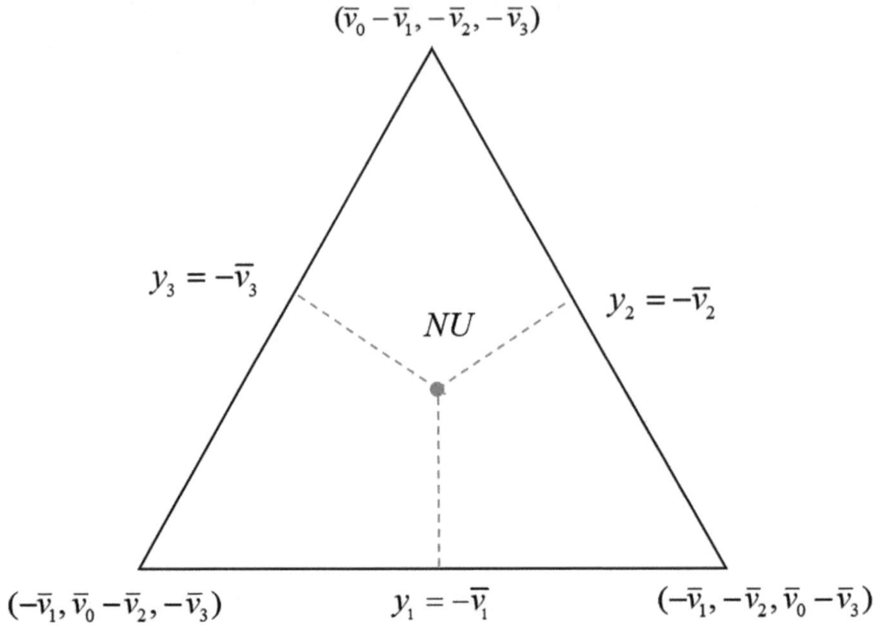

Fig. 4.26 Core of a 3-player data game

Example 4.21 (continued) In the 3-player data game, we have $\overline{M}_1 = \emptyset$, $\overline{M}_2 = \{1\}$, $\overline{M}_3 = \{2\}$, and $\overline{M}_0 = \{1, 2\}$. Hence, $\overline{v}_0 = 15$, $\overline{v} = (0, 6, 9)$ and the core is given by:

$$C(N, c) = \{y \in \mathbb{R}^n | y_1 + y_2 + y_3 = 0,\ \ y_1 \geq 0,\ \ y_2 \geq -6,\ \ y_3 \geq -9\}.$$

Its vertices are $a^1 = (15,\ -6,\ -9)$, $a^2 = (0,\ 9,\ -9)$ and $a^3 = (0,\ -6,\ 6)$, and its center of gravity is the allocation $(5, -1, -4)$. Because the core is a simplex, the nucleolus coincides with its center of gravity, as illustrated by Fig. 4.26.

Proposition 4.24 *The* nucleolus *of a* data game *is the average of its* core vertices:

$$NU_i(N, c) = \frac{\overline{v}_0}{n} - \overline{v}_i \quad (i = 1, .., n).$$

A firm is compensated if and only if the value of the data it is alone to detain ($\overline{v}_i$) exceeds the per capita value of the data detained by single firms ($\overline{v}_0$). Because a data sharing game can be written as a sum of elementary games, *additivity* allows for an easy computation of the Shapley value: it suffices to compute the Shapley value of an elementary game.[39]

[39] Béal et al. (2010) have axiomatized the Shapley value on the basis of properties specific to data games.

Proposition 4.25 *The* Shapley value *of a* data game *is given by:*

$$SV_i(N, c) = \frac{v_0}{n} - \sum_{h \in M_i} \frac{d_h}{t_h} \quad (i = 1, ..., n).$$

Proof For any given subset $T \subset N$, we define the game (N, e_T) by[40]:

$$e_T(S) = \begin{cases} 0 \text{ if } S \cap T = \emptyset, \\ 1 \text{ if } S \cap T \neq \emptyset. \end{cases}$$

Players in T are substitutable and players outside de T are null. Using the axioms of efficiency, symmetry and null player, we get:

$$SV_i(N, e_T) = \begin{cases} \frac{1}{t} \text{ for all } i \in T, \\ 0 \text{ for all } i \notin T. \end{cases}$$

An elementary game (N, c_h) can then be written $c_h(S) = \big(1 - e_{T_h}(S)\big)d_h$. As the Shapley value is a linear operator, the Shapley value of the elementary game (N, c_h) is given by

$$SV_i(N, c_h) = \begin{cases} \frac{d_h}{n} - \frac{d_h}{t_h} \text{ for all } i \in T_h, \\ \frac{d_h}{n} \qquad\quad \text{for all } i \notin T_h, \end{cases}$$

where $t_h = |T_h|$. The Shapley value of the complete game then follows by simple addition. ♦

According to the Shapley value, the worth of the data set is allocated uniformly among the firms and the worth of each individual data is *redistributed* among the firms that detain them.

Example 4.21 (continued) In the 3-player data game, we have $v_0 = 27$ and the Shapley value is given by $SV(N, c) = (9, -3, -6)$ to be compared to the nucleolus $(5, -1, -4)$.

Looking at the two compensation rules

$$SV_i(N, c) = \frac{v_0}{n} - \sum_{h \in M_i} \frac{d_h}{t_h},$$

[40] These games are used in Dehez (2011) to axiomatize the Shapley value in a cost-sharing framework.

$$NU_i(N,c) = \frac{\overline{v}_0}{n} - \sum_{h \in \overline{M}_i} d_h,$$

we observe that they coincide *if and only if* each data is detained by only one firm, i.e., $t_h = 1$ for all $h \in M_0$ or, equivalently, $M_i = \overline{M}_i$ for all $i \in N$.

By definition, the nucleolus belongs to the core: no coalition is in a position to object. The Shapley value instead may be subject to objections. In the framework of the REACH legislation, the possibility to leave the system and play jumper alone exists under the term "opt out". It is the weak point of the Shapley value. But does the nucleolus define an acceptable rule? The answer is negative because the core only considers the data that are detained by single firms, and not all the data. The weakness of the nucleolus is illustrated by the situation where only the players n and n–1 detain data and their data sets differ by a single data:

$$M_i = \emptyset \;\; (i = 1, \ldots, n-2), \;\; M_{n-1} = \{2, \ldots, m\} \text{ and } M_n = \{1, \ldots, m\}.$$

In this situation, the core compensates only the last firm and the other firms, firm $n - 1$ included, may have to pay up to d_1. The nucleolus goes further, by imposing to the $n - 1$ first players to pay d_1/n each. The Shapley value instead prescribes a system of compensation that is more acceptable:

$$\begin{aligned}
y_i &= \frac{v_0}{n} \quad (i = 1, \ldots, n-2),\\
y_{n-1} &= \frac{v_0}{n} - \sum_{h=2}^{m} \frac{d_h}{2} = -\frac{n-2}{2n} v_0 + \frac{d_1}{2},\\
y_n &= \frac{v_0}{n} - \sum_{h=2}^{m} \frac{d_h}{2} - d_1 = -\frac{n-2}{2n} v_0 - \frac{d_1}{2}.
\end{aligned}$$

The firms without data all pay the per capita value of the entire database, without compensation, while the last two firms are both compensated, the difference between what they get being precisely equal to d_1. The particular case where the individual data sets form a *partition* of the entire data set deserves that we look at it: $M_i \cap M_j = \emptyset$ for all $i \neq j$. In such a situation, $\overline{M}_i = M_i$ and $\overline{v}_i = v_i$ for all i. The data game and the associated surplus sharing game are then given by:

$$c(S) = v_0 - \sum_{i \in S} v_i \;\text{ and }\; v(S) = (s-1)\, v_0.$$

for all $S \neq \emptyset$. The latter is a symmetric and convex game. Indeed, the marginal contribution of a player i is always equal to 1 except for coalition $\{i\}$ where it is zero. The data game is therefore concave. The symmetry of the surplus sharing game implies that equal division is the natural allocation:

$$x_i = \frac{1}{n} v(N) = \frac{1}{n}(n-1) v_0$$

and, in terms of cost-sharing, the allocation is given by:

$$y_i = c(i) - x_i = c(i) - \frac{1}{n}(n-1)v_0 = \frac{v_0}{n} - v_i.$$

By the axiom of symmetry, it defines the Shapley value *and* the nucleolus.

Example 4.22 Data Game with Disjoint Data Sets. Consider the case of three firms and three data, with $d = (6, 9, 12)$, $M_1 = \emptyset$, $M_2 = \{1\}$ and $M_3 = \{2, 3\}$. The data game and the associated surplus game are given by:

$$\begin{aligned} c(1) &= v_0 = 27, \\ c(2) &= c(1,2) = d_2 + d_3 = 21, \\ c(3) &= c(1,3) = d_1 = 6, \\ c(2,3) &= c(1,2,3) = 0. \end{aligned} \qquad \begin{aligned} &v(1) = v(2) = v(3) = 0, \\ &v(1,2) = v(1,3) = v(2,3) = 27, \\ &v(1,2,3) = 54. \end{aligned}$$

The resulting compensation system follows from the equal division of the surplus. It is given by $(9, 3, -12)$: only firm 3 is compensated.

Patents and royalties (Dehez & Poukens, 2014).
Augustin Cournot (1838) was the first to observe that merging firms that produce complementary goods leads to higher profits and lower prices. That argument can be applied to the case of firms detaining patents that are essential for the development of a new product: if they fail to coordinate, each patent owner will apply an excessive tariff for the use of its patents, without considering the impact on his sales nor on the revenue of all the sector. Such a fragmentation of the intellectual property rights may eventually lead to the underutilization of the associated technological norm.

Over the last decades, *standard-setting organizations* have played an increasing role in the development and marketing of new technologies, for instance, the *International Telecommunications Union* (ITU), the *European Telecommunications Standard Institute* (ETSI) or the *American National Standards Institute* (ANSI). Beyond these organizations, there are agreements between firms willing to promote technological norms ensuring compatibility and interoperability of the associated devices, for instance, MPEG-k, nG and RFID.[41] The patents covering these norms are grouped and commercialized as a single package. That assumes that an agreement exists on the amount of *royalties* that will be imposed on users and on the division of the proceeds among the patent owners. Standard-setting organizations tend to evaluate the rights of use according to a ***F****air,* ***R****easonable* ***A****nd* ***N****on-****D****iscriminatory* (FRAND) scheme in order to avoid the risk of "hold-up" due to the temptation to impose excessive royalties.

Dehez and Poukens (2014) have proposed to define royalties in a cooperative game framework while distinguishing two types of patents, depending on the existence or

[41] For instance, MPEG-4 is a norm of video compression used in digital television. 4G is a norm of mobile telephony. RFID is the acronym of *Radio Frequency Identification.*

absence of substitutes. Here, to simplify, we will assume that all patents are essential and have no substitute.

We denote by $N = \{1, ..., n\}$ the set of firms that are concerned by the standard. There are m firms and by M the subset of the firms that detain one or several essential patents. The remaining firms without patents are *users*. We know the profit that each firm expects to obtain by using the associated technology or norm, π_i for firm i.[42] The question then concerns the division of the *total profit* $\pi(N)$ among the n firms. Any given division then defines the royalties that the users will pay to the patent owners as a part of their profit. We assume that $\pi_i > 0$ for all $i \notin M$. The cooperative game (N, v) associated to the situation (N, M, π) is defined by the characteristic function given by:

$$v(S) = \begin{cases} \pi(S) \text{ if } M \subset S, \\ 0 \quad\ \ \text{ if } M \not\subset S. \end{cases}$$

It defines a *patent game*. Notice that the number of patents does not matter. Indeed, all patents are essential and detaining at least one is enough: patent owners are necessary (veto) players.

There is an implicit hypothesis: firms operate on *disjoint markets*, allowing profits to be added. The total profit $v(N) = \pi(N) > 0$ is then the amount to be redistributed.

Proposition 4.26 Patent games *are essential and convex.*

Proof For $m \geq 2$, $v(i) = 0$ for all i and the game is essential. For $m = 1$, say $M = \{1\}$, the game is essential because $\pi_i > 0$ for all $i \neq 1$. Given two arbitrary subsets S and T, there are three cases.

$$\text{(i) } M \subset S \text{ and } M \not\subset T : \begin{cases} v(S \cap T) = 0 \text{ and } v(T) = 0, \\ v(S) = \pi(S), \\ v(S \cup T) = \pi(S) + \pi(T) - \pi(S \cap T) \\ \qquad\qquad = \pi(S) + \pi(T \backslash S) \geq \pi(S). \end{cases}$$

$$\text{(ii) } M \not\subset S \text{ and } M \not\subset T : \begin{cases} v(S) = v(T) = v(S \cap T) = 0, \\ v(S \cup T) \geq 0. \end{cases}$$

(iii) $M \subset S \cap T : v(S) + v(T) - v(S \cup T) - v(S \cap T) = \pi(S) + \pi(T) - \pi(S \cup T) - \pi(S \cap T) = 0.$

The inequalities characterizing convexity are verified in all three cases. ♦

The core of a patent game is defined by only $2n - m$ inequalities: beyond non-negativity, an allocation belongs to the core if no firm without a patent obtains more than its profit.

---

[42] The case $\pi_i = 0$ corresponds to non-profit organizations like for instance universities. For instance, Columbia University (New York) was part of the MPEG-2 consortium along with SONY.

Proposition 4.27 *The* core of the *patent game* (N, v) *associated to* (N, M, π) *is given by*

$$C(N, M, \pi) = \{x \in \mathbb{R}^n_+ | x(N) = \pi(N), \quad x_i \leq \pi_i \text{ for all } i \in N \setminus M\}.$$

Proof We know that a core allocation x satisfies the following inequalities:

$$x_i \leq v(N) - v(N \setminus i) \text{ for all } i \in N.$$

where $v(N) - v(N \setminus i) = \pi_i$ for all $i \notin M$. Hence, if x is a core allocation, $x_i \leq \pi_i$ for all $i \notin M$. Now, consider an allocation $x \in \mathbb{R}^n_+$ such that $x_i \leq \pi_i$ for all $i \notin M$ and a coalition S. If $M \not\subset S$, we have $v(S) = 0 \leq \pi(S)$.

If instead $M \subset S$, we have $x(S) = \pi(N) - x(N \setminus S) \geq \pi(N) - \pi(N \setminus S) = \pi(S) = v(S)$. It confirms that x is a core allocation. ♦

We observe that the allocation $(\pi_1, ..., \pi_n)$ belongs to the core, as well as the allocation that gives to the patent owners the totality of the profits of the users. The condition $x_1 \geq \pi_1$ that applies in the case where $M = \{1\}$ is redundant. Indeed, it is a consequence of the inequality $x(N \setminus M) \leq \pi(N \setminus M)$. In the case where there are no users, $n = m$ and the core includes all possible divisions of the total profit.

Example 4.23 Patent Game. Consider the case of three firms where the first two detain patents while the third one is a user. The associated characteristic function is given by $v = (0, 0, 0 | \pi_1 + \pi_2, 0, 0 | \pi_1 + \pi_2 + \pi_3)$. Figure 4.27 confirms that, beyond non-negativity, only one inequality defines the core, namely $x_1 + x_2 \geq \pi_1 + \pi_2$ or equivalently $x_3 \leq \pi_3$.

The marginal contributions of a firm i to a coalition S containing M are given by:

$$v(S) - v(S \setminus i) = \begin{cases} \pi(S) \text{ if } i \in M, \\ \pi_i \quad \text{ if } i \notin M. \end{cases}$$

Marginal contributions are equal to 0 for the coalitions not containing M and patent owners are substitutable. The following proposition gives the division derived from Shapley value.

Proposition 4.28 *The* Shapley value *of the game associated to* (N, M, π) *is given by*

$$\text{for } i \notin M\colon SV_i(N, M, \pi) = \frac{1}{m+1} \pi_i,$$
$$\text{for } i \in M\colon SV_i(N, M, \pi) = \frac{1}{m} \pi(M) + \frac{1}{m+1} \pi(N \setminus M).$$

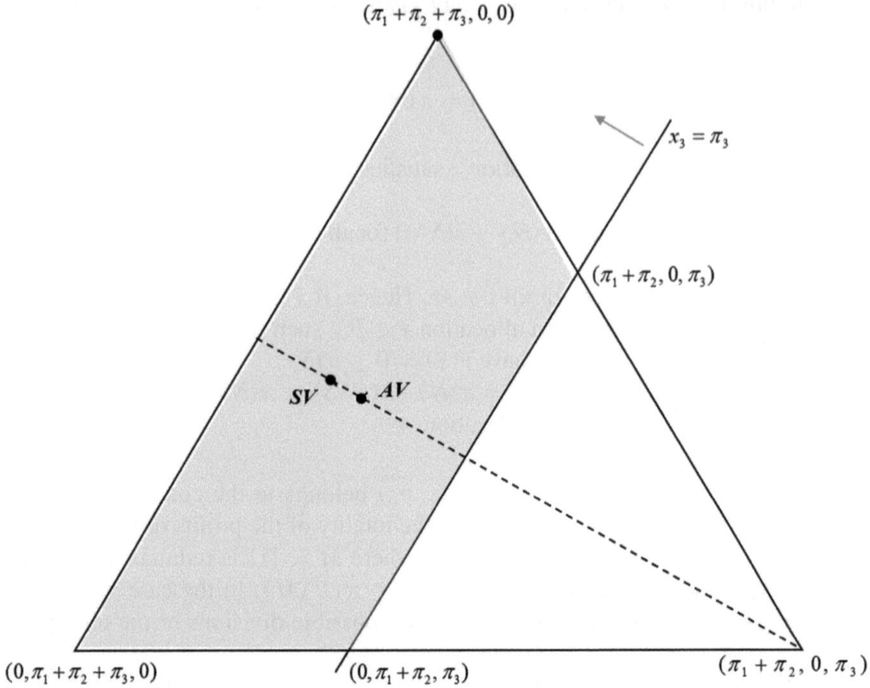

Fig. 4.27 Core of the 3-player patent game ($m = 2$)

Proof To compute the Shapley value, we only need to compute what a user receives. The marginal contribution of a firm $i \notin M$ is either zero or equal to π_i. Therefore, for a given ordering, firm i gets π_i if it is preceded by all firms in M. There are C_n^{m+1} ways to place the set $M \cup \{i\}$. As the ordering within M or outside M does not matter, the number of orderings σ such that $M \subset S_i^\sigma$ is given by[43]:

$$C_n^{m+1}\ m!\ (n-m-1)! = \frac{n!}{(m+1)!(n-m-1)!}\ m!\ (n-m-1)! = \frac{n!}{m+1}.$$

Hence, the amount allocated by the Shapley value to a user is given by

$$SV_i(N, v) = \frac{1}{m+1}\pi_i \text{ for all } i \notin M.$$

The amount of royalties paid to the patent owners is then given by $m\pi(N\backslash M)/(m+1)$ and the complete formula then follows from efficiency and symmetry: patent owners share equally the total profit and the royalties. ◆

[43] Remember that S_i^σ denotes the set of players who precede i in the ordering σ, i included.

We may add users, each one paying the same proportion of its profit. We observe that the share of profit given up by users increases with the number of patent owners and tends to 1. The amount of royalties becomes clearly excessive when there are many patent owners. If instead they form an organization, we fall in the case $m = 1$ where users have to pay half of their profits, a reasonable amount in agreement with the FRAND approach. This is what we obtain by taking the simple average of the marginal contribution vectors that do not take their multiplicity into account. In general, the simple average of the marginal contribution vectors is given by:

$$\begin{aligned}&\text{for } i \notin M\colon AV_i(N, M, \pi) = \tfrac{1}{2}\,\pi_i,\\ &\text{for } i \in M\colon AV_i(N, M, \pi) = \tfrac{1}{m}\,\pi(M) + \tfrac{1}{2m}\,\pi(N\backslash M).\end{aligned}$$

Users keep half of their profits independent of the number of patent owners. Both formulas, SV and AV, coincide only in the case where $m = 1$.

Example 4.23 (continued) Players 1 and 2 are the patent owners: only the coalitions $\{1, 2\}$ and $\{1, 2, 3\}$ have a positive worth while the user only contributes to the grand coalition. His contribution is equal to π_3 and therefore, the Shapley value gives to that firm a third of its profit. There are four distinct vectors that, by convexity, correspond to the vertices of the core. Modifying the example by assuming that $M = \{1\}$, the characteristic function becomes $v = (\pi_1, 0, 0|\pi_1 + \pi_2,\ \pi_1 + \pi_3,\ 0|\pi_1 + \pi_2 + \pi_3)$. Figure 4.28 represents the core and the Shapley value that is given by:

$$SV(N, M, \pi) = \left(\pi_1 + \frac{\pi_2 + \pi_3}{2}, \frac{\pi_2}{2}, \frac{\pi_3}{2}\right) = AV(N, M, \pi).$$

What about the nucleolus? It turns out that it may be inappropriate for the determination of royalties. Indeed, the royalties paid by a user happen to depend on the comparison between its profit and the profits of the patent owners. This is illustrated by Fig. 4.29 where $M = \{1, 2\}$.

Because patent owners are substitutable, the nucleolus depends on a single parameter and has the following form:

$$\left(\frac{\pi(N) - a}{2}, \frac{\pi(N) - a}{2}, a\right)$$

where $a \in [0, \pi(N)]$. The losses $e(x, S) = v(S) - x(S)$, as functions of the parameter a, are given by:

$$\begin{aligned}e(a, \{1\}) &= e(a, \{2\}) = \frac{a}{2} - \frac{\pi(N)}{2},\\ e(a, \{3\}) &= -a,\end{aligned}$$

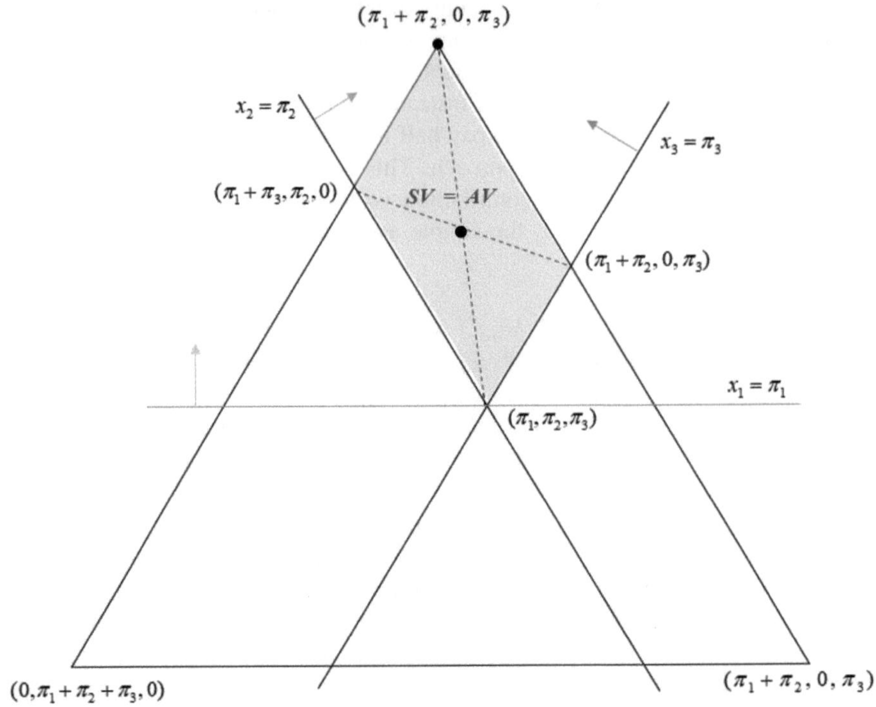

Fig. 4.28 Core of the 3-player patent game ($m = 1$)

$$e(a,\{1,2\}) = a - \pi_3,$$
$$e(a,\{1,3\}) = e(a,\{2,3\}) = -\frac{a}{2} - \frac{\pi(N)}{2}.$$

We may ignore the losses $e(a,\{1,3\})$ and $e(a,\{2,3\})$ because they are both located below $e(a,\{1\})$. The position of $e(a,\{1,2\})$ depends on the value of π_3 compared to $\pi_1+\pi_2$. In Fig. 4.29, assuming $\pi_3 = 2(\pi_1+\pi_2)$, $e(a,\{1,2\})$ is the dotted line passing through the intersection between $e(a,\{1\})$ and $e(a,\{3\})$ defined by $a = \pi(N)/3.a = \pi(N)/3$.

The value of the parameter a that defines the nucleolus is given by the intersection between $e(a,\{3\})$ and $e(a,\{1,2\})$ in the case where $\pi_3 < 2(\pi_1+\pi_2)$, and by the intersection between $e(a,\{3\})$ and $e(a,\{1\})$ in the case where $\pi_3 > 2(\pi_1+\pi_2)$:

$$a = \begin{cases} \frac{\pi_3}{2} & \text{if } 0 \le \pi_3 \le 2(\pi_1+\pi_2), \\ \frac{\pi_1+\pi_2+\pi_3}{3} & \text{if } \pi_3 \ge 2(\pi_1+\pi_2). \end{cases}$$

If the user's profit if low relative to the sum of the profits of the patent owners, the nucleolus coincides with *AV*, the average of the marginal contribution vectors: the user then gives up half of its profit. In the opposite case where the user's profit

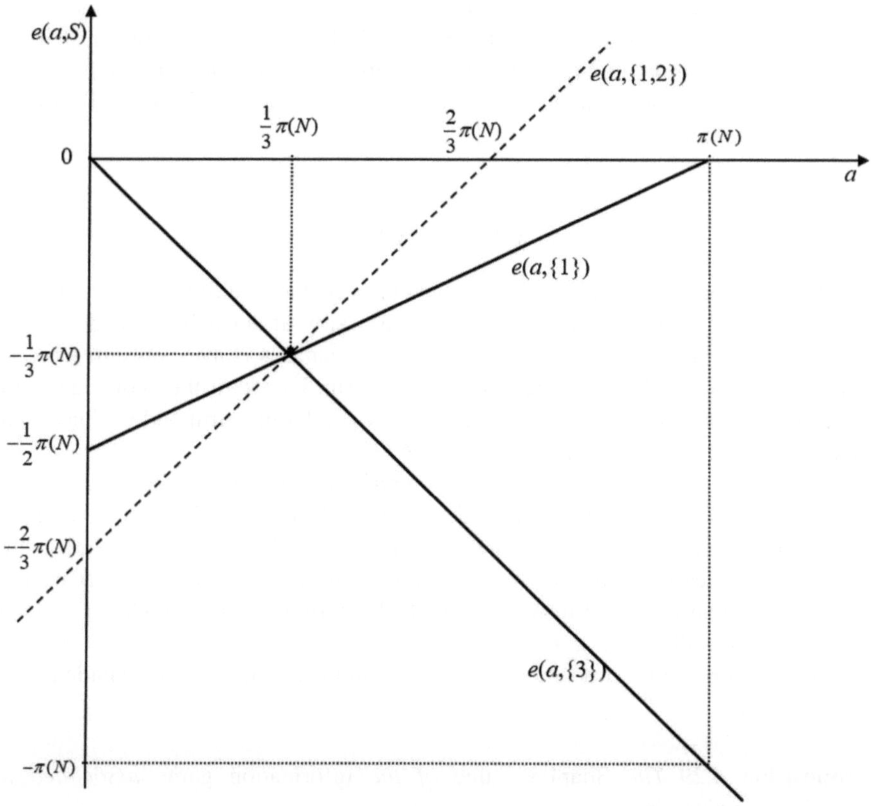

Fig. 4.29 Nucleolus of the 3-player patent game ($m = 2$)

if high, the nucleolus coincides with the equal division: the royalties paid by the user then exceed the sum of the profits of the patent owners:

$$\pi_3 - \frac{\pi_1 + \pi_2 + \pi_3}{3} = \frac{2\pi_3 - (\pi_1 + \pi_2)}{3} \geq \pi_1 + \pi_2.$$

Sharing information (Muto et al., 1989).
There is a link between the patent games and the *information games* introduced by Muto et al. (1989).[44] In information games, some firms possess an essential information that could be a patent. It differs from a patent situation except in the case where the information is held by a single firm. Unlike the data sharing problem, the question here concerns the redistribution of the profits that firms generate when they share the information. In particular, how much should uninformed firms pay to informed firms.

[44] See also Moulin (1986, p. 431).

Like for patent games, we denote by M, $M \neq N$, the subset of informed firms with $1 \leq m < n$, and by $\pi_i > 0$ the profit that firm i expects to obtain if it has access to the information. Without that information, a firm cannot expect to obtain a positive profit. The associated cooperative game is then described by the following characteristic function:

$$v(S) = \begin{cases} \sum_{i \in S} \pi_i & \text{if } S \cap M \neq \emptyset, \\ 0 & \text{if } S \cap M = \emptyset. \end{cases}$$

The case where $m = n$ has been excluded because the resulting game would then be additive and no redistribution would be necessary. It is easily verified that this defines a superadditive and essential game. The game is convex only in the case where the information is detained by only one firm. Indeed, it then coincides with the patent game where the essential patent is owned by that firm and we know that patent games are convex by Proposition 4.26.

The core is nonempty: it always contains the no-compensation allocation $(\pi_1, \pi_2, \ldots, \pi_n)$. Once several firms detain the information, the core reduces to that allocation and it therefore coincides with the nucleolus: in such a case, the information loses its value due to the competition between its owners. If instead there is only one informed firm, say firm 1, the core is given by $C(N, v) = \{x \in \mathbb{R}^n_+ \mid x_i \leq \pi_i \text{ for all } i = 2, \ldots, n\}$.

This is in line with Proposition 4.27: we are indeed in the case of a single patent holding firm.

Proposition 4.29 *The* Shapley value *of the* information game *associated to* (N, M, π) *is given by:*

$$SV_i(N, M, \pi) = \begin{cases} \frac{m}{m+1}\pi_i & \text{if } i \notin M, \\ \pi_i + \frac{1}{m(m+1)}\pi(N \backslash M) & \text{if } i \in M. \end{cases}$$

Proof We proceed in three steps. We first show that informed firms keep their profit and receive all the same compensation. Indeed, in the 0-normalized game, informed firms are substitutable and Shapley value gives them an identical amount, say b. So, we have $SV_i(N, M, \pi) = \pi_i + b$ for all $i \in M$.

We then show that the uninformed firms keep an equal proportion of their profits that is independent of the number of uninformed firms. Given an arbitrary vector of marginal contributions, we observe that a firm $i \notin M$ receives π_i or 0, whether it is preceded or not by an informed firm. Hence, there is a α such that $SV_i(N, M, \pi) = \alpha\,\pi_i$ for all $i \notin M$. We then observe that adding an uninformed firm multiplies the number of orderings favorable to an uninformed firm by $n + 1$: they were $\alpha\, n!$ and are now $\alpha\,(n + 1)!$ confirming that the coefficient α only depends on m.

It remains to compute the value of α in the case where there is only one uniformed firm, say firm n. It receives its profit in all orderings in which it is *not first*. There are $n! - (n-1)!$ such orderings and the Shapley value allocates to firm n an amount equal to

$$SV_n(N, M, \pi) = \frac{n! - (n-1)!}{n!}\pi_n = \frac{n-1}{n}\pi_n.$$

From that, we deduce the value of the proportionality coefficient as a function of m:

$$\alpha(m) = \frac{m}{m+1}. \quad \blacklozenge$$

As for patents, the Shapley value imposes to the uninformed firms to pay a proportion equal to $1/(m+1)$ of their profits. That proportion is equal to 1/2 when there is a single informed firm and it *decreases* with the number of informed firms.

Example 4.24 Information Game. The 3-player information game where $M = \{1, 2\}$ is given by:

$$v(1) = \pi_1,\ v(2) = \pi_2,\ v(3) = 0,$$
$$v(i, j) = \pi_i + \pi_j,\ \text{for } i \neq j,$$
$$v(1, 2, 3) = \pi_1 + \pi_2 + \pi_3.$$

The marginal contribution vectors are given by Table 4.17.

Table 4.17 Marginal contribution vectors: case where the first two firms are informed

	1	2	3
123	π_1	π_2	π_3
132	π_1	π_2	π_3
213	π_1	π_2	π_3
231	π_1	π_2	π_3
312	$\pi_1 + \pi_3$	π_2	0
321	π_1	$\pi_2 + \pi_3$	0

If instead $M = \{1\}$, we fall back to a patent game with a single patent holding firm. The marginal contribution vectors are given by Table 4.18.

The Shapley values in these two situations are given by:

$$SV(N, M, \pi) = \left(\pi_1 + \frac{\pi_2 + \pi_3}{2}, \frac{\pi_2}{2}, \frac{\pi_3}{2}\right) = AV(N, M, \pi),$$

$$SV(N, M, \pi) = \left(\pi_1 + \frac{\pi_3}{6},\ \pi_2 + \frac{\pi_3}{6},\ \frac{2}{3}\pi_3\right).$$

Table 4.18 Marginal contribution vectors: case where only firm 1 is informed

	1	2	3
123	π_1	π_2	π_3
132	π_1	π_2	π_3
213	$\pi_1 + \pi_2$	0	π_3
231	$\pi_1 + \pi_2 + \pi_3$	0	0
312	$\pi_1 + \pi_3$	π_2	0
321	$\pi_1 + \pi_2 + \pi_3$	0	0

Apportionment of damages (Ferey and Dehez 2013, 2016a and 2016b)
In law, the question of sharing damage that result from the action of several actors (physical or moral)—called *tortfeasors* in some legal texts—has been and still is the object of intense discussions, philosophical as well as juridical. It opens the problem of *causality*.

There are many examples. Here is a first. A pedestrian is run down by a car and one of his legs is broken. He is moved to a hospital where he undergoes surgery. Nothing goes as planned and he ends up losing his leg. He is entitled to compensation, to be determined. Two parties are involved, the car driver and the hospital. How much should each party contribute? Here is a second. A railway bridge is provided to support a maximum of 20 tons. The trains that take it have a weight of 18 tons. Three actors, maybe ill-intentioned, abandon on the deck goods of a certain weight. They act independently. The first one places 2 tons of goods while the other two place 3 tons each. At the passage of the train, the total weight is 26 tons and the bridge collapses, causing several casualties. How to share damage between the three actors? These two examples have a different structure. There is sequentiality in the first: without the intervention of the car driver, no damage would have resulted. Is he then fully responsible? This is not the case in the second: alone the first actor would not have caused the catastrophe while each of the other two actors would have caused it alone.

It is important to specify that we are in an *ex-post* perspective. Damage has been caused and the question concerns the compensation of the victims. We are in civil law, not in criminal law.

To capture causality, we construct a cooperative game (N, v) where N is the set of actors and the characteristic function v measures *potential damage*. More precisely, $v(S)$ measures the damage that would have resulted from the intervention of the members of coalition S, $S \neq N$, while $v(N)$ measures the total damage D actually observed; it is the amount that has to be divided among the actors. This defines a *liability game*. Knowledge of $v(S)$ allows the computation of the additional damage caused by coalition S, $v(N) - v(N\backslash S)$, as well as of the additional damage caused by an individual actor, $v(N) - v(N\backslash i)$ for actor i.

By definition, the core of a liability game (N, v) is the set of contributions $(x_1, ..., x_n)$ that are *acceptable* in the sense that each coalition contributes at least its *potential damage* and *at most its* additional damage:

$$v(S) \leq x(S) \leq v(N) - v(N \backslash S) \quad \text{for all } S \subset N.$$

This extends to coalitions the legal principle that imposes that each individual actor pays at least his potential damage and at most his additional damage:

$$v(i) \leq x_i \leq v(N) - v(N \backslash i) \quad \text{for all } S \subset N.$$

Being based on the additional damage $Cm_i(S) = v(S) - v(S \backslash i)$, the Shapley value provides a neutral and equitable solution to the question of damage sharing.

We distinguish different situations. In the case where no damage result in the absence of any one of the actors, we are in a unanimity game where all actors are substitutable. As a consequence, the Shapley value leads to an equal division.

In a *sequential* situation, actors are identified by their position in the sequence of actions and their immediate damage, $d_i \geq 0$ for actor i. An immediate damage may be null: if $d_i = 0$ for some $i < n$, i is an actor who has caused an *indirect* damage. If the victim is one of the actors, it appears in the first position. Two actors are substitutable if one follows the other in the sequence while the first does not cause any immediate damage.

The corresponding liability game is then entirely defined by the list of immediate damage $d = (d_1, d_2, ..., d_n)$.

Example 4.25 Sequential Damage Game. In the case of two or three actors, we have:

$$\begin{aligned}
&v(1) = v(1, 3) = d_1, \\
&v(2) = v(3) = v(2, 3) = 0, \\
&v(1, 2) = d_1 + d_2, \\
&v(1, 2, 3) = d_1 + d_2 + d_3 = D.
\end{aligned}$$

We easily verify that core allocations are such that $x_1 \geq d_1$: the first actor, the initiator, has to contribute at least his immediate damage. Furthermore, the core contains the allocation $(D, 0, ..., 0)$ that imposes to the first actor to pay alone the total damage. It also contains the damage vector d that imposes to each actor to pay his immediate damage. More generally the core of a sequential liability game is given by:

$$C(N, d) = \left\{ x \in \mathbb{R}^n_+ \,\middle|\, x(N) = \sum_{j=1}^{n} d_j \text{ and } \sum_{j=1}^{i} x_j \geq \sum_{j=1}^{i} d_j \text{ for all } i \in N \right\}.$$

We observe that no actor has to pay for damages caused *upstream*.

Table 4.19 Vectors of marginal contributions of a 3-player sequential liability game

	1	2	3
123	d_1	d_2	d_3
132	d_1	$d_2 + d_3$	0
213	$d_1 + d_2$	0	d_3
231	$d_1 + d_2 + d_3$	0	0
312	d_1	$d_2 + d_3$	0
321	$d_1 + d_2 + d_3$	0	0

The sequential liability games are closely related to the airport games.[45] They are convex and, as a consequence, their core is nonempty and contains the Shapley value.

Example 4.25 (continued) In the 3-actor sequential game, the vectors of marginal contributions are given in Table 4.19.

In terms of marginal contributions, d_2 is the marginal damage of actor 2 to coalition $\{1, 2\}$ while $D = d_1 + d_2 + d_3$ is the marginal damage of actor 1 to the grand coalition. For instance, 2 and 3 are substitutable actors if and only if $d_2 = 0$.

The Shapley value follows from Table 4.19. It is given by:

$$\begin{aligned} x_1 &= \frac{1}{3}d_3 + \frac{1}{2}d_2 + d_1, \\ x_2 &= \frac{1}{3}d_3 + \frac{1}{2}d_2, \\ x_3 &= \frac{1}{3}d_3. \end{aligned} \tag{4.27}$$

No surprise, like for the airport games, we obtain a triangular formula. It is a natural division such that no actor pays for upstream damage. The Shapley value can be axiomatized on the set of sequential liability games using the following properties.

A9 *Null immediate damage* If an actor causes no immediate damage, his contribution and his successor's contribution must coincide:

$$\text{for all } d \in \mathbb{R}^n_+ : d_i = 0,\ i < n \ \Rightarrow\ \varphi_i(N, d) = \varphi_{i+1}(N, d).$$

[45] More precisely, one is the *dual* of the other (see Dehez and Ferey, 2013). The characteristic function v^d that defines the dual of a game (N,v) associates to any coalition S its marginal contribution: $v^d(S) = v(N) - v(N\backslash S)$.

A10 *Upstream independence* The contribution of an actor does not depend on damages caused by actors that precede him:

$$\text{for all } d,\ d' \in \mathbb{R}^n_+ : \ d_j = d'_j,\ j = i, \ldots, n \ \Rightarrow \ \varphi_i(N, d) = \varphi_i(N, d').$$

Null immediate damage is nothing but a consequence of symmetry. Indeed, if $d_i = 0$ for some $i < n$, then i and $i + 1$ are substitutable actors.

Proposition 4.30 *The* Shapley value *is the unique efficient allocation rule that satisfies* Null immediate damage *and* Upstream independence *on the set of all sequential* liability games.

Proof Consider the case where $n = 3$. If $d = (0, 0, d_3)$, Efficiency and null immediate damage imply:

$$\varphi_1(N, (0, 0, d_3)) = \varphi_2(N, (0, 0, d_3)) = \varphi_3(N, (0, 0, d_3)) = \frac{d_3}{3}.$$

Upstream independence then implies $\varphi_3(d) = d_3/3$ for all $d \geq 0$. If $d = (0, d_2, d_3)$, Efficiency and null immediate damage imply:

$$\varphi_1(N, (0, d_2, d_3)) = \varphi_2(N, (0, d_2, d_3)) = \frac{1}{2}(d_2 + d_3 - \frac{1}{3}d_3) = \frac{1}{2}d_2 + \frac{1}{3}d_3.$$

Using again Upstream independence, one gets $\varphi_2(d) = d_2/2 + d_3/3$ for all $d \geq 0$. It then remains d_1 that must be covered by the first actor:

$$\varphi_1(N, d) = d_1 + \frac{1}{2}d_2 + \frac{1}{3}d_3 \text{ for all } d \geq 0.$$

We have retrieved (4.27) and these arguments can be extended to any number of actors, by proceeding backward, starting from the last actor. Hence, A1, A9 and A10 define a unique allocation rule. Because the Shapley value satisfies these properties, that rule must be the Shapley value. ◆

Example 4.25 (continued) In the 3-actor sequential game, if $d_2 > 0$, there are four distinct marginal contribution vectors:

$$\begin{aligned}
\mu^1 &= (d_1, d_2, d_3), \\
\mu^2 &= (d_1, d_2 + d_3, 0), \\
\mu^3 &= (d_1 + d_2, 0, d_3), \\
\mu^4 &= (d_1 + d_2 + d_3, 0, 0).
\end{aligned}$$

By convexity, they correspond to the vertices of the core, as illustrated by Fig. 4.30.

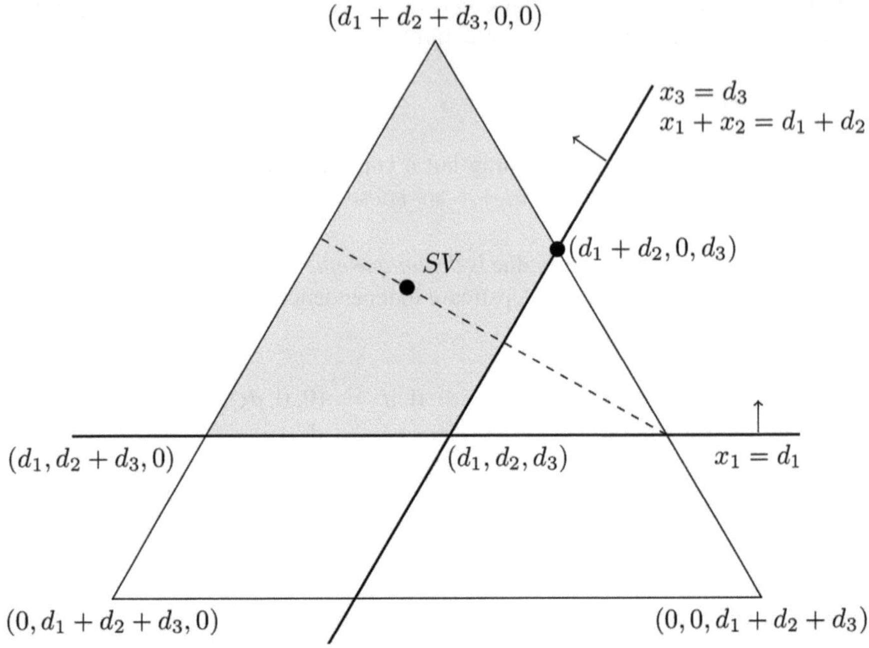

Fig. 4.30 Core of a 3-player sequential liability game

Example 4.26 Railway Bridge. The railway bridge mentioned earlier can sustain at most 20 tons while trains weigh 18 tons. The associated liability game is neither simultaneous nor sequential. Knowing that the first actor placed 2 tons while the last two actors placed 3 tons each, is given by:

$$\begin{aligned} v(1) &= 0, \\ v(2) &= v(3) = D, \\ v(1,2) &= v(1,3) = v(2,3) = v(1,2,3) = D. \end{aligned}$$

The first actor is a null player while the other two are substitutable. The Shapley value then exempts the first actor and allocates half of the damage to the last two actors. The core is empty: there is no acceptable division of the damages. In such circumstances, it is likely that a judge will consider the three participants in solidarity and impose on them to pay each one third of the damage.

If instead the weights had been 0.5 and 1.5 tons respectively, the game becomes:

$$\begin{aligned} v(1) &= v(2) = v(3) = 0, \\ v(1,2) &= v(1,3) = 0, \\ v(2,3) &= v(1,2,3) = D. \end{aligned}$$

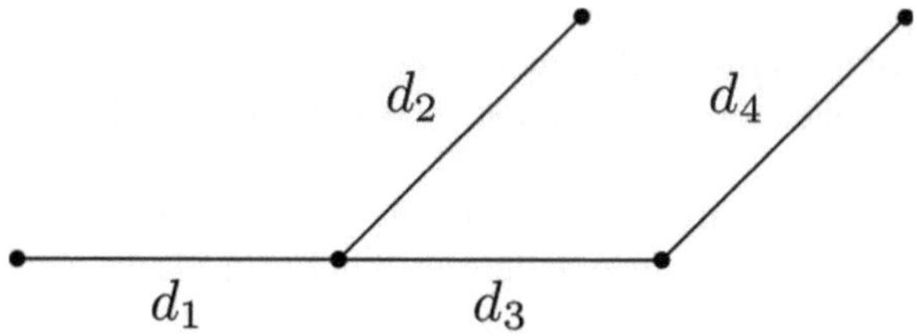

Fig. 4.31 Sequential tree structure

The core is still empty while the Shapley value is unchanged.

If weights were 2 tons and 1 ton, respectively, we would end up with a simple majority game where actor 1 is a necessary player. In this case, the core is nonempty and reduces to the allocation (D, 0, 0) while the Shapley value allocates 2/3 of the damages to the first actor.

Example 4.27 Falling Infant: Talmud Ruling. The Talmud contains an interesting ruling.[46] It says what the law should be if someone throws an infant from a roof and someone else "receives" the infant on a sword, thus killing him before he reaches the ground. While neither party is absolved, the ruling says that neither party is guilty of violating the biblical injunction against murder. A minority opinion holds that the person with the sword is liable on the biblical count of murder because he hastened the infant's death, even if by a fraction of a second. Framing the story as a liability game, we have

$$v(1) = D,$$
$$v(2) = 0,$$
$$v(1, 2) = D.$$

The Shapley value and the nucleolus coincide: they consider that the first person is the only liable person.

Oishi et al. (2023) have analyzed more complex situations of sequential liability that can be represented in a directed tree where each branch is associated to an actor.

Example 4.28 Sequential Tree Structure. Figure 4.31 illustrates a 4-player sequential tree structure.

The simple sequential case is therefore a tree that goes along a single line, without bifurcations. The computation of the Shapley value remains, however, easy. It starts from terminal nodes and proceeds backward towards the initial node:

[46] That story was reported to me by Robert Aumann. The precise source is Bav Kamma 26B.

- for a given path, identify the number of branches, say k,
- allocate $1/k$ of the terminal damages to the actors present along the path,
- repeat the sequence for each terminal node and eliminate them.

We then proceed identically on the pruned tree, and repeat the operation until the initial node. Applied to the situation described in Fig. 4.31, we get:

$$\begin{aligned}
x_4 &= \frac{1}{3}d_4 + 0 + 0 + 0 = \frac{1}{3}d_4,\\
x_3 &= \frac{1}{3}d_4 + 0 + \frac{1}{2}d_3 + 0 = \frac{1}{3}d_4 + \frac{1}{2}d_3,\\
x_2 &= 0 + \frac{1}{2}d_2 + 0 + 0 = \frac{1}{2}d_2,\\
x_1 &= \frac{1}{3}d_4 + \frac{1}{2}d_3 + \frac{1}{2}d_2 + d_1.
\end{aligned}$$

The corresponding liability game is given by

$$\begin{aligned}
&v(1) = v(1,4) = d_1,\\
&v(2) = v(3) = v(4) = v(2,3) = v(2,4) = v(3,4) = v(2,3,4) = 0,\\
&v(1,2) = v(1,2,4) = d_1 + d_2,\\
&v(1,3) = d_1 + d_3,\\
&v(1,2,3) = d_1 + d_2 + d_3,\\
&v(1,3,4) = d_1 + d_3 + d_4,\\
&v(1,2,3,4) = d_1 + d_2 + d_3 + d_4.
\end{aligned}$$

The Shapley value can be computed from Table 4.20 that gives the marginal contributions for coalitions with positive worth.

Adding a branch can easily be accommodated. Figure 4.32 illustrates the situation that includes a fifth actor.

Table 4.20 Marginal contributions of the sequential tree structure

	1	2	3	4
$\{1\}$	d_1	0	0	0
$\{1,2\}$	$d_1 + d_2$	d_2	0	0
$\{1,3\}$	$d_1 + d_3$	0	d_3	0
$\{1,4\}$	d_1	0	0	0
$\{1,2,3\}$	$d_1 + d_2 + d_3$	d_2	d_3	0
$\{1,2,4\}$	$d_1 + d_2$	d_2	0	0
$\{1,3,4\}$	$d_1 + d_3 + d_4$	0	$d_3 + d_4$	d_4
$\{1,2,3,4\}$	$d_1 + d_2 + d_3 + d_4$	d_2	$d_3 + d_4$	d_4

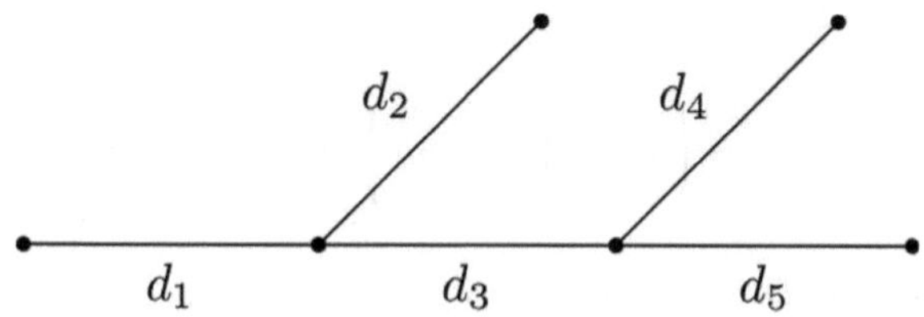

Fig. 4.32 Augmented sequential tree structure

The allocation derived from the Shapley value allocates one third of d_5 to the new actor, and the same amount is added to the contributions of 1 and 3. The contributions of 2 and 4 remain unchanged.

Dehez and Ferey (2013) show that it is possible to assign weights to actors to account for the severity of their misconduct. The choice of weights is then the decision of the judge who may have reasons to deviate from the symmetric Shapley value.[47]

Dividing a collective probability of success (Hou et al., 2018)
We consider situations where different actors have a common target. The probability with which each actor attains the target is known. Assuming that they act independently, the joint probability of success can be computed. The question is then to determine the share of every actor in this collective probability of success. These shares can then be used for allocation purposes. Budget allocation for a missile interception system or for vaccine research units are two examples. Another example is the division of damage in a probabilistic framework. And actors could be factors, like those that influence a particular disease or a fatal car accident.

Assume that players are facing an attainable target. By his actions, each player *alone* can reach the target with a known probability p_i, $0 < p_i \leq 1$, for player i. Players' actions are coordinated, but the success of a player is assumed to be independent of the success of another player. Consequently, the probability that a coalition $S \subset N$ fails is given by[48]:

$$\prod_{j \in S} (1 - p_j)$$

where, *by* convention, a product over an empty set is equal to 1.

We define a *probability game* (N, v) whose characteristic function associates to each coalition S the probability that *at least one* of its members succeeds, assuming

[47] They use the notion of *weighted value* introduced by Shapley (1953) and the fact that, for games convex, the set of allocations obtained as weighted values coincides with the core (see Monderer et al., 1992).

[48] See the Mathematical appendix for basic probability concepts.

that players outside S *all* fail[49]:

$$v(S) = \left(1 - \prod_{j \in S} (1 - p_j)\right) \prod_{j \in N \setminus S} (1 - p_j).$$

It indeed corresponds to the worse case.

The marginal contribution of player i to the success of coalition S is the probability that player i succeeds while players *outside* S all fail:

$$MC_i^v(S) = p_i \prod_{j \in N \setminus S} (1 - p_j).$$

Proposition 4.31 *Probability games are convex and thereby superadditive.*

Proof Marginal contributions are *increasing* with respect to set inclusion. Indeed, if $i \in S \subset T$, we have:

$$p_i \left(\prod_{j \in N \setminus S} (1 - p_j) - \prod_{j \in N \setminus T} (1 - p_j) \right)$$

$$= p_i \prod_{j \in N \setminus T} (1 - p_j) \left(\prod_{j \in T \setminus S} (1 - p_j) - 1 \right) > 0.$$

Convexity then follows from Proposition 4.2. ◆

To compute the Shapley value, we shall use the formula based on the Harsanyi dividends. Dividends are given by (4.5):

$$\alpha_T(N, v) = \prod_{j \in T} p_j \prod_{j \in N \setminus T} (1 - p_j).$$

It is the probability that all players in T succeed while players outside T all fail. Dividends of probability games are nonnegative: probability games are positive games. Using (4.16), the Shapley value is given by:

$$SV_i(N, p) = \sum_{\substack{T \subset N \\ i \in T}} \frac{(-1)^{t-1}}{t} \prod_{j \in T} p_j$$

$$= p_i \sum_{\substack{T \subset N \\ i \in T}} \frac{(-1)^{t-1}}{t} \prod_{j \in T \setminus i} p_j \; (i = 1, \ldots, n). \tag{4.28}$$

[49] This is the dual of the game used by Hou et al. (2018).

Example 4.29 Probability Game. The 3-player probability game is defined by:

$$\begin{aligned} v(i) &= p_i(1-p_j)(1-p_k) && \text{for } i,j,k \in \{1,2,3\}, j,k \neq i, j \neq k, \\ v(i,j) &= (p_i+p_j-p_ip_j)(1-p_k) && \text{for } i,j,k \in \{1,2,3\}, j,k \neq i, j \neq k, \\ v(1,2,3) &= 1-(1-p_1)(1-p_2)(1-p_3). \end{aligned}$$

Its Shapley value is given by:

$$SV_1(N,v) = p_1 - \frac{1}{2}(p_1p_2+p_1p_3) + \frac{1}{3}p_1p_2p_3 = p_1\left(1-\frac{1}{2}(p_2+p_3)+\frac{1}{3}p_2p_3\right)$$
$$SV_2(N,v) = p_2 - \frac{1}{2}(p_1p_2+p_2p_3) + \frac{1}{3}p_1p_2p_3 = p_2\left(1-\frac{1}{2}(p_1+p_3)+\frac{1}{3}p_1p_3\right)$$
$$SV_3(N,v) = p_3 - \frac{1}{2}(p_1p_3+p_2p_3) + \frac{1}{3}p_1p_2p_3 = p_3\left(1-\frac{1}{2}(p_1+p_2)+\frac{1}{3}p_1p_2\right)$$

Looking at (4.28), we observe that the Shapley value allocates to a player a share that is *proportional* to his probability of success:

$$SV_i(N,p) = p_i f(p_{-i})$$

where p_{-i} denotes the vector of probabilities of which the coordinate i has been eliminated and the function $f : \mathbb{R}_+^{n-1} \to \mathbb{R}_+$ is *player-independent* and *symmetric*. We then introduce the following axiom.

A11 *Proportionality* There exist n functions $f_1, ..., f_n : \;]0,1]^{n-1} \to \mathbb{R}$ such that:

$$\varphi_i(N,p) = p_i f_i(p_{-i}) \text{ for all } i \in N.$$

The following proposition is proven in Dehez (2023).

Proposition 4.32 *There is a unique efficient allocation rule φ defined on the set of probability games that satisfies symmetry (A2) and proportionality (A11).*

Together with symmetry, proportionality characterizes the Shapley value on the class of probability games: it is the property that differentiates the Shapley value from other symmetric allocation rules. This is not proportionality in the Aristotelian sense: the ratio between the amounts allocated by the Shapley value does not coincide with the ratio between the individual probabilities. However, under symmetry, A11 can be reformulated:

$$p_j = q_j \text{ for all } j \neq i \;\Rightarrow\; \frac{\varphi_i(N,p)}{\varphi_i(N,q)} = \frac{p_i}{q_i}.$$

By symmetry, we know that two players with the same probability of success get the same shares but, in the present context, the converse is also true:

$$SV_i(N,p) = SV_j(N,p) \text{ if and only if } p_i = p_j.$$

Probability games can be used to solve damage apportionment in a probabilistic framework. The idea is the following. Damage results from the joint and independent actions of several actors, each one being assigned a probability of causing *alone* the damage. Damage have occurred and a possible apportionment could simply be proportional to the individual probabilities. This is, however, a crude way of proceeding. Applying the Shapley value to the corresponding probability game gives a more correct distribution of probabilities among the players.

Example 4.29 (continued) Based on the probabilities $p = (0.9, 0.4, 0.1)$, the division of the damages would follow the shares (0.64, 0.29, 0.07). Applying (4.28), the Shapley value is given by (0.69, 0.21, 0.05), leading to the shares (0.73, 0.22, 0.05): almost 3/4 of the damages would then be covered by the first actor. If instead $p =$ (1, 0.4, 0.1), the Shapley value gives directly the shares: (0.76, 0.19, 0.04) to be compared to (0.67, 0.27, 0.07).

Elections and approval voting (Ginsburgh & Zang, 2012).
There are plenty of methods for electing one or several candidates to a position, for instance, the mayor of a city or the president of a country. *Majority voting* is the simplest and most common method: voters are asked to choose one candidate and the candidate obtaining the largest number of votes is then elected.[50] This is a rudimentary method that does not consider the preferences of the voters over the candidates. To quote Duncan Black (1958), "*Which candidate ought to be elected in a single-member constituency if all we consider is* the order *in which each of the electors ranks the candidates? ... At the very outset of the argument, we try to move from the is to the ought and to jump the unbridgeable chasm between the universe of science and that of morals*".

Alternative methods exist among which *approval voting* was introduced in the 1970s by Weber (1977), and Brams and Fishburn (1978).[51] Under approval voting, the number of candidates an elector is allowed to list is not limited and there is no cost in listing additional candidates. Approval voting has not been implemented very often, except in some scientific societies such as the *American Mathematical Society* or the *Institute of Electrical and Electronics Engineers.* A few other exceptions exist, such as the election of the United Nations Secretary General. In France, several experiments have been conducted, in particular by Baujard and Igersheim (2010) following the 2002 and 2007 French presidential.

[50] In cases where more than one candidate obtains the largest number of votes, a mechanism must be put in place to eventually select a unique winner, for instance by random drawing.
[51] See also Weber (1995), Brams & Fishburn (2005, 2007), Brams (2008) and Laslier & Sanver (1995).

Under approval voting, voters who list several candidates carry more weight and, in that sense, approval voting violates the *one-person-one-vote* principle often emphasized by the advocates of political equality. A modified method, *equal-and-even cumulative voting* (also called block approval voting), reconciles approval voting with that principle by dividing the votes of each elector by the number of candidates retained. For instance, if an elector lists three candidates, each gets 1/3 of a vote instead of 1. Hence, electors have an incentive to limit the sizes of their ballots: adding a candidate reduces the chances that those already present will be elected. If the objective of an elector is to see elected one of the candidates that she places high in her preferences, she will tend to submit a limited number of candidates. Cumulative voting is also used in multiwinner elections when electors can spread a fixed number of votes—usually equal to the number of seats to be filled—over one or more candidates.

Equal-and-even cumulative voting corresponds to the concept of *Shapley ranking*, introduced by Ginsburgh and Zang (2012) as the Shapley value of a transferable utility game derived from approval ballots. It also corresponds to the concept of *satisfaction approval voting* introduced by Brams and Kilgour (2014). A distinction must be made between voting, ranking and ordering: voting is the procedure by which electors submit ballots; ranking aggregates the voters' choices by assigning a score to each candidate; and a ranking induces an ordering, which is the ordinal relation on the set of candidates induced by the ranking.

Consider a set N of candidates and a set M of voters. Under approval voting, a *ballot profile* is a mapping π that associates to each subset S of candidates, the number of electors whose approval set coincides with S:

$$\pi(S) = |\{h \in M \mid N_h = S\}| \quad \text{for all } S \subset N.$$

where N_h is the *approval set* or *ballot* of elector h, that is the set of candidates listed by elector h. We assume that $N_h \neq \emptyset$ for all h and we do not exclude the case where $N_h = N$ for some h.

A ballot profile can be arranged in a $n \times m$ matrix whose rows are attributed to candidates and columns to electors. The *approval score* of candidate i is the number of electors who have included i in their ballot:

$$AR_i(N, \pi) = |\{h \in M \mid i \in N_h\}| = \sum_{S:\, i \in S} \pi(S) \quad (i = 1, \ldots, n).$$

Under equal-and-even cumulative voting, each of the candidates listed by elector h receives a fraction $1/n_h$, where $n_h = |N_h|$ is the size of elector h's ballot. The scores are then obtained by summing the fractions allocated to each candidate:

$$SR_i(N, \pi) = \sum_{S:\, i \in S} \frac{1}{s} \pi(S) = \sum_{h\,:\, i \in N_h} \frac{1}{n_h} \quad (i = 1, \ldots, n). \tag{4.29}$$

Example 4.30 A Four-Candidate—Five-Voter Election. Consider an election involving 4 candidates and 5 voters. Assuming that approval voting prevails, ballots are given by Table 4.21. The approval scores are obtained by summing the votes horizontally resulting in the ordering $1 \succ 4 \succ 2 \sim 3$. It differs from the ranking resulting from equal-and-even cumulative voting given by $4 \succ 1 \succ 2 \succ 3$.

Table 4.21 Four-candidate—five-voters

	1	2	3	4	5	*AR*	*SR*
1	0	1	1	1	1	4	1.67
2	0	0	1	0	1	2	0.83
3	0	0	0	1	1	2	0.66
4	1	1	0	1	0	3	1.83

Equal-and-even cumulative voting coincides with the concept of Shapley ranking introduced by Ginsburgh and Zang (2012). They show that it corresponds to the Shapley value of a well-defined transferable utility game associated to ballot profiles.

To each subset S of candidates, we associate the number of electors whose approval set is *included* in S given by $v(S) = |\{h \in M \mid N_h \subset S\}|$. It defines a *ranking game* where the players are the candidates. $v(N)$ is the number of voters and $v(i)$ is the number of electors who have only listed candidate i. Equivalently, $v(S)$ can be written in terms of the ballot profile:

$$v(S) = \sum_{T \subset S} \pi(T) \quad \text{for all } S \subset N. \tag{4.30}$$

Hence, there is a one-to-one relation between ballot profiles and ranking games.

The set $RG(N)$ of all ranking games on a given set N of candidates forms a remarkable class of games. The characteristic functions defining ranking games are monotonic (increasing), convex (thereby superadditive) and positive. Furthermore, the set $RG(N)$ is *closed under addition*: starting from any two ballot profiles (N, π') and (N, π'') on a common set of candidates, and their associated ranking games (N, v') and (N, v''), the ranking game $(N, v'+v'')$ is associated to the ballot profile $(N, \pi' + \pi'')$, assuming that the sets of voters are disjoint.[52]

Looking at (4.4) that expresses the worth of a coalition in terms of Harsanyi dividends, we observe that the dividends of the ranking game are precisely given by the ballot profiles:

$$\alpha_T(N, v) = \pi(T).$$

[52] See Dehez and Ginsburgh (2020) for a proof.

Hence, given (4.16) that defines the Shapley value in terms of the Harsanyi dividends, (4.29) and (4.30) together imply $SR(N, \pi) = SV(N, v).SR(N, \pi) = SV(N, v)$.

Example 4.30 (continued) The ballot game of the four candidates—five-voters voting situation is given by $\pi(4) = \pi(1, 2) = \pi(1, 4) = \pi(1, 2, 3) = \pi(1, 3, 4) = 1$ and $\pi(S) = 0$ for all other subsets S. The associated game is given by $v = (0, 0, 0, 0|1, 0, 2, 0, 1, 1|2, 3, 3, 1|5)$ and its Shapley value is given (1.67, 0.83, 0.66, 1.83).

Dehez and Ginsburgh (2020) have axiomatized the Shapley ranking using the following axioms.

A1′ *One-person-one-vote* (efficiency) The scores add-up to the number of electors:

$$\sum_{i \in N} \varphi_i(N, \pi) = \sum_{S \subset N} \pi(S).$$

A2′ *Anonymity* If candidates' names are permuted, the scores are permuted accordingly.

A3′ *Null candidate* (null player) Candidates appearing in no ballot get a zero score:

$$\pi(S) = 0 \text{ for all } S \subset N \text{ such that } i \in S \;\Rightarrow\; \varphi_i(N, \pi) = 0.$$

A4′ *Additivity* The scores associated to a sum of ballot profiles defined over a common set of candidates equal the sum of the scores associated with each ballot profile: for any two ballot profiles π' and π'' on N, $\varphi(N, \pi' + \pi'') = \varphi(N, \pi') + \varphi(N, \pi'')$.

Proposition 4.33 Shapley ranking *is the unique ranking rule that* satisfies one-person-one-vote, anonymity, *null candidate and* additivity *on the set of ranking games.*

4.7 Concluding Remarks

Many examples have shown that the concept of core covers strategic aspects that are implicit in the cooperative approach by bringing to light existing competitive forces. The many cases where the core is empty characterize situations where these competitive forces lead to deadlock. While the core is a set of allocations, the nucleolus and the Shapley value are division rules that have a normative content. The nucleolus offers a benevolent compromise when the core is empty or contains many allocations. However, it does not satisfy to some desirable properties that are instead satisfied by the Shapley value. Moreover, we have seen that the Shapley value often leads to allocations that are natural. It may not be the case like for instance in the following problem. A community of towns decides to build a sewage treatment plant. Each town is willing to host the plant provided it is compensated for the nuisances caused. The solution is clearly to install the plant in the town that has the lowest nuisance cost. The associated cooperative game is an inverted airport game whose core has a simple structure allowing for an easy calculation of its nucleolus. In this context, the Shapley value happens to be inappropriate because it compensates other towns. The case of a family in which children have to care for their elderly is another such a situation. Who's going to take care of them? It should, of course, be the one who lives closest to the parents and he should then be compensated by the others.[53]

In this chapter, we have considered the case where utility is transferable. In Chap. 3 on bargaining, transferability was ruled out but we were limited to two players. Beyond two players, there exists a vast literature on *non-transferable* cooperative games in which the possibilities of a coalition are represented by a set instead of a number. The notion of core can be easily transposed into this framework, but this is not the case of all concepts. In particular, there exist several definitions of value.[54]

A cooperative game may be the reduced form of some non-cooperative game. It is, however, not the case for most of the examples we have seen in this chapter. Looking at a particular solution concept, the question is "What are its non-cooperative foundations" or "How can it be non-cooperatively implemented". The idea is to transform a cooperative game into a bargaining problem specified as a non-cooperative game. This is the so-called *Nash program* initiated by Nash in his 1953 paper where he proves that the Nash solution is an equilibrium of the non-cooperative "demand game" described in the concluding remarks of Chap. 3. The problem is that there are many other equilibria (actually an infinity) beyond the Nash solution. By introducing uncertainty, Nash then proves that there is a unique equilibrium at the limit when uncertainty becomes negligible. In the same vein, Rubinstein (1982) has proposed an alternative game where impatience leads to a unique subgame perfect equilibrium that tends to the Nash solution as impatience vanishes. Hart and Mas-Colell (1996) have proposed a non-cooperative procedure that leads to the Shapley value. Other concepts, in particular the core, have been given various non-cooperative foundations.[55]

---

[53] See Dehez (2013) for details.

[54] See Hart (2004) and the chapter by McLean in the third volume of the *Handbook of game theory* edited by Aumann and Hart (2002).

[55] See for instance Serrano (2005).

References

Algaba, E., Fragnelli, V., & Sanchez-Soriano, J. (2020). *Handbook of the Shapley value*. Routledge.

Aumann, R. J., & Drèze, J. H. (1974). Cooperative games with coalition structure. *International Journal of Games Theory, 3*, 217–237.

Aumann, R. J., & Maschler, M. (1964). The bargaining set for cooperative ames. In M. Dresher, L. S. Shapley, & A. W. Tucker (Eds.), *Advances in game theory* (pp. 443–476). Princeton University Press.

Aumann, R. J., & Maschler, M. (1985). Game theoretic analysis of a bankruptcy problem from the Talmud. *Journal of Economic Theory, 36*, 195–213.

Aumann, R.J. and S. Hart. (2002). *Handbook of game theory* (3 volumes), Elsevier, Amsterdam.

Baujard, A., & Igersheim, H. (2010). Framed-field experiments on approval voting in political contexts. Some teachings. In J. F. Laslier & Sanver, M.R. (eds.), *Handbook of approval voting*. Springer.

Béal, S., & Navarro, F. (2020). Necessary versus equal players in axiomatic studies. *Operations Research Letters, 48*, 385–391.

Béal, S., Deschamps, M., Ravix, J. T., & Sautel, O. (2010). Les informations exigées par la législation REACH : Analyse du partage des coûts. *Revue D'economie Politique, 120*, 991–1014.

Black, D. (1958). *The theory of committees and elections*. Cambridge University Press.

Bondareva, O. N. (1963). Some applications of linear programming methods to the theory of cooperative games (in Russian). *Problemy Kybernetiki, 10*, 119–139.

Brams, S. J. (2008). *Mathematics and democracy*. Princeton University Press.

Brams, S. J., & Fishburn, P. C. (1978). Approval voting. *American Political Science Review, 72*, 831–847.

Brams, S. J., & Fishburn, P. C. (2005). Going from theory to practice: The mixed success of approval voting. *Social Choice and Welfare, 25*, 457–474.

Brams, S. J., & Fishburn, P. C. (2007). *Approval voting* (2nd edn.). Springer. (1st edition dated 1983, Bell Telephone Laboratories).

Brams, S. J., & Kilgour, D. M. (2014). Satisfaction approval voting. In R. Fara et al. (eds.) *Voting power and procedures. Essays in honor of Dan Fesenthal and Moshé Machover* (pp. 323–346). Springer.

Cournot, A. (1838). *Recherches sur les principes mathématiques de la théorie des richesses*. Hachette. English translation by N. T. Bacon (1927). *Researches into the mathematical principles of the theory of wealth*. MacMillan.

Dehez, P. (2011). Allocation of fixed costs: Characterization of the (dual) weighted Shapley value. *International Game Theory Review, 13*, 1–16.

Dehez, P. (2013). Cooperative provision of indivisible public goods. *Theory and Decision, 74*, 13–29.

Dehez, P. (2017). On Harsanyi dividends and asymmetric values. *International Game theory Review, 19* (reprinted as chapter 26 in L. A. Petrosyan & D. W. K. Yeung (eds.), *Game theoretic analysis* (pp. 523–558). World Scientific Publishing).

Dehez, P. (2021). 1-convex transferable utility games, a reappraisal, *CORE-Discussion Paper* 2021-16.

Dehez, P. (2023). Sharing a collective probability of success. *Mathematical Social Sciences, 123*(2023), 122–127.

Dehez, P. (2024). Cooperative product games. *International Game Theory Review* 26/01.

Dehez, P., & Ferey, S. (2013). How to share joint liability: A cooperative game approach. *Mathematical Social Sciences, 66*, 44–50.

Dehez, P., & Ginsburgh, V. (2020). Approval voting and Shapley ranking. *Public Choice, 184*, 415–428.

Dehez, P., & Pacini, P. M. (2024). A note on the relation between the Shapley value and the core of 3-player transferable utility games, *Economics Bulletin, 44*, 611–619.

Dehez, P., & Poukens, S. (2014). The Shapley value as a guide to FRAND licensing agreements. *Review of Law and Economics, 10*, 265–284.
Dehez, P., & Tellone, D. (2013). Data games: Sharing public goods with exclusion. *Journal of Public Economic Theory, 15*(2013), 654–673.
Driessen, T. (1985). Properties of 1-convex games. *Or Spektrum, 7*, 19–26.
Dubey, P. (1975). On the uniqueness of the Shapley value. *International Journal of Game Theory, 4*, 131–139.
Dutta, B., Debraj, R., Sengupta, K., & Vohra, R. (1989). A consistent bargaining set. *Journal of Economic Theory, 49*, 93–112.
Edgeworth F.Y. (1881). *Mathematical Psychics: An Essay on the Application of Mathematics to the Moral Sciences*, Kegan and co, London.
Einy, E., Holzman, R., & Monderer, D. (1999). On the least core and the Mas-Colell bargaining set. *Games and Economic Behavior, 28*, 181–188.
Faulhaber, G. (1975). Cross-subsidization: Pricing in public enterprises. *American Economic Review, 65*, 966–977.
Ferey, S., & Dehez, P. (2016a). Multiple causation, apportionment and the Shapley value. *Journal of Legal Studies, 45*, 143–171.
Ferey, S., & Dehez, P. (2016b). Overdetermined causation causes, contributions and the Shapley value. *Chicago-Kent Law Review, 91*, 637–658.
Gillies, D. B. (1953). *Some theorems on n-person games*. Ph.D. Thesis, Princeton University.
Gillies, D. B. (1959). Solutions to general non-zero-sum games. In A. W. Tucker & R. D. Luce (Eds.), *Contributions to the theory of games IV, Annals of mathematical studies* (pp. 47–85). Princeton University Press.
Ginsburgh, V., & Zang, I. (2012). Shapley ranking of wines. *Journal of Wine Economics, 7*, 169–180.
Gonzáles-Díaz, J., & Sánchez-Rodríguez, E. (2007). A natural selection from the core of a TU game: The core-centre. *International Journal of Game Theory, 36*, 27–46.
Hansen, T., & Gabszewicz, J. J. (1972). Collusion of factor owners and distribution of the social output. *Journal of Economic Theory, 4*, 1–18.
Harsanyi, J.C. (1959). A bargaining model for the cooperative n-person game. In Tucker, A.W. and Luce, D.R. (Eds.) *Contributions to the theory of games (Vol. IV)*, Annals of Mathematics Study 40, Princeton University Press, 325–355.
Harsanyi, J. C. (1963). A simplified bargaining model for the *n*-person game. *International Economic Review, 4*, 194–220.
Harsanyi, J., & Selten, R. (1988). *A general theory of equilibrium selection in games*. The MIT Press.
Hart, S. (2004). A Comparison of non-transferable utility values. *Theory and Decision, 56*, 35–46.
Hart, S., & Mas-Colell, A. (1996). Bargaining and value. *Econometrica, 64*, 357–380.
Hou, D., Xu, G., Sun, P., & Driessen, T. (2018). The Shapley value for the probability games. *Operations Research Letters, 46*, 457–461.
Ichiishi, T. (1981). Super-modularity: Applications to convex games and to the greedy algorithm. *Journal of Economic Theory, 25*, 283–286.
Izquierdo, J. M., & Rafels, C. (2012). A characterization of convex TU games by means of the Mas-Colell bargaining set (*à la* Shimomura). *International Journal of Game Theory, 41*, 381–395.
Kohlberg, E. (1972). The nucleolus as a solution of a minimization problem. *SIAM Journal on Applied Mathematics, 23*, 34–39.
Laslier, J.F. & Sanver, M.R. (eds.), Handbook of approval voting, Springer.
Littlechild, S. C., & Owen, G. (1973). A simple expression for the Shapley value in a special case. *Management Science, 20*, 370–372.
Littlechild, S. C., & Thompson, G. F. (1977). Aircraft landing fees: A game theory approach. *The Bell Journal of Economics, 8*, 186–204.
Luce, D., & Raiffa, H. (1957). *Games and decisions*. Wiley.

Maschler, M., Peleg, B., & Shapley, L. S. (1979). Geometric properties of the kernel, nucleolus and related solution concepts. *Mathematics of Operations Research, 4*, 303–338.

Maschler, M., Solan, E., & Zamir, S. (2020). *Game theory* (2nd ed.). Cambridge University Press.

Mas-Colell, A. (1989). An equivalence theorem for a bargaining set. *Journal of Mathematical Economics, 18*, 129–139.

Megiddo, N. (1974). On the nonmonotonicity of the bargaining set, the kernel and the nucleolus of a game. *SIAM Journal on Applied Mathematics, 27*, 355–358.

Milnor, J. W. (1952). Reasonable outcomes for *n*-person games, *Research Memorandum* 916, Rand Corporation, Santa Monica.

Monderer, D., Samet, D., & Shapley, L. S. (1992). Weighted values and the core. *International Journal of Game Theory, 21*, 27–39.

Moulin, H. (1986). *Game theory for the social sciences* (2nd ed.). NYU Press.

Moulin, H. (1988). *Axioms of cooperative decision making*. Cambridge University Press.

Muto, S., Potters, J., & Tijs, S. (1989). Information market games. *International Journal of Game Theory, 18*, 209–226.

Myerson, R. B. (1977). Graphs and cooperation in games. *Mathematics of Operations Research, 2*, 225–229.

Myerson, R. B. (1980). Conference structures and fair allocation rules. *International Journal of Game Theory, 9*, 169–182.

Oishi, T., van der Laan, G. R., & van den Brink, R. (2023). Axiomatic analysis of liability problems with rooted-tree networks in tort law. *Economic Theory, 75*, 229–258.

O'Neill, B. (1982). A problem of right arbitration from the Talmud. *Mathematical Social Sciences, 2*, 345–371.

Peleg, B. (1986). On the reduced game property and its converse. *International Journal of Game Theory, 15*, 187–200.

Rawls, J. (1971). *Theory of justice*. Harvard University Press.

Rosales, D. (2014). *Cooperative product games*. unpublished mimeo.

Rubinstein, A. (1982). Perfect equilibrium in a bargaining model. *Econometrica, 50*, 97–109.

Schmeidler, D. (1969). The nucleolus of a characteristic function game. *SIAM Journal of Applied Mathematics, 17*, 1163–1170.

Serrano, R. (2005). Fifty years of the Nash program, 1953–2003. *Investigaciones Economicas, 29*, 219–258.

Shapley, L. S. (1951). Notes on the n-person game II: The value of an n-person game. Research Memoreandum 670, The Rand Corporation, Santa Monica.

Shapley, L. S. (1953). A value for *n*-person games. In H. Kuhn & A. W. Tucker (eds.) (pp. 307–317), Reproduced in A. Roth (ed.), *The Shapley value. Essays in honor of Lloyd Shapley* (pp. 31–40). Cambridge University Press.

Shapley, L. S. (1955). *Market as cooperative games*, Discussion Paper P-629, Rand Corporation, Santa Monica.

Shapley, L. S. (1967). On balanced sets and cores. *Naval Research Logistics Quarterly, 14*, 453–460.

Shapley, L. S. (1968). N-person game theory, text of a talk given at the Rand Corporation, Santa Monica, in November 1967. https://www.rand.org/pubs/papers/P3752.html.

Shapley, L. S. (1971). Cores of convex games. *International Journal of Game Theory, 1*, 11–26.

Shapley, L. S. (1973). Let's block block. *Econometrica, 41*, 1201–1202.

Shapley, L. S. (1981a). Discussion comments on "Equity considerations in traditional full cost allocation practices: An axiomatic approach". In S. Moriarity (ed.), *Joint cost allocation, Proceeding of the University of Oklahoma conference on costs allocations* (pp. 131–136). Centre for Economic and Management Research, University of Oklahoma.

Shapley, L. S. (1981b). Valuation of games. In W. F. Lucas (ed.), *Game theory and its applications. Proceedings of symposia in applied mathematics* (vol. 24, pp. 55–67). American Mathematical Society, Providence - Rhode Island.

Shapley, L. S., & Shubik, M. (1954). A method for evaluating the distribution of power in a committee system. *American Political Science Review, 48*, 787–792. Reproduced in A. Roth (ed.), *The Shapley value. Essays in honor of Lloyd Shapley* (pp. 41–48), Cambridge University Press.

Shapley, L. S., & Shubik, M. (1966). Quasi-cores in a monetary economy with nonconvex preferences. *Econometrica, 34*, 805–827.

Shapley, L. S., & Shubik, M. (1967). Ownership and the production function. *Quarterly Journal of Economics, 81*, 88–111.

Shapley, L. S., & Shubik, M. (1969). On the core of an economic system with externalities. *American Economic Review, 59*, 678–684.

Shimomura, K. (1997). Quasi-cores in barganing sets. *International Journal of Game Theory, 26*, 283–302.

Shubik, M. (1959). Edgeworth market games. In A. W. Tucker & R. D. Luce (Eds.), *Contributions to the theory of games IV, Annals of mathematical studies* (pp. 267–278). Princeton University Press.

Shubik, M. (1982). *Game theory in the social sciences.* The MIT Press.

Shubik, M. (1984). *A game-theoretic approach to political economy*, The MIT Press, Cambridge.

Sobolev, A.I. (1975). The characterization of optimality principles in cooperative games by functional equations. In N. N. Vorobjev (ed.), *Matematischeskie Metody v Socialnix Naukax*, Proceedings of the Seminar, Issue 6, Institute of Physics and Mathematics, Academy of Sciences of the Lithuanian SSR, Vilnius, 94–151 (in Russian, with English summary).

Sönmez, T. O. (1993). Population-monotonicity of the nucleolus on a class of public good problems, *mimeo*, Department of Economics, University of Rochester.

Sprumont, Y. (1990). Population monotonic allocation schemes for cooperative games with transferable utility. *Games and Economic Behavior, 2*, 378–394.

Thompson, G. F. (1971). *Airport costs and pricing*, Ph.D. Thesis. University of Birmingham.

Thomson, W. (1983). The fair division of a fixed supply among growing population. *Mathematics of Operations Research, 8*, 319–326.

Vohra, R. (1991). An existence theorem for a bargaining set. *Journal of Mathematical Economics, 20*, 19–34.

von Neumann, J. (1928). Zur Theorie der Gesellschaftspiel, *Mathematische Annalen, 100*, 295–320 (translated in Tucker A.W. and R.D. Luce, 1959).

von Neumann, J., & Morgenstern, O. (1944). *Theory of games and economic behavior*. Princeton University Press (latest edition dated 1953).

Weber, R. J. (1977). Comparison of voting systems, mimeo (reproduced in Comparison of public choice systems, *Cowles Foundation Discussion Paper* 498, 1979, Yale University).

Weber, R. J. (1988). Probabilistic values for games. In A. Roth (Ed.), *The Shapley value* (pp. 101–119). Cambridge University Press.

Weber, R. J. (1995). Approval voting. *Journal of Economic Perspectives, 9*, 39–49.

Young, H. P. (1985a). *Cost allocation: Methods, principles, applications*. North-Holland.

Young, P. Y. (1985b). Monotonic solutions of cooperative games. *International Journal of Game Theory, 14*, 65–72.

Zhao, J. (2018). Three little-known and yet still significant contributions of Lloyd Shapley. *Games and Economic Behavior, 108*, 592–599.

Voting and Power

5

Political science, as an empirical discipline, is the study of the shaping and sharing of power (Lasswell & Kaplan, 1950).

As the quote above suggests, the question of power is central to the analysis of political processes. But what do we mean by power? Can it be measured? This is the purpose of this chapter. We will limit ourselves to the analysis of collective decisions within committees. A committee is a group of decision-makers in which decisions are made according to well-established rules. These rules translate into the list of winning coalitions, the coalitions of decision-makers who, according to the rules, are able to decide. The set of decision-makers and the list of winning coalitions define a voting game. We do not intend to describe the decision procedures as such: a proposal is put on the table and the question is which subsets of decision-makers, if they agree, can together impose a decision, that is, accept or reject the proposal.

Decision-makers do not necessarily have the same weight in the decision-making process. They may have a different number of votes, some may have a veto right and special restrictions may be added, such as, for example, the protection of a minority. A general meeting of shareholders, a parliament (where decision-makers are identified with the parties) and international organizations such as the European Council or the United Nations Security Council, are all examples of such committees.

The problem addressed in this chapter is the measurement of the relative power of each member of a committee, beyond the apparent power conferred on them by the rules: we want to measure the ability of each decision-maker to influence the outcome of a vote given the rules in force.

P. Dehez, *Game Theory for the Social Sciences*, Springer Series in Game Theory,
https://doi.org/10.1007/978-3-031-58241-7_5

5.1 Voting Games

Winning coalitions
Decisive players
Voting games as simple games.

A voting game is defined by a list of voters (players) together with the list of winning coalitions, those subsets of voters that are in a position to take a decision.

Winning coalitions
Formally, a voting game is defined by a set N of players and the list W of winning coalitions that verify the following natural assumptions.

W1 The grand coalition is always winning: $N \in W$.

W2 Two disjoint coalitions are never simultaneously winning: $S, T \in W \Rightarrow S \cap T \neq \emptyset$.

W3 Enlarging a winning coalition does not make it lose $[S \subset T$ and $S \in W] \Rightarrow T \in W$.

W1 says that if everybody agrees, what has been proposed passes or is rejected. Condition W2 implies that the complement of a winning coalition is necessarily losing:

$$S \in W \;\Rightarrow\; N \backslash S \notin W.$$

Condition W3 is a *monotonicity* condition. A game that does not satisfy W2 is said to be *improper*: the underlying rules are incomplete.[1]

Example 5.1 Unanimity If, whatever is the number of players, unanimity is required for a decision to be taken, only the grand coalition is winning: $W = \{N\}$. In the bargaining problem studied in Chap. 2, decisions are taken unanimously. An agreement between both players is indeed required in order to implement a particular solution.

Example 5.2 Simple Majority, With or Without Veto Player With n voters, simple majority means that any coalition S of size greater than $n/2$ is winning. In the 3-player case, any coalition consisting of two or three players is winning:

$$W = \{\{1, 2\}, \{1, 3\}, \{2, 3\}, \{1, 2, 3\}\}.$$

If the first player is alone to have a veto right, the number of winning coalitions decreases:

$$W = \{\{1, 2\}, \{1, 3\}, \{1, 2, 3\}\}.$$

[1] To be complete, we should add that the empty coalition is losing: $\emptyset \notin W$.

Beyond the grand coalition, only the coalitions of size equal to 2 that contain player 1 are winning. Several decision-makers may detain a veto right. In the case where two of the three players have a veto right, we may just ignore the third player: his opinion does not count. Unanimity is a situation where all players have a veto right.

Veto right and dictatorship should not be confused. A dictator is such that a coalition is winning once he is present: $S \in W \quad \Leftrightarrow \quad i \in S$. A player has a veto right if (and only if) he is a member of all winning coalitions: $S \in W \quad \Rightarrow \quad i \in S$. Players with a veto right are veto players. In the 3-player case where player 1 is alone to have a veto right, the list of winning coalition is given by $\{\{1\}, \{1, 2\}, \{1, 3\}, \{1, 2, 3\}\}$. Veto players are necessary players. They can be identified easily.

Proposition 5.1 *Player i has a veto right in a* voting game (N, W) if and only if *the coalition $N \backslash i$ is losing.*

Proof By W1, $N \subset W$. Hence, if i is a veto player, $N \backslash i \notin W$. If $N \backslash i$ is loosing but i is not a veto player, there exists $T \in W$ such that $i \notin T$. Then $T \subset N \backslash i$, contradicting W3. ♦

A winning coalition is *minimal* if removing one of its members makes it to lose

$$[S \in W \text{ and } T \subsetneq S] \Rightarrow T \notin W.$$

By W3, the knowledge of the set W_{min} of minimal winning coalitions suffices to construct the set of all winning coalitions.

A coalition is *blocking* if it is losing and so is his complement. The existence of blocking coalitions may lead to a deadlock.

A voting game is said to be *decisive* if a coalition is winning *if and only if* the complementary coalition is losing: $S \in W$ *if and only if* $N \backslash S \notin W$. Consequently, in a decisive game, there is no blocking coalition.

Example 5.1 (continued) If unanimity applies, all coalitions, except the grand coalition, are blocking.

Example 5.2 (continued) In the 3-voter simple majority game, W_{min} is the set of coalitions of size 2. And if player 1 has a veto right, $W_{min} = \{\{1, 2\}, \{1, 3\}\}$. No coalition is blocking in the simple majority game when n is odd. If instead n is even, coalitions counting half of the members are blocking. By definition of the veto right, the losing coalitions of which at least one member has a veto right is blocking. In the 3-voter game where voter 1 has a veto right, the coalitions $\{1\}$ and $\{2, 3\}$ are blocking.

Example 5.3 General Assembly of Shareholders I (Owen, 2013) Consider a firm owned by four shareholders. The share distribution is given by 10, 20, 30 and 40. If simple majority applies, there are 7 winning coalitions:

$$W = \{\{2, 4\}, \{3, 4\}, \{1, 2, 3\}, \{1, 2, 4\}, \{1, 3, 4\}, \{2, 3, 4\}, \{1, 2, 3, 4\}\}$$

three of which are minimal: $W_{min} = \{\{2, 4\}, \{3, 4\}, \{1, 2, 3\}\}$. There are two blocking coalitions, namely $\{1, 4\}$ and $\{2, 3\}$.

Example 5.4 US Federal System The US Federal System is a bicameral system with the House of Representatives and the Senate that group respectively 435 representatives and 100 senators. On top, the President and the Vice President play a role. The latter can intervene in case of a tie in the Senate. For a bill to pass, a majority is needed in both chambers. The President has, however, a veto right but it can be overturned by 2/3 of the vote in both chambers. Hence there are 537 players. Making the list of winning coalitions is not a simple task! It is simplified if the players are identified with parties.

We will consider the simplified version of this system that has been analyzed by Shapley and Shubik (1954), without Vice President and a President who has an absolute veto right. The set of players is then given by $N = \{1\} \cup A \cup B$ where the President is player 1 while A and B are the subsets of representatives and senators respectively. In this framework, S is a winning coalition if $1 \in S$, $|S \cap A| > a/2$ and $|S \cap B| > b/2$. Shapley and Shubik consider nine players: the President, three senators and five representatives: $a = 5, b = 3$ and $n = 9$. The winning coalitions are therefore those that include the President, at least three representatives and at least two senators.[2]

Example 5.5 UN Security Council The UN Security Council includes fifteen member states, five of which are "*permanent members*", China, United Kingdom, France, Russia and the United States. These five members have a veto right and for a proposition to pass, nine votes are required. The *minimal* winning coalitions are therefore of the following form: {5 permanent members, 4 non-permanent members}.

Example 5.6 Canadian Constitution The Canadian constitution can be modified with the support of at least seven provinces, provided these provinces count for at least half of the Canadian population. This formula is known as "7 + 50". More precisely, an amendment is promulgated if it is supported by a majority in the Parliament and in the Senate, and at least 2/3 of the ten provincial assemblies provided they represent at least 50% of the total population.[3] Table 5.1 lists the provinces and their share in the total population, according to the last census dated 2016.

---

[2] This example appears also in Shubik (1982) and in Dubey and Shapley (1979).

[3] Notice that the representation of provinces and territories in the Canadian Parliament is proportional to the population.

Table 5.1 Canadian population in 2016

Ontario	38.26%
Québec	23.23%
British Columbia	13.22%
Alberta	11.57%
Manitoba	3.64%
Saskatchewan	3.12%
Nova Scotia	2.63%
New Brunswick	2.13%
Newfoundland and Labrador	1.48%
Prince Edward Island	0.41%

Example 5.7 Minority Protection In some situations, decision rules may contain a minority protection clause. For instance, if $M \subset N$ is the subset of minority players, the rules may specify that a majority in both N and M is required for a decision to be taken.

Decisive players

A player i is decisive in a coalition S if S is winning and it turns losing without i:

$$i \in S \in W \text{ and } S \backslash i \notin W.$$

Equivalently, player i is decisive in a coalition S of which he is not a member if S is losing and turns winning if i joins it:

$$i \notin S \notin W \text{ and } S \cup i \in W.$$

A coalition is *minimal winning* if all its members are decisive. A player has a *veto right* if he is decisive in all winning coalitions. And a *dictator* is decisive in *all* the coalitions of which he is a member.

A player i that is never decisive is a *null player*: $S \backslash i \in W$ for all $S \in W$. Two players i and j that are decisive in all coalitions of which they are members are *substitutable*:

$$\text{for all } S \in W \text{ such that } i, j \in S\text{: } S \backslash i \notin W \text{ and } S \backslash j \notin W.$$

Voting games as simple games

A voting game (N, W) can be associated to an equivalent transferable utility game (N, v) where winning coalition have worth 1 and losing coalition have worth 0.

So, the characteristic function v has values in $\{0, 1\}$ and $v(N) = 1$ by W1. It is superadditive by W2 and W3. Indeed, if $S \cap T = \emptyset$, there are two possible situations. Either the two coalitions are losing and their union is possibly winning. Or, one is winning and the other is losing, in which case their union must be winning. Hence, the inequality $v(S) + v(T) \leq v(S \cup T)$ is always satisfied once $S \cap T = \emptyset$. If we

Table 5.2 Marginal contribution vectors of the simple majority game with veto

π	1	2	3
123	0	1	0
132	0	0	1
213	1	0	0
231	1	0	0
312	1	0	0
321	1	0	0

exclude the case of a dictator, $v(i) = 0$ for all i. The associated game is then essential and the imputation set coincides with the unit simplex $\Delta_n = \left\{x \in \mathbb{R}^n_+ \mid x(N) = 1\right\}$.

Condition W3 implies that the characteristic function is monotonic:

$$[S \subset T \text{ and } v(S) = 1] \Rightarrow v(T) = 1.$$

Notice that, following Proposition 4.1, this is a consequence of superadditivity.

This equivalence allows the use of the transferable utility game concepts seen in Chap. 4. The problem is to divide “1” (100%) between the players and what a player receives is then interpreted as a *measure of his relative power*.

In a voting game, marginal contributions are equal to 0 or 1, and the marginal contribution of a player to a winning coalition equals 1 *if and only if* he is decisive in that coalition. The case where $v(S) - v(S\backslash i) = -1$ is indeed excluded.

The marginal contribution vectors have all coordinates *but one* equal to zero. Only one player gets 1 in a given ordering π, depending on his position and the identity of the players preceding him. He is the *key player* in the ordering π.

Example 5.2 (continued) The marginal contribution vectors of the simple majority game with veto right are given in Table 5.2. Player 1 has a veto right and he is key in all orderings in which he is not first. The other two are decisive in one ordering each, the one where they appear in the second position, preceded by the first player.

5.2 Weighted Majority Games

Weights and quotas
Normalization
Voting games equivalent to weighted majority games.

We have seen many examples of voting games where players were not equal. Is it possible to formalize the differences between the actors by assigning them weights?

Weights and quotas

In a weighted majority game, each player is endowed with a number of votes, w_i for player i, and a minimum of Q votes is necessary for a proposition to pass. The w_i nonnegative, at least one is positive and the quota Q is positive. We will use the notation $(Q|w_1, ..., w_n)$. A coalition is then winning *if and only if* the sum of the weights of its members is not inferior to the quota:

$$S \in W \quad \Leftrightarrow \quad \sum_{i \in S} w_i \geq Q.$$

To qualify as a voting game, two inequalities must be satisfied:

$$\frac{1}{2}\sum_{i \in N} w_i < Q \leq \sum_{i \in N} w_i. \tag{5.1}$$

They ensure that W1 and W2 are satisfied. We could add the inequalities $w_i < Q$ for all i if we want to exclude a dictator.

Example 5.2 (continued) In a simple or qualified majority voting game with n players, the w_i are all equal to 1. In the simple majority case, the quota is given by $Q = n/2 + 1$ if n is even, and by $Q = (n + 1)/2$ if n is odd.

Weighted majority games may be used to represent a parliament where players are assimilated into parties, each with a weight equal to its number of seats. General assemblies of shareholders are also weighted majority games where the weight of a shareholder is equal to the number of shares he owns.

Example 5.3 (continued) In the general assembly of shareholders I, given the shares 10, 20, 30 and 40, the corresponding weighted majority game can be written as $(51|10, 20, 30, 40)$. We will see that players 2 and 3 are actually substitutable and have therefore the same relative power.

Example 5.8 European Union Council of Ministers. The Council of Ministers brings together the government ministers from each EU country. They meet to discuss, amend or adopt laws, and coordinate policies in various areas (agriculture, justice, economic and financial affairs, foreign affairs, environment, ...).

Table 5.3 lists weights and quotas since the origin until 2003. We observe that, when expressed in the percentage of the total weight, the quota has progressively moved from 70 to 73%. For propositions coming from the European Commission, it is a pure weighted majority game. We observe that in EU-6, also called "Inner Six", Luxembourg was never decisive. It was certainly not wanted even if it is obvious given the quota! For other propositions, it goes a bit differently. In EU-15, 64 votes were needed with the support of at least eleven member states. Following the Nice Treaty of 2003, the decision rules have been made more complicated. To be accepted a proposition then needed 255 votes out of 345 and the support of at least 15-member states (18 for propositions not emanating from the Commission), counting for at least 65% of the total population.[4] The Lisbon Treaty of 2007 has introduced further changes.

Example 5.9 United Nations General Assembly. In the UN General Assembly, simple or qualified majority applies according to the nature of the resolution. Under the present rules, one country = one vote. This was not the case at the time of the Soviet Union. Until the early 1980s, the General Assembly counted 138 states, each endowed with one vote, except the Soviet Union that had three votes. A qualified majority of 2/3 applied, hence a quota of 98.

Normalization

Weights and quotas can be normalized by dividing them by the sum of the weights:

$$\lambda_i = \frac{w_i}{\sum w_j} \text{ and } q = \frac{Q}{\sum w_j}.$$

The number λ_i then represents the relative weight of player i: $0 \leq \lambda_i \leq 1$ for all i and $\sum \lambda_i = 1$. A coalition S is then winning if $\lambda(S) \geq q$, and the inequalities (5.1) become $1/2 < q \leq 1$.

The number λ_i is not a correct measure of the relative power of the player i. Relative power indeed depends on the distribution of weights and on the quota.

Example 5.2 (continued) In the 3-player simple majority, players have the same power: $\lambda_i = 1/n$ for all i.

Voting games equivalent to weighted majority games

Can all voting games be transformed into weighted majority games? The answer is negative. It turns out that the US Federal System in its complete version is not a weighted system. The revision of the Canadian constitution is also not a weighted system.[5] However, the fact that some players have a veto right does not necessarily exclude the equivalence, as illustrated by the following two examples.

Example 5.2 (continued) If we choose the weights $w = (2, 1, 1)$ and the quota $Q = 3$, we obtain the same set of winning coalition as in the 3-player simple majority game where player 1 has a veto right: $W = \{\{1, 2\}, \{1, 3\}, \{1, 2, 3\}\}$. Actually there is an infinity of solutions. For instance, the weighted majority game $(51|50, 49, 1)$ produces the same set of winning coalitions! This confirms that weights do not reveal anything on the distribution of power among players.

[4] See for instance Laruelle, Martinez and Valenciano (2006).

[5] See Taylor and Pacelli (2008) for necessary and sufficient conditions under which a voting game can be written as a weighted majority game.

Table 5.3 EU Council of Ministers: weights assigned to the member states

	1958	1973	1981	1986	1995	2003
Germany	4	10	10	10	10	29
France	4	10	10	10	10	29
Italy	4	10	10	10	10	29
Netherlands	2	5	5	5	5	13
Belgium	2	5	5	5	5	12
Luxembourg	1	2	2	2	2	4
United Kingdom		10	10	10	10	29
Denmark		3	3	3	3	7
Ireland		3	3	3	3	7
Greece			5	5	5	12
Spain				8	8	27
Portugal				5	5	12
Sweden					4	10
Finland					3	7
Austria					4	10
Romania						14
Poland						27
Czech Republic						12
Hungary						12
Bulgaria						10
Slovakia						7
Lithuania						7
Slovenia						4
Latonia						4
Estonia						4
Cyprus						4
Malta						3
Total weight	17	58	63	76	87	345
Quota	12	41	45	54	64	255
Quota in %	70%	70%	71%	71%	73%	74%

Example 5.5 (continued) Consider the UN Security Council and assign weight 1 to the non-permanent members. We then look for the weight x of the permanent members and the quota Q that reproduces the same winning coalitions. The argument goes as follows. The *heaviest losing* coalitions include 10 non-permanent members and four permanent members. Their weight is $10 + 4x$ and it must be inferior to the quota Q. The *lightest* winning coalitions include five permanent members together with four non-permanent members. Their weight is $5x + 4$ and it must exceed the quota Q. Hence, we have the inequalities $10 + 4x < Q \leq 5x + 4$.

The smallest integer that verifies the inequality $10+4x < 5x+4$ is $x = 7$. Fixing the quota at 39 then reproduces the same winning coalitions. The corresponding weighted majority game is given by $(39 \mid 7, 7, 7, 7, 7, 1, 1, \ldots, 1)$. There is an absolute equivalence although one may figure out that the permanent members would never give up their veto right to adopt the weighted formulation...

5.3 Core of a Voting Game *

Emptiness of the core in the absence of veto players
Characterization of the core of a voting game

As a voting game can be written as a transferable utility game, we can look at its core although it will turn out to be inappropriate for power measurement.

Emptiness of the core in the absence of veto right
We will see that the core of a voting game is nonempty *if and only if* at least one player has a veto right. Put differently, the core is empty in the absence of veto right.

Example 4.3 (continued) The core of the simple majority game is empty as illustrated by the normalized luggage game. If now player 1 is endowed with a veto right, the core is nonempty and reduces to the single allocation (1, 0, 0). Indeed, we have:

$$x_1 + x_2 \geq 1 \Rightarrow x_3 = 0,$$
$$x_1 + x_3 \geq 1 \Rightarrow x_2 = 0 \Rightarrow x_1 = 1.$$

All the power lies in the hand of the veto player who can exploit his dominant position to eventually obtain a power equivalent to the one of a dictator. The core makes no difference between a dictator and a veto right when it is detained by a single player.

Consider a voting game (N, v). We denote by V the set of players endowed with a veto right, i.e., $S \in W \Rightarrow V \subset S$.

We have the following proposition.

Proposition 5.2 *The* core *of a* voting game *is nonempty* if and only if $V \neq \emptyset$.

Proof We proceed in two steps. If $V = \emptyset$, we have $v(N\backslash i) = 1$ for all $i \in N$. If there exists an imputation x in the core, the following inequalities must be satisfied:

$$0 \leq x_i \leq v(N) - v(N\backslash i) = 0 \quad \text{for all } i \in N$$

implying $x_i = 0$ for all $i \in N$, a contradiction. The core is therefore empty.

Inversely, suppose that $V \neq \emptyset$. We then construct an allocation x by imposing $x_i = 0$ for all $i \notin V$ and $x_i \geq 0$ for all $i \in V$. If S is a winning coalition, $V \subset S$ and therefore $x(S) = x(V) = 1$. Hence, x belongs to the core. ◆

Characterization of the core of a voting game

The second part of the above proof shows that the core of a voting game can be defined in terms of the players having a veto right: the core is the set of allocations assigning 0 to players without veto right while the veto players arbitrarily share the value of the game. That is the object of the following proposition.

Proposition 5.3 *The* core *of a* voting game (N, v) *where the set* V *of players with a veto right is nonempty is given by:*

$$C(N, v) = \left\{x \in \mathbb{R}^n_+ \mid x_i = 0 \text{ for all } i \notin V \text{ and } x(V) = 1 \right\}. \tag{5.2}$$

Proof We have to show that an imputation x belongs to the core *if and only if* the following conditions are satisfied:

$$\begin{aligned} x_i &= 0 \quad \text{for all } i \notin V, \\ x_i &\geq 0 \quad \text{for all } i \in V, \\ x(V) &= 1. \end{aligned}$$

In the proof of Proposition 5.2, we have seen that such an allocation belongs to the core. It then remains to show that these allocations are the *only* core allocations. Assume that there exists an imputation y that offers a positive amount to a non-veto player. We then have $y(V) < 1$, calling for an objection from the coalition of veto players. Hence, y cannot belong to the core: core allocations assign 0 to the non-veto players. ◆

Example 5.10 Consider the five-player game where the first two players have a veto right: $V = \{1, 2\}$. Core allocations are of the form $x = (\alpha, 1 - \alpha, 0, 0, 0)$ with $0 \leq \alpha \leq 1$. The argument can be extended to 3 or 4 veto players. We exclude 5 because otherwise, it would be an unanimity game, in which case, all players have a veto right.

In general, the definition of the core of a voting game is independent of the minimum number of players required to obtain a majority. Indeed, that number does not enter into consideration in the definition of the core (5.2).

5.4 Power Indices

Shapley–Shubik power index
Banzhaf power index
Paradoxes of power indices.

The power of a player depends on his capacity to change the nature of coalitions. Put differently, the power of a player depends on his capacity to make losing a winning coalition or, alternatively, on his capacity to make winning a losing coalition. Power indices are precisely based on that. They give an idea of the distribution of power that is induced by the decision rules and they can be used to compare different sets of decision rules.

There is a large number of definitions of power indices. However, we will limit ourselves to the most important ones, namely the Shapley–Shubik and the Banzhaf power indices.

Shapley–Shubik power index
We have seen that a voting game can be written as a cooperative game with transferable utility..We may therefore apply the concepts that were developed in Chap. 4. This idea goes back to the 1954 paper of Shapley and Shubik. It consists of interpreting the allocation obtained by applying the Shapley value as a distribution of power among the players. This is the so-called Shapley–Shubik power index.

Formula (4.15) that gives the Shapley value is greatly simplified when applied to simple games, for marginal contributions are then equal to 0 or 1. More precisely, the marginal contribution of a player is equal to 1 for all coalitions in which he is decisive, hence the following proposition.

Proposition 5.4 *Given a* simple game (N, v), *the Shapley–Shubik power index is given by*

$$SSI_i(N, v) = \sum \alpha_n(s) \tag{5.3}$$

where the sum applies only to (winning) coalitions in which player i is decisive.

SSI is an application that associates an element in the unit simplex Δ_n to any simple game.

Example 5.2 (continued) In the simple majority voting game with veto right, player 1 is decisive in all winning coalitions, namely $\{1, 2\}$, $\{1, 3\}$ and $\{1, 2, 3\}$. Hence, his relative power according to the Shapley value is given by

$$SSI_1(N, W) = 1/6 + 1/6 + 1/3 = 2/3$$

As the other players are substitutable, they share equally what remains and are then assigned a power equal to 1/6 each. They are indeed decisive in a single coalition, $\{1, 2\}$ and $\{1, 3\}$ respectively. Hence, the Shapley–Shubik index is given by $SSI(N, W) = (2/3, \ 1/6, \ 1/6)$. It is also the Shapley–Shubik index of the weighted majority game $(51|50, 49, 1)$ that has the same winning coalitions. We observe that, in contrast to the core, the Shapley value differentiates dictatorship from the situation where there is a unique veto player. A dictator gets full power by definition, the other player being null.

What about using formula (4.14) based on marginal contribution vectors associated with players' orderings? Following a given ordering, all players get 0 except one that gets 1: it is the player that is decisive in the coalition formed with those that precede him. He is the key player in the ordering π. Hence, we have the equivalent formulation of the Shapley–Shubik power index:

$$SSI_i(N, W) = \frac{\text{number of permutations where } i \text{ is key}}{n!}. \tag{5.4}$$

Quoting Shapley and Shubik (1954): "*There is a group of individuals all willing to vote for some bill. They vote* in order. *As soon as a majority has voted for it, it is declared passed, and the member who voted last is given credit for having passed it. Let us choose the* voting order *of the members randomly. Then we may compute the frequency with which an individual belongs to the group whose votes are used and, of more importance, we may compute how often he is pivotal. This latter number serves to give us our index. It measures the number of times that the action of the individual actually changes the state of affairs*".

Example 5.2 (continued) We have seen in Table 5.2 that in the simple majority voting game with veto rights, the veto player is decisive in all the orders where he is not the first. This happens 4 times out of 6, hence the power index is 2/3.

Using formula (5.4) makes computing heavier, especially beyond four players. With formula (5.3), we only have to look at winning coalitions while (5.4) requires to consider all $n!$ orderings. In addition, we may use the properties of efficiency, symmetry and null player to simplify further the computation: the total must be 1, substitutable players get identical amounts and null players get zero.

One must keep in mind that additivity cannot be invoked in the context of simple games simply because the sum of two simple games is not a simple game.[6]

Example 5.3 (continued) In the general assembly of shareholders I, there are seven winning coalitions: $W = \{\{2,4\}, \{3,4\}, \{1,2,3\}, \{1,2,4\}, \{1,3,4\}, \{2,3,4\}, \{1,2,3,4\}\}$. Table 5.4 collects the marginal contributions associated to winning coalitions. Given

[6] An axiomatic based on simple games has been proposed by Dubey (1975). It is unfortunately not easy to interpret. See the book of Laruelle and Valenciano (2008).

Table 5.4 Marginal contributions of the general assembly of shareholders I

	1	2	3	4	
$\{2, 4\}$	0	1	0	1	1/12
$\{3, 4\}$	0	0	1	1	1/12
$\{1, 2, 3\}$	1	1	1	0	1/12
$\{1, 2, 4\}$	0	1	0	1	1/12
$\{1, 3, 4\}$	0	0	1	1	1/12
$\{2, 3, 4\}$	0	0	0	1	1/12

the absence of a veto player, the grand coalition has been omitted. Weighting the marginal contributions, we get

$$SSI(N, W) = (1/12,\ 3/12,\ 3/12,\ 5/12) \simeq (8.3,\ 25.0,\ 25.0,\ 41.6) \text{ in } \%.$$

We observe that the second and third shareholders have the same power while the third has 10 shares more. They are indeed substitutable.

Compared to the a priori power given by the distribution of shares (10, 20, 30, 40), we observe that the actual power of the first and third are lower, giving more power to the other two shareholders.

If we modify the distribution of shares, by transferring one share from the first to the second, the distribution of shares becomes (9, 21, 30, 40) and there are eight winning coalitions:

$$W' = \{\{2, 3\}, \{2, 4\}, \{3, 4\}, \{1, 2, 3\}, \{1, 2, 4\}, \{1, 3, 4\}, \{2, 3, 4\}, \{1, 2, 3, 4\}\}$$

With this distribution of shares, the first shareholder is a null player while the other three become substitutable! Using symmetry and efficiency, we obtain the Shapley–Shubik index (0, 1/3, 1/3, 1/3).

Example 5.4 (continued) In the simplified version of the US Federal System analyzed by Dubey and Shapley (1979), with five representatives and three senators, a senator is decisive in three types of coalitions:

{the president, three representatives, one senator, himself},
{the president, four representatives, one senator, himself},
{the president, five representatives, one senator, himself}.

If $k \in \{3, 4, 5\}$ is the number of representatives, the number of coalitions is given by the combinations of k elements among five: we get successively 10, 5 and 1. As there are two other senators, there are 20 coalitions of the first type, 10 of the second and 2 of the third. The associated Shapley weights are $\alpha_9(6) = 1/504$, $\alpha_9(7) = 1/252$ and

$\alpha_9(8) = 1/72$. Hence, the Shapley–Shubik index assigns to each senators a power equal to $54/504 \simeq 0.107$. A representative is decisive in two types of coalitions:

$$\{\text{the president, two representatives, two senators, himself}\},$$
$$\{\text{the president, two representatives, three senators, himself}\}.$$

There are six combinations of two representatives along with the remaining four and three combinations of two senators. Hence, there are 18 coalitions of the first type and 6 of the second type. The Shapley–Shubik index then assigns to a each representative a power equal to $30/504 \simeq 0.06$. As a consequence, the power of the President is given by 0.38, to be compared to the power of the Senate and the House of Representatives, given by 0.32 and 0.30 respectively.

Example 5.11 Apex Game The Apex game is a voting game involving three players or more, with a majority player (called Apex), and a number of minority players (called Bases).[7] Minority players are substitutable. The majority player, say player 1, has a limited veto right, like the US President. Either player 1 gets the support of at least one minority player or all minority players agree, in which case they don't need the first. Hence, if n is the number of players, there are n minimal winning coalitions: the coalitions of the form $\{1, i\}$ where i is a minority player, and the coalition of all minority players.

This game is actually equivalent to the weighted majority game defined by weights $w = (n-2,\ 1,\ 1, ..., 1)$ and a quota $Q = n - 1$. Indeed, if x is the weight assigned to the first player while 1 is assigned to the minority players, the heaviest losing coalition weights $n - 2$ and the lightest winning coalition weights $x + 1$. Hence, we must have $n - 2 < Q \leq x + 1$.

In the case where $n = 5$, a coalition S is winning if $1 \in S$ and $|S| \geq 2$, or $|S| \geq 4$. Referring to the definition (5.4) of the Shapley–Shubik index in terms of players' orderings, the majority player is decisive in all orderings except those where he is first or last. This happens 48 times out of 120, i.e., a probability equal to 2/5. There are indeed $4! = 24$ orderings in which a player occupies a given place while there are altogether $5! = 120$ possible orderings. The Shapley–Shubik index then assigns 3/5 to the majority player and, by efficiency and symmetry, it assigns 1/10 to each minority player. The majority player has therefore six times more power than a minority player, with a power index exceeding 1/2.

The same arguments can be used to compute the Shapley–Shubik index for an arbitrary number of players exceeding 2. Player 1 is first or last $2(n-1)!$ times out of $n!$, giving a probability equal to $2/n$. Hence, the Shapley value assigns $(n-2)/n$ to the majority player and, by efficiency and symmetry, it assigns $2/n(n-1)$ to each minority player. Taken together, minority players have a power equal to $2/n$

[7] The Apex game was introduced by von Neumann and Morgenstern (1944) and has been studied extensively since, especially in connection with coalition formation.

while the power of the first player tends to 1 when the number of minority players tends to infinity.

Example 5.12 General Assembly of Shareholders II (Shubik, 1982). Consider an assembly of 601 shareholders. One of them holds 40 shares while all the others hold a single share each. Simple majority applies. Let's compute the Shapley–Shubik index of the majority shareholder using (5.4). He is *not* decisive in the orders where:

- he is preceded by *at most* 100 minority shareholders (positions 1–101),
- he is preceded by *at least* 501 minority shareholders (positions 502–601).

That makes a total of 201 positions out of 601. The Shapley–Shubik index therefore assigns to the majority shareholders 400/601, i.e., a power almost equal to 2/3. The remaining third is distributed equally between the minority shareholders. They clearly have an advantage to form a syndicate!

In general, considering a weighted majority game $(Q|\ \lambda, 1, ..., 1)$ where the parameters Q and λ satisfy the inequalities $\lambda < Q \leq n-1$: the first player cannot decide alone while the $n-1$ remaining players can impose a decision. The Shapley–Shubik index then assigns a power equal to λ/n to the first player and

$$SSI_i = \frac{n-\lambda}{n(n-1)}$$

to the remaining players. Altogether, their power is equal to $(n-\lambda)/n$. If $\lambda > 1$, they have an interest to form a syndicate. Applied to the *UN General Assembly* of the early 1980 (Example 5.9), the Soviet Union had a power of 2.17% against 0.7% for the other member states.

Other examples will be analyzed after having defined the Banzhaf power index and the comparison between the two indices will then be made.

Banzhaf power index

In 1965, John Banzhaf has proposed to measure the power of a decision-maker exclusively on the basis of the number of coalitions in which he is decisive.[8] Being decisive in a coalition is all what matters, independently of its size. He writes, "*…the appropriate measure of a legislator's power is simply the number of different situations in which he is able to determine the outcome. More explicitly, in a case in which there are n legislators, each acting independently and each capable of influencing the outcome only by means of his votes, the ratio of the power of legislator x to the*

[8] Banzhaf is a jurist. He has proposed that method following a problem in a US electoral system. See his papers published in 1965, 1966 and 1968.

power of legislator y is the same as the ratio of the number of possible voting combinations *of the entire legislature in which X can alter the outcome by changing his vote to the number of* combinations *in which Y can alter the outcome by changing his vote*" (Banzhaf, 1965). Banzhaf index is the power index that is most often used in political science.

Practically, we only have to count for each player the number of coalitions in which that player is decisive. This defines the "*raw*" Banzhaf index $BI_i(N, W)$. By definition of marginal contributions in a simple game, the number of coalitions in which player i is decisive equals the sum of its marginal contributions:

$$BI_i(N, W) = \sum_{S \subset N} (v(S) - v(S \backslash i))$$

The ratio $BI_i(N, W)/BI_j(N, W)$ then measures the power relationships between decision-makers i and j.

Clearly, nothing ensures that the sum of the $BI_i(N, W)$ be equal to 1: efficiency is generally not satisfied.

Example 5.2 (continued) In the simple majority voting game with veto right, the raw Banzhaf index is given by $BI(N, W) = (3, 1, 1)$. The veto player is indeed decisive in three coalitions, $\{1, 2\}$, $\{1, 3\}$ and $\{1, 2, 3\}$, while the other two are each decisive in only one coalition. The ratio of power between player 1 and player 2 (or 3) is equal to 3, to be compared to the Shapley–Shubik index that gives a ratio equal to 4.

To have a distribution of power comparable to the Shapley–Shubik index, we normalize the raw index by dividing each $BI_i(N, W)$ by their sum. The *normalized Banzhaf index* is then given by:

$$NBI_i(N, W) = \frac{BI_i(N, W)}{B(N, W)} \tag{5.5}$$

where $B(N, W) = \sum_{i \in N} BI_i(N, W)$.

By construction, the Banzhaf power index $NBI(N, W)$ is an imputation: the $NBI_i(N, W)$ are nonnegative and their sum is equal to 1. Like the Shapley–Shubik index, NBI is an application from the set of simple games into the unit simplex Δ_n.

Being based on marginal contributions—like the Shapley–Shubik index—the normalized Banzhaf index satisfies the symmetry and null player properties: equal players have the same power and null players have no power. As a consequence, both indices coincide in voting games where players are equal, and the majority games, simple or special, including unanimity.

Example 5.2 (continued) By symmetry, the two power indices coincide in 3-player voting games when there is no veto nor null players. If player 1 is the only one to detain a veto right, we have seen that the raw Banzhaf index was given by $BI(N, W) =$ (3, 1, 1). The normalized Banzhaf power index is therefore given by (3/5, 1/5, 1/5). It differs significantly from the Shapley–Shubik index given by (2/3, 1/6, 1/6).

Example 5.3 (continued) In the general assembly of shareholders I, the raw Banzhaf index is obtained from Table 5.4: $BI(N, W) = (1, 3, 3, 5)$. It happens that here the power indices coincide.

Example 5.11 (continued) In the Apex game, the first player is decisive in 14 coalitions: $\{1, 2\}$, $\{1, 3\}$, $\{1, 4\}$, $\{1, 5\}$, $\{1, 2, 3\}$, $\{1, 2, 4\}$, $\{1, 2, 5\}$, $\{1, 3, 4\}$, $\{1, 3, 5\}$, $\{1, 4, 5\}$, $\{1, 2, 3, 4\}$, $\{1, 2, 3, 5\}$, $\{1, 2, 4, 5\}$, $\{1, 3, 4, 5\}$. The minority players are each decisive in two coalitions. For instance, player 2 is decisive in the coalitions $\{1, 2\}$, $\{2, 3, 4, 5\}$. Hence, the raw Banzhaf index is given by (14, 2, 2, 2, 2) and the normalized Banzhaf assigns almost 64% of the power to the majority player. It is to be compared to the 60% assigned by the Shapley–Shubik index given by $(3/5,\ 1/10,\ 1/10,\ 1/10,\ 1/10) \simeq (60,\ 10, \ldots, 10)$ in %.

Example 5.13 Consider the 5-player voting game defined by the *minimal* winning coalitions $\{1, 4, 5\}$, $\{2, 4, 5\}$, $\{3, 4, 5\}$, $\{2, 3, 5\}$, $\{1, 2, 3, 4\}$. It is equivalent to the weighted majority (8 | 1, 2, 2, 3, 4) where players 2 and 3 are substitutable, and no player has a veto right. There are 10 winning coalitions. Leaving aside the grand coalition, the marginal contributions are given in Table 5.5.

Table 5.5 Marginal contributions of the 5-player voting game

	1	2	3	4	5	
$\{1, 4, 5\}$	1	0	0	1	1	1/30
$\{2, 4, 5\}$	0	1	0	1	1	1/30
$\{3, 4, 5\}$	0	0	1	1	1	1/30
$\{2, 3, 5\}$	0	1	1	0	1	1/30
$\{1, 2, 3, 4\}$	1	1	1	1	0	1/20
$\{1, 2, 4, 5\}$	0	0	0	1	1	1/20
$\{1, 3, 4, 5\}$	0	0	0	0	1	1/20
$\{1, 2, 3, 5\}$	0	1	1	0	1	1/20
	2	4	4	6	8	24

The resulting normalized Banzhaf index happens to coincide with the Shapley–Shubik index: $NBI = (2/24,\ 4/24,\ 4/24,\ 6/24,\ 8/24) \approx$ (8.3, 16.6 , 16.6 , 25.0, 33.3) expressed in %.

Example 5.4 (continued) What about the distribution of power in the simplified version of the US Federal System? We have already computed that a senator is decisive in 32 coalitions and a representative is decisive in 24 coalitions. The President has veto right and is decisive in all coalitions of the form {the President, a senators, b representatives} where $a \geq 2$ and $b \geq 3$. Hence, there are $C_3^2 + C_3^3 = 4$ possibilities for a senator and $C_5^3 + C_5^4 + C_5^5 = 16$ possibilities for a representative. The President is therefore decisive in 64 coalitions and the raw Banzhaf index is $BI = (64, 32, ..., 24, ...)$. The total being 280, the normalized index is given by:

$$NBI = \left(\frac{64}{280}, \frac{32}{280}, ..., \frac{24}{280}, ...\right) \simeq (22.9, 11.4, ..., 8.6) \text{ in } \%$$

to be compared to the Shapley–Shubik index

$$SSI = \left(\frac{192}{504}, \frac{54}{504}, ..., \frac{30}{504}, ...\right) \simeq (38.1, 10.7, ..., 6.0) \text{ in } \%.$$

The two measures differ significantly, but the order is identical: the President comes first followed by the senators. The difference is actually deeper as observed by Brams (1975): the distribution of power between the three bodies according to Banzhaf is reversed compared Shapley–Shubik, (23, 34, 43) against (38, 32, 30).[9]

The two power indices may give different measures of relative power. In some instances, the difference may be surprisingly high as for instance in the UN Security Council.

Example 5.5 (continued) Considering the UN Security Council, a non-permanent member i is decisive in coalitions of the form {5 P, 3 NP, i}. The number of these coalitions is equal to the number of combinations of 3 elements among 9. Hence, we have:

$$SSI_{NP} = C_9^3\, \alpha_{15}(9) = \frac{9!}{3!6!}\frac{8!6!}{15!} \simeq 0.0019.$$

By efficiency and symmetry, the power of a permanent member is given by $SSI_P \simeq 0.196$. To compute the Banzhaf index, we need to compute the number of coalitions in which permanent and non-permanent members are decisive. We already know that a non-permanent member is decisive in $C_9^3 = 84$ coalitions. A permanent member is decisive in coalitions of the form $\{4P,\ i,\ kNP\}$ where $k = 4, ..., 10$. As a consequence, a permanent member is decisive in $C_{10}^4 + C_{10}^5 + C_{10}^6 + C_{10}^7 + C_{10}^8 + C_{10}^9 + C_{10}^{10} = 848$ coalitions and, altogether, members are decisive $848 \times 5 + 84 \times 10 = 5080$ times. The normalized Baindices are therefore given by:

$$NBI_{\text{NP}} = \frac{84}{5080} \simeq 0.016,$$
$$NBI_{\text{P}} = \frac{848}{5080} \simeq 0.167.$$

[9] See the discussion in Dubey and Shapley (1979).

We observe that the power ratio between a permanent member and a non-permanent member is close to 100 according to Shapley–Shubik while it is only 10 according to Banzhaf ! We may verify these results using the equivalent weighted majority game (39 | 7, 7, 7, 7, 1, …, 1).

Example 5.8 (continued) The analysis of the decision procedures within the EU is another interesting application of the power indices. For the Council of Ministers, the Shapley–Shubik index (expressed in %) corresponding to the weights and quotas given in Table 5.3 are given in Table 5.6.[10] In EU-6, Belgium and the Netherlands recover the weight of Luxembourg. In the period 1981–1985, we observe that Denmark and Ireland had the same power as Luxembourg. These three members were indeed substitutable. This analysis applies to propositions emanating from the Commission. It goes differently for propositions emanating from members of the Council. For instance, in EU-6, beyond a quota of 12, the support of four members was needed. The three large members could not impose a decision and Luxembourg was not a null player: it was decisive in the coalition formed with the three large members.

It is possible to analyze the distribution of power among political parties within a parliament by assimilating parties to players, each with a weight equal to their number of seats. Here is an example.

Example 5.14 German Parliament. Table 5.7 gives the distribution of seats and the distribution of power as given by the Banzhaf index in the German Parliament (Bundestag) from 1994 to 2021.[11] The actual coalitions are underlined. There are two large parties, CDU/CSU on the right and SPD on the left. We observe that the 2009 elections have led to the same coalition (CDU/CSU–FDP) than in 1994, while it was different in terms of power distribution: the SPD, the liberals (FDP) and the left (Linke) were substitutable, while the Green was a null player. In 2013, the 2005 coalition came back with a quite different power distribution. The cartel CDU/CSU has a near majority and cannot get the support of its liberal partner that has disappeared as a result of the 5% minimum rule. The others (SPD, Green and Linke) are now substitutable and share equally the remaining 50%. The SDP was the only possible coalition partner for the Chancellor, Angela Merkel, at the cost of a shift in its policy towards the left. After the last election of 2017, the arrival of Alternative für Deutschland (AfD) has upset the political chessboard. The same coalition was eventually replicated. It took a while to form although there was no real alternative. Notice that CDU/CSU and SPD have lost seats, while in terms of power, only CDU/CSU lost. In the 2021 elections, CDU/CSU has again lost seats while the SPD has regained seats and power. However, the two parties got the same power. Grüne has seen its score increased both in terms of seats and power, while

[10] The two indices differ by at most 10%.

[11] We observe that there is not much difference between Shapley-Shubik and Banzhaf indices.

Linke has disappeared. These results opened up alternative coalitions, beyond the existing two-party that prevailed in the past, namely SPD or CDU/CSU, together with Grüne and FDP. The SPD, FDP and Grüne finally arrived at an agreement to form a "traffic light coalition" with Olaf Scholz from SPD as Chancellor (Table 5.7).

Table 5.6 EU Council of Ministers: Shapley–Shubik indices

	1958	1973	1981	1986	1995	2003
Germany	23.81	16.72	15.77	12.87	10.99	8.67
France	23.81	16.72	15.77	12.87	10.99	8.67
Italy	23.81	16.72	15.77	12.87	10.99	8.67
Netherlands	14.29	9.15	8.20	6.66	5.91	3.68
Belgium	14.29	9.15	8.20	6.66	5.91	3.40
Luxembourg	0	1.58	4.10	1.80	2.54	1.10
United Kingdom		16.72	15.77	12.87	10.99	8.67
Denmark		6.62	4.10	4.59	3.53	1.96
Ireland		6.62	4.10	4.59	3.53	1.96
Greece			8.20	6.66	5.91	3.40
Spain				10.89	9.10	7.99
Portugal				6.66	5.91	3.403
Sweden					5.08	2.82
Finland					3.53	1.96
Austria					5.08	2.82
Romania						3.99
Poland						7.99
Czech Republic						3.40
Hungary						3.40
Bulgaria						2.82
Slovakia						1.96
Lithuania						1.96
Slovenia						1.10
Latonia						1.10
Estonia						1.10
Cyprus						1.10
Malta						0.82

In the 2021 elections, CDU/CSU has again lost seats while the SPD has regained seats and power. However, the two parties got the same power. Grüne has seen its score increased both in terms of seats and power, while Linke has disappeared. These results opened up alternative coalitions, beyond the existing two-party that prevailed in the past, namely SPD or CDU/CSU, together with

Table 5.7 German parliament: shares in seats and Banzhaf indices

Seats *BNI*	CDU CSU	SPD	FDP	GRÜNE	LINKE	AfD
1994	44 50	37 17	7 17	7 17	4 0	–
1988	37 13	44 55	6 13	7 13	5 5	–
2002	41 33	42 33	8 0	9 33	0 0	–
2005	36 50	36 30	10 13	8 13	9 13	–
2009	38 50	23 17	15 17	11 0	12 17	–
2013	49 50	31 17	0 0	10 17	10 17	–
2017	35 39	22 18	11 11	9 11	10 11	13 11
2021	27 29	28 29	12.5 14	16 14	5.5 0.0	11 14

Grüne and FDP. The SPD, FDP and Grüne finally arrived at an agreement to form a "traffic light coalition" with Olaf Scholz from SPD as Chancellor.

The number of winning coalitions that turn losing if a player leaves coincides with the number of losing coalitions that turn winning if that player joins. We can therefore use indifferently one definition or the other to compute both power indices, Shapley–Shubik or Banzhaf. Coleman (1971) has used these two ways to apprehend decisiveness to build two distinct indices, one based on the *capacity to block* a decision and one based on the *capacity to initiate* a decision. In the first case, he divides by the number of winning coalitions (denoted γ^+), while in the second case, he divides by the number of losing coalitions (denoted γ^-) that include the empty set. Hence, we have $\gamma^+ + \gamma^- = 2^n$.

Example 5.2 (continued) In the simple majority game with veto right $BI = (3,\ 1,\ 1)$. Referring to Tables 5.8 and 5.9, the two Coleman indices, BI/γ^+ and BI/γ^-, are given by (1, 1/3, 1/3) for the capacity to block and (3/5, 1/5, 1/5) for the capacity to initiate.

Table 5.8 Capacity to block

	1	2	3
$\{1, 2\}$	1	1	0
$\{1, 3\}$	1	0	1
$\{1, 2, 3\}$	1	0	0

Table 5.9 Capacity to initiate

	1	2	3
∅	0	0	0
{1}	0	1	1
{2}	1	0	0
{3}	1	0	0
{2, 3}	1	0	0

Dubey and Shapley (1979) have proposed an alternative normalization obtained by dividing $BI(N, W)$ by 2^{n-1}. The idea is the following. Consider a player i and the set of all subsets of N, including the empty set. We then compute the number of subsets in which that player makes a difference either because it is a winning coalition that turns losing if i leaves it or if it is a losing coalition that turns winning if i joins it. That number equals $2BI_i(N, W)$. Picking at random a subset of N, the expected number of subsets in which player i makes a difference is therefore equal to $BI_i(N, W)/2^{n-1}$. It is the probability that player i will be decisive, assuming that all coalitions have the same probability of forming. It defines the Dubey-Shapley power index. In contrast, the Shapley–Shubik index is the probability that a player will be decisive, assuming that coalitions of the same size are equally likely and coalitions' size have the same probability to occur. This is what we have seen when introducing the alternative formulation (4.15) of the Shapley value. Applied to the simple majority game with veto right (Example 5.2), $BI = (3,\ 1,\ 1)$ and therefore, the index proposed by Dubey and Shapley is given by (3/4, 1/4, 1/4).

Paradoxes of power indices

Brams (1975) has identified three types of paradoxes: the coalition paradox, the new member paradox and the quarreling members paradox.

What happens when several players decide to form a coalition and act as a single player? Consider for instance the weighted majority games (4 | 2, 2, 1, 1, 1) and (4 | 2, 2, 3). In the latter, the last three players of the first game have formed a coalition and added their weights. We would expect the power of the coalition to be greater than the combined power of the isolated players or at least not smaller. Actually, it is not the case. In the second game, players are substitutable and share equally the power. In the first game, the last three players obtain 2/15 according to Shapley–Shubik and 1/7 according to Banzhaf. Multiplied by 3, we get 2/5 = 0.4 and 3/7 $\simeq$ 0.43 respectively, scores that are both greater than 1/3. Brams (1975, p. 178) concludes that "*gains in power may also motivate the defection of coalition members*".

Looking at the evolution of the power of the EU member states along the successive enlargements, we observe that it goes down for all but one country, Luxemburg, whose power increases. Of course, the conditions change, the quota being adjusted at each enlargement. However, we observe the same phenomenon if we compare the weighted majority games (5 | 3, 2, 2) and (5 | 3, 2, 2, 1). The power of those detaining 2 votes increases with the addition of a new player: it was 1/6 according to Shapley–Shubik and 1/5 according to Banzhaf, and goes up to 1/4. The power of the first player instead decreases from $2/3 \simeq 0.66$ to $5/12 \simeq 0.42$.

Assume that two players refuse to appear together in a winning coalition. This could be expected to be detrimental to both of them. Actually, it is not necessarily the case as in the 3-player weighted majority game $(5 \mid 3, 2, 2)$. If the last two players are excluded to be members of the same coalition, only the coalitions $\{1, 2\}$ and $\{1, 3\}$ enter into account.[12] The resulting Banzhaf index assigns 1/4 to these players against 1/5 in the original game. Their power increases. Viewing the Shapley–Shubik index as an expectation, if the first player chooses at random his partner, we obtain a power equal to:

$$SSI = \frac{1}{2}\left(\frac{1}{2}, \frac{1}{2}, 0\right) + \frac{1}{2}\left(\frac{1}{2}, 0, \frac{1}{2}\right) = \left(\frac{1}{2}, \frac{1}{4}, \frac{1}{4}\right) = NBI.$$

They obtained 1/4, compared to their power in the original game that was equal to 1/6.

Other paradoxes are proposed by Straffin (1982): if two players quarrel, one may gain while the other loses; a quarrel between two players may not affect them but arm other players; worse, if a player quarrels with a null player, he may lose!

5.5 Concluding Remarks

If we compare the two definitions of the power indices given by (5.3) and (5.5), we observe that they differ by the weighting of marginal contributions. It is a uniform weighting in the Banzhaf case while weights depend on coalitions' size in the case of Shapley–Shubik. They correspond to two different models of coalition formation. For Shapley–Shubik, the power of a player is proportional to the number of orderings in which he is key and the index measures his probability of being key. For Banzhaf instead, the power of a player is simply proportional to the number of coalitions in which he is decisive.

We have seen that the distributions of power resulting from both indices could be quite different and sometimes very different like for the UN Security Council.

The various paradoxes that have been highlighted do not discredit power indices. On the contrary, as Brams (1975) puts it: "*They illustrate their usefulness in showing up aspects of voting power whose existence would have been difficult to demonstrate convincingly in the absence of precise quantitative concepts. Taken together, (they) suggest that there may be instabilities in power relationships and structures that have heretofore not been evident. Related to these instabilities are opportunities for effecting changes in the* status quo *to the benefit of certain players—which will, of course, be pleasing to some but disturbing to others*".

[12] Formally, we leave the framework of cooperative games. Power indices remain, however, well defined.

References

Banzhaf, J. F. (1965). Weighted voting does not work: A mathematical analysis. *Rutgers Law Review, 19*, 317–343.

Banzhaf, J. F. (1966). Multimember electoral districts. Do they violate the 'One man one vote' principle? *Yale Law Journal, 75*, 1309–1388.

Banzhaf, J. F. (1968). One man, 3312 votes: A mathematical analysis of the electoral college. *Villanova Law Review, 14*, 304–332.

Brams, S. J. (1975). *Game theory and politics*. The Free Press (republished in 2003 by Dover).

Coleman, J. S. (1971). Control of collectivities and the power of a collectivity to act. In B. Lieberman (Ed.), *Social choice* (pp. 269–300). Gordon and Breach.

Dubey, P. (1975). On the uniqueness of the shapley value. *International Journal of Game Theory, 4*, 131–139.

Dubey, P., & Shapley, L. S. (1979). Mathematical properties of the Banzhaf power index. *Mathematics of Operations Research, 4*, 99–131.

Laruelle, A., & Valenciano, F. (2008). *Voting and collective decision making*. Cambridge University Press.

Laruelle, A., Martinez, R., & Valenciano, F. (2006). Success versus decisiveness: Conceptual discussion and case study. *Journal of Theoretical Politics, 18*, 185–205.

Lasswell, H. D., & Kaplan, A. (1950). *Power in society*. Yale University Press.

Owen, G. (2013). *Game theory* (4th ed.). Emerald Group Publishing.

Shapley, L. S., & Shubik, M. (1954). A method for evaluating the distribution of power in a committee system. *American Political Science Review,* 48, 787–792. Reproduced in A. Roth (ed.), *The shapley value. Essays in honor of Lloyd Shapley* (pp. 41–48), Cambridge University Press.

Shubik, M. (1982). *Game theory in the social sciences*. The MIT Press.

Straffin, P. (1982). Power indices in politics. In S. Brams, W. Lucas, & P. Straffin (Eds.), *Political and related models* (pp. 256–321). Springer.

Taylor, A. D., & Pacelli, A. M. (2008). *Mathematics and politics. Strategy, voting, power and proof*. Springer.

von Neumann, J., & Morgenstern, O. (1944). *Theory of games and economic behavior*. Princeton University Press (latest edition dated 1953).

References

Mathematical Appendix

Sets and Subsets

A *set* can be defined in two ways, either by enumerating its elements or by characterizing the common properties of its elements, for instance:

$$T = \{a, b, c, x, y\},$$
$$T = \{\text{natural numbers multiple of } 3\} = \{3, 6, 9, 12, \ldots\}.$$

An element of a set is said to *belong* to that set and a set may be contained in another set:

$a \in A$	a *belongs* to A or a is an *element* of A.
$A \subset B$	B *contains* A or A is a *subset* of B,
$A \subset B$	A is a *subset* of B, but different from B.

A distinction must be made between an element a of a set A and the subset $\{a\}$ of A. Both are equivalent: $a \in A \Leftrightarrow \{a\} \subset A$.

The *cardinal* of a set refers to the number of its elements. It can be *finite* or *infinite*, and it can be *countable* or not. A set is countable if it is possible to count its elements, possibly without an end: a countable set has the same cardinality as any subset of the set of *natural numbers* $\mathbb{N} = \{0, 1, 2, 3, \ldots\}$ Finite sets are definitely countable but infinite sets can be countable too. A *singleton* is a set containing a single element.

P. Dehez, *Game Theory for the Social Sciences*, Springer Series in Game Theory,
https://doi.org/10.1007/978-3-031-58241-7

For a finite set T, $|T|$ denotes the number of its elements, called *cardinal* of T. We will systematically use the corresponding lower-case letter to denote the cardinal of a finite set: $t = |T|, n = |N|, \ldots$. The empty set is denoted by $\emptyset$: it contains no element and is a subset of all sets. Sets can be combined:

$A \cup B$ *union*: the set of elements in A *and/or* in B,
$A \cap B$ *intersection*: the set of elements common to A and B,
$B \backslash A$ *difference*: the set of elements in B but not in A,
$A \times B$ *Cartesian product* of A and B: $\{(a, b) |\ a \in A \text{ and } b \in B\}$.

Two sets A and B are *disjoints* if they have no element in common: $A \cap B = \emptyset$. In case of a family of sets $(A_1, \ldots, A_n)$, their union, intersection and Cartesian products are written as follows:

$$\bigcup_{i=1}^{n} A_i \text{ or } \bigcup_{i \in N} A_i,$$
$$\bigcap_{i=1}^{n} A_i \text{ or } \bigcap_{i \in N} A_i,$$
$$\prod_{i=1}^{n} A_i \text{ or } \prod_{i \in N} A_i.$$

where $N = \{1, 2, \ldots, n\}$. A *partition* of a set X is a collection of *disjoints* subsets de X whose union is equal to X. Starting from a finite set N of cardinal n, we denote by 2^N the set of all its subsets. It includes the empty set $\emptyset$ and the set N itself. There are 2^n subsets—explaining the notation 2^N a number that becomes quickly astronomical!

Here is an illustration involving the sets $A = \{a, b, c, d\}$ and $B = \{a, \{b, c\}, d\}$ whose cardinal are 4 and 3 respectively:

$$a, b, c, d \in A \text{ and } \{a\}, \{b\}, \{c\}, \{d\} \subset A,$$
$$a, \{b, c\}, d \in B \text{ and } \{a\}, \{b, c\}, \{d\} \subset B,$$
$$A \cap B = \{a, d\} \text{ and } A \cup B = \{a, b, c, d, \{b, c\}\},$$
$$A \backslash B = \{b, c\} \text{ and } B \backslash A = \{\{b, c\}\},$$
$$2^B = \{\emptyset, \{a\}, \{b, c\}, \{d\}, \{a, \{b, c\}\}, \{a, d\}, \{\{b, c\}, d\}, B \text{ and } |2^B| = 2^3 = 8.$$

Natural Numbers and Beyond

We often work with the set $\mathbb{R}$ of real numbers that includes the set $\mathbb{N}$ of *natural* numbers, the set $\mathbb{Z} = \{\ldots, -3, -2, -1, 0, 1, 2, 3, \ldots\}$ of *integers* and the set $\mathbb{Q} = \{x = a/b | a, b \in \mathbb{Z}, b \neq 0\}$ of *rational* numbers: $\mathbb{N} \subset \mathbb{Z} \subset \mathbb{Q} \subset \mathbb{R}$. The set $\mathbb{R} \backslash \mathbb{Q}$ is the set of *irrational numbers*, those numbers that cannot be written as a ratio of two integers like for instance. $\sqrt{2}$, π, ... These are numbers that can only be approximated: their decimal part is an infinite sequence of numbers without repetition. The sets $\mathbb{N}$, $\mathbb{Z}$, $\mathbb{Q}$ and $\mathbb{R}$ have an *infinite cardinal*. However, $\mathbb{N}$, $\mathbb{Z}$, and $\mathbb{Q}$ are countable while $\mathbb{R}$ is not. The *real line* is the geometric representation of the set of real numbers. It runs from $-\infty$ to $+\infty$, with the origin being zero. It is a *continuum*: there are real numbers between any two real numbers. We denote by $\mathbb{R}_+$ the set *non-negative* real numbers.

Binary Relations: Orders and Preorders

A *binary relation* R on the elements a and b of set A applies or not: aRb or bRa. For example, the binary relation on the set of integers "is not smaller than" is denoted by $\geq$: $a \geq b$.

A *preorder* is a binary relation R that is *reflexive* and *transitive*:

- aRa for all $a \in A$,
- aRb and $bRc \Rightarrow aRc$.

A binary relation R on a set A is *anti-symmetric* if aRb and $bRa \Rightarrow a = b$. A preorder that is anti-symmetric is an *order*. The relation $\geq$ on the set of real numbers $\mathbb{R}$ is an order.

Vectors and the Euclidian Space

A point in the plane $\mathbb{R} \times \mathbb{R} = \mathbb{R}^2$ is defined by its Cartesian coordinates: $x = (x_1, x_2)$. It is sometimes referred to as the *vector* x, the line segment joining the origin to the point x. Beyond dimension 2, a vector $x = (x_1, x_2, ..., x_n)$ is an element of the $\mathbb{R}^n$. Equipped with *Euclidian distance*

$$D(x, y) = \sqrt{\sum_{i=1}^{n} (x_i - y_i)^2}$$

it is referred to as the *Euclidian space* of dimension n.[1]

The *scalar product* of two vectors x and y in $\mathbb{R}^n$ is defined by:

$$x \cdot y = \sum_{i=1}^{n} x_i y_i.$$

[1] This definition of distance results from the famous *theorem of Pythagoras*.

Simple and Weighted Sums

Variables are denoted by lower-case letters like x, y, z, p, q,... Variables can be differentiated by an index: x_i, x_j, x_k... For instance, x_i can be the share of person i in a cake to be divided, p_i can be the price of commodities i,... A collection of n variables corresponds to a point in the n-dimensional Euclidian space: $x = (x_1, x_2, ..., x_n) \in \mathbb{R}^n$. The *sum* de n numbers $x_1, x_2, ..., x_n$ is denoted by:

$$\sum_{i=1}^{n} x_i.$$

The partial sum associated with a subset $S \subset \{1, ..., n\}$ is given by:

$$\sum_{i \in S} x_i \text{ or } x(S).$$

The notation $\sum x_i$ is sometimes used for a sum that covers all variables. The *average* or *mean* of n numbers $x_1, x_2, ..., x_n$ is defined by:

$$\mu = \frac{1}{n} \sum_{i=1}^{n} x_i.$$

In probabilistic terms, the mean corresponds to the *mathematical expectation* associated with a random experiment that produces any one of these numbers with a probability $1/n$. It is a *random variable*. Throwing a die is a simple example of a random variable: it produces a result in the set $\{1, 2, 3, 4, 5, 6\}$, each with a probability 1/6, and its mathematical expectation is given by $21/6 = 3.5$.

More generally, a (discrete) random variable is defined by weights λ_i such that $0 \leq \lambda_i \leq 1$ for all i and $\sum \lambda_i = 1$. It produces the result x_i with a probability λ_i and its mathematical expectation is given by the weighted average

$$\mu = \sum_{i=1}^{n} \lambda_i \, x_i.$$

Lines, Planes and Hyperplanes

A *vector* is a point in a Euclidian space. In the plane $\mathbb{R} \times \mathbb{R} = \mathbb{R}^2$, a *line* is defined by the set of points $x = (x_1, x_2)$ satisfying the equation $p_1 x_1 + p_2 x_2 = a$. Alternatively, the equation of a line can be written as:

$$x_2 = \frac{a}{p_2} - \frac{p_1}{p_2} x_1.$$

Its *slope* is given by $-p_1/p_2$ and its *intercept* (intersection with the x_2 axis) is given by a/p_2.

Moving into $\mathbb{R}^3$ a *plane* is defined by the set of points $x = (x_1, x_2, x_3)$ satisfying the equation $p_1x_1 + p_2x_2 + p_3x_3 = a$. In $\mathbb{R}^n$ a *hyperplane* is defined by the set H of points $x = (x_1, x_2, \ldots, x_n)$ such that $p_1x_1 + p_2x_2 + \cdots + p_nx_n = a$ or, using the Cartesian product, $H = \{x \in \mathbb{R}^n | p \cdot x = a\}$.

The p_i's and a are the *coefficients* that define the hyperplane: the p_i's define the *orientation* of the hyperplane and a defines its *position* in the space. Notice that the coefficients are defined up to a factor: if $a \neq 0$, a hyperplane is defined by n coefficients $(q_1, ..., q_n)$ where $q_i = p_i/a,\ i = 1, ..., n$. If $a = 0$, the hyperplane passes through the origin.

The sets $\{x \in \mathbb{R}^n | p \cdot x \leq a\}$ and $\{x \in \mathbb{R}^n | p \cdot x \geq a\}$ are the *half-spaces* associated to the hyperplane $p \cdot x = a$.

Closed and Bounded Sets

Intervals in the real line $\mathbb{R}$ are of the following forms: the closed interval $[a, b]$ that contains its *boundary points* a and b; the *open* interval $]a, b[$ that contains all the points between a and b except a and b; the interval $[a, b[$ that contains all the points between a and b, except b; the interval $[a, +\infty[$ that contains all the points greater or equal to a. The real line is itself an interval: $\mathbb{R} =]-\infty, +\infty[$. A set is *closed* if it contains the points of its boundary: the interval $[-10, 120[$ is not closed while the intervals $[-10, +\infty[$ and $[-20, 50]$ are closed. This extends to sets in $\mathbb{R}^n$: a set is closed if it contains its boundary points.

Nothing excludes that a closed set extend to infinity in some of its coordinates. A set is *bounded* if it is not the case. It can be framed "within a box": no coordinate escape to infinity.

Convex Sets[2]

A *linear combination* of two points x and y in $\mathbb{R}^n$ is a point given by $z = \alpha x + \beta y$ where α and β are real numbers. The case where $\alpha \in [0, 1]$ and $\beta = 1-\alpha$ defines a particular type of linear combination, called *convex combination*: varying α in $[0, 1]$ generates the *line segment* joining x and y. Linear and convex combinations generalize to any number of points: $\alpha x + \beta y + \gamma z + ...$ In the case of a convex combination, the coefficients $\alpha, \beta, \gamma, ...$ are non-negative numbers that sum up to one.

A set X is *convex* if it contains the line segment joining any two of its points:

$$x, y \in X \;\Rightarrow\; \lambda x + (1 - \lambda)y \in X \;\text{ for all } \lambda \in [0, 1].$$

[2] For more information, see for instance Lay, S.R. (1982), *Convex sets and their applications*, Dover Publications, New York.

Alternatively, a set is convex if it contains all convex combinations of its points.

The *convex hull* of an arbitrary set X in $\mathbb{R}^n$ is the smallest convex set containing it. The convex hull of two distinct points is a line segment. In the case of three distinct points, it is a triangle provided that these points do not belong to a line. In general, the term *polytope* is used to designate the convex hull of a finite number of points. A *polyhedral set* is the intersection of a finite number of half-spaces. A bounded polyhedral set is a *polytope*.

Consider $m + 1$ dimensional vectors $(x^1, ..., x^{m+1})$ forming a set of dimension m.[3] The polytope generated by these $m + 1$ points is called a *simplex* (or m-simplex) and the points $\lambda f(x) + (1 - \lambda)f(y) \leq f(\lambda x + (1 - \lambda)y)$ are its vertices. It has a dimension equal to m and any of its points is a convex combination of its *vertices*. Actually, each point x in a simplex is associated to a *unique* convex combination of its vertices and the coefficients define the *barycentric coordinates* of x. A one-dimensional simplex is a line segment, a two-dimensional simplex is a triangle, a three-dimensional simplex is a tetrahedron, ... The *unit-simplex* is a particular simplex defined by:

$$\Delta_n = \left\{ x \in \mathbb{R}^n_+ \middle| \sum_{i=1}^{n} x_i = 1 \right\}.$$

It has dimension $n – 1$. For instance, Δ is the set of probability distributions of a (discrete) random variable taking n different values.

Mappings, Functions and Correspondences

In general, a *mapping* f associates the elements of a set A (called the *domain* of f) to elements of a set B (called the *image* of A through f): $f : A \rightarrow B$. The mapping f is a *function* if, to each element of A, is associated one and only one element of B. The mapping f is a *correspondence* if, to each element of A, is associated a subset of B. It is a point-to-set mapping.

The inverse mapping $f^{-1} : B \rightarrow A$ is not necessarily a function: different points in A may have the same image. When each point in A has a unique image in B, f is a *one-to-one function*.

[3] It means that the $m + 1$ points are *affinely independent*: no element is a linear combination of the others.

Given a function $f : A \to B$, the set of elements $(a, b) \in A \times B$ such that $b = f(a)$ is the *graph* of f. Given a correspondence $f : A \to B$, the set of elements $\{(a, b) \in A \times B | b \in f(a)\}$ is the graph of f.

Convex, Concave and Continuous Functions

A real-valued function $f : X \to \mathbb{R}$ where X is a convex subset of $\mathbb{R}^n$ is *concave* if the line segment joining any two of its points on its graph lies entirely below the graph:

$$\lambda f(x) + (1 - \lambda)f(y) \leq f(\lambda x + (1 - \lambda y)).$$

A function f is *convex* if the function $-f$ is concave.

A function f is *continuous* if infinitesimal changes in x induce infinitesimal change in $f(x)$.

Combinatorial Analysis

Given a set of n elements, there are $n!$ different ways to order them, where $n!$ is the *factorial* of n that is given by the product of the first n natural and positive numbers:

$$n! = n \times (n - 1) \times (n - 2) \times \cdots \times 2 \times 1.$$

$n!$ is the number of *orderings* or *permutations* of n elements. Given a set of n elements, how many subsets of k elements can be formed? If $n = 3$ and $k = 2$, the answer is immediate, it is 3: $\{1, 2\}$, $\{1, 3\}$ and $\{2, 3\}$. In general, the answer is given by the following formula:

$$C_n^k = \frac{n!}{k!\,(n - k)!}.$$

It is the number of *combinations* of k elements among n elements. For instance, we have:

$$C_6^3 = \frac{6!}{3!\,3!} = \frac{6 \times 5 \times 4 \times 3 \times 2}{3 \times 2\ \ 3 \times 2} = 20.$$

In combinations, the order of the elements does not matter. If the order does matter, we have to take all orderings into account. This leads to the following formula

$$A_n^k = k!\,C_n^k = \frac{n!}{(n - k)!} = n \times (n - 1) \times \cdots \times (n - k + 1).$$

It is the number of *arrangements* of k elements among n elements. For instance, we have:

$$A_6^3 = \frac{6!}{3!} = \frac{6 \times 5 \times 4 \times 3 \times 2}{3 \times 2} = 120.$$

Events and Probabilities

An *event* is the description of the outcome of an experiment. We denote by $P[A]$ the probability that event A occurs. The event "*non-A*" occurs if A does *not* occur. It occurs with a probability $P[non\,A] = 1 - P[A]$.

Considering two events A and B, the event $A \cup B$ occurs if A *or* B occurs, possibly both. The event $A \cap B$ occurs if A *and* B occur. The probability that *at least one* of the two events occurs is given by $P[A \cup B] = P[A] + P[B] - P[A \cap B]$. If they are *independent*, the probability that both events occur is the product of the probabilities $P[A \cap B] = P[A]\,P[B]$ and the probability that one of the events occurs then simplifies as follows:

$$\begin{aligned} P[A \cup B \cup C] &= P[A] + P[B] + P[C] - P[A]P[B] - P[A]P[C] \\ &\quad - P[B]P[C] + P[A]P[B]P[C] \\ &= 1 - (1 - P[A])(1 - P[B])(1 - P[C]). \end{aligned}$$

This formula generalizes to any number of independent events. For instance, in the case of three independent events, we have:

$$\begin{aligned} P[A \cup B \cup C] &= P[A] + P[B] + P[C] - P[A]\,P[B] - P[A]\,P[C] \\ &\quad - P[B]\,P[C] + P[A]\,P[B]\,P[C] \\ &= 1 - (1 - P[A])(1 - P[B])(1 - P[C]). \end{aligned}$$

Propositional Logic

Consider two statements P and Q. We then have:

An important proposition to be remembered: [$A \Rightarrow B$] implies [*non-B* $\Rightarrow$ *non-A*].

$P \Rightarrow Q$	P implies Q: if P is true, then Q is true as well, P is a *sufficient condition* for Q (Q if P), Q is a *necessary condition* for P (P only if Q)
$P \Leftrightarrow Q$	P and Q are *equivalent*, P is a *necessary* and *sufficient condition* for Q, *P if and only if Q*

Greek Alphabet (Extract)

α = alpha	β = beta	γ = gamma	δ = delta	ε = epsilon
λ = lambda	μ = mu	π = pi	φ = phi	ω = omega

List of Examples

P. Dehez, *Game Theory for the Social Sciences*, Springer Series in Game Theory,
https://doi.org/10.1007/978-3-031-58241-7

List of Propositions

2.1. Complete and continuous preorderings can be represented by a continuous utility function.
2.2. Among the utility functions that represent the preferences over lotteries, there exists a utility function such that a lottery is preferred to another lottery if and only if the expected utility of the first is greater than the expected utility of the second.
2.3. If a utility function satisfies the Expected Utility Hypothesis, then any positive affine transformation defines a utility function that satisfies the Expected Utility Hypothesis.
2.4. Behavioral strategies and mixed strategies are equivalent.
2.5. Dominant strategies are part of the definition of any equilibrium and, if both players have a dominant strategy, their combination defines the unique equilibrium.
2.6. For games with finite strategy spaces, all sequences of successive eliminations of dominated strategies end up at the same reduced game.
2.7. In a zero-sum game, an equilibrium exists if and only if it has a value.
2.8. In zero-sum games, if two pairs of strategies define equilibria, then the pairs obtained by interchanging the strategies also define equilibria and the utility levels are all equal.
2.9. Games defined by finite strategy spaces have an equilibrium.
2.10. At an equilibrium in mixed strategies, each player is indifferent between the pure strategies to which he assigns a positive probability.
2.11. Every two-person game has a strong mediated equilibrium.

3.1. Nash axioms define one and only one rule. It is given by the maximization of the product of gains.
3.2. The Nash solution combines equality of gains and their maximization.
3.3. If the Nash solution is egalitarian, it coincides with the utilitarian solution.
3.4. Kalai-Smorodinski axioms define one and only one rule. It is the proportional solution.

P. Dehez, *Game Theory for the Social Sciences*, Springer Series in Game Theory,
https://doi.org/10.1007/978-3-031-58241-7

4.1. If individual worth is nonnegative, superadditivity implies that the characteristic function is monotonic and nonnegative valued.
4.2. A game is convex if and only if the marginal contributions are nondecreasing with respect to coalition size.
4.3. The core allocations of a 3-player game are the efficient allocations that give to players at least their individual worth and at most their contribution to the grand coalition.
4.4. In a core allocations, a null player obtains a zero amount and a dummy player obtains his worth.
4.5. If two players are substitutable in a game, core allocations obtained by exchanging their coordinates are also core allocations. Moreover, the core contains allocations that allocate equal amounts to substitutable players.
4.6. Convex games have a nonempty core.
4.7. A constant-sum game has a nonempty core if and only if it is inessential.
4.8. The core of a balanced game is a bounded and convex set.
4.9. The vertices of the core of a convex game are the marginal contributions vectors.
4.10. A game is convex if and only if its core is the convex polyhedra whose vertices are marginal contributions vectors.
4.11. The bargaining set coincides with the core if and only if the game is convex.
4.12. The weighted sum of marginal contributions and the average of the marginal contribution vectors are equivalent formulations of the Shapley value.
4.13. There is one and only one efficient allocation rule that satisfies equal treatment of substitutable players, null player and additivity. It is the Shapley value.
4.14. There is one only one efficient allocation rule that satisfies equal treatment of substitutable players and monotonicity. It is the Shapley value.
4.15. There is one only one efficient allocation rule that satisfies balanced contributions. It is the Shapley value.
4.16. There is one only one efficient allocation rule that satisfies simultaneously equal treatment of necessary players and additivity. It is the Shapley value.
4.17. The Shapley value defines a Milnor-reasonable imputation.
4.18. The nucleolus is a well-defined singleton for all superadditive game.
4.19. A game is concave if and only if marginal costs are nonincreasing with respect to coalition size.
4.20. Bankruptcy games are convex.
4.21. Airport games are concave.
4.22. Data games are subadditive and monotone decreasing.
4.23. The core of a data sharing game is a regular simplex.
4.24. The nucleolus of a data sharing game is the average of its core vertices.
4.25. Derivation of the Shapley value of a data game.
4.26. Patent games are essential and convex.
4.27. Derivation of the core of a patent game.
4.28. Derivation of the Shapley value of a patent game.
4.29. Derivation of the Shapley value of an information game.

4.30. Unicity of the Shapley value on the set of sequential liability games.
4.31. Probability games are convex.
4.32. Unicity of the Shapley value on the set of probability games.
4.33. Unicity of the Shapley ranking on the set of ranking games.

5.1. A player has a veto right if and only if the grand coalition is losing in his absence.
5.2. The core of a voting game is non-empty if and only if there is at least one veto player.
5.3. The core of a voting game allocates 1 between the veto players, if any.
5.4. Derivation of the Shapley-Shubik power index.

Resources

Many websites cover to game theory. Here are some of them.

- Alvin Roth's Game Theory, Experimental economics and market design page stanford.edu/~alroth/alroth.html
- Ariel Rubinstein's and Martin Osborne's pages www.economics.utoronto.ca/osborne and arielrubinstein.tau.ac.il also give access to some of their books,
- www.gametheory.net

A number of sites offer online computations or software:

- gte.csc.liv.ac.uk is an online toolbox devoted to non-cooperative games,
- www.gambit-project.org a software dedicated to non-cooperative games,
- www.tuglabweb.uvigo.es is a rich toolbox devoted to 3- and 4-player cooperative games,
- www.warwick.ac.uk/~ecaae and powerslave.val.utu.fi offer online algorithms for the computation of power indices for weighted majority games.

There are online course, for instance: www.youtube.com/user/gametheoryonline or www.edx.org/learn/game-theory

See also the page www.gtcenter.org of the Stony Brook *Center for Game Theory* and the page ratio.huji.ac.il of the *Federmann Center for the Study of Rationality*.

The authors' page https://perso.uclouvain.be/pierre.dehez contains various documents and information.

There are also packages devoted to cooperative games that use well-known softwares.

The packages developed by Holger Meinhardt from the Karlsruhe Institute of Technology for both *Matlab* and *Mathematica*: https://github.com/himeinhardt

The package developed by Jochen Staudacher et al. form the Hochschule für angewandte Wissenschaften Kempten for *R*: rbasics.org/packages/coopgame-package-in-r.

P. Dehez, *Game Theory for the Social Sciences*, Springer Series in Game Theory,
https://doi.org/10.1007/978-3-031-58241-7

Books Covering Game Theory

There are many books covering Game Theory. Here is a list that includes books that may not be explicitly referred to in the text but have inspired the author.

Alos-Ferrer, C. and K. Ritzberger (2018), *The theory of extensive form games*, Springer, Heidelberg.

Aumann, R.J. (1989), *Lectures on game theory*, Westview Press, Boulder.

Aumann, R.J. and S. Hart (eds. 1992, 1994, 2002), *Handbook of game theory* (Vols. 1, 2 and 3), Elsevier, Amsterdam.

Binmore, K. (1992), *Fun and games*, Heath, London, 1992.

Brams, S.J. (1975), *Game theory and politics*, The Free Press, New York (republished in 2003 by Dover, New York).

Brams S.J. and A.D. Taylor (1996), *Fair division. From cake cutting to dispute resolution*, Cambridge University Press, Cambridge.

Camerer, C.F. (2003), *Behavioral game theory: experiments in strategic interaction*, Princeton University Press, Princeton.

Davis, M. (1970), Game theory: a nontechnical introduction (2nd edition), Basic Books, New York.

Driessen, T. (1988), *Cooperative games. Solutions and applications*, Kluwer Academic Publishers, Dordrecht.

Kuhn, H. (1997), *Classics in game theory*, Princeton University Press, Princeton.

Luce, D. and H. Raiffa (1957), *Games and decisions*, Wiley, New York.

Maschler, M., E. Solan and S. Zamir (2020), *Game theory* (2nd edition), Cambridge University Press, Cambridge.

Moulin, H. (1986), *Game Theory for the Social Sciences (2nd edn.), NYU Press, New York.*

Moulin, H. (1988), Axioms of cooperative decision making, Cambridge University Press, Cambridge.

Moulin, H. (1995), *Cooperative microeconomics. A game theoretic introduction*, Princeton University Press, Cambridge.

Moulin, H. (2003), *Fair division and collective welfare*, The MIT Press, Cambridge, Massachusetts.

Nash, J. (1996), *Essays on game theory*, Edward Elgar,

P. Dehez, *Game Theory for the Social Sciences*, Springer Series in Game Theory,
https://doi.org/10.1007/978-3-031-58241-7

Myerson, R. (1991), *Game theory, analysis of conflict*, Harvard University Press, Cambridge.

Osborne, M. (2004), *An introduction to game theory*, Oxford University Press, London.

Osborne, M.J. and A. Rubinstein (1994), *A course in game theory*, The MIT Press, Cambridge, Massachusetts.

Owen, G. (2013), *Game theory* (4th édition), Emerald Group Publishing, Bingley.

Peleg, B. and P. Sudhölter (2007), *Introduction to the theory of cooperative games*, Springer, Heidelberg.

Rasmussen, E. (2001), *Games and information. An introduction to game theory* (3rd ed), Basil Blackwell, London.

Roth, A. (1988), *The Shapley value. Essays in honor of Loyd Shapley*, Cambridge University Press, Cambridge.

Schelling, T. (1960), *The strategy of conflict*, Harvard University Press, Cambridge.

Shubik, M. (1982), *Game theory in the social sciences*, The MIT Press, Cambridge.

Shubik, M. (1984), *A game-theoretic approach to political economy*, The MIT Press, Cambridge, Massachusetts.

Umbhauer, G. (2016), *Game theory and exercices*, Routledge, London.

Young, H.P. (1994), *Equity. In theory and practice*, Princeton University Press, Princeton.

Young, H.P. and S. Zamir (2015), *Handbook of game theory*, Vol. 4, Elsevier, Amsterdam.

Name Index

P. Dehez, *Game Theory for the Social Sciences*, Springer Series in Game Theory, https://doi.org/10.1007/978-3-031-58241-7

Subject Index

P. Dehez, *Game Theory for the Social Sciences*, Springer Series in Game Theory,
https://doi.org/10.1007/978-3-031-58241-7

D

E

MIX
Papier aus verantwortungsvollen Quellen
Paper from responsible sources
FSC® C105338

If you have any concerns about our products,
you can contact us on
ProductSafety@springernature.com

In case Publisher is established outside the EU,
the EU authorized representative is:
Springer Nature Customer Service Center GmbH
Europaplatz 3, 69115 Heidelberg, Germany

Printed by Libri Plureos GmbH
in Hamburg, Germany